California and *Hawaii*
PUBLISHING
MARKET
PLACE

California
and Hawaii

PUBLISHING MARKET PLACE

*A comprehensive directory
of markets, resources, and
opportunities for writers.*

Compiled by: Marjorie Gersh

Writers
Connection

Cupertino, California

California and Hawaii Publishing Marketplace
1991 Edition

Published by: Steve Lester

Compiled by: Marjorie Gersh

Edited by: Meera Lester, Jan Stiles

Cover Designed by: Detta Penna

Books from Writers Connection Press:

California and Hawaii Publishing Marketplace
Southwest Publishing Marketplace

To order copies, see page 281.

Writers Connection
1601 Saratoga-Sunnyvale Road, Suite 180
Cupertino, CA 95014
(408) 973-0227, FAX (408) 973-1219

Printed and bound in the United States of America

ISBN 0-9622592-1-7

Table of Contents

Acknowledgements

For their conscientious and diligent work verifying information, typesetting, and proofreading the manuscript, we thank Writers Connection staff members Cheryl Bowlin, Arlene Di Salvo, Mardeene Mitchell, Dean Stark, Julee Stiles, Burton Sukhov, and Nancy Tamburello. We extend our thanks also to Jayson Loam for additional help in verifying information.

We deeply appreciate the suggestions, support, and advice given to us by our friends and colleagues. They include Cliff Feldman, Phyllis Taylor Pianka, Robert Scott Milne, Tom McFadden, and Michael Crisp.

For sharing our belief that "writers helping writers strengthens our West Coast and Hawaiian Islands writing and publishing community," and for supporting our work over the years, we extend a heartfelt thanks to all our Writers Connection members.

This book is dedicated to writers everywhere, but especially to those in California and Hawaii who have long needed and frequently requested a definitive guide to publishing markets, information, and resources in these states.

Introduction

We know what writers need. Writers Connection has been in the business of providing information and services to writers, organizations, small presses, and self-publishers for nearly a decade. *California Publishing Marketplace*, lead book in our *Marketplace* series, sold out two printings in 1989-90. Now expanded to include Hawaii, this newly revised and updated 1991 edition of *California and Hawaii Publishing Marketplace* offers writers hundreds of markets for their work.

The second book in the series, *Southwest Publishing Marketplace*, provides similar information for the rapidly growing areas of writing and publishing in the states of Arizona, Colorado, Nevada, New Mexico, Texas, and Utah. Many new opportunities and markets, some relatively untapped as yet, make up this comprehensive new resource available for the first time in 1991 from Writers Connection Press. Together, these books can help writers expand their horizons.

Markets

California, the birthplace of the small press movement in the 1960s, and Hawaii, with markets often overlooked by writers, are expected to increase publishing activity in the 1990s. That means more opportunities than ever before for writers wanting to sell to these relatively untapped markets. Because we designed and developed this book specifically for writers, we've included the names of book and magazine submissions editors along with editorial guidelines and submission information, acceptance policies, preferred method of query, rights purchased, and tips for writers from the respective editor or publisher. For newspapers, we've listed addresses and names of general, book review, and travel editors.

Professional Organizations

For those interested in expanding their professional network, we've included wherever possible the address, phone number, and contact for the national headquarters of each organization and then listed information on local chapters. You're sure to find one in your area.

Writers' Conferences

Writers' conferences are prime sources of information, professional contacts, and motivational renewal. In the conference section, you'll find listings for locations, dates, themes, formats, fees, number of faculty members, and special events. If you're serious about writing, plan to attend at least one conference this year.

Literary Agents

One question we are frequently asked is, "Where can I find a literary agent to represent my work?" While our list does not include every agent in California and Hawaii, it does include those who responded to our request for information. We sent out hundreds of surveys and spent weeks verifying information on the phone. The result is a list of agents that includes not only names, addresses, and phone numbers, but substantial information on the kinds of literary properties the agencies are seeking, agency commission fees, and rights handled by the agency.

Books and Resources

For many years, Writers Connection teachers, members, and seminar participants have offered insights and suggestions about the kinds of books they need for honing their skills. Writers Connection has responded by creating a bookstore filled with how-to-write books, style guides, reference books, market books, and business writing books. Since these books have proved so helpful to our writers, we thought you'd like to know about them, too. An annotated list of books is included in this directory, as well as other resources you, the writer, might need.

Updates

We realized from its inception that this book would require regular updating of information. Some of that information will appear in the monthly 16-page *Writers Connection* newsletter. In addition, we plan to issue a new edition yearly.

In the process of compiling and verifying information for the book, we mailed thousands of questionnaires. If any publishers, agents, organizations, or conferences are not listed, it is likely that their surveys were not returned, they requested deletion, or their information could not be verified.

We realize much of the information in this book will change with time—organizations elect new officers each year; book publishers, magazines, and newspapers hire new editors; and conference directors find new locations, change formats, and offer new speakers.

When using this book, if you come across information that is incomplete or has changed, please let us know. If you know of a book, magazine, or newspaper publisher that should be included, tell us—we'll send the appropriate survey forms. Let us know if you would like your organization or conference listed. Listings are free.

If you wish to be notified of future editions of *California and Hawaii Publishing Marketplace*, please send us your name and address. Finally, we appreciate feedback. Let us know if the book works well for you, or if it doesn't, and why.

Meera Lester, Editor
Co-founder Writers Connection

About Writers Connection

Writers Connection was founded in 1983 by Steve and Meera Lester to serve writers and publishing professionals in California. Writers Connection has 2,000 members and provides a wide range of services, including seminars, a job shop specializing in contract or full-time placement of technical and other writers and editors, a bookstore offering a wide selection of titles on writing- and publishing-related topics, the annual Selling to Hollywood weekend conference, and a 16-page monthly newsletter.

With the establishment of the small press arm of the company, Writers Connection will be increasing its publishing activity. At present the company publishes the *Marketplace* series books and the *Writing for Hollywood* and *Selling to Hollywood* documentary videotapes.

Writers Connection memberships offer discounts on seminars, conferences, and book and tape purchases, and access to a wide range of resource material.

The monthly *Writers Connection* newsletter features updated information on markets, events, contests, and industry news as well as articles on various aspects of writing and publishing. Members receive the newsletter free, and subscriptions are available to nonmembers.

The company's seminar offerings target professional writers as well as hobbyists, average three to six hours in length, and cover subjects such as "Constructing the Novel," "Writing Mystery and Suspense," "Basic Grammar," "Travel Writing," "Integrating Spirituality in Your Writing," "Developing a Technical Style Guide," and "Writing User-Friendly Documentation."

If you would like to join Writers Connection or subscribe to the monthly newsletter, an order form appears on page 282. The form may also be used to request seminar information, a free sample newsletter, or additional information about Writers Connection and future editions of the *Southwest Publishing Marketplace* and *California and Hawaii Publishing Marketplace* books.

Book Publishers

We assume that you have a manuscript (or an idea for one) that you wish to have published. We have obtained and organized the following information to help you decide where to send your submission, what to include in and on the envelope, when to anticipate an initial response, and in general, what to expect in terms and payment if you are offered a publishing contract.

How to Use the Information in This Section

The first paragraph of each entry identifies the publishing company, lists its location, and describes its publishing history. Your initial contact should be directed to the submissions editor named in the entry.

Subjects of Interest

We divided this section into three main fields: fiction, nonfiction, and other. We listed the publishers' areas of interest within each field and included titles of recent publications. What publishers don't want is as important as what they do want; don't waste your time trying to force through an exception.

Initial Contact

Follow the instructions. Send editors what they want. There are many resources in the Books for Writers section that will help you prepare an effective query letter or persuasive book proposal. Include any additional material requested. When sending a requested resumé, biography (bio), or curriculum vitae, include only those details of your life that are relevant to your authority and ability to write the book. Always include a self-addressed, stamped envelope (SASE) for the editor's response or return of your materials.

Acceptance Policies

Unagented manuscripts: Many medium to large publishers will look only at manuscripts submitted by an agent. To find an agent, turn to the Literary Agents section, send a query about your project to several of the agents listed, then choose the agent you feel will best represent you and your project.

Simultaneous submissions: If the publisher's information says "yes" to simultaneous submissions, you may submit your manuscript to several different publishers at the same time, but you should inform each publisher that the manuscript is being simultaneously submitted.

Disk submissions: Many publishers are willing to accept your *final* manuscript on a disk compatible with the publisher's computer system, but almost all of them prefer the initial contact be in the form of hard copy (a printout on paper).

Response time to initial inquiry: Response time varies greatly. Be patient and avoid phoning the publisher unless you've been instructed to do so by the publisher in question. A week or two *after* the specified response time (listed in the publisher's entry), you are entitled to send a written request for information concerning the status of your submission.

Average time until publication: This information (always dependent upon a number of factors) provides an approximate idea of how long the process takes after the publisher has received the completed manuscript.

Advance: When dealing with small or mid-size presses, the advances (if given at all) tend to be small. The money goes primarily into production and promotion. An advantage of working with small presses is that your book is not "just another on their big list." The lists tend to be smaller, and thus your book gets more attention.

Royalty: Some royalties are computed on the retail cover price, but most are computed on the publisher's gross sales income, which combines discounted sales (usually 40 percent off retail) to distributors and retailers. If your personal negotiations with a publisher have reached the contract stage, pay an agent or a publishing attorney to review and evaluate the contract before you sign.

First run: The number of copies to be printed is usually based on the publisher's best estimate of the number of copies that can be sold in the initial one- to two-year period.

Subsidy basis: In general, this means that the author pays some portion of the production and promotion costs and potentially stands to earn more than a basic royalty if the book sells well. Many legitimate small publishing houses simply do not have the money to finance all costs, and for that reason they encourage author investment. Subsidy deals take many forms, so obtain all the facts, get the terms in writing, and seek legal advice before signing.

Marketing Channels

Most publishers market books through direct mail sales to individuals and libraries, rep sales to bookstores, and distributor sales (distributors stock, sell, and distribute books to bookstores and libraries). In addition, some publishers promote special sales through book clubs, professional and social organizations, and special interest groups. If your book has such special sales potential, be sure to mention that fact in your initial contact with the publisher.

Subsidiary Rights: If the publisher lists "all," that means he/she is buying and handling all sub rights to ensure that the publishing house realizes as much profit from the book as possible. Often, however, subsidiary rights are negotiable. An experienced agent or publishing attorney can advise you if you're unsure whether or not to sell all these rights.

Additional Information

This is the publisher's opportunity to supply any supplemental information not covered in the preceding sections. Tips are specific recommendations from the publisher to the author and should be seriously considered.

Catalog: We suggest that your first step toward any publisher be to send for the catalog of books already published. This will give you the "flavor" of that press and enable you to draft a more focused query or submission.

Abbreviations

n/i means no information was given to us by the publisher.

n/a means that this particular question did not apply to the publisher.

AAMES-ALLEN PUBLISHING COMPANY. 1106 Main St. Huntington Beach, CA 92648-2719. (714) 536-4926. Submissions Editor: Peggy Glenn. Not accepting manuscripts.

ACCENT ON MUSIC. PO Box 417. Palo Alto, CA 94302. (415) 856-0987. Submissions Editor: Mark Hanson. Founded: 1987. Number of titles published: cumulative—2, 1991—1. Softback 100%.

Subjects of Interest. Nonfiction—how-to, music instructions. Recent publications: *Art of Contemporary Travis Picking; Solo Style Contemporary Travis Picking* (both instructional book plus audio cassette). Do not want: nonmusic subjects.

Initial Contact. Query letter; outline of book. Include author bio.

Acceptance Policies. Unagented manuscripts: yes. Simultaneous submissions: yes, query letter first. Disk submissions: no. Response time to initial inquiry: 4 weeks. Average time until publication: n/i. **Advance:** none. **Royalty:** negotiable. First run: 2000.

Marketing Channels. Distribution houses; mail orders. Subsidiary rights: English language publication outside United States and Canada.

Additional Information. We are looking for other high-quality books to distribute in our catalog. Catalog: upon request.

ACROBAT BOOKS. PO Box 1170. Los Angeles, CA 90294. (213) 578-1055. Submissions Editor: Anthony Cohan. Founded: 1975. Number of titles published: cumulative—22, 1991—2. Hardback 25%, softback 75%.

Subjects of Interest. Nonfiction—instruction and interviews in the creative arts (film, music, video, etc.). Recent publications: *Selling Your Film: A Guide to the Contemporary Marketplace; Directing the Film* (interviews with 75 famous film directors); *Stolen Moments* (conversations with contemporary musicians). Do not want: poetry; children's books.

Initial Contact. Query letter.

Acceptance Policies. Unagented manuscripts: yes. Multiple submissions: yes. Disk submissions: no. Response time to initial inquiry: 4 weeks. Average time until publication: 6 months. **Advance:** none. **Royalty:** 15-20%. First run: 3000-4000.

Marketing Channels. Distribution houses; direct mail; independent reps; in-house staff. Subsidiary rights: all.

Additional Information. Catalog: upon request.

ACS PUBLICATIONS. PO Box 34487. San Diego, CA 92116. (619) 297-9203. Submissions Editor: Maritha Pottenger. Founded: 1976. Number of titles published: cumulative—80, 1989—8. Hardback 5%, softback 95%.

Subjects of Interest. Nonfiction—astrology; metaphysical; holistic health. Recent publications: *The Inner Sky; Tables of Planetary Phenomenon; Book of Neptune.* Do not want: fiction or thinly disguised autobiographies.

Initial Contact. Query letter; outline of book.

Acceptance Policies. Unagented manuscripts: yes. Simultaneous submissions: query letter first. Disk submissions: no. Response time to initial inquiry: 1 month. Average time until publication: 2 years. **Advance:** none. **Royalty:** 15% of monies received. First run: 3000.

Marketing Channels. Distribution houses; direct mail; in-house staff; special sales. Subsidiary rights: all.

Additional Information. We do not accept deterministic (the planets are doing it to you) astrology; personal power and responsibility vital. Tips: Request "Guidelines for Potential Authors." Catalog: 8 1/2 x 11 manila envelope, 3 first class stamps.

AFCOM PUBLISHING. PO Box H. Harbor City, CA 90710-0330. (213) 326-7589. Submissions Editor: Greg Cook. Founded: 1986. Number of titles published: cumulative—7, 1991—4. Softback 100%.

Subjects of Interest. Fiction—children's books. Recent publications: *The Twelve Powers of Animals.* Nonfiction—how-to activity books. Recent publications: *Foundations of Continuous Measurable Improvement; Why Do I Eat More Than I Want Diet Book?; Why Do I Drink More Than I Want?; Over 101 Inexpensive Ways to Entertain Children.*

Initial Contact. Query letter; sample chapters.

Acceptance Policies. Unagented manuscripts: no. Disk submissions: no. Response time to initial inquiry: 4-6 weeks. Average time until publication: 6-8 months. **Advance:** n/i. **Royalty:** n/i. First run: n/i. Subsidy basis: price negotiable based on edition, graphics, printing, and binding.

Marketing Channels. Distribution houses; direct mail; independent sales reps; in-house staff; special sales. Subsidiary rights: none.

Additional Information. We are looking for books which are directed to an easily reached market. Catalog: write to publisher.

ALCHEMIST/LIGHT PUBLISHING. PO Box 5183. San Jose, CA 95150-5183. (408) 723-6108. Submissions Editor: Bil Paul. Founded: 1972. Number of titles published: cumulative—4, 1991—1. Softback 100%.

Subjects of Interest. Nonfiction—bicycle route guides. Recent publications: *Bicycling California's Spine.* Do not want: fiction; poetry.

Initial Contact. Query letter only. Include the geographical area covered and information about books previously published by the author.

Acceptance Policies. Unagented manuscripts: yes. Simultaneous submissions: yes. Disk submissions: prefer IBM Microsoft Word. Response time to initial inquiry: 2 weeks. Average time until publication: n/i. **Advance:** n/i. **Royalty:** n/i. First run: n/i.

Marketing Channels. n/i. Subsidiary rights: n/i.

ALLEN PUBLISHING COMPANY. PO Box 1889. Reseda, CA 91337.
(818) 344-6788. Submissions Editor: Michael Wiener. Founded: 1979. Number of titles published: cumulative—20, 1991—2. Softback 100%.

Subjects of Interest. Nonfiction—self-help book aimed at the "opportunity seeker" market. Recent publications: *A Consumer's Guide to Multi-Level Marketing.* Do not want: any other subject than our specialty.

Initial Contact. Query letter; SASE is mandatory.

Acceptance Policies. Unagented manuscripts: yes. Simultaneous submissions: yes. Disk submissions: no. Response time to initial inquiry: 2 weeks. Average time until publication: 6 months. **Advance:** negotiable. **Royalty:** negotiable. First run: varies.

Marketing Channels. Mail order only. Subsidiary rights: none.

Additional Information. Our audience consists of people, usually with limited financial assets, who want to start a business or find some other way to make money. Catalog: SASE.

ALTA NAPA PRESS. (Imprints: Gondwana Books). 1969 Mora Ave.
Calistoga, CA 94515. (707) 942-4444. Submissions Editor: Carl T. Endemann. Founded: 1976. Number of titles published: cumulative—16, 1991—2. Hardback 10%, softback 90%.

Subjects of Interest. Nonfiction—history; philosophy; poetry. Recent publications: *Wherever I Went* (travel sketches). **Other**—poetry (Gondwana Books). Recent publications: *Crossroads at the Antipodes* (experimental poetry in 7 languages, all originals). Do not want: sentimental personal gusts or pornography.

Initial Contact. Query letter and 2 sample chapters. Poetry: 3 poems. Include biographical background and philosophy; poetic goals and principles; and hour, date, and place of your birth. Include SASE.

Acceptance Policies. Unagented manuscripts: yes. Simultaneous submissions: no. Disk submissions: no. Response time to initial inquiry: 6 weeks. Average time until publication: 6 months. **Advance:** none. **Royalty:** n/i. First run: 500. Subsidy basis: yes.

Marketing Channels. Direct mail. Subsidiary rights: translation and foreign.

Additional Information. We want material on any subject of universal appeal which is clear and concise. Tips: Read our catalog. Catalog: $1.30.

American Astronautical Society *see* **UNIVELT, INC.**

AMERICAN BUSINESS CONSULTANTS. 1540 Nuthatch Lane.
Sunnyvale, CA 94087. (408) 738-3011. Submissions Editor: Wilfred F. Tetreault. Founded: n/i. Number of titles published: cumulative—100, 1991—2. Hardback 1%, softback 99%.

Subjects of Interest. Nonfiction—appraising, buying, selling, and financing all types of businesses; start-up companies; fraud in business. Recent publications: *Buying and Selling Business Opportunities; Starting Right in Your New Business.* Do not want: anything other than the above.

Initial Contact. Entire manuscript.

Acceptance Policies. Unagented manuscripts: yes. Simultaneous submissions: yes. Disk submissions: no. Response time to initial inquiry: 15 days. Average time until publication: 3 months. **Advance:** open. **Royalty:** open. First run: open.

Marketing Channels. Direct mail; special sales. Subsidiary rights: none.

Additional Information. I conduct weekly seminars throughout the country. Tips: It would be a good idea to attend a seminar. Catalog: write and ask.

AMERICAN INDIAN STUDIES. 3220 Campbell Hall, UCLA. Los Angeles, CA 90024. (213) 825-7315. Submissions Editor: Dr. Duane Champagne. Founded: 1970. Number of titles published: cumulative—39, 1991—6. Softback 100%.

Subjects of Interest. Nonfiction—scholarly approach to American Indian culture. Recent publications: *Contemporary Issues in Native American Health; Exemplar of Liberty; The Light on the Tent Wall.* Do not want: poetry.

Initial Contact. Query letter; book proposal with sample chapters or entire manuscript; precis. Include author bio.

Acceptance Policies. Unagented manuscripts: yes. Simultaneous submissions: no. Disk submissions: IBM; Macintosh. Response time to initial inquiry: 1 month. Average time until publication: 3-6 months. **Advance:** none. **Royalty:** none. First run: 1000-2500.

Marketing Channels. Cooperative distribution; direct mail; in-house staff. Subsidiary rights: none.

Additional Information. We seek primarily to publish scholarly research on American Indian topics. Tips: Submit 4 double-spaced copies; follow *Chicago Manual of Style* for end notes. Catalog: upon request.

AMERICAN INSTITUTE OF COMPUTER TECHNOLOGY. PO Box 2615. Pasadena, CA 91102. (818) 793-8429. Submissions Editor: Russell Simpson. Founded: 1984. Number of titles published: cumulative—5, 1991—2. Softback 100%.

Subjects of Interest. Nonfiction—how to make money at home with computers. Recent publications: *Make Money Moonlighting; Insider Secrets for the Desktop Publisher.*

Initial Contact. Query letter with synopsis/outline and book proposal. Include 2-4 page outline including chapter headings and itemized list of major topics or content of each chapter. Also include author's experience and expertise.

Acceptance Policies. Unagented manuscripts: yes. Simultaneous submissions: no. Disk submissions: ASCII; MS DOS; Macintosh. Response time to initial inquiry: 2 weeks. Average time until publication: 1 year. **Advance:** $1000-$2000. **Royalty:** 10%, based on actual monies received by the publisher. First run: 5000-10,000.

Marketing Channels. Direct mail; in-house staff; special sales. Subsidiary rights: n/i.

Additional Information. Catalog: Fall 1990, write for catalog. Writer's guidelines: write for brochure.

AMERICAN POETRY ASSOCIATION. 250 A Potrero St. PO Box 1803. Santa Cruz, CA 95061. (408) 429-1122. Submissions Editor: Richard Elliot. Founded: 1981. Number of titles published: cumulative—36, 1991—5. Hardback 100%.

Subjects of Interest. Other—poetry. Recent publications: *Up, Down, and Up Again.* Do not want: prose.

Initial Contact. 1 poem, no more than 20 lines. Include name and address on each.

Acceptance Policies. Unagented manuscripts: yes. Simultaneous submissions: yes; prefer previously unpublished. Disk submissions: no. Response time to initial inquiry: 3 weeks. Average time until publication: 6-9 months. **Advance:** none. **Royalty:** none. 152 contest winners receive $11,000 in prizes including $1000 grand prize. Four contests per year. First run: 2000.

Marketing Channels. Direct mail. Subsidiary rights: none; all rights remain with poet.

Additional Information. Every poet who sends poems automatically enters the poetry contest. Every poet receives a copy of the *Poet's Guide to Getting Published*.

AMERICA WEST PUBLISHERS. PO Box 6451. Tehachapi, CA 93582.
(805) 822-9655. Submissions Editor: George Green. Founded: 1987. Number of titles published: cumulative—19, 1990—20. Hardback 10%, softback 90%.

Subjects of Interest. Nonfiction—metaphysical; health and medicine; UFOs; holistic; self-help; new age. Recent publications: *Spacegate: The Veil Removed; Spiral to Economic Disaster; AIDS: The Last Great Plague; Violet Flame and Other Meditations; Conversations with Nostradamus U-1*.

Initial Contact. Query letter with synopsis/outline.

Acceptance Policies. Unagented manuscripts: yes. Simultaneous submissions: no. Disk submissions: no. Response time to initial inquiry: 1 month. Average time until publication: 6 months. **Advance**: $300+/-. **Royalty**: 10-15% based on actual monies received by publisher. First run: 3000.

Marketing Channels. Distribution houses; cooperative distribution; direct mail; in-house staff. Subsidiary rights: all.

Additional Information. Catalog: upon request. Writer's guidelines: upon request.

APPLETON AND LANGE. (Subsidiary of Simon and Schuster). 2755 Campus
Dr. San Mateo, CA 94403. (415) 377-0977. Submissions Editors: Ruth Weinberg (basic science); Nancy Evans (clinical science). Founded: 1938. Number of titles published: cumulative—40, 1991—12. Softback 100%.

Subjects of Interest. Nonfiction—medical. Do not want: anything outside of medicine.

Initial Contact. Book proposal with 2 sample chapters. Include table of contents; affiliations.

Acceptance Policies. Unagented manuscripts: yes. Simultaneous submissions: no. Disk submissions: yes. Response time to initial inquiry: 3 months. Average time until publication: depends on subject. **Advance**: none. **Royalty**: yes. First run: n/i.

Marketing Channels. Distribution houses; direct mail; independent reps; in-house staff; special sales. Subsidiary rights: direct mail or direct sales; book club; translation and foreign; English language publication outside the United States and Canada.

Additional Information. The authors and editors of our books are practicing physicians or Ph.D.s on the faculty of medical schools and hospitals. Tips: We publish brief, concise, practical, quick references in basic sciences and clinical medicine. Catalog: upon request.

APPLEZABA PRESS. PO Box 4134. Long Beach, CA 90804. (213) 591-0015.
Submissions Editor: D. H. Lloyd. Founded: 1977. Number of titles published: cumulative—32, 1991—4. Hardback 10%, softback 90%.

Subjects of Interest. Fiction—modern novels; short story collections. Recent publications: *The Gold Rush*. Nonfiction—cookbooks. Recent publications: *College Quickies Cookbook* (second enlarged edition). Poetry. Recent publications: *Gridlock: Poetry About Southern California*. Do not want: genre fiction (romance, detective, etc.).

Initial Contact. Query for fiction and nonfiction; entire manuscript for poetry.

Acceptance Policies. Unagented manuscripts: yes. Simultaneous submissions: yes; inform us. Disk submissions: no. First novels: yes. Response time to initial inquiry: 5-8 weeks. Average time until publication: 3 years. **Advance**: up to $100. **Royalty**: 8-12%. First run: 1000-3000.

Marketing Channels. Distribution houses; cooperative distribution; direct mail. Subsidiary rights: all.
Additional Information. Catalog: #10 SASE.

ARIEL VAMP PRESS. PO Box 3496. Berkeley, CA 94703. (415) 654-4849. Submissions Editor: Jolene Babyak. Founded: 1987. Number of titles published: 1988—1. Softback 100%.
Subjects of Interest. Nonfiction—prison; prisoners; serious jazz musicians. Recent publications: *Eyewitness on Alcatraz: Interviews with Guards, Families and Prisoners Who Lived on the Rock*.
Initial Contact. Query letter.
Acceptance Policies. Unagented manuscripts: no. Simultaneous submissions: yes. Disk submissions: no. Response time to initial inquiry: 4-6 weeks. Average time until publication: 18 months. **Advance**: n/i. **Royalty**: n/i. First run: n/i.
Marketing Channels. Distribution houses; direct mail. Subsidiary rights: n/i.

Asian Humanities Press *see* **JAIN PUBLISHING COMPANY.**

ASTRONOMICAL SOCIETY OF THE PACIFIC. 390 Ashton Ave. San Francisco, CA 94112. (415) 337-1100. Submissions Editor: Andrew Fraknoi. Founded: 1889. Number of titles published: cumulative—25.
Subjects of Interest. Nonfiction—space science; astronomy. Recent publications: *The Extragalactic Distance Scale, Synthesis Imaging in Radio Astronomy*.
Initial Contact. Very little work by outsiders accepted; authors must have track record in science or science writing.
Acceptance Policies. Unagented manuscripts: yes. Simultaneous submissions: no. Disk submissions: WordPerfect. Response time to initial inquiry: depends on project. Average time until publication: depends. **Advance:** n/i. **Royalty:** n/i. First run: n/i.
Marketing Channels. n/i. Subsidiary rights: n/i.
Additional Information. We are a nonprofit scientific educational organization publishing educational materials. We publish *Mercury* magazine as well as a newsletter for teachers, a series of conference proceedings, and a catalog of educational materials.

ATHLETIC PRESS. (Subsidiary of Golden West Books). PO Box 80250. San Marino, CA 91118. (818) 283-3446. Submissions Editor: Donald Duke. Founded: 1971. Number of titles published: cumulative—20, 1991—0. Softback 100%.
Subjects of Interest. Nonfiction—conditioning for sports. Recent publications: *Stretching for All Sports*.
Initial Contact. Query letter; general description.
Acceptance Policies. Unagented manuscripts: yes. Simultaneous submissions: no. Disk submissions: no. Response time to initial inquiry: 4-6 months. Average time until publication: 1 year. **Advance:** none. **Royalty:** 10%. First run: 3000.
Marketing Channels. Distribution houses; direct mail; independent sales reps. Subsidiary rights: none.

AUTHORS UNLIMITED. 3324 Barham Blvd. Los Angeles, CA 90068.
(213) 874-0902. Submissions Editors: Renais Hill, Jon Rappaport, S. E. Bernstein.
Founded: 1981. Number of titles published: cumulative—200,1991—30. Hardback
10%, softback 90%.

Subjects of Interest. Fiction—Recent Publications: *The President's Black Bag; One Eye Cries.* Nonfiction—Recent Publications: *Diverse Forces in Yugoslavia 1941/1945; Wahoosi, True Tale of an Indian Missionary.* Poetry. Do not want: anything pornographic.

Initial Contact. Query letter and complete manuscript.

Acceptance Policies. Unagented manuscripts: yes. Simultaneous submissions: yes, if informed who else submitted to. Disk submissions: no. First novels: yes. Response time to initial inquiry: 2 weeks. Average time until publication: 9 months. **Advance**: none. **Royalty**: scale. First run: 2000.

Marketing Channels. Distribution houses; cooperative distribution; direct mail; in-house staff; special sales. Subsidiary rights: all.

Additional Information. Send clean manuscript in proper format. Catalog: SASE plus $.90.

AUTO BOOK PRESS. PO Bin 711. San Marcos, CA 92069. (619) 744-3582.
Submissions Editor: William Carroll. Founded: 1955. Number of titles published:
cumulative—20, 1991—4. Hardback and softback.

Subjects of Interest. Nonfiction—automotive material; technical or definitive how-to. Recent publications: *The Singles' Philosopher.*

Initial Contact. Query letter.

Acceptance Policies. Unagented manuscripts: yes. Simultaneous submissions: yes. Response time to initial inquiry: 2 weeks. Average time until publication: 1 year. **Advance**: varies. **Royalty**: 15%.

Marketing Channels. Direct mail. Subsidiary rights: none.

Additional Information. Tips: Take time to research the market. Catalog: write and request.

Avant *see* **SLAWSON COMMUNICATIONS, INC.**

AVIATION BOOK COMPANY. 25133 Anza Dr., Unit E. Santa Clarita, CA
91355. (805) 294-0101. Submissions Editor: W. P. Winner. Founded: 1964.
Number of titles published: cumulative—17, 1991—2. Hardback and softback.

Subjects of Interest. Nonfiction—technical aviation; pilot training; aeronautical history. Recent publications: *Instrument Flight Training Manual; 1990 Federal Aviation Regulations for Pilots; 1990 Airman's Information Manual; Tips on Buying Cessna Singles.*

Initial Contact. Query letter; outline.

Acceptance Policies. Unagented manuscripts: yes. Response time to initial inquiry: 2 months. Average time until publication: 9 months. **Advance**: none. **Royalty**: paid on retail price.

Marketing Channels. n/i. Subsidiary rights: n/i.

Additional Information. Tips: Let us know what is unique about your book and why it's better than its competition. We are willing to look at artwork and photos. Catalog: 9x12 SASE, $1 postage.

BALLENA PRESS. 823 Valparaiso Ave. Menlo Park, CA 94025. Submissions Editor: Sylvia Vane. Founded: 1971. Number of titles published: cumulative—50, 1991—4-6. Hardback, some; softback, all.

Subjects of Interest. Nonfiction—anthropology of the western United States; Indian cultures.

Initial Contact. Entire manuscript. Manuscript will not be returned and therefore should be only a photocopy of the original. Include identification of author.

Acceptance Policies. Unagented manuscripts: yes. Simultaneous submissions: no. Disk submissions: If accepted, we shall ask that the manuscript be submitted on WordPerfect. Response time to initial inquiry: 1 week to 6 months. Average time until publication: 6 months to 2 years. **Advance:** none. **Royalty:** 5-10%. First run: 500-1500.

Marketing Channels. Direct mail; distribution houses; cooperative distribution with institutions (usually museums). Subsidiary rights: all.

Additional Information. We have a considerable number of accepted manuscripts and are generally not on the lookout for manuscripts except from those who know our reputation and what we are looking for. Catalog: upon request.

BARR-RANDOL PUBLISHING COMPANY. 136A N. Grand Ave. West Covina, CA 91791. (818) 339-0270. Submissions Editor: G. F. Coats. Founded: 1985. Number of titles published: cumulative—1. Softback 100%.

Subjects of Interest. Nonfiction—real estate and mortgage investment. Recent publications: *Smart Trust Deed Investment in California, 2nd Edition.* Do not want: manuscripts that require more than minor editing.

Initial Contact. Book proposal with sample chapters.

Acceptance Policies. Unagented manuscripts: yes. Simultaneous submissions: yes. Disk submissions: no. Response time to initial inquiry: 3 weeks. Average time until publication: n/i. **Advance:** n/i. **Royalty:** n/i. First run: n/i.

Marketing Channels. Distribution houses; cooperative distribution; direct mail; in-house staff. Subsidiary rights: all.

Additional Information. We have a very narrow focus and know exactly what we want.

BAY VIEW ASSOCIATES. PO Box 5281. San Mateo, CA 94402. (415) 344-5509. Submissions Editor: Barbara Duffy. Founded: 1989. Number of titles published: 1991—3. Softback 100%.

Subjects of Interest. Nonfiction—occult; self-help. Do not want: Satanism.

Initial Contact. Query letter with synopsis/outline.

Acceptance Policies. Unagented manuscripts: yes. Simultaneous submissions: yes. Disk submissions: Apple IIC, E. Response time to initial inquiry: 1 month. Average time until publication: 6 months. **Advance:** varies. **Royalty:** varies. First run: varies.

Marketing Channels. Distribution houses; special sales. Subsidiary rights: all.

Additional Information. We are a brand new company. Catalog: none. Writer's guidelines: call and request.

BEDFORD ARTS, PUBLISHERS. 301 Brannan St. #410. San Francisco, CA 94107. (415) 882-7870. Submissions Editor: Stephen Vincent. Founded: 1986. Number of titles published: cumulative—15, 1991—4. Hardback 65%, softback 35%.

Subjects of Interest. Nonfiction—art books; books on typography; illustrated biographies; reprints of art and criticism. Recent publications: *Facing History: The Black Image in American Art; O California!; The Futurist Cookbook.*

Initial Contact. Book proposal with sample chapters; art work, if possible.

Acceptance Policies. Unagented manuscripts: yes. Simultaneous submissions: yes. Disk submissions: WordPerfect; MultiMate; IBM DW3; Wang; WordStar; Volksriter; Microsoft Word; Smana; ASCII. Response time to initial inquiry: 1 month. Average time until publication: varies. **Advance:** varies. **Royalty:** 4% of gross sales. First run: 5000+/-.

Marketing Channels. Distribution houses; cooperative distribution; direct mail; special sales. Subsidiary rights: first serialization; second serialization; reprint rights; direct mail or sales rights; book club rights; translation and foreign rights; English language publication outside the United States and Canada.

Additional Information. Catalog: upon request.

BENMIR BOOKS. 2512 9th St., Ste. 8. Berkeley, CA 94710. (415) 849-9117. Submissions Editor: Boris Bresler. Founded: 1983. Number of titles published: cumulative—6 , 1991—2. Hardback 25%, softback 75%.

Subjects of Interest. Fiction—Jewish themes. Recent publications: *Imaginary Number* (short stories); *From Leningrad to Jerusalem.* Nonfiction—Jewish themes. Recent publications: *One and One Make Three* (dual autobiography). Do not want: poetry.

Initial Contact. Sample chapters; entire manuscript; biographical information.

Acceptance Policies. Unagented manuscripts: yes. Simultaneous submissions: yes. Disk submissions: no. First novels: yes. Response time to initial inquiry: 2 months. Average time until publication: 12 months. **Advance:** varies. **Royalty:** 15% on net. First run: 3000.

Marketing Channels. Distribution houses; cooperative distribution; direct mail; in-house staff. Subsidiary rights: none; for now, no policy.

Additional Information. We only want books on Jewish themes. Tips: No poetry. Catalog: upon request.

Benziger *see* **GLENCOE/MCGRAW-HILL EDUCATIONAL DIVISION.**

BICYCLE BOOKS, INC. 32 Glen Dr. PO Box 2038. Mill Valley, CA 94941. (415) 381-0172. Fax: (415) 381-6912. Submissions Editor: Christina Nau. Founded: 1985. Number of titles published: cumulative—15, 1991—4. Hardback 33%, softback 67%.

Subjects of Interest. Nonfiction—how-to, sports, recreational, and travel books related to bicycling. Recent publications: *In High Gear* (international bike racing); *Tour of the Forest* (bike racing comic); *The New Bike Book* (beginners grade); *Mountain Bike Maintenance; Bicycle Fitness Book; Bicycle Commuting Book.*

Initial Contact. Entire manuscript; photographs and art work.

Acceptance Policies. Unagented manuscripts: yes. Simultaneous submissions: yes. Disk submissions: IBM PC formatted discs in 360KB; ASCII files. Response time to initial inquiry: 6 weeks. Average time until publication: 1 year. **Advance:** none. **Royalty:** 7 1/2%. First run: 5000-8000.

Marketing Channels. Distribution houses; cooperative distribution; direct mail; in-house sales. Subsidiary rights: all.

Additional Information. Catalog: SASE.

Billiard Books *see* **MONEYTREE PUBLISHING.**

BIOFEEDBACK PRESS. (Subsidiary of Biofeedback Institute of San Francisco). 3428 Sacramento St. San Francisco, CA 94118. (415) 921-6500. Submissions Editor: Dr. George von Bozzay, president. Founded: 1973. Number of titles published: 1991—no new titles. Hardback 25%, softback 75%.

Subjects of Interest. Nonfiction—stress management; behavioral medicine; biofeedback. Recent publications: *Biofeedback Methods and Procedures* (introductory manual); *Behavioral Medicine, Stress Management and Biofeedback* (clinician's desk reference); *Projects in Biofeedback* (text/workbook); *What is Biofeedback?* (information paperback for students and patients).

Initial Contact. Query letter.

Acceptance Policies. Unagented manuscripts: yes. Simultaneous submissions: no. Disk submissions: no. Response time to initial inquiry: 30 days. Average time until publication: 1 year. **Advance:** negotiable. **Royalty:** negotiable. First run: varies.

Marketing Channels. Direct mail; independent reps. Subsidiary rights: none.

Additional Information. Most titles are specifically targeted to health professionals specializing in behavioral health. Catalog: upon request.

BLAKE PUBLISHING. (Subsidiary of The Graphic Center). 2222 Beebee St. San Luis Obispo, CA 93401. (805) 543-6843. Submissions Editor: Vicki Leon. Founded: 1983. Number of titles published: cumulative—17, 1991—3. Softback 100%.

Subjects of Interest. Nonfiction—nature; regional travel; food and cooking. Recent publications: *The Coral Reef; The Kelp Forest.* Do not want: poetry; fiction.

Initial Contact. Query letter. Include credits.

Acceptance Policies. Unagented manuscripts: no. Simultaneous submissions: no. Disk submissions: no. Response time to initial inquiry: 4-6 weeks. Average time until publication: 6-12 months. **Advance:** varies. **Royalty:** varies. First run: varies.

Marketing Channels. Distribution houses; independent reps; in-house staff. Subsidiary rights: none.

Additional Information. Catalog: upon request.

BLUE DOLPHIN PUBLISHING, INC. 12380 Nevada City Hwy. Grass Valley, CA 95945. (916) 265-6925. Submissions Editor: Paul M. Clemens. Founded: 1985. Number of titles published: cumulative—22, 1991—5. Hardback 10%, softback 90%.

Subjects of Interest. Nonfiction—psychology (lay and professional); comparative spiritual traditions (Zen, Tibetan, Sufi); health; death and dying; video and audio cassettes. Recent publications: *Do Less . . . And Be Loved More; Blatant Raw Foodist Propaganda; The Middle Path of Life; A Practical Guide to Creative Senility.*

Initial Contact. Query letter; book proposal with sample chapters; or entire manuscript. Include author biography and references.

Acceptance Policies. Unagented manuscripts: yes. Simultaneous submissions: yes; inform us. Disk submissions: IBM; ASCII. Response time to initial inquiry: 6 weeks to 3 months.

Average time until publication: 6-9 months. **Advance**: none. **Royalty**: 10% on invoice total. First run: 2000-5000.

Marketing Channels. Distribution houses; direct mail. Subsidiary rights: all.

Additional Information. We also own and operate Blue Dolphin Press, Inc., and produce all productions in-house. Tips: We are looking for only the very best manuscripts, concise and practical, to help people become better individuals. Catalog: upon request.

BLUESTOCKING PRESS. PO Box 1014-wc. Placerville, CA 95667. (916) 621-1123. Submissions Editor: Jane A. Williams. Founded: 1987. Number of titles published: cumulative—4, 1991—3. Softback 100%.

Subjects of Interest. **Fiction**—children's and young adult; biographies for children on United States and colonial history figures, 1700-1900; adult historical fiction, 1700-1900; fiction stressing self-reliance, reasoning, and independence. **Nonfiction**—alternatives in education; Austrian free market economies; family issues. Do not want: textbooks; contrived and forced poetry.

Initial Contact. Query letter and sample chapters. Include SASE for returning sample and our response.

Acceptance Policies. Unagented manuscripts: yes. Simultaneous submissions: yes. Disk submissions: no. Response time to initial inquiry: 3-4 months. Average time until publication: 12-18 months. **Advance**: none. **Royalty**: negotiable based on gross. First run: 1000-5000.

Marketing Channels. Cooperative distribution; direct mail; special sales. Subsidiary rights: n/i.

Additional Information. Everything we do involves individuals having the right to choose (consumer products, work, education). Catalog: SASE.

Body Press *see* **PRICE STERN SLOAN, INC.**

BORGO PRESS. Box 2845. San Bernardino, CA 92406. (714) 884-5813. Submissions Editor: Robert Reginald. Founded: 1975. Number of titles published: cumulative—1000, 1991—100. Hardback, softback, we do everything in both versions.

Subjects of Interest. **Nonfiction**—scholarly books and reference works for the library and academic markets; scholarly monographs. Recent publications: *The Work of Colin Wilson: An Annotated Bibliography and Guide; To Kill or Not to Kill: Thoughts on Capital Punishment.* Do not want: fiction; poetry; children's books; trade books; popular nonfiction; etc.

Initial Contact. Query letter. Include some evidence the author has looked at our books, not our catalog.

Acceptance Policies. Unagented manuscripts: yes. Simultaneous submissions: no. Disk submissions: no. Response time to initial inquiry: 2 months plus. Average time until publication: 2 years plus. **Advance**: none. **Royalty**: 10%. First run: 100-1000.

Marketing Channels. Direct mail. Subsidiary rights: all.

Additional Information. We throw away submissions without SASEs. All of our books are published in open-ended, numbered, monographic series. Tips: Do not submit manuscripts unless you have seen our books. Catalog: SASE with $.85 postage.

BOXWOOD PRESS. 183 Ocean View Blvd. Pacific Grove, CA 93950. (408) 375-9110. Submissions Editor: Dr. Buchsbaum. Founded: 1952. Number of titles published: cumulative—100; 1991—5. Hardback 50%, softback 50%.

Subjects of Interest. Nonfiction—biology; natural history; area studies; psychology; psychiatry; mathematics; economics; biography. Recent publications: *Living Invertebrates; Beyond the Birding; Hydra.*

Initial Contact. Entire manuscript (no proposals). Include curriculum vitae (indicate your expertise).

Acceptance Policies. Unagented manuscripts: yes. Simultaneous submissions: yes. Disk submissions: yes. Response time to initial inquiry: 3 weeks approximately. Average time until publication: 5 months from clean manuscript. **Advance:** none. **Royalty:** 10%. First run: 1000 (up to 5000). Subsidy basis: Project must be sound and have an identifiable market.

Marketing Channels. Distribution houses; direct mail; independent reps; in-house staff; special sales. Subsidiary rights: all.

Additional Information. Tips: Have it neat, double-spaced, and clean. Catalog: upon request.

BRANDYWYNE BOOKS. (Subsidiary of Affaire de Coeur). 1555 Washington Ave. San Leandro, CA 94577. (415) 357-5665. Submissions Editor: Barbara Keenan. Number of titles published: cumulative—4, 1991—4. Hardback 100%. We publish reprints only; authors must have all rights.

Subjects of Interest. Fiction—romance; mystery; science fiction. Recent publications: *Ring of Fear.* Nonfiction—cookbooks. Do not want: unpublished books unless author queries first.

Initial Contact. Query letter and book. Include SASE for return. We will print unpublished books with our charges and setup costs added to the printing.

Acceptance Policies. Unagented manuscripts: yes. Simultaneous submissions: yes. Disk submissions: no. Response time to initial inquiry: 3-4 months. Average time until publication: 6 months. **Advance:** only on accepted reprints. **Royalty:** after first 60,000. First run: 65,000. Subsidy basis: yes.

Marketing Channels. Distribution houses; direct mail. Subsidiary rights: none.

Additional Information. We are a very small press, and most of our books go through the library. Tips: Always send SASE. We will agent a manuscript out to larger houses if it is good. Catalog: send SASE.

BRENNER INFORMATION GROUP. (Subsidiary of Brenner Microcomputing, Inc.). 13223 Black Mountain Rd., Ste. 430. San Diego, CA 92129. (619) 693-0355. Submissions Editor: Robert C. Brenner. Founded: 1982/1988. Number of titles published: cumulative—9, 1991—8. Softback 100%.

Subjects of Interest. Nonfiction—how-to; self-help; reference. Recent publications: *How to Start Your Own Desktop Publishing; Checklist for First Time Publishers; The 1990 Index for Desktop Publishing.* Do not want: novels.

Initial Contact. Query letter; book proposal with sample chapters. Include biography.

Acceptance Policies. Unagented manuscripts: yes. Simultaneous submissions: yes; inform us. Disk submissions: MS-DOS; Macintosh. Response time to initial inquiry: 2-4 weeks. Average time until publication: 2-6 months. **Advance:** variable. **Royalty:** 9-17%. First run: 2000-5000. Subsidy basis: Will produce finished product from initial manuscript; will consult on marketing and sales; also do share-cost publishing.

Marketing Channels. Distribution houses; direct mail; in-house staff; special sales. Subsidiary rights: all.

Additional Information. Our purpose is to collect, process, format, package, and distribute information of value to people. Tips: Request guidelines. Catalog: upon request.

Broadway Books *see* **HUNTER HOUSE, INC., PUBLISHERS.**

BRISTOL PUBLISHING ENTERPRISES. (Imprints: Bristol; Nitty Gritty).
PO Box 1737. San Leandro, CA 94577. (415) 895-4461; 1-800-346-4889. Submissions Editor: Patricia J. Hall. Founded: 1987; purchased Nitty Gritty 1988. Number of titles published: cumulative—47, 1991—10. Softback 100%.

Subjects of Interest. Nonfiction—cookbooks; books for people over 50. Recent publications: *Turkey, the Magic Ingredient; The Encyclopedia of Grandparenting*.

Initial Contact. Query letter with synopsis/outline. Include resumé, sample of published writing.

Acceptance Policies. Unagented manuscripts: yes. Simultaneous submissions: yes. Disk submissions: IBM compatible; Microsoft Word; ASCII. Response time to initial inquiry: 60-90 days. Average time until publication: 6-12 months. **Advance**: negotiable. **Royalty**: negotiable. First run: negotiable.

Marketing Channels. Distribution houses; direct mail; independent reps; special sales. Subsidiary rights: n/i.

Additional Information. Tips: Authors of cookbooks must have a proven track record in the food industry—writing, cooking, teaching, other. Catalog: upon request. Writer's guidelines: SASE.

BUDDHA ROSE PUBLICATIONS. PO Box 902. Hermosa Beach, CA
90254. (213) 543-3809. Submissions Editor: Eliot Sebastian. Founded: 1989. Number of titles published: cumulative—28, 1991—15. Hardback 25%, softback 75%.

Subjects of Interest. Fiction—literary. Recent publications: *The Passionate Kiss of Illusion*. Nonfiction—philosophy; metaphysics; cultural studies; poetry. Recent publications: *Cambodian Refugees* in Long Beach, California.

Initial Contact. Entire manuscript.

Acceptance Policies. Unagented manuscripts: yes. First novels: yes. Simultaneous submissions: yes. Disk submissions: no. Response time to initial inquiry: 3 months. Average time until publication: 6 months. **Advance**: none. **Royalty**: 15% of total sales. First run: 1000. Subsidy basis: with new authors.

Marketing Channels. Distribution houses; direct mail; in-house staff. Subsidiary rights: all.

Additional Information. Catalog: upon request.

BULL PUBLISHING COMPANY. 110 Gilbert. Menlo Park, CA 94025.
(415) 322-2855. Submissions Editor: David C. Bull. Founded: 1974. Number of titles published: cumulative—85, 1991—6. Hardback 5%, softback 95%.

Subjects of Interest. Nonfiction—health; nutrition; fitness; cancer care and prevention. Recent publications: *Print That Works: The First Step-by-Step Guide that Integrates Writing, Design, and Marketing; Great Shape: The First Fitness Guide for Large Women; Fitness and Sports Medicine: An Introduction*. Do not want: books with only trade potential; must have some crossover to professional markets (medical and allied health).

Initial Contact. Book proposal with sample chapters. Include listing of potential markets.

Acceptance Policies. Unagented manuscripts: yes. Simultaneous submissions: no. Disk submissions: no. Response time to initial inquiry: 2 weeks. Average time until publication: 9 months. **Advance**: varies. **Royalty**: 10-15% of net. First run: 5000+ (depending on the book).

Marketing Channels. Distribution houses; direct mail; special sales. Subsidiary rights: all.

Additional Information. Catalog: upon request.

BURNING GATE PRESS. PO Box 6015. Mission Hills, CA 91395-1015. (818) 896-8780. Submissions Editor: Mark H. Kelly. Founded: 1990. Number of titles published: 1991—5. Hardback 80%, softback 20%.

Subjects of Interest. Fiction—mainstream; suspense; techno-thrillers. **Nonfiction**—art; business; science and technology; photography; travel; general. Do not want: nothing excluded.

Initial Contact. Query letter with synopsis/outline and sample chapters. Include author resumé.

Acceptance Policies. Unagented manuscripts: yes. First novels: yes. Simultaneous submissions: yes. Disk submissions: no. Response time to initial inquiry: 4 weeks. Average time until publication: 3-6 months. **Advance**: less than $10,000. **Royalty**: 20% flat, based on publisher's net revenue. First run: 5000, average.

Marketing Channels. Distribution houses; direct mail; special sales. Subsidiary rights: all.

Additional Information. We are committed to publishing only the highest caliber original works of general interest nonfiction and fiction by new and established authors. Tips: Call first. Catalog: call or write. Writer's guidelines: call or write.

CADMUS EDITIONS. Box 687. Tiburon, CA 94920. (707) 431-8527. Submissions Editor: Jeffrey Miller. Founded: 1979. Number of titles published: cumulative—18, 1991—2. Hardback 20%, softback 80%.

Subjects of Interest. Fiction—Recent publications: *The Hungry Girls and Other Stories*; *The Pigeon Factory; Early Routines*. **Nonfiction**—poetry. Recent publications: *How a City Sings* (Federico Garcia Lorca); *The Wandering Fool*.

Initial Contact. Query letter. Include curriculum vitae with list of publications to date. Also include SASE.

Acceptance Policies. Unagented manuscripts: yes. Simultaneous submissions: no. Disk submissions: no. First novels: yes. Response time to initial inquiry: 30-45 days. Average time until publication: 12 to 18 months. **Advance**: usually none. **Royalty**: negotiable. First run: 2000.

Marketing Channels. Distribution houses; independent reps. Subsidiary rights: all.

Additional Information. Catalog: upon request.

CALGRE PRESS. PO Box 711. Antioch, CA 94509. (415) 754-4916. Submissions Editor: Diane Power. Founded: 1988. Number of titles published: cumulative—4, 1991—4. Hardback 3%, softback 97%.

Subjects of Interest. Fiction—children's illustrated stories. **Nonfiction**—how-to; self-help parenting; education; business. Recent publications: *Raising Kids for Success; The Defiant Ones* (parenting); *PC Ordeal* (how-to computer).

Initial Contact. Query letter only.

Acceptance Policies. Unagented manuscripts: yes. Simultaneous submissions: yes. Disk submissions: no. First novels: yes. Response time to initial inquiry: 2 months. Average time until publication: 1 year. **Advance**: negotiable. **Royalty**: 10-15%. First run: n/i.

Marketing Channels. Distribution houses; cooperative distribution; direct mail; independent sales; in-house staff; special sales. Subsidiary rights: first serialization; second serialization; newspaper syndication; dramatization, motion picture, and broadcast rights; video distribution; direct mail or direct sales; book club.

Additional Information. We cater to first-time and little-known authors. Tips: Our books are aimed at parents and children from preschool age up through high school. Catalog: upon request. Writer's guidelines: upon request.

C & T PUBLISHING. PO Box 1456. Lafayette, CA 94549. 5021 Blum Rd., #1. Martinez, CA 94553. (415) 937-0605; (800) 284-1114. Submissions Editor: Todd Hensley. Founded: 1983. Number of titles published: cumulative—34, 1991—4. Hardback 5%, softback 95%.

Subjects of Interest. Nonfiction—how-to quilting books. Recent publications: *Baltimore Beauties and Beyond; Perfect Pineapples; Wearable Art for Real People; Crosspatch* (all how-to-quilt books); *Visions: Quilts of a New Decade* (catalog from a juried show). Do not want: any material outside quilting field.

Initial Contact. Query letter; perhaps photos of quilts to be included.

Acceptance Policies. Unagented manuscripts: yes. Simultaneous submissions: no. Disk submissions: ASCII file. Response time to initial inquiry: 1 week. Average time until publication: 9-12 months. **Advance**: negotiable; subsidizes author's photographic expenses. **Royalty**: 8% retail. First run: 10,000-15,000.

Marketing Channels. Direct mail; independent reps; craft product distributors. Subsidiary rights: all.

Additional Information. We only publish quilting books. Tips: Send for author's packet.

CANTERBURY PRESS. Box 2151C. Berkeley, CA 94702. (415) 843-1860. Submissions Editor: Ian Faircloth and Norine Brogans. Number of titles published: cumulative—10; 1991—2.

Subjects of Interest. Fiction—adventure; experimental; fantasy; humor; needs to have a social, political, or cultural insight. Recent publications: *Perigrina* (children's bilingual). Nonfiction—philosophy; social justice; sociology; studies on the "third world"; minorities; underprivileged. Recent publications: *Living Outside Inside* (problems of the disabled). Do not want: books which do not exhibit our philosophy.

Initial Contact. Query letter; outline.

Acceptance Policies. Unsolicited manuscripts: query first; all unsolicited manuscripts are returned unopened. Unagented manuscripts: yes. Disk submissions: query. Response time to initial inquiry: 1 month, queries; 2 months, manuscripts. Average time until publication: 4 months. **Advance**: $500. **Royalty**: 5-8%. Subsidy basis: yes; 50%.

Marketing Channels. n/i. Subsidiary rights: n/i.

Additional Information. We are appealing to a mature audience that appreciates innovative writing, new ideas, and insights. Tips: Send for manuscript guidelines; #10 SASE. Catalog: #10 SASE.

CAPRA PRESS. PO Box 2068. Santa Barbara, CA 93120. Submissions Editor: Noel Young. Founded: 1969. Number of titles published: cumulative—300, 1991—15. Hardback 33%, softback 67%.

Subjects of Interest. Fiction—general trade with a focus on the west. Nonfiction—birdwatching, outdoor, natural history; folklore; creative writing; essays. Do not want: poetry; children's books; cookbooks; first novels.

Initial Contact. Book proposal. Include sample chapters, professional background of the author, and evaluation of the uniqueness of this particular book.

Acceptance Policies. Unagented manuscripts: yes. Simultaneous submissions: yes. Disk submissions: yes. Response time to initial inquiry: 6 weeks. Average time until publication: 2 years. **Advance:** varies. **Royalty:** 12% based on net sales. First run: 5000-10,000.

Marketing Channels. Consortium book sales; direct mail; special sales. Subsidiary rights: all.

Additional Information. Tips: Read our catalog first. Catalog: call us directly.

CAREER PUBLISHING, INC. 910 N. Main St. PO Box 5486. Orange, CA 92613-5486. (714) 771-5155. Submissions Editor: Marilyn Martin. Founded: 1972. Number of titles published: cumulative—65, 1991—10. Softback 100%.

Subjects of Interest. Nonfiction—vocational courses; medical; computer, word processing; truck driving textbooks. Recent publications: handbook/workbook for Wordstar, WordPerfect, HyperCard; *Occupational Outlook Handbook; CDL Bus/Truck Guides; PFS: First Publisher*. Do not want: fiction or poetry.

Initial Contact. Query letter.

Acceptance Policies. Unagented manuscripts: yes. Simultaneous submissions: no. Disk submissions: yes; Apple and IBM compatibles. Response time to initial inquiry: 30 days. Average time until publication: 1 year. **Advance:** none. **Royalty:** 10%. First run: 3000-5000.

Marketing Channels. Cooperative distribution; in-house staff. Subsidiary rights: all.

Additional Information. Write for guidelines. Catalog: upon request.

CAROUSEL PRESS. PO Box 6061. Albany, CA 94706. (415) 527-5849. Submissions Editor: Carole T. Meyers. Founded: 1976. Number of titles published: cumulative—10, 1989—1. Hardback 5%, softback 95%.

Subjects of Interest. Nonfiction—family travel; California travel. Recent publications: *San Francisco Family Fun; Weekend Adventures for City-Weary People: Overnight Trips in Northern California*.

Initial Contact. Book proposal with sample chapters. Include SASE.

Acceptance Policies. Unagented manuscripts: yes. Simultaneous submissions: no. Disk submissions: no. Response time to initial inquiry: 2 weeks. Average time until publication: 1 year. **Advance:** no. **Royalty:** standard. First run: 5000.

Marketing Channels. Distribution houses; direct mail; in-house staff; special sales. Subsidiary rights: all.

Additional Information. Catalog: SASE with $.45 postage.

CASSANDRA PRESS. PO Box 868. San Rafael, CA 94915. (415) 382-8507. Submissions Editor: Gurudas. Founded: 1985. Number of titles published: cumulative—19, 1991—5. Softback 100%.

Subjects of Interest. Nonfiction—new age; metaphysical; holistic health; astrology; psychology.

Initial Contact. Query letter; or book proposal with sample chapters.

Acceptance Policies. Unagented manuscripts: yes. Simultaneous submissions: yes. Disk submissions: no. Response time to initial inquiry: 1-2 months. Average time until publication: 9-12 months. **Advance**: none. **Royalty**: 6% on retail; higher as sales increase. First run: 8000-14,000.

Marketing Channels. Distribution houses; direct mail. Subsidiary rights: all.

Additional Information. Catalog: upon request.

CATALYSTS PUBLICATIONS. 143 Dolores St. San Francisco, CA 94103. (415) 552-5045. Submissions Editor: Bonnie Weiss. Founded: 1985. Number of titles published: cumulative—3. Softback 100%.

Subjects of Interest. Nonfiction—how-to's: publicity, promotion, writing. Recent publications: *How to Publicize Your Way to Success: A Step by Step Guide; The Power of Publicity* (cassette album); *Spotlight* (a newsletter on musical theater/film).

Initial Contact. Query letter.

Acceptance Policies. Unagented manuscripts: yes. Simultaneous submissions: no. Disk submissions: no. Response time to initial inquiry: 3 weeks. Average time until publication: n/i. **Advance**: n/i. **Royalty**: n/i. First run: n/i.

Marketing Channels. n/i. Subsidiary rights: n/i.

Additional Information. Catalog: upon request.

CCC PUBLICATIONS. 20306 Tau Place. Chatsworth, CA 91311. (818) 407-1661. Submissions Editor: Cliff Carle. Number of titles published: cumulative—16 books and 7 cassettes, 1991—8-10. Softback 100%.

Subjects of Interest. Nonfiction—humorous how-to/self-help. Recent publications: *How to Talk Your Way Out of a Traffic Ticket; Hormones From Hell.*

Initial Contact. Query letter or complete manuscript. Include SASE.

Acceptance Policies. Unagented manuscripts: yes. Simultaneous submissions: yes. Disk submissions: no. Response time to initial inquiry: 1 month, queries; 3 months, manuscripts. Average time until publication: 1 year. **Advance**: n/i. **Royalty**: 5-10% on wholesale.

Marketing Channels. Radio interviews; public relations firm.

Additional Information. We have a reputation for humor titles that have a long shelf life and will appeal to the impulse buyer. Catalog: 8 1/2 x 11 SASE, 2 first class stamps.

Celestial Arts *see* **TEN SPEED PRESS.**

CHALLENGER PRESS. (Subsidiary of A. Wallace and Associates, Inc.). 540 Alisal Rd., Ste. 8. Solvang, CA 93463. (805) 688-2434. Submissions Editor: Marilyn White-Munn. Founded: 1989. Number of titles published: cumulative—2, 1991—5. Softback 100%.

Subjects of Interest. Nonfiction—self help; personal growth; psychology. Recent publications: *Loving Tough, Loving Smart, Loving You; Successfully Different.* Do not want: religious; poetry.

Initial Contact. Query letter with synopsis/outline. Include sample chapters and SASE.

Acceptance Policies. Unagented manuscripts: yes. Simultaneous submissions: yes. Disk submissions: no. Response time to initial inquiry: 14 working days. Average time until publication: 9-12 months. **Advance**: n/i. **Royalty**: n/i. First run: n/i.

Marketing Channels. Distribution houses; direct mail; independent reps; in-house staff. Subsidiary rights: reprint; book club; English language publication outside the United States and Canada.

Additional Information. We publish short (25,000 words or less) fundamental psychology books. Writer's guidelines: write for "Instructions for Authors."

CHANDLER & SHARP PUBLISHERS, INC. 11 A Commercial Blvd.

Novato, CA 94949. (415) 883-2353. Submissions Editor: Jonathan Sharp. Founded: 1972. Number of titles published: cumulative—40, 1991—3. Hardback 5%, softback 95%.

Subjects of Interest. Nonfiction—an occasional trade book with subject matter related to our textbook interests. **Other**—college-level texts in anthropology and political science. Recent publications: *Understanding Politics: The Culture of Societies and the Structures of Government; The Bittersweet Century: Speculations on Modern Science and American Democracy.*

Initial Contact. Query letter; book proposal with sample chapters. Include author's resumé or vitae.

Acceptance Policies. Unagented manuscripts: yes. Simultaneous submissions: yes; we request that author listen to our best offer before making a final decision. Disk submissions: no (we hope to in the future). Response time to initial inquiry: 10 days to 2 weeks. Average time until publication: 9 months to 2 years. **Advance:** small, but negotiable. **Royalty:** 15% of net (cash received). First run: 3000-6000 copies. Subsidy basis: yes; negotiable, but author is expected to pay at least one-half of costs.

Marketing Channels. Direct mail; independent reps; in-house staff. Subsidiary rights: all.

CHICANO STUDIES LIBRARY PUBLICATIONS UNIT. 3404 Dwinelle

Hall. University of California. Berkeley, CA 94720. (415) 642-3859. Submissions Editor: Lillian Castillo-Speed. Founded: 1971. Number of titles published: cumulative—13, 1991—2. Hardback 80%, softback 20%.

Subjects of Interest. Nonfiction—reference books. Recent publications: *Spanish-Language Reference Books: An Annotated Bibliography.* Do not want: poetry; travel; cookbooks.

Initial Contact. Query letter with synopsis/outline. Include author's vitae or bio.

Acceptance Policies. Unagented manuscripts: yes. Simultaneous submissions: no. Disk submissions: no. Response time to initial inquiry: 2 weeks. Average time until publication: 9 months. **Advance:** none. **Royalty:** none. First run: n/i.

Marketing Channels. Distribution houses; direct mail. Subsidiary rights: all.

Additional Information. We are interested in book-length Mexican-American reference manuscripts: bibliographies, indexes, etc. Tips: Material must be accurate, complete, and as comprehensive as possible. Catalog: upon request.

CHILDREN'S BOOK PRESS. 1461 Ninth Ave. San Francisco, CA 94122.

Submissions Editor: Harriet Rohmer. Founded: 1975. Number of titles published: cumulative—17, 1991—6.

Subjects of Interest. Fiction—multicultural literature for children; picture books only. Recent publications: *Baby Rattlesnake* (Native American); *Uncle Nacho's Hat* (Nicaragua); *Nine-In-One* (Laos); *Family Pictures* (Mexican-American).

Initial Contact. Entire manuscript; explain why you feel it is important to publish the story at this time.

Acceptance Policies. Unagented manuscripts: yes. Simultaneous submissions: yes. Disk submissions: no. Response time to initial inquiry: 4-6 months. Average time until publication: 1 year. **Advance**: varies. **Royalty**: 5% author; 5% artist. First run: 7500.

Marketing Channels. Distribution houses; direct mail; independent reps; special sales. Subsidiary rights: all.

Additional Information. We publish bilingual and multicultural folk tales and contemporary stories reflecting the traditions and culture of Third World communities both in the United States and in the Third World. Tips: Send for editorial guidelines. Catalog: upon request.

CHINA BOOKS AND PERIODICALS, INC. 2929 24th St. San Francisco, CA 94110. (415) 282-2994. Submissions Editor: Bob Schildgen. Founded: 1965. Number of titles published: cumulative—45, 1991—12. Hardback 20%, softback 80%.

Subjects of Interest. **Fiction**—mostly translations from Chinese literature; new Chinese fiction series dedicated to the publishing of contemporary works. **Nonfiction**—books about China and the autonomous regions of China; Chinese topics; Chinese-Americans. Recent publications: *Buddhist Art of the Tibetan Plateaus; 5000 Years of Chinese Costumes; Easy Tao* (on Chinese exercise). Do not want: books that are not related to China.

Initial Contact. Query letter.

Acceptance Policies. Unagented manuscripts: yes. Simultaneous submissions: yes. Disk submissions: MS-DOS (preferably WordPerfect or Microsoft Word). Response time to initial inquiry: 1 month. Average time until publication: 8 months. **Advance**: $1000. **Royalty**: 8% of retail. First run: 5000 average. Subsidy basis: yes; occasionally.

Marketing Channels. Distribution houses; direct mail; independent reps. Subsidiary rights: all.

Additional Information. Catalog: upon request.

CHRONICLE BOOKS. 275 5th St. San Francisco, CA 94103. (415) 777-7240. Submissions Editors: Nion McEvoy, Executive Editor; Bill LeBlond (nonfiction); Victoria Rock (children's); David Barich (cookbooks); Jay Schaefer (fiction and topical nonfiction). Founded: 1966. Number of titles published: cumulative—600, 1991—100. Hardback 25%, softback 75%.

Subjects of Interest. **Fiction**—children's (we are just entering this field); reprint fiction. **Nonfiction**—high-quality, full-color coffee-table books; cookbooks; craft books (new to our list); regional California: art, cooking, foods, design, nature, photography, recreation, travel; some poetry. Recent publications: *Frieda Kahlo: The Brush of Anguish; Visions from the Twilight Zone; The Rainforests; James McMair's Pasta Cookbook; James McMair's Soups.*

Initial Contact. Query letter; book proposal with sample chapters. Include sample artwork.

Acceptance Policies. Unagented manuscripts: yes. Simultaneous submissions: yes. Response time to initial inquiry: 6 weeks. Average time until publication: 18 months. **Advance**: $3000-$10,000, average. **Royalty**: 6-10% of retail.

Marketing Channels. Independent reps; in-house staff. Subsidiary rights: first serialization; second serialization; newspaper syndication; reprint; book club; translation and foreign.

Additional Information. We are in the process of expanding our nonfiction and children's line and welcome submissions. Catalog: 9x12 SASE, 4 first class stamps.

CITY LIGHTS BOOKS. 261 Columbus Avenue. San Francisco, CA 94133. (415) 362-1090. Submissions Editor: Robert Sharrard. Founded: 1953. Number of titles published: cumulative—120, 1991—10. Hardback 10%, softback 90%.

Subjects of Interest. Fiction—alternative, unconventional novels; fiction in translation. Recent publications: *The White Book; Memoirs of a Woman Doctor*. **Nonfiction**—philosophy, art, and history studies. Recent publications: *Indians in Overalls; The Gnostics*. Poetry. Recent publications: *Resistance; Poems of Arab Adalusia*.

Initial Contact. Query letter; book proposal with sample chapters; SASE.

Acceptance Policies. Unagented manuscripts: 50%. Simultaneous submissions: yes. Disk submissions: no. First novels: yes; very few. Response time to initial inquiry: 6 weeks. Average time until publication: 18 months. **Advance**: $500-$2000. **Royalty**: 7% annual payment. First run: 2500. Subsidy basis: yes.

Marketing Channels. Cooperative distribution. Subsidiary rights: all.

CLEIS PRESS. PO Box 14684. San Francisco, CA 94114. Submissions Editor: Frederique Delacoste. Founded: 1980. Number of titles published: cumulative—16, 1991—7. Softback 100%.

Subjects of Interest. Fiction—feminist; gay/lesbian; literary. Recent publications: *Night Train to Mother*. Do not want: romance. **Nonfiction**—human rights; feminist; gay/lesbian; women's issues; by and about Latin American women; government/politics. Recent publications: *Sex Work: Writings by Women in the Sex Industry* (anthology of essays). Do not want: religious or spiritual works; topics that have been overworked.

Initial Contact. Query letter; or outline and sample chapters; or complete manuscript. Send complete manuscript for fiction.

Acceptance Policies. Unagented manuscripts: yes. Simultaneous submissions: yes; inform us as to who and when. Disk submissions: query. Response time to initial inquiry: 1 month. Average time until publication: 6 months. **Advance**: n/i. **Royalty**: varies.

Marketing Channels. n/i. Subsidiary rights: n/i.

Additional Information. We are interested in books which will sell in feminist and progressive bookstores and will sell in Europe for translation rights. Tips: Author should spend time in a bookstore whose clientele resembles her audience. Know your market. Catalog: #10 SASE and 2 first class stamps.

CLIFFHANGER PRESS. Box 29527. Oakland, CA 94604-9527. (415) 763-3510. Submissions Editor: Nancy Chirich. Founded: 1986. Number of titles published: cumulative—7, 1991—12. Softback 100%.

Subjects of Interest. Fiction—mystery; suspense. Recent publications: *The Druze Document*. Do not want: spy stories; hard-boiled detective-type characters.

Initial Contact. Send for author's guidelines first. Include SASE.

Acceptance Policies. Unagented manuscripts: yes. Simultaneous submissions: yes. Response time to initial inquiry: 2 months. Average time until publication: 9-12 months. Advance: none. **Royalty**: 10%. First run: n/i.

Marketing Channels. Distribution houses. Subsidiary rights: working on it.

Additional Information. Our focus is mystery/suspense with a strong regional or foreign feel, a strong plot, and believable characters. Writer's guidelines: SASE. Catalog: #10 SASE.

CLOTHESPIN FEVER PRESS. 5529 N. Figueroa. Los Angeles, CA 90042. (213) 254-1373. Submissions Editor: Jenny Wren. Founded: 1985. Number of titles published: cumulative—10, 1991—3. Softback 100%.

Subjects of Interest. Fiction—anthologies; short stories. Recent publications: *Leaving Texas. Self-Portraits Anthology: From a Different Light; Shitkickers and other Texas Stories.* Nonfiction—autobiography; how-to. Recent publications: *Guide to Women's Book Publishing in the United States; A Dykes Bike Repair Handbook.* Do not want: works on AIDS; gay male works.

Initial Contact. Query letter; book proposal with sample chapters.

Acceptance Policies. Unagented manuscripts: yes. Simultaneous submissions: yes; inform us. Disk submissions: Macintosh Word 3.0. First novels: yes. Response time to initial inquiry: 1 month. Average time until publication: 1 year. **Advance:** none. **Royalty:** negotiable. First run: 250-500.

Marketing Channels. Distributors; direct mail; in-house staff; special sales at conventions. Subsidiary rights: none.

Additional Information. We are a lesbian publisher, and our audience is primarily lesbian. Heterosexual material is not of interest to us. Tips: Read one of our books. Catalog: upon request.

COMMUNICATION UNLIMITED. (Imprint: Write to Sell). PO Box 6405. Santa Maria, CA 93456. Submissions Editor: Gordon Burgett. Founded: 1980. Number of titles published: cumulative—7, 1991—1. Hardback 40%, softback 60%.

Subjects of Interest. Nonfiction—information dissemination by writing and speaking. Recent publications: *Self-Publishing to Tightly-Targeted Markets; Empire Building by Writing and Speaking; Query Letters/Cover Letters: How They Sell Your Writing; How to Sell 75% of Your Freelance Writing; Speaking for Money.* Do not want: anything but information dissemination by writing and speaking.

Initial Contact. Query letter. Include explanation of who would buy the book, why, and what else like it exists.

Acceptance Policies. Unagented manuscripts: yes. Simultaneous submissions: no. Disk submissions: yes; if book accepted, we want copy on disk; will discuss format. Response time to initial inquiry: to query, quickly; no response to any other form. Average time until publication: varies. **Advance:** varies. **Royalty:** varies. First run: depends on perceived market.

Marketing Channels. Distribution houses; direct mail. Subsidiary rights: none.

Additional Information. We are very small by intention and are closely linked with seminars, plus audio cassette production. Tips: Try someone else unless it serves the speaking and writing market directly. Catalog: upon request.

COMSOURCE PUBLISHING. PO Box 26216. San Francisco, CA 94126. (415) 775-5879. Submissions Editor: J.R. Pierce. Founded: 1972. Number of titles published: cumulative—30, 1991—5. Hardback 20%, softback 80%.

Subjects of Interest. Nonfiction—food and wine; travel guides; horse racing; computers and software; parapsychology and paranormal. Recent publications: *Little Restaurants of San Francisco; Computers in Business; Out of This World* (parapsychological phenomenon). Do not want: fiction.

Initial Contact. Query letter; author biography; outline or table of contents. Include writing sample.

Acceptance Policies. Unagented manuscripts: yes. Simultaneous submissions: no. Disk submissions: no. Response time to initial inquiry: 2 months. Average time until publication: varies to 1 year. **Advance:** negotiable. **Royalty:** varies. First run: 10,000.

Marketing Channels. Distribution houses; direct mail; independent reps. Subsidiary rights: all.

Additional Information. Catalog: upon request.

CONARI PRESS. 713 Euclid Avenue. Berkeley, CA 94708. (415) 527-9915. Submissions Editor: Mary Jane Ryan. Founded: 1987. Number of titles published: cumulative—9, 1991—10. Hardback 50%, softback 50%.

Subjects of Interest. Nonfiction—psychology; self-help. Recent publications: *Working with the Ones You Love: How to Create Healthy Relationships for a Successful Family Business; Coming Apart: Why Relationships End and How to Live Through the Ending of Yours.* Do not want: fiction.

Initial Contact. Entire manuscript.

Acceptance Policies. Unagented manuscripts: yes. Simultaneous submissions: yes; just tell us. Disk submissions: IBM WordPerfect. Response time to initial inquiry: 1-2 months. Average time until publication: 1 year. **Advance:** varies. **Royalty:** varies. First run: 5000-20,000.

Marketing Channels. Distribution houses; direct mail. Subsidiary rights: all.

Additional Information. Catalog: SASE.

CONTEMPORARY ARTS PRESS. PO Box 3123, Rincon Station. San Francisco, CA 94119. (415) 431-7672. Submissions Editor: Carl Loeffler. Founded: 1975. Number of titles published: cumulative—20, 1991—5.

Subjects of Interest. Nonfiction—experimental arts and new communication technology; contemporary art; new forms of art; performance art; art and video; telecom and art. Recent publications: *Performance Anthology: Sourcebook for a Decade of California Performance Art; Correspondence Art: Art Sent through the Mail.* Also publishes a quarterly magazine via electronic publishing.

Initial Contact. Query letter; manuscript.

Acceptance Policies. Unagented manuscripts: yes. Simultaneous submissions: no. Disk submissions: yes. Response time to initial inquiry: 3-6 months. Average time until publication: 1-2 years. **Advance:** negotiable. **Royalty:** negotiable.

Marketing Channels. 70-country electronic network.

CRAFTSMAN BOOK COMPANY. 6058 Corte Del Cedro. Carlsbad, CA 92009. (619) 438-7828. Submissions Editor: Laurence D. Jacobs. Founded: 1953. Number of titles published: cumulative—60, 1991—12. Softback 100%.

Subjects of Interest. Nonfiction—how-to construction manuals for professional builders. Recent publications: *National Construction Estimator; The 1990 Painting Cost Guide; Residential Electricians Handbook; Drywall Contracting; Running Your Remodeling Business; Masonry Estimating.* Do not want: anything not for professional builders.

Initial Contact. Query letter; book proposal. Include author's qualifications.

Acceptance Policies. Unagented manuscripts: yes. Simultaneous submissions: yes. Disk submissions:; MS-DOS (IBM compatible). Response time to initial inquiry: 3 weeks. Average time until publication: 1 year. **Advance:** none to $500. **Royalty:** 12 1/2% of gross. First run: 5000.

Marketing Channels. Direct mail. Subsidiary rights: reprint; video distribution; sound reproduction and recording; direct mail or direct sales; book clubs; translation and foreign; computer and other magnetic and electronic media; commercial; English language publication outside the United States and Canada.

Additional Information. Must be straight how-to material. Catalog: upon request.

CREATIVE MEDIA SERVICES. 2936 Domingo Ave., Ste. 5. Berkeley, CA 94705. (415) 843-3408. Submissions Editor: Linda Harris. Number of titles published: cumulative—39, 1991—4. Softback 100%.

Subjects of Interest. Other—clip art; camera-ready art. Recent publications: *1990 Clip Art; CMS Custom Clip Art.*

Initial Contact. Query letter; samples of artwork.

Acceptance Policies. Unagented manuscripts: yes. Simultaneous submissions: n/i. Disk submissions: n/i. Response time to initial inquiry: immediate. Average time until publication: 6 months. **Advance**: n/i. **Royalty**: n/i. First run: n/i.

Marketing Channels. Direct mail. Subsidiary rights: none.

Additional Information. Catalog: upon request.

CREATIVE WITH WORDS PUBLICATIONS. PO Box 223226. Carmel, CA 93922. (408) 649-1682. Submissions Editor: Brigitta Geltrich. Founded: 1975. Number of titles published: cumulative—79, 1991—2. Softback 100%.

Subjects of Interest. Fiction—folklore genres (e.g. Christmas tales, Easter tales; lore around the world); creative writing and language arts work of children. Recent publications: *Children in Folklore/Children and Their Folklore; We Are Poets and Authors, Too!* (annual anthology of children's writings). Do not want: pornography; controversial issues.

Initial Contact. Query letter; book proposal with sample chapters; always include cover letter stating to which project author is submitting (see writer's guidelines).

Acceptance Policies. Unagented manuscripts: yes. Simultaneous submissions: no. Disk submissions: TRS 80 or Xerox 6085/8010. Response time to initial inquiry: 1 month; then according to deadline. Average time until publication: deadline is observed. **Advance**: none. **Royalty**: none. First run: n/i.

Marketing Channels. In-house staff. Subsidiary rights: none.

Additional Information. We offer authors a 20% price reduction on 1-9 copies ordered and 30% reduction on orders 10 and above. Tips: Be creative, be proficient, be brief. Catalog: SASE.

CREATIVITY UNLIMITED. 30819 Casilina. Rancho Palos Verdes, CA 90274. (213) 541-4844. Submissions Editor: Shelley Stockwell. Founded: 1983. Number of titles published: cumulative—12 videos, 11 tapes, and 3 books; 1991—3. Softback 100%.

Subjects of Interest. Nonfiction—new age; love yourself; hypnosis; self-hypnosis tapes. Recent publications: *Insides Out; Sex and Other Touchy Subjects.* Poetry. Recent publications: *Enlightenment Poetry.*

Initial Contact. Query.

Acceptance Policies. Unagented manuscripts: yes. Simultaneous submissions: n/i. Disk submissions: no. Response time to initial inquiry: 2 weeks. Average time until publication: 6 months. **Advance**: no. **Royalty**: n/i. First run: 2000.

Marketing Channels. n/i. Subsidiary rights: n/i.

Additional Information. We have a poetry contest for easy to understand poetry with a first prize of $500. Write for information.

Crime and Social Justice *see* **SOCIAL JUSTICE.**

CRISP PUBLICATIONS. 95 First St. Los Altos, CA 94022. (415) 949-4888.
Submissions Editor: Michael G. Crisp. Founded: 1984. Number of titles published: cumulative—125, 1991—30. Softback 100%.

Subjects of Interest. Nonfiction—management training; communications; office management; self-management; sales training/customer service; entrepreneurship; career guidance; study skills; retirement and life planning. Recent publications: *Fifty-Minute Series: Increasing Employee Productivity; Selecting and Working with Consultants; Your First Thirty Days on the Job; Personal Wellness; Business Etiquette and Professionalism.*

Initial Contact. Query letter. Include table of contents; preface.

Acceptance Policies. Unagented manuscripts: yes. Simultaneous submissions: no. Disk submissions: no. Response time to initial inquiry: 3 weeks. Average time until publication: 6 months. **Advance:** none. **Royalty:** 10%. First run: 5000 +/-.

Marketing Channels. Distribution houses; cooperative distribution; direct mail; independent reps; special sales.

Additional Information. Most books are from experienced trainers/authors. Tips: If subject is unique and author has developed a widely attended workshop, chances for placement are improved. Catalog: upon request.

CROSSING PRESS, THE. PO Box 1048. Freedom, CA 95019. (408) 722-0711. Submissions Editors: John or Elaine G. Gill. Founded: 1972. Number of titles published: cumulative—350, 1991—28. Hardback 10%, softback 90%.

Subjects of Interest. Fiction—literary; feminist; general; mysteries; sci-fi feminist. Recent publications: *Married Life and Other Adventures; Trespassing.* Nonfiction—cookbook series; women's health series; parenting series; men's series; gay men's series; women's spirituality series. Recent publications: *Island Cooking: Recipes from the Caribbean; Sun-Dried Tomatoes; Men and Intimacy; All Women Are Healers.* Do not want: romance novels; historical fiction; children's stories.

Initial Contact. Query letter with synopsis/outline. Include sample chapters.

Acceptance Policies. Unagented manuscripts: yes. Simultaneous submissions: yes. Disk submissions: IBM/DOS. First novels: yes. Response time to initial inquiry: 3-4 weeks. Average time until publication: 6-12 months. **Advance:** negotiable. **Royalty:** 7-10% of net. First run: 5000-10,000. Subsidy basis: negotiable.

Marketing Channels. Distribution houses; direct mail; independent reps; in-house staff; special sales. Subsidiary rights: all.

Additional Information. We recently moved to new offices, expanded our production facility, and expanded our seasonal releases. Tips: Study our catalog and contact us one year prior to desired release. Writer's guidelines and catalog: call (800) 777-1048.

Crystal Clarity *see* **DAWN PUBLICATIONS.**

DAHLIN FAMILY PRESS. 5339 Prospect Rd., #300. San Jose, CA 95129-5020. (408) 554-2863. Submissions Editor: T. Dahlin. Founded: 1989. Number of titles published: cumulative—1, 1991—5. Hardback 100%.

Subjects of Interest. Fiction—general. **Nonfiction**—general. Recent publications: *The Gods of Eden.*

Initial Contact. Query letter with synopsis/outline and entire manuscript.

Acceptance Policies. Unagented manuscripts: yes. Simultaneous submissions: yes. Disk submissions: no. First novels: yes. Response time to initial inquiry: 4 weeks. Average time until publication: 1 year. **Advance:** none. **Royalty:** 10-15%. First run: 3000, minimum. Subsidy basis: negotiable.

Marketing Channels. Distribution houses; in-house staff. Subsidiary rights: all.

Additional Information. We are a brand new press with a highly successful first title in hardback. Tips: We cannot take too many new titles at once, but we are very aggressive in marketing those we do take. Catalog: write to us.

JOHN DANIEL AND COMPANY. PO Box 21922. Santa Barbara, CA 93121. (805) 962-1780. Submissions Editor: John Daniel. Founded: 1985. Number of titles published: cumulative—46, 1991—8. Hardback 10%, softback 90%.

Subjects of Interest. Fiction—short stories; novels. Recent publications: *A Problem of Plumbing* (short stories about disability). **Nonfiction**—memoirs; essays. Recent publications: *The Times of Our Lives* (guide to writing autobiography). Poetry (very little). Recent publications: *Letters from Los Angeles, Poems.*

Initial Contact. Query letter.

Acceptance Policies. Unagented manuscripts: yes. Simultaneous submissions: yes. Disk submissions: Macintosh or IBM compatible. First novels: yes. Response time to initial inquiry: 6-8 weeks. Average time until publication: 6-12 months. **Advance:** none. **Royalty:** 10% of net receipts. First run: 2000.

Marketing Channels. Cooperative distribution. Subsidiary rights: all.

Additional Information. We are very small, specializing in belles lettres. We are particularly interested in essays, literary memoirs, and short fiction dealing with social issues. Tips: Query first. Writer's guidelines: upon request. Catalog: SASE.

MAY DAVENPORT, PUBLISHERS. 26313 Purissima Rd. Los Altos Hills, CA 94022. (415) 948-6499. Submissions Editor: May Davenport. Founded: 1975. Number of titles published: cumulative—35, 1991—2-3. Hardback and softback.

Subjects of Interest. Fiction—children's (elementary, secondary): fantasy, adventure. Recent publications: *Creeps; Chase of the Sorceress.* **Nonfiction**—coloring books for children: animals, art, music, nature. Do not want: picture books.

Initial Contact. Query letter. Include SASE.

Acceptance Policies. Unagented manuscripts: yes. Simultaneous submissions: no. Disk submissions: no. Response time to initial inquiry: 3 weeks. Average time until publication: 1-3 years. **Advance:** none. **Royalty:** 15% on retail. First run: 2000. Subsidy basis: will consider for special junior or senior high textbooks, i.e. economics, international markets, finance, and money and banking. 50% cash down for editing/illustration/layout/dummy for approval; 25% down for printing/binding; 25% before delivery of books.

Marketing Channels. Distribution houses; direct mail; independent reps. Subsidiary rights: 50/50 negotiable.

Additional Information. We will contract for small business or club newsletter: collect news, edit, illustrate, layout, and see to the printing, binding, and mailing. Tips: Be yourself! Your talent with words will speak for itself. And if you can make people laugh or smile, that's precious. Catalog: SASE.

DAWN PUBLICATIONS. (Imprint: Crystal Clarity). 14618 Tyler Foote. Nevada City, CA 95959. (916) 292-3482. Submissions Editor: Bob Rinzler. Founded: 1969. Number of titles published: cumulative—40, 1991—4. Hardback 5%, softback 95%.

Subjects of Interest. Nonfiction—nature; self-help; children's; healing. Recent publications: n/i. Do not want: n/i.

Initial Contact. Query letter with synopsis/outline.

Acceptance Policies. Unagented manuscripts: yes. Simultaneous submissions: yes. Disk submissions: no. Response time to initial inquiry: n/i. Average time until publication: n/i. **Advance**: n/i. **Royalty**: n/i. First run: n/i.

Marketing Channels. Distribution houses; cooperative distribution; direct mail; in-house staff; special sales. Subsidiary rights: all.

Additional Information. Tips: We may not write back if there is no interest. Catalog: n/i. Writer's guidelines: n/i.

DELLEN PUBLISHING COMPANY. (Subsidiary of Macmillan Inc.). 400 Pacific Ave., 3rd Fl. East. San Francisco, CA 94133. (415) 433-9900. Submissions Editor: Donald E. Dellen. Founded: 1976. Number of titles published: cumulative—40. Hardback 90%, softback 10%.

Subjects of Interest. Other—college textbooks; mathematics; statistics; computer science.

Initial Contact. Query letter; book proposal.

Acceptance Policies. Unagented manuscripts: n/a. Simultaneous submissions: n/i. Disk submissions: yes. Response time to initial inquiry: 2 weeks. Average time until publication: depends on state of manuscript. **Advance**: n/i. **Royalty**: n/i. First run: n/i.

Marketing Channels. In-house staff. Subsidiary rights: all.

Additional Information. Catalog: write or phone.

Dodo Bird Books (1991) *see* **QUIKREF PUBLISHING.**

Don't Call it Frisco Press *see* **LEXIKOS.**

DOUBLE M PRESS. 16455 Tuba St. Sepulveda, CA 91343. (818) 360-3166. Submissions Editor: Charlotte M. Stein. Founded: 1975. Number of titles published: cumulative—12, 1991—3. Hardback, softback, simultaneous production.

Subjects of Interest. Fiction—children's (preschool through young adult): history; contemporary problems; humor; fantasy. Nonfiction—history and biography, geared to the school market, libraries, and parents. Do not want: gratuitous violence or sex.

Initial Contact. Query letter first.

Acceptance Policies. Unagented manuscripts: yes. Simultaneous submissions: yes. Disk submissions: no. First novels: yes. Response time to initial inquiry: 1 month. Average time until publication: 1 year. **Advance**: none. **Royalty**: 8% minimum of gross. First run: 1000.

Marketing Channels. Direct mail; special sales. Subsidiary rights: first serialization; newspaper syndication; book club; translation and foreign; English language publication outside the United States and Canada.

Additional Information. Catalog: not until fall.

DOWN THERE PRESS/YES PRESS. (Subsidiary of Open Enterprises, Inc.).
PO Box 2086. Burlingame, CA 94011-2086. (415) 550-0912, 342-2536.
Submissions Editor: Joani Blank. Founded: 1975. Number of titles published:
cumulative—10, 1991—2. Softback 100%.

Subjects of Interest. Fiction—erotica. Recent publications: *Herotica: A Collection of Women's Erotic Fiction*. Nonfiction—sexual self-help, education, and awareness. Recent publications: *Good Vibrations: Complete Guide to Vibrators* (revised, second edition); *Kids First Book About Sex*.

Initial Contact. Query letter; book proposal with 1-3 sample chapters; chapter outline.

Acceptance Policies. Unagented manuscripts: yes. Simultaneous submissions: yes; please advise. Disk submissions: prefer hard copy for initial contact. First novel: maybe. Response time to initial inquiry: 2 months. Average time until publication: 1 year. **Advance**: minimal. **Royalty**: 8-10% of cover price. First run: 2000-5000.

Marketing Channels. Distribution houses; cooperative distribution; direct mail; special sales. Subsidiary rights: all.

Additional Information. We are a very small press with very specific views of the kind of sex information and erotica to be made available. Catalog: #10 SASE.

DROPZONE PRESS. PO Box 882222. San Francisco, CA 94188.
(415) 776-7164. Fax (415) 921-6776. Submissions Editor: Roy T. Maloney.
Founded: 1978. Number of titles published: cumulative—5, 1991—4. Softback
100%.

Subjects of Interest. Nonfiction—real estate; business; science; golf course books. Recent publications: *Winning the IRS Game: Secrets of a Tax Attorney; Real Estate Quick and Easy*. Other—video. Do not want: novels.

Initial Contact. Query letter or Fax.

Acceptance Policies. Unagented manuscripts: call first. Simultaneous submissions: yes; call first. Disk submissions: no. Response time to initial inquiry: 2 weeks. Average time until publication: 3 months. **Advance**: negotiable. **Royalty**: negotiable. First run: negotiable.

Marketing Channels. Distribution houses; direct mail; special sales. Subsidiary rights: none.

Additional Information. My books are in their tenth edition. Catalog: phone.

DUSTBOOKS. Box 100. Paradise, CA 95967. (916) 877-6110; (800) 477-6110.
Submissions Editor: Len Fulton. Founded: 1963. Number of titles published:
cumulative—100+, 1991—6. Hardback and softback.

Subjects of Interest. Nonfiction—microcomputers; writing and publishing. Recent publications: *Small Press Record of Books in Print; Black and Blue Guide to Literary Magazines; International Directory of Little Magazines and Small Presses; Associated Writing Programs Official Guide to Writing Programs*.

Initial Contact. Outline; sample chapters.

Acceptance Policies. Unagented manuscripts: yes. Simultaneous submissions: yes; inform us. Disk submissions: no. Response time to initial inquiry: 2 months. Average time until publication: 1 year. **Advance**: $500+\. **Royalty**: 15%. First run: n/i.

Marketing Channels. Mail order. Subsidiary rights: all.

Additional Information. We have a small general trade list. Our energy is directed toward directories dealing with small press book/magazine directories. Tips: Writer's guidelines available; #10 SASE. Catalog: upon request.

ECLIPSE BOOKS/ECLIPSE COMICS. (Imprints: Eclipse Comics; Eclipse Books; Independent Comics Group; Cohan and Cohen Publishers). PO Box 1099. Forestville, CA 95436. (707) 887-1521. Submissions Editors: Greg Gaisden (comics/graphic albums); Catherine Yvonwode (graphic journalism). Founded: 1978. Number of titles published: cumulative—1000, 1991—120. Hardback 20%, softback 80%.

Subjects of Interest. Fiction—graphic albums: science fiction, dark fantasy, crime, adventure, funny animal, fantasy, etc. Recent publications: J. R. R. Tolkien's *The Hobbit* (adapted for comics); Clive Barker's *Tapping the Vein* (horror/fantasy). **Nonfiction**—graphic albums: political and social history, graphic journalism, trading cards, political journalism. Recent publications: *Brought to Light* (political journalism). Do not want: super hero comics; pornography.

Initial Contact. Book proposal with sample chapters. Include sample art for graphic albums.

Acceptance Policies. Unagented manuscripts: yes. Simultaneous submissions: yes, but as a reluctant necessity. Disk submissions: no. Response time to initial inquiry: 3 months. Average time until publication: 6 months to 2 years. **Advance:** based on page rate ($35—50 page/script; $100—250 page/art). **Royalty:** 8% (split among all creators, writers, artists, etc.) First run: n/i.

Marketing Channels. Distribution houses; cooperative distribution; direct mail; independent reps; in-house staff; special sales. Subsidiary rights: varies by contract from "first serialization" to "all," depending on the project.

Additional Information. We work primarily with freelance, independent authors and artists, unlike the larger comic book companies that hire them contractually for series work. Tips: Become familiar with one line of material and see if what you've got in mind is a good "fit." Catalog and writer's guidelines: SASE and ask for "promo pack, catalog, and writer's guidelines."

EDUCATIONAL INSIGHTS. (Imprints: Laurel Park Publishing). 19560 S. Rancho Way. Dominguez Hills, CA 90220. (213) 637-2131. Submissions Editor: Debra Hays. Founded: 1962. Number of titles published: cumulative—600, 1991—70. Softback 100%.

Subjects of Interest. Nonfiction—educational only, preschool through junior high. Recent publications: *The Adventures of Dandy Duck; Making Smart Choices About Drugs.*

Initial Contact. Book proposal with sample chapters or entire manuscript.

Acceptance Policies. Unagented manuscripts: yes. Simultaneous submissions: yes. Disk submissions: no. Response time to initial inquiry: 30 days. Average time until publication: 9 months. **Advance:** varies. **Royalty:** varies. First run: varies. Subsidy basis: yes; terms vary.

Marketing Channels. Distribution houses; direct mail; in-house staff. Subsidiary rights: all.

Additional Information. Catalog: upon request.

ELECTRONIC TREND PUBLICATIONS. 12930 Saratoga Ave., Ste. D-1. Saratoga, CA 95070. (408) 996-7416. Submissions Editor: Gene Selven. Founded: 1978. Number of titles published: cumulative—75, 1991—15. Softback perfect bound.

Subjects of Interest. Nonfiction—all technology subjects; technology market reports. Recent publications: *Start Up: Founding a High Tech Company and Securing Multi-Round*

Financing; Critical Trends in Contract Assembly (impact of parallel processing on high-performance computing); *Mimic Program; SMT Surface Mail Technology.*

Initial Contact. Call first.

Acceptance Policies. Unagented manuscripts: yes. Simultaneous submissions: yes. Disk submissions: Wordstar; WordPerfect. Response time to initial inquiry: immediately (on phone). Average time until publication: 6 months. **Advance:** negotiable. **Royalty:** might be royalty or payment in full. First run: 75-150.

Marketing Channels. Direct mail; promote through magazine and newspaper reviews. Subsidiary rights: none.

Additional Information. This is a market research company, and its needs are exclusively in that field. Catalog: upon request.

ELYSIUM GROWTH PRESS. (Imprints: Golden Eagle; Sun West).
700 Robinson Rd. Topanga, CA 90290. (213) 455-1000. Submissions Editor: Ed Lange. Founded: 1961. Number of titles published: cumulative—21, 1991—4. Hardback 40%, softback 60%.

Subjects of Interest. Nonfiction—source for books about the human body with and without clothes. Nudist travel guides, United States and international. Recent publications: *International Naturist Federation Guide to Nude Recreation; Importance of Wearing Clothes; Family Naturism in America; Body Package.*

Initial Contact. Query letter; book proposal.

Acceptance Policies. Unagented manuscripts: yes. Simultaneous submissions: yes. Disk submissions: yes; Macintosh. Response time to initial inquiry: 10 days. Average time until publication: 12 months. **Advance:** $2000+. **Royalty:** 10%. First run: 5000.

Marketing Channels. Distribution houses; cooperative distribution; direct mail; special sales. Subsidiary rights: all.

Additional Information. Tips: Review our catalog for type of material sought. Catalog: SASE.

EMPIRE PUBLISHING SERVICE. 7645 Le Berthon St. Tujunga, CA 91042.
(818) 784-8918. Submissions Editor: Wendy Landes. Founded: 1970. Number of titles published: cumulative—193, 1991—5. Hardback 20%, softback 80%.

Subjects of Interest. Nonfiction—how to; texts; technical; entertainment industry. Recent publications: *Producing Your First Film; Television Production Techniques; Young Directors and Their Films.* Other—dramas; musicals; poetry. Do not want: novels.

Initial Contact. Query letter. Include #10 SASE.

Acceptance Policies. Unagented manuscripts: yes. Simultaneous submissions: no. Disk submissions: no. Response time to initial inquiry: 60-90 days. Average time until publication: 90-180 days. **Advance:** varies. **Royalty:** varies. First run: 2000-20,000.

Marketing Channels. Distribution houses; direct mail; independent reps; in-house staff; special sales. Subsidiary rights: all.

Additional Information. Catalog: $1.00 plus SASE with $.65 postage.

ENCORE MUSIC PUBLISHING COMPANY. PO Box 315. Orinda, CA 94563. (415) 376-4902. Submissions Editor: E. D'Amante. Founded: 1977. Number of titles published: cumulative—2, 1991—1. Softback 100%.

Subjects of Interest. Nonfiction—college theory textbooks; music theory books of general interest. Recent publications: *All About Chords; Music Fundamentals.* Do not want: bibliographies; historical.

Initial Contact. Query letter with synopsis/outline. Include market.

Acceptance Policies. Unagented manuscripts: yes. Simultaneous submissions: yes, include expected time frame of response. Disk submissions: no. Response time to initial inquiry: 7-15 days. Average time until publication: flexible. **Advance:** none. **Royalty:** based on wholesale price. First run: n/i.

Marketing Channels. Distribution houses; cooperative distribution; direct mail; independent reps; in-house staff. Subsidiary rights: none.

Additional Information. We publish quality textbooks on music theory.

Enrich *see* **PRICE STERN SLOAN, INC.**

EPISTEMICS INSTITUTE PRESS. PO Box 77508. Los Angeles, CA 90007. (213) 389-0307. Submissions Editor: Leonora K. Petty. Founded: 1983. Number of titles published: cumulative—1. Hardback 40%, softback 60%.

Subjects of Interest. Nonfiction—philosophy; epistemology; epistemological historical philosophies. Recent publications: *Prisoners of Aristotle; The Miracle of Abduction.*

Initial Contact. Query letter; entire manuscript.

Acceptance Policies. Unagented manuscripts: yes. Simultaneous submissions: yes. Disk submissions: no. Response time to initial inquiry: 1 week. Average time until publication: 2 months. **Advance:** none. **Royalty:** 40%. First run: varies. Subsidy basis: yes; 50/50 author/publisher.

Marketing Channels. Direct mail. Subsidiary rights: none.

Additional Information. Small press confined to nonfiction. Interdisciplinary with epistemological method of inquiry dealing with language as a vehicle. Tips: Make sure your manuscript has originality and has been researched. Catalog: upon request.

ESOTERICA PRESS. PO Box 170. Barstow, CA 92312. Submissions Editor: Yoly Zentella. Founded: 1985. Number of titles published: cumulative—3, 1991—2. Softback 100%.

Subjects of Interest. Fiction—novellas dealing with humanist themes; universal issues; women in and out of United States, especially Latinos; traditional stories. Recent publications: *Blood at the Roots* (novella based on true story by Aisha Eshe). **Nonfiction**—biographies, history dealing with travel or human situations; food. Recent publications: *An American Indian Remembers* (an American Indian cookbook). Poetry on humanist themes. Recent publications: *Proud Ones: Poems by Koryne Ortega.* Do not want: frivolities; stories with emphasis on sex, but will accept erotica.

Initial Contact. Query letter; sample chapters; must include SASE; source for contact with Esoterica Press.

Acceptance Policies. Unagented manuscripts: yes. Simultaneous submissions: yes; on condition that if we are first to accept, writer withdraws manuscript from other presses, gives us first rights. Disk submissions: no. First novels: yes. Response time to initial inquiry: 6-12 weeks. Average time until publication: 6-12 months. **Advance:** none. **Royalty:** after expenses, 60/40 author/publisher. First run: depends on market.

Marketing Channels. Distribution houses; cooperative distribution; direct mail; in-house staff. Subsidiary rights: first serialization; second serialization; reprint; book club; translation and foreign; English language publication outside United States and Canada.

Additional Information. Our emphasis is on fiction writing by women, Latino-Americans, Asian-Americans, Arab-Americans, Black-Americans, and Native-Americans. This of course does not exclude others. Tips: We encourage authors to also submit manuscripts for publication in our literary journal, *Notebook/Cuaderno*. Catalog and writer's guidelines: legal-size SASE.

ETC PUBLICATIONS. Drawer ETC. Palm Springs, CA 92263. (619) 325-5352. Submissions Editor: LeeOna S. Hostrop. Founded: 1972. Number of titles published: cumulative—120, 1989—6. Hardback and softback.

Subjects of Interest. Nonfiction—business management; educational management; gifted education, texts.

Initial Contact. Complete manuscript.

Acceptance Policies. Unagented manuscripts: yes. Simultaneous submissions: yes. Disk submissions: no. Response time to initial inquiry: 3 weeks. Average time until publication: 1 year. **Advance:** none. **Royalty:** standard. First run: 2500. Subsidy basis: will consider.

Marketing Channels. n/i. Subsidiary rights: all.

Additional Information. Catalog: upon request.

EVERGREEN COMMUNICATIONS. 2085-A Sperry Ave. Ventura, CA 93003. (805) 650-9248. Submissions Editor: Mary Beckwith. Founded: 1989. Number of titles published: cumulative—6, 1991—8. Softback 100%.

Subjects of Interest. Fiction—adult, children's, and young adult.
Nonfiction—devotionals/inspirationals; parenting; self-help. Recent publications: *Time Out!* and *Songs from the Heart* (men's and women's inspirational, respectively); *Help for Hurting Moms. . . and Hurting Kids, Too.*

Initial Contact. Book proposal. Include 3 sample chapters.

Acceptance Policies. Unagented manuscripts: yes. Simultaneous submissions: yes. Disk submissions: no. First novels: yes. Response time to initial inquiry: 6-8 weeks. Average time until publication: 18 months. **Advance:** $500. **Royalty:** 12% based on net sales. First run: 10,000.

Marketing Channels. Distribution houses; independent reps; in-house staff; special sales. Subsidiary rights: all.

Additional Information. Writer's guidelines: SASE.

EZ NATURE BOOKS. PO Box 4206. San Luis Obispo, CA 93402. (805) 528-5292. Submissions Editor: Ed Zolkoski. Founded: 1983. Number of titles published: cumulative—12, 1991—4. Softback 100%.

Subjects of Interest. Nonfiction—local history; local nature; local guide books; Californiana. Recent publications: *Making the Most of San Luis Obispo; Santa Barbara Companion; Ventura Companion; Mountain Biking the Central Coast; History of San Luis Obispo; Hearst's Dream; California Indian Watercraft; California's Chumash Indians; Bicycling SLO*. Do not want: fiction; poetry.

Initial Contact. Query letter with synopsis/outline. Include information about previously written books.

Acceptance Policies. Unagented manuscripts: yes. Simultaneous submissions: yes, inform us. Disk submissions: no. Response time to initial inquiry: a few weeks. Average time until publication: difficult to pin down. **Advance:** prefer not. **Royalty:** 10%, based on sales. First run: usually 4000-5000.

Marketing Channels. Distribution houses; independent reps; in-house staff. Subsidiary rights: none.

Additional Information. We are a very small operation trying to fill important niches. Catalog: upon request.

FALLEN LEAF PRESS. PO Box 10034. Berkeley, CA 94709. (415) 848-7805. Submissions Editor: Ann Basart. Founded: 1984. Number of titles published: cumulative—7, 1991—3. Hardback 12.5%, softback 87.5%

Subjects of Interest. Nonfiction—music reference books; monographs on contemporary composers. Recent publications: *Writing About Music* (directory); *The Solo Cello: A Bibliography*. Do not want: anything not related to music.

Initial Contact. Query letter; book proposal with sample chapters; front matter, sample indexes (if ref. book); author's background and expertise, current position, interest in and knowledge of subject, published works.

Acceptance Policies. Unagented manuscripts: yes; unagented: 100%. Simultaneous submissions: no. Disk submissions: IBM compatible. Response time to initial inquiry: 1-2 months. Average time until publication: varies. **Advance:** none to $500. **Royalty:** 10%, except for esoteric books with none. First run: 300-750.

Marketing Channels. Distribution houses, direct mail. Subsidiary rights: vary; usually not relevant, except in case of foreign translation; English language publication outside United States and Canada; direct mail or sales.

Additional Information. At this time we are requesting camera-ready copy for our reference books. Tips: Look at our catalog and our published books. Catalog: upon request.

MICHEL FATTAH. 933 Pico Blvd. Santa Monica, CA 90405. (213) 450-9777. Submissions Editor: Darrell Houghton. Founded: 1982. Number of titles published: cumulative—40, 1991—unsure. Hardback 75%, softback 25%.

Subjects of Interest. Fiction—historical fiction. Recent publications: *Eternal Fire* (historical novel of Persia). Nonfiction—celebrity biographies; how-to; self-help. Recent publications: *My Days with Errol Flynn; The Senator Must Die: The Murder of Robert F. Kennedy; Earthquake Ready*. Other—children's books. Do not want: pornography/erotica.

Initial Contact. Query letter.

Acceptance Policies. Unagented manuscripts: no. Simultaneous submissions: no. Disk submissions: no. Response time to initial inquiry: varies. Average time until publication: 1 year. **Advance:** varies. **Royalty:** varies. First run: 5000. Subsidy basis: no.

Marketing Channels. Distribution houses; independent reps. Subsidiary rights: all.

Additional Information. Do not send any fiction at this time. Tips: SASE is very important. Catalog: 8 1/2 x 11 SASE; $1.00.

Fax-Files *see* **PACIFIC AERO PRESS.**

FELS AND FIRN PRESS. 33 Scenic Ave. San Anselmo, CA 94960.
(415) 457-4361. Submissions Editor: John M. Montogomery. Founded: 1967. Number of titles published: cumulative—4, 1991—0.

Subjects of Interest. **Fiction**—would consider if on Jack Kerouac. **Nonfiction**—Jack Kerouac. Recent publications: *Jack Kerouac at the Wild Boar, and Other Skirmishes.*

Initial Contact. Query letter.

Acceptance Policies. Unagented manuscripts: yes. Simultaneous submissions: yes. Disk submissions: no. Response time to initial inquiry: 10 days. Average time until publication: 6 months. **Advance**: varies. **Royalty**: 10% of wholesale price of run. First run: 1500. Subsidy basis: yes, I could.

Marketing Channels. Distribution houses; direct mail. Subsidiary rights: none.

Additional Information. Distributor for Black Dog press. Two poetry titles by Robert Peterson. Catalog: upon request.

FESTIVAL PUBLICATIONS. 7944 Capistrano Ave. West Hills, CA 91304.
(818) 340-0175. Submissions Editor: Alan Gadney. Founded: 1976. Number of titles published: cumulative—15 books, 1991—8; 20 audio tapes. Hardback 50%, softback 50%.

Subjects of Interest. **Nonfiction**—reference books and audio cassette tapes in the fields of film, video, television, screenwriting, and related subjects. Recent publications: series of books on contests, festivals, grants, scholarships, and fellowships in film, video, television broadcasting, writing.

Initial Contact. Query letter.

Acceptance Policies. Unagented manuscripts: yes. Simultaneous submissions: yes. Disk submissions: IBM PC. Response time to initial inquiry: 3-6 months. Average time until publication: 6-12 months. **Advance**: negotiable. **Royalty**: negotiable. First run: 3000-5000. Subsidy basis: yes.

Marketing Channels. Distribution houses; cooperative distribution; direct mail; in-house staff; special sales. Subsidiary rights: all.

Additional Information. We are interested in manuscripts, seminars, courses, and other materials that can be offered on audio cassette tapes in the fields of film, video, television, and screenwriting. We are also interested in short manuscripts that can be offered as "special reports" on specific areas in the above categories. Catalog: upon request.

FIESTA CITY PUBLISHERS. PO Box 5861. Santa Barbara, CA 93150. (805) 733-1984. Submissions Editor: Frank E. Cooke. Founded: 1980. Number of titles published: cumulative—5, 1991—1. Hardback 25%, softback 75%.

Subjects of Interest. Nonfiction—music; cooking; how-to. Recent publications: *Anything I Can Play, You Can Play Better* (self-taught guitar method); *Kids Can Write Songs, Too!* (for young teens). Do not want: personal accounts of difficult situations.

Initial Contact. Query letter; brief description of proposed material.

Acceptance Policies. Unagented manuscripts: yes. Simultaneous submissions: yes. Disk submissions: no. Response time to initial inquiry: 2-4 weeks. Average time until publication: 6 months (varies). **Advance:** none. **Royalty:** varies. First run: 1000.

Marketing Channels. Distribution houses; direct mail; special sales. Subsidiary rights: none.

Additional Information. Catalog: upon request.

Firehole Press *see* **NATURE'S DESIGN.**

FITHIAN PRESS. PO Box 1525. Santa Barbara, CA 93102. (805) 962-1780. Submissions Editor: Eric Larson. Founded: 1986. Number of titles published: cumulative—60, 1991—20. Hardback 75%, softback 25%.

Subjects of Interest. Fiction—literary (novels, short stories). Recent publications: *Snow Shadows*; *The Scorpion Sapphire* (suspense novels). Nonfiction—all subjects (general, memoirs); poetry. Recent publications: *Rancho Santa Margarita Remembered* (memoir, history); *Sentinels of Love* (a guide to California rural churches). Poetry. Recent publications: *The Waiting Land*; *Coming to This*. Do not want: books in bad taste.

Initial Contact. Query letter; book proposal with 2 sample chapters; length of manuscript.

Acceptance Policies. Unagented manuscripts: yes. Simultaneous submissions: yes. Disk submissions: IBM compatible, Macintosh. First novels: yes. Response time to initial inquiry: 2 weeks. Average time until publication: 9 months. **Advance:** none. **Royalty:** 50-75% of net receipts. First run: 1000. Subsidy basis: yes, author pays production costs in return for larger royalty.

Marketing Channels. Distribution houses; direct mail; special sales. Subsidiary rights: all, nonexclusive.

Additional Information. Fithian Press books are copublished with their authors. Member, Publishers Marketing Association. Catalog: write for free brochure and catalog. Include SASE.

FLUME PRESS. 644 Citrus Ave. Chico, CA 95926. (916) 342-1583. Submissions Editor: Casey Huff. Founded: 1984. Number of titles published: cumulative—6, 1991—1. Softback 100%.

Subjects of Interest. Nonfiction—poetry chapbooks. Recent publications: *The Centralia Mine Fire; Common Waters, Running Patterns.*

Initial Contact. Through our annual chapbook contest; send for information.

Acceptance Policies. Unsolicited manuscripts: just through contest. Unagented manuscripts: n/a. Simultaneous submissions: yes; if chosen by Flume Press, author must withdraw from other publisher. Disk submissions: no. Response time to initial inquiry: 6 weeks after contest deadline. Average time until publication: 3 to 4 months. **Advance:** n/a. **Royalty:** contest prize—$100 + 25 copies. First run: 250.

Marketing Channels. Distribution houses; direct mail.

Additional Information. Flume is a not-for-profit press. Catalog: upon request.

FOGHORN PRESS. 212 Prentiss St. San Francisco, CA 94110.
PO Box 77845. San Francisco, CA 94107. (415) 641-5777. Submissions Editor: Vicki I. Morgan. Founded: 1985. Number of titles published: cumulative—14 (including second, third editions), 1991—6. Softback 100%.

Subjects of Interest. Nonfiction—sports and recreation. Recent publications: *California Camping* (guidebook describing more than 1500 campgrounds, third edition); *California Golf* (guidebook to 725 courses, second edition); *Rocky Mountain Camping; Forty Niners: Collector's Edition*. Do not want: fiction; children's books.

Initial Contact. Query with cover letter; book proposal with a few sample chapters.

Acceptance Policies. Unagented manuscripts: yes. Simultaneous submissions: yes. Disk submissions: no. Response time to initial inquiry: 4-6 weeks. Average time until publication: 9-18 months. **Advance**: none. **Royalty**: 10-14% of net. First run: 6000-12,000 (depends on title).

Marketing Channels. Distribution houses; in-house staff; special sales. Subsidiary rights: all.

Additional Information. We believe in promoting as fully as possible every title we take on. The marketability of a book is a major consideration. We also have a line of professional football team histories on the Forty Niners, Raiders, Rams, and Broncos. Tips: At this time, we are oriented toward the western states. We are looking for recreational titles that are not overly narrow in scope. Catalog: call or write.

FORMAN PUBLISHING, INC. 2932 Wilshire Blvd., Ste. 201. Santa Monica,
CA 90403. (213) 453-8553. Submissions Editor: Len Forman. Founded: 1979. Number of titles published: cumulative—5. Hardback 50%, softback 50%.

Subjects of Interest. Nonfiction—art; business; calendars; decorating; design; family issues; health; self-help. Recent publications: *PMS; Stepmothering; After 50*. Do not want: fiction.

Initial Contact. Book proposal with entire manuscript. Include why your book is unique.

Acceptance Policies. Unagented manuscripts: yes. Simultaneous submissions: yes. Disk submissions: no. Response time to initial inquiry: 4 weeks. Average time until publication: 1 year. **Advance**: yes. **Royalty**: standard. First run: n/i.

Marketing Channels. Distribution houses; independent reps. Subsidiary rights: all.

Additional Information. We own the distribution company. We have 18 reps and 250 titles from 35 publishers. Catalog: $1.50.

FROG IN THE WELL. PO Box 170052. San Francisco, CA 94117.
(415) 431-2113. Submissions Editor: Susan Hester. Founded: 1980. Number of titles published: cumulative—7, 1991—1. Softback 100%.

Subjects of Interest. Fiction—feminist social change. Recent publications: *The Honesty Tree* (12-year-old discovers her employers/friends are lesbians). **Nonfiction**—feminist social change. Recent publications: *Once I Was a Child and There Was Much Pain* (drawings giving a glimpse into the soul of an incest survivor). Do not want: pornography.

Initial Contact. Query letter; book proposal with sample chapters. Include short list of published works.

Acceptance Policies. Unagented manuscripts: yes. Simultaneous submissions: yes; inform us. Disk submissions: yes; Apple compatible. First novels: yes. Response time to initial inquiry: 3-4 months. Average time until publication: up to 1 year. **Advance**: none. **Royalty**: 50% of net after expenses have been paid. First run: 2500+. Subsidy basis: open to possibility.

Marketing Channels. Distribution houses; cooperative distribution; direct mail; in-house staff; special sales. Subsidiary rights: all.

Additional Information. Catalog: upon request.

FRONT ROW EXPERIENCE. (Imprints: Kokono). 540 Discovery Bay Blvd. Byron, CA 94514. (415) 634-5710. Submissions Editor: Frank Alexander. Founded: 1974. Number of titles published: cumulative—24, 1991—2-3. Softback 100%.

Subjects of Interest. Nonfiction—special education; perceptual-motor development with emphasis in movement education; lesson plans and teacher guidebooks for pre-K and elementary school teachers. Recent publications: *Peaceful Playgrounds, Plays, Pageants and Programs; Perceptual-Motor Development Guide*. Do not want: authors who are not active in their field and not conducting workshops, seminars, talks, etc., that promote their ideas.

Initial Contact. Query letter; convincing case why book will do well.

Acceptance Policies. Unagented manuscripts: yes. Simultaneous submissions: yes. Disk submissions: no. Response time to initial inquiry: 2-3 weeks. Average time until publication: 9-12 months. **Advance**: none. **Royalty**: 5% of first 2000; 10% thereafter. First run: 500 minimum; more if author convinces us their promotional efforts will result in larger sales.

Marketing Channels. Direct mail. Subsidiary rights: all.

Additional Information. Tips: Authors must be willing to sell and promote their own books. Catalog: upon request.

GATEWAY BOOKS. 31 Grand View Ave. San Francisco, CA 94114. (415) 821-1928. Submissions Editor: Donald Merwin. Founded: 1985. Number of titles published: cumulative—10, 1991—4. Softback 100%.

Subjects of Interest. Nonfiction—relationships (senior audience); self-help in retirement field; United States, foreign, or seasonal living sites. Recent publications: *The Grandparent Book; Get Up and Go; To Love Again: Intimate Relationships After 60*. Do not want: unrelated self-help or travel works.

Initial Contact. Query letter; table of contents.

Acceptance Policies. Unagented manuscripts: yes. Simultaneous submissions: yes. Disk submissions: check first. Response time to initial inquiry: 1 month. Average time until publication: 1 year. **Advance**: small. **Royalty**: 12% of net; negotiated. First run: 2500-5000.

Marketing Channels. Distribution houses.

Additional Information. Catalog: upon request.

GAY SUNSHINE PRESS. (Imprint: Leyland Publications). Box 40397. San Francisco, CA 94140. (415) 824-3184. Submissions Editor: Winston Leyland. Founded: 1970. Number of titles published: cumulative—70, 1991—8. Hardback (limited) and softback.

Subjects of Interest. Fiction—erotica; ethnic; historical; mystery; science fiction; short stories. Recent publications: *Crystal Boys*. Nonfiction—how-to and gay lifestyle; creative literary nonfiction. Recent publications: *Twenty Years of Gay Sunshine: An Anthology of Gay History*. Do not want: any topic too limited or academic; long personal narratives.

Initial Contact. Query letter first; then outline and sample chapters if we request. Include SASE.

Acceptance Policies. Unsolicited manuscripts: we return them unopened. Unagented manuscripts: yes. Disk submissions: no. Response time to initial inquiry: 1 month. Average time until publication: n/i. **Advance**: none. **Royalty**: standard or outright purchase. First run: 5000.

Marketing Channels. Distribution houses; direct mail; special sales. Subsidiary rights: all.

Additional Information. We also take translations. Catalog: $1.

GEM GUIDE BOOK COMPANY. 3677 San Gabriel Parkway. Pico Rivera, CA 90660. (213) 692-5492. Submissions Editors: Al Mayerski, George Wilson. Founded: 1965. Number of titles published: cumulative—66. Softback 100%.

Subjects of Interest. Nonfiction—Gem Trail of (several Southwest states); Ghost Towns of . . . ; Hiking and Backpacking In . . . . Recent publications: *Midwest Gem, Fossil and Mineral Trails; Gem Trails of Oregon; Day Hikes and Trail Rides In and Around Phoenix*.

Initial Contact. Query letter.

Acceptance Policies. Unagented manuscripts: yes. Simultaneous submissions: yes. Disk submissions: no. Response time to initial inquiry: 2 weeks. Average time until publication: 6-9 months. **Advance**: n/i. **Royalty**: n/i. First run: n/i.

Marketing Channels. Distribution houses; direct mail; independent reps; in-house staff. Subsidiary rights: none.

Additional Information. We are currently seeking to expand our outdoor recreation list, e.g. bicycling, off-road travel, children's travel books. Catalog: send request to George Wilson, editor.

J. PAUL GETTY TRUST PUBLICATIONS. 17985 Pacific Coast Highway. Malibu, CA 90265. (213) 459-7611. Submissions Editor: Leslee Holderness. Clothback 50%, softback 50%.

Subjects of Interest. Nonfiction—art; art history; photography; conservation; art education. Recent publications: *Vision of Tondal* (illuminated manuscript); *The Conservation of Tapestries*. Do not want: fiction; poetry.

Initial Contact. Query letter only.

Acceptance Policies. Unagented manuscripts: yes. Simultaneous submissions: yes. Disk submissions: yes. Response time to initial inquiry: n/i. Average time until publication: n/i. **Advance**: n/i. **Royalty**: n/i. First run: n/i.

Marketing Channels. Cooperative distribution. Subsidiary rights: none.

GHOST TOWN PUBLICATIONS. PO Drawer 5998. Carmel, CA 93921. (408) 373-2885. Not accepting manuscripts.

GLENCOE/MCGRAW-HILL EDUCATIONAL DIVISION. (Subsidiary of Macmillan/McGraw-Hill School Publishing Company. Imprints: Benziger). 15319 Chatsworth St. Mission Hills, CA 91345. (818) 898-1391. Submissions Editor: Murray Giles, Editorial Director. Founded: 1971. Number of titles published: cumulative—425, 1989—80. Hardback 75%, softback 25%.

Subjects of Interest. Nonfiction—Benziger Imprint: Catholic religious education texts for preschool through adult. Glencoe Imprint: junior high/high school; junior college text in vocational subjects (business, home economics, technical/industrial education, careers); junior high/high school texts in selected general curriculum subjects (English, math, social studies, health, art). Do not want: trade books, fiction or nonfiction.

Initial Contact. Query letter; book proposal with 1 sample chapter. Include curriculum vitae.

Acceptance Policies. Unagented manuscripts: yes. Simultaneous submissions: yes. Disk submissions: only by prior arrangement. Response time to initial inquiry: 2 weeks. Average time until publication: 1 year. **Advance**: varies. **Royalty**: varies. First run: varies.

Marketing Channels. Direct mail; in-house staff. Subsidiary rights: all.

Additional Information. We are interested only in textbooks for established courses offered by public schools, parochial schools, or private business/trade schools. Tips: We frequently employ writers, copyeditors, indexers, etc., on a freelance or for-hire basis. Catalog: upon request.

GLGLC MUSIC. (Subsidiary of La Costa Music Business Consultants). PO Box 147. Cardiff, CA 92007. (619) 436-7219. Submissions Editor: Robert Livingston. Founded: 1979. Number of titles published: cumulative—15, 1991—2. Hardback 10%, softback 90%.

Subjects of Interest. Nonfiction—music business; music trade; tax law; contracts; copyright law. Recent publications: *Livingston's Complete Music Business Directory*.

Initial Contact. Query letter. Include SASE.

Acceptance Policies. Unagented manuscripts: yes. Simultaneous submissions: no. Disk submissions: yes; IBM PC. Response time to initial inquiry: 30 days. Average time until publication: 2-3 months. **Advance**: varies. **Royalty**: standard 6-12%. First run: varies; specialize in short run.

Marketing Channels. Direct mail. Subsidiary rights: none.

Additional Information. Catalog: upon request.

Golden Eagle *see* **ELYSIUM GROWTH PRESS.**

GOLDEN WEST BOOKS. (Subsidiary of Pacific Railroad Publications, Inc.). PO Box 80250. San Marino, CA 91118. (213) 283-3446. Submissions Editor: Donald Duke. Founded: 1961. Number of titles published: cumulative—153, 1991—3. Hardback 100%.

Subjects of Interest. Nonfiction—railroad transportation histories; American transportation. Recent publications: *RDC: The Budd Diesel Rail Car; Beaumont Hill of the Southern Pacific*.

Initial Contact. Query letter; general description.

Acceptance Policies. Unagented manuscripts: yes. Simultaneous submissions: no. Disk submissions: yes. Response time to initial inquiry: 4-6 months. Average time until publication: 1 year. **Advance**: none. **Royalty**: 10%. First run: 3000-4000.

Marketing Channels. Distribution houses; direct mail; independent reps. Subsidiary rights: none.

Additional Information. Catalog: upon request.

Gondwana Books *see* **ALTA NAPA PRESS.**

H. M. GOUSHA. (Subsidiary of Simon and Schuster). PO Box 49006. San Jose, CA 95161. In-house only.

GREENHAVEN PRESS, INC. PO Box 289009. San Diego, CA 92198-0009. (619) 485-7424. Submissions Editor: Bruno Leone. Founded: 1970. Number of titles published: cumulative—440, 1991—35. Softback 100%.

Subjects of Interest. **Nonfiction**—children's and young adult. Adult *Opposing Viewpoint Series* in the field of crime; contemporary social issues; controversial topics; government/politics; politics/world affairs. Recent publications: *Opposing Viewpoint Series: American Values; America's Future; Crime and Criminals; The Elderly; Euthanasia; The Homeless; Genetic Engineering; Japan; Male/Female Roles; Sexual Values; Third World.*

Initial Contact. Query letter with sample chapter.

Acceptance Policies. Unagented manuscripts: yes. Simultaneous submissions: yes, inform us. Disk submissions: no. Response time to initial inquiry: 1 month. Average time until publication: 1 year. **Advance:** none. **Royalty:** flat fee. First run: varies.

Marketing Channels. Distribution houses; direct mail. Subsidiary rights: English language publication outside the United States and Canada.

Additional Information. Catalog: write or call. Writer's guidelines: write or call.

GREENHOUSE REVIEW PRESS. 3965 Bonny Doon Rd. Santa Cruz, CA 95060. (408) 426-4355. Submissions Editor: Gary Young. Founded: 1975. Number of titles published: cumulative—22, 1991—2. Hardback 10%, softback 90%.

Subjects of Interest. **Nonfiction**—poetry; broadside series, single sheets, illustrated poems. Recent publications: *A Throw of the Dice; Life as a Two Act Play.*

Initial Contact. Entire manuscript. Include SASE.

Acceptance Policies. Unagented manuscripts: yes. Simultaneous submissions: no. Disk submissions: no. Response time to initial inquiry: 1 month. Average time until publication: 2 years. **Advance:** none. **Royalty:** pays in copies. First run: 350.

Marketing Channels. Direct mail. Subsidiary rights: none.

Additional Information. Limited edition, finely printed, letter press, hand-made paper for book collectors, libraries, and museums.

GREEN TIGER PRESS, INC. 435 E. Carmel St. San Marcos, CA 92069. (619) 744-7575. Submissions Editor: Editorial Committee. Founded: 1970. Number of titles published: cumulative—75, 1991—12. Hardback and softback.

Subjects of Interest. **Fiction**—illustrated picture books for children and adults; words must evoke visual sense of wonder. Do not want: science fiction; novels.

Initial Contact. Query letter; entire manuscript (never send the original).

Acceptance Policies. Unagented manuscripts: yes. Simultaneous submissions: yes. Disk submissions: n/i. Response time to initial inquiry: allow 3 months. Average time until publication: n/i. **Advance:** n/i. **Royalty:** percent of retail. First run: 3000-10,000.

Marketing Channels. Distribution houses; independent reps; direct mail. Subsidiary rights: vary according to project.

Additional Information. We also publish greeting cards, calendars, and posters. Tips: Words should stimulate the imaginative world of children; evoke a mythical quality. Catalog: upon request.

GURZE DESIGNS AND BOOKS. Box 2238. Carlsbad, CA 92008.
(619) 434-7533. Submissions Editor: Leigh Cohn. Founded: 1980. Number of titles
published: cumulative—10, 1991—3. Softback 100%.

Subjects of Interest. Nonfiction—health; pop-psych; self-help. Recent publications: *Self-Esteem Tools for Recovery; Bulimia: A Guide to Recovery.* Do not want: poetry; fiction;
heavily academic works.

Initial Contact. Query letter.

Acceptance Policies. Unagented manuscripts: yes. Multiple submissions: yes. Disk
submissions: MAC; Osborne. Response time to initial inquiry: 6-8 weeks. Average time until
publication: 6-8 months. **Advance:** $1000. **Royalty:** 10% net. First run: 7500.

Marketing Channels. Distribution houses; cooperative distribution; direct mail; special
sales. Subsidiary rights: direct mail or direct sales; book club; sound reproduction and
recording.

Additional Information. Catalog: upon request.

**HARCOURT BRACE JOVANOVICH, CHILDREN'S BOOKS
DIVISION.** 1250 6th Ave. San Diego, CA 92101. (619) 699-6810. Submissions
Editor: Linda King. Number of titles published: cumulative—445, 1991—95.
Hardback and softback.

Subjects of Interest. Fiction—picture books; novels for all ages. Recent publications:
Elbert's Bad Word; Dixie Storms; Fish Eyes; The Dark Way: Stories from the Spirit World.
Nonfiction—juvenile.

Initial Contact. Nonfiction: query first. Fiction: query; or submit outline and sample
chapters. Picture books: complete manuscript.

Acceptance Policies. Unagented manuscripts: yes. Simultaneous submissions: no. Disk
submissions: no. Response time to initial inquiry: 6-8 weeks. Average time until publication:
1-2 years. **Advance:** varies. **Royalty:** varies; some outright purchases. First run: varies.

Marketing Channels. Distribution houses; independent reps. Subsidiary rights: all.

Additional Information. Tips: Send for manuscript guidelines for #10 SASE, 1 first class
stamp. Catalog: 9x12 SASE, 4 first class stamps.

HARPER AND ROW. 151 Union St. Ice House One, Ste. 401. San Francisco,
CA 94111. (415) 477-4400. Submissions Editor: Thomas Grady. Founded: 1870.
Number of titles published: cumulative—190, 1991—12. Hardback 60%, softback
40%.

Subjects of Interest. Nonfiction—religions (all denominations); self-help; new age;
psychology. Recent publications: *Caring and Commitment: Learning to Live the Love We
Promise; The Addictive Organization; Women and the Blues; Harper's Bible Commentary;
The Enneagram; The Chalice and the Blade; Codependent No More.* Do not want: fiction.

Initial Contact. Query; or outline and sample chapters.

Acceptance Policies. Unagented manuscripts: no. Simultaneous submissions: yes; inform
us. Disk submissions: no. Response time to initial inquiry: 2-3 months. Average time until
publication: 12-18 months. **Advance:** varies. **Royalty:** standard. First run: varies.

Marketing Channels. Direct mail; in-house staff; special sales. Subsidiary rights: all.

Additional Information. Catalog: upon request.

HARPER JUNIOR BOOKS GROUP, WEST COAST. (Moved to Portland, Oregon.)

HAY HOUSE, INC. PO Box 2212. Santa Monica, CA 90406. (213) 394-7445. Submissions Editor: Dan Olmos. Founded: 1985. Number of titles published: cumulative—25, 1991—8. Hardback 10%, softback 90%.

Subjects of Interest. Nonfiction—self-help; psychology; biography; metaphysical; new age. Recent publications: *Your Heart, Your Planet; Love Yourself, Heal Your Life Workbook.* Do not want: negative books; satanism; psychic occurrences.

Initial Contact. Book proposal with sample chapters or entire manuscript. Include previous writing experience: articles, books, etc.

Acceptance Policies. Unagented manuscripts: yes. Simultaneous submissions: no. Disk submissions: no. Response time to initial inquiry: 4-6 weeks. Average time until publication: 1 year. **Advance:** $2000-$15,000. **Royalty:** 5-10%. First run: 7500.

Marketing Channels. Distribution houses; direct mail; in-house staff; special sales. Subsidiary rights: all (except computer, magnetic, and electronic media).

Additional Information. Tips: Typewritten manuscripts only—no handwriting will be accepted. Catalog: upon request.

Health Media *see* **SLAWSON COMMUNICATIONS, INC.**

HERE'S LIFE PUBLISHERS, INC. (Subsidiary of Campus Crusade for Christ). Box 1576. San Bernardino, CA 92402-1576. (714) 886-7981. Submissions Editor: Dan Benson. Number of titles published: 1988—25. Hardback 5%, softback 95%.

Subjects of Interest. Nonfiction—self-help; evangelism; Christian campus ministry; family; personal growth. Recent publications: *How to Prepare for the Coming Persecution; When Victims Marry.* Do not want: new age; metaphysical; missionary biography; poetry; booklets; songs.

Initial Contact. Query; or outline with sample chapters.

Acceptance Policies. Unagented manuscripts: yes. Simultaneous submissions: yes. Disk submissions: yes; query. Response time to initial inquiry: 1-3 months. Average time until publication: 1 year. **Advance:** n/i. **Royalty:** 15% of wholesale. First run: 5000.

Marketing Channels. Independent reps; special sales. Subsidiary rights: all.

Additional Information. Tips: Writers have the best chance to sell to us if they use a Biblical approach to problem solving. Catalog: 8 1/2 x 11 SASE, $1.45 postage. Writer's guidelines: #10 SASE.

HEYDAY BOOKS. Box 9145. Berkeley, CA 94709. (415) 549-3564. Submissions Editor: Malcolm Margolin. Founded: 1974. Number of titles published: cumulative—25, 1991—4. Hardback 5%, softback 95%.

Subjects of Interest. Nonfiction—California Indians; natural history; history and travel (must have California focus). Recent publications: *East Bay Out: A Guide to East Bay Regional Parks; Cyclists Route Atlas: A Guide to the Gold Country and High Sierra; The Harvest Gypsies: On the Road to the Grapes of Wrath* by John Steinbeck (a series of newspaper articles originally published in 1936 about migrant farm workers). Do not want: fiction; poetry; books not about California.

Initial Contact. Query letter (minimal).

Acceptance Policies. Unagented manuscripts: yes. Simultaneous submissions: no. Disk submissions: no. Response time to initial inquiry: 10 days. Average time until publication: 6 months. **Advance**: rarely more than $1000. **Royalty**: 8-10% of list. First run: 4000-7000. Subsidy basis: no.

Marketing Channels. Distribution houses; independent reps; in-house staff. Subsidiary rights: all.

Additional Information. Manuscript should be literate, sensitive, and useful. Catalog: manila envelope, $.45 postage.

HOLDEN DAY, INC. 523 47th St. Oakland, CA 94609. (415) 428-9400. Submissions Editor: Martha Murphy. Founded: 1959. Number of titles published: 1991—5. Hardback 50%, softback 50%.

Subjects of Interest. Nonfiction—operations research; physics; college-level market software. Recent publications: *Storm: Personal Version 2.0* (quantitative modeling for decision support); *VP Expert for Business Applications*. Do not want: trade books.

Initial Contact. Query letter. Include biography, markets, and table of contents.

Acceptance Policies. Unagented manuscripts: yes. Simultaneous submissions: yes. Disk submissions: ASCII code. Response time to initial inquiry: 2-3 weeks. Average time until publication: contract dependent. **Advance**: negotiable. **Royalty**: negotiable. First run: market dependent.

Marketing Channels. In-house staff; direct mail; data base of users. Subsidiary rights: none.

Additional Information. Tips: Include a representative or unique chapter. Catalog: upon request.

HOLLOWAY HOUSE PUBLISHING COMPANY. 8060 Melrose Ave. Los Angeles, CA 90046. (213) 653-8060. Submissions Editor: Raymond F. Locke. Number of titles published: cumulative—1500; 1991—30-35. Softback 100%.

Subjects of Interest. Fiction—Black Experience literature; contemporary stories. Recent publications: *Letters from a Little Girl* (biography). **Nonfiction**—games (i.e., backgammon, gin rummy); gambling (how to win).

Initial Contact. Outline; 3 sample chapters.

Acceptance Policies. Unagented manuscripts: yes. Simultaneous submissions: yes. Disk submissions: query first. Response time to initial inquiry: 8 weeks. Average time until publication: 6 months. **Advance**: n/i. **Royalty**: standard. First run: 15,000-20,000.

Marketing Channels. Distribution houses; direct mail; independent reps. Subsidiary rights: n/i.

Additional Information. We are the largest publisher of Black Experience literature. Tips: Check guidelines. Catalog: and guidelines; SASE.

HOOVER INSTITUTION PRESS. (Subsidiary of Hoover Institution on War, Revolution and Peace). Stanford University. Stanford, CA 94305-6010. (415) 723-3373. Submissions Editor: Patricia A. Baker, Executive Editor. Number of titles published: 1989—12, 1990—16. Hardback 50%, softback 50%.

Subjects of Interest. Nonfiction—international studies; domestic studies; political science; history; public policy; arms control; Soviet-U.S. relations. Recent publications: *The New Wealth of Nations*; *The Modern Uzbeks*; *Breaking With Communism: The Intellectual Odyssey of Bertram D. Wolfe*. Do not want: fiction of any type—all manuscripts must be scholarly.

Initial Contact. Query letter; book proposal with 3 sample chapters. Or query letter with abstract and 3 sample chapters with footnotes.

Acceptance Policies. Unagented manuscripts: yes. Simultaneous submissions: to be discussed with managing editor. Disk submissions: check with managing editor. Response time to initial inquiry: 4-6 weeks. Average time until publication: to be discussed with managing editor. **Advance**: negotiable. **Royalty**: negotiable. First run: negotiable.

Marketing Channels. Independent sales reps; in-house staff; direct mail; special sales. Subsidiary rights: first serialization; newspaper syndication; reprint; book club; translation and foreign; English language publication outside the United States and Canada.

Additional Information. Catalog: upon request.

HP Books *see* **PRICE STERN SLOAN, INC.**

HUNTER HOUSE, INC., PUBLISHERS. (Imprints: Broadway Books; Light Wave Press; Saturday Books; Sufi Publishing). PO Box 847. Claremont, CA 91711. (714) 624-2277. Fax (714) 624-9028. Submissions Editor: Corrine Sahli. Founded: 1978. Number of titles published: cumulative—70, 1989—8. Hardback 10%, softback 90%.

Subjects of Interest. **Fiction**—womanist/mythical, historical. Recent publications: *On the Road to Baghdad*. **Nonfiction**—women's health; family health; psychology. Recent publications: *Sexual Healing; Menopause Without Medicine; The Enabler; Trauma in the Lives of Children; Healthy Aging; Writing From Within*. **Other**—"infobooks" for teens. Do not want: erotica; science fiction; illness biographies.

Initial Contact. Query letter; book proposal with 2-3 sample chapters. Include author's background and resumé.

Acceptance Policies. Unagented manuscripts: yes. Simultaneous submissions: yes; we request author notify us immediately if he/she decides to sign with another publisher. Disk submissions: no. Response time to initial inquiry: 1-2 months. Average time until publication: 12-18 months. **Advance**: $100-$500. **Royalty**: 12% of net, rising to 15%. First run: varies. Subsidy basis: yes; common interest.

Marketing Channels. Distribution houses; cooperative distribution; direct mail; in-house staff; special sales. Subsidiary rights: all.

Additional Information. We offer comprehensive book production services to both self-publishing authors and other publishers. Tips: Do not send full manuscripts unless requested. SASE required. Writer's guidelines: upon request. Catalog: upon request.

ILLUMINATIONS PRESS. 2110-B 9th St. Berkeley, CA 94710. (415) 849-2102. Submissions Editors: Norman Moser (poetry); Randy Fingland (prose). Founded: 1965. Number of titles published: cumulative—9, 1991—1. Softback 100%.

Subjects of Interest. **Nonfiction**—personal essays on art, Zen, mysticism, etc. Recent publications: *El Grito del Norte* (stories and tales); *The Illuminations Reader: Anthology of Writing and Art* (limited run of cloth copies). Poetry; plays. Recent publications: *Cleft Between Heaven and Earth* (poetry); *Between Me and Thee* (poetry); *Forester Whacks* (poetry). Do not want: Christian verse.

Initial Contact. Query letter; book proposal with 10-15 pages of prose; 5-10 pages of poetry. Include subscription to anthology; author bio; credits. We can be contacted by phone.

Acceptance Policies. Unagented manuscripts: yes. Simultaneous submissions: yes. Disk submissions: no. Response time to initial inquiry: 2-3 months. Average time until publication: 12-18 months. **Advance**: none. **Royalty**: percent of profits based on investment. First run:

400-800 (poetry); 800-1500 (prose). Subsidy basis: 50% or less of costs plus $43 submission fee to new '80s-'90s book series.

Marketing Channels. Distribution houses; direct mail; special sales; subscription. Subsidiary rights: all.

Additional Information. We'll stick with quality even in these hard times called the '90s. Tips: Fiction needs convincing specificity; nonfiction needs authenticity. Writer's guidelines: SASE. Catalog: SASE.

INFO NET PUBLISHING. PO Box 3789. San Clemente, CA 92672. (714) 492-7219. Submissions Editor: Herb Wetenkamp, Jr. Founded: 1987. Number of titles published: cumulative—3, 1991—5. Softback 100%.

Subjects of Interest. Fiction—general; mainstream; modern; sports. **Nonfiction**—bicycling how-to; senior citizens how-to; cooking. Recent publications: *Bicycle Retailers Guide to Getting Rich in the Recession; Principles of Bicycle Retailing; The Race Across America Book.*

Initial Contact. Query letter with synopsis/outline. Include bio plus published pieces.

Acceptance Policies. Unagented manuscripts: yes. Simultaneous submissions: yes, offer of exclusivity to be accepted. Disk submissions: yes. Response time to initial inquiry: 2 months. Average time until publication: 6 months. **Advance:** negotiable. **Royalty:** negotiable, 8%. First run: inquire. Subsidy basis: fee plus commission.

Marketing Channels. Distribution houses; direct mail; independent reps; in-house staff; special sales. Subsidiary rights: first serialization; video distribution; direct mail or direct sales; commercial; English language publication outside the United States and Canada.

Additional Information. We are open to consider any how-to or semiprofessional subject. Tips: Be expert and thorough. Catalog: SASE. Writer's guidelines: SASE.

IN ONE EAR PRESS. 3527 Voltaire St. San Diego, CA 92106. (619) 223-1871. Submissions Editor: Elizabeth Reid. Founded: 1989. Number of titles published: cumulative—2, 1991—4. Softback 100%.

Subjects of Interest. Nonfiction—language books (Spanish, English); how-to books; poetry (6-8 lines maximum). Recent publications: *Border Spanish; Spanish Lingo for the Savvy Gringo.* Do not want: epic poetry.

Initial Contact. Query letter only. Include author's bio and qualifications.

Acceptance Policies. Unagented manuscripts: yes. Simultaneous submissions: yes. Disk submissions: IBM compatible; 5 1/4. Response time to initial inquiry: 1 month. Average time until publication: 6 months. **Advance:** none. **Royalty:** buy either all rights or publishing rights. First run: 500 copies. Subsidy basis: negotiated.

Marketing Channels. Cooperative distribution; direct mail; special sales. Subsidiary rights: reprint; book club.

Additional Information. We will consider short how-to books (75-100 pages) on topics of general interest. Tips: We like a light, humorous approach where appropriate, with simple to understand language. Catalog: SASE.

INTEGRATED PRESS. 526 Comstock Dr. Tiburon, CA 94920. (415) 435-2446. Submissions Editor: Jack Gaines. Founded: 1979. Number of titles published: 1989—3. Hardback 30%, softback 70%.

Subjects of Interest. Nonfiction—psychology, biography. Recent publications: *Fritz Perls: Here and Now.* Do not want: anything which is not quality.

Initial Contact. Query letter.

Acceptance Policies. Unagented manuscripts: yes. Simultaneous submissions: no. Disk submissions: no. Response time to initial inquiry: 3 weeks. Average time until publication: n/i. **Advance**: $500. **Royalty**: 6/10/12%. First run: 2500.
Marketing Channels. n/i. Subsidiary rights: n/i.

International Academy of Astronautics *see* **UNIVELT, INC.**

INTERURBAN PRESS/TRANS ANGLO BOOKS. Box 6444. Glendale, CA 91225. (818) 240-9130. Submissions Editor: Paul Hammond. Number of titles published: cumulative—90, 1991—15. Hardback and softback.
Subjects of Interest. Nonfiction—transportation and transportation history (emphasis on railroads); Western Americana (logging, gold rush, mining); preservation movement; business and economics; travel. Recent publications: *Deisels Over Donner; The Surfliners; Cajun Album; Illinois Terminal—The Electric Years; Rails Through the Orange Groves; The Feather River Route; Main Streets of the Northwest; Monterey and Pacific Grove Streetcar Era*.
Initial Contact. Query letter.
Acceptance Policies. Unagented manuscripts: yes. Simultaneous submissions: no. Disk submissions: query first. Response time to initial inquiry: 4-6 weeks. Average time until publication: 1-3 years. **Advance**: none. **Royalty**: 5-10% on gross. First run: 2500.
Marketing Channels. Distribution houses; special sales. Subsidiary rights: n/i.
Additional Information. Catalog: upon request.

Irio I O *see* **STRAWBERRY HILL PRESS.**

ISLAND PRESS. Star Route 1, Box 38. Covelo, CA 95428. (707) 983-6432. Submissions Editor: Barbara Dean. Founded: 1978. Number of titles published: cumulative—125, 1991—35. Hardback and softback. We do simultaneous editions.
Subjects of Interest. Nonfiction—practical information and analysis for professionals and concerned citizens on the conservation and management of natural resources. Recent publications: *War on Waste; Shading Our Cities; Ancient Forests of the Pacific Northwest*. Do not want: anything outside our carefully defined niche.
Initial Contact. Book proposal with 2 sample chapters. Send for author information packet.
Acceptance Policies. Unagented manuscripts: yes. Simultaneous submissions: yes; if author informs us. Disk submissions: final manuscript can be on disk; initial submission must be hard copy. Response time to initial inquiry: 1-3 months. Average time until publication: 9 months from finished manuscript. **Advance**: none. **Royalty**: 5-7.5% net. First run: varies considerably.
Marketing Channels. Distribution houses; independent reps; direct mail; special sales. Subsidiary rights: all.
Additional Information. Tips: Send for author information packet. Catalog: upon request.

ISM PRESS. PO Box 12447. San Francisco, CA 94112. (415) 333-7641. Submissions Editor: Daniel Fogel. Founded: 1982. Number of titles published: cumulative—8, 1991—0. Hardback 33%, softback 67%.
Subjects of Interest. Nonfiction—history; third world cultures and struggles; women's studies. Recent publications: *Love and Politics; This Bridge Called Me Back* (Spanish translation). Do not want: "new age" metaphysics; manuscripts containing only poetry.

Initial Contact. Query letter with synopsis/outline.

Acceptance Policies. Unagented manuscripts: yes. Simultaneous submissions: yes; if we contract to publish the book, we'll want an exclusive deal. Disk submissions: IBM compatible, 5 1/4. Response time to initial inquiry: 1 month. Average time until publication: 18 months. **Advance:** yes. **Royalty:** yes, based on net income. First run: 1500-5000.

Marketing Channels. Distribution houses; direct mail or direct sales. Subsidiary rights: book club; translation and foreign; English language publication outside the United States and Canada.

Additional Information. We publish some books in Spanish and some bilingual. Tips: We favor broad but rigorous coverage of a field of nonfiction. Catalog: upon request.

JAIN PUBLISHING COMPANY. (Imprints: Asian Humanities Press; AHP Paperbacks). PO Box 3523. Fremont, CA 94539. (415) 659-8272. Submissions Editor: Mukesh K. Jain. Founded: 1976. Number of titles published: cumulative—52, 1991—10. Hardback 60%, softback 40%.

Subjects of Interest. Nonfiction—Asian studies: religions, cultures, philosophies, and literature. Recent publications: *Tower of Myriad Mirrors: A Supplement to Journey to the West; Zibo: The Last Great Zen Master of China.* Do not want: fiction.

Initial Contact. Book proposal with 2 sample chapters. Include curriculum vitae.

Acceptance Policies. Unagented manuscripts: yes. Simultaneous submissions: no. Disk submissions: IBM/Apple compatible; coding instructions available. Response time to initial inquiry: 4-8 weeks. Average time until publication: 9-12 months. **Advance:** none. **Royalty:** 6-7.5%; usually offered with second and successive printings. First run: 1000-2000 copies. Subsidy basis: yes; whereas we do not ask for direct subsidy from the author, occasionally we do expect author cooperation with third party subventions.

Marketing Channels. Distribution houses; direct mail. Subsidiary rights: all.

Additional Information. Tips: Manuscripts should be no more than 400 pages and preferably with no color art. Catalog: upon request.

JALMAR PRESS. (Subsidiary of B.L. Winch and Assoc.). 45 Hitching Post Dr., Bldg. 2. Rolling Hill Estates, CA 90274-4297. (213) 547-1240. Submissions Editor: B.L. Winch. Founded: 1971. Number of titles published: cumulative—44, 1991—4. Hardback 10%, softback 90%.

Subjects of Interest. Nonfiction—positive self-esteem; drug and alcohol abuse prevention; peaceful conflict resolution; whole brain learning. Recent publications: *Esteem Builders* (kindergarten-eighth grade curriculum); *Feel Better Now: 30 Ways to Relieve Frustrations in Three Minutes or Less.* Do not want: novels.

Initial Contact. Book proposal with sample chapters; survey of why product is needed; evidence author is visible and can sell the book; information on competitive products; who the market is. SASE must be enclosed for any response.

Acceptance Policies. Unagented manuscripts: yes. Simultaneous submissions: yes. Disk submissions: no. Response time to initial inquiry: 6-8 weeks. Average time until publication: 12-18 months. **Advance:** small, but negotiable. **Royalty:** 7.5-15%. First run: 5000-25,000. Subsidy basis: yes; open to discussion.

Marketing Channels. Distribution houses; cooperative distribution; direct mail; independent reps; special sales. Subsidiary rights: all.

Additional Information. Have 5 best-sellers (over 100,00 copies sold) out of 20 current titles. Very strong back list. Keep books in stock if sales justify. Tips: Present strong proposal covering market and competition for the book. Catalog: upon request.

Kazan Books *see* **VOLCANO PRESS.**

Kokono Books *see* **FRONT ROW EXPERIENCE.**

KIMCO COMMUNICATIONS. 424 W. Dayton. Fresno, CA 93722. (209) 275-0893. Submissions Editor: John Kimbrough. Founded: 1989. Number of titles published: 1990—3. Softback 100%.
Subjects of Interest. Nonfiction—travel related to home/hospitality exchanging; personal travel experiences. Recent publications: *Vacation Home Exchanging and Hospitality Guide*; Newsletter: *Vacation Home Exchanging*.
Initial Contact. Query letter with book proposal. Query for article guidelines. Include SASE for return of material.
Acceptance Policies. Unagented manuscripts: yes. Simultaneous submissions: yes. Disk submissions: no. Response time to initial inquiry: 2-3 weeks. Average time until publication: 1 year. Advance: $500. Royalty: 10%, or will buy outright. First run: 2000-5000.
Marketing Channels. Cooperative distribution; direct mail; special sales. Subsidiary rights: none.
Additional Information. We self-publish and market travel books and a newsletter related to home and hospitality exchange (articles pay $25-$100). Tips: Peripheral material is sometimes used, e.g., bed and breakfast, independent travel abroad, travel tips with emphasis on the how-to, cost, and personal experience of such experience. Writer's guidelines: upon request.

KONOCTI BOOKS. Rt. I, Box 216. Winters, CA 95694. (916) 662-3364. Not currently accepting submissions.

KOSTELLO DESIGN AND PUBLISHING COMPANY. PO Box 11606. Oakland, CA 94611. (415) 652-1286. Submissions Editor: Delores C. Booth. Founded: 1978. Number of titles published: cumulative—7, 1991—3. Softback 100%. Not accepting submissions at this time.
Subjects of Interest. Nonfiction—time management. Other—educational workbooks and books, K-10; artwork for children; short stories (2-12 pages). Recent publications: *The Success is Best* (series). Do not want: novels.
Initial Contact. Query letter (short is better).
Acceptance Policies. Unagented manuscripts: yes. Simultaneous submissions: yes. Disk submissions: no. Response time to initial inquiry: 2 weeks. Average time until publication: depends. Advance: varies. Royalty: none. First run: 2500-5000.
Marketing Channels. Direct mail; independent reps; in-house staff. Subsidiary rights: n/i.
Additional Information. We are interested in purchase of artwork and short stories for K-10. Tips: Type on one side of page; address on manuscript. Catalog: upon request.

LAHONTAN IMAGES. PO Box 1093. Susanville, CA 96130. (916) 257-6747. Submissions Editor: Tim I. Purdy. Founded: 1986. Number of titles published: cumulative—6, 1991—2. Softback 100%.
Subjects of Interest. Nonfiction—general interest, specializing in the history of Northeastern California and the Great Basin. Recent publications: *Eagle Lake; Flanigan: Anatomy of a Railroad Ghost Town; Frontier Times: The 1874-1875 Journals of Sylvester Daniels*. Do not want: fiction.

Initial Contact. Query letter.

Acceptance Policies. Unagented manuscripts: yes. Simultaneous submissions: yes. Disk submissions: no. Response time to initial inquiry: 1 month. Average time until publication: 6 months. **Advance:** none. **Royalty:** 10% on retail and wholesale. First run: 1500.

Marketing Channels. Cooperative distribution; direct mail; in-house staff. Subsidiary rights: none.

Additional Information. We are a small regional publisher, specializing on topics of Northeastern California and Nevada. Catalog: upon request.

Laurel Park Publishing *see* **EDUCATIONAL INSIGHTS.**

LET'S GO TRAVEL PUBLICATIONS. 135 W. Nuevo Rd., Ste. B. Perris, CA 92370. (714) 943-4459. Submissions Editor: Keith A. Evans. Founded: 1987. Number of titles published: cumulative—7, 1991—5. Softback 100%.

Subjects of Interest. Nonfiction—travel, guidebooks, and regional. Recent publications: *Invitation to Guam.* Do not want: books with sexual connotations.

Initial Contact. Query letter with synopsis/outline and book proposal.

Acceptance Policies. Unagented manuscripts: yes. Simultaneous submissions: no. Disk submissions: MS DOS; Wordstar 5.5; WordPerfect 5.1. Response time to initial inquiry: 6 weeks. Average time until publication: 1 year. **Advance:** none. **Royalty:** 10% based on number sold. First run: 5000.

Marketing Channels. Distribution houses; direct mail. Subsidiary rights: none.

Additional Information. We deal mainly with travel guidebooks on off-the-beaten-path destinations (foreign or domestic). Tips: Please include SASE. Very professional-looking work and a hot topic will catch the eye. Catalog: SASE. Writer's guidelines: SASE.

LEXIKOS. (Imprints: Don't Call It Frisco Press). PO Box 296. Lagunitas, CA 94938. (415) 488-0401. Submissions Editor: Michael R. Witter. Founded: 1982. Number of titles published: cumulative—42, 1991—6. Hardback 10%, softback 90%.

Subjects of Interest. Nonfiction—regional and local histories; walking guides. Recent publications: *A Short History of Santa Fe; Shipwrecks at the Golden Gate.* Do not want: self-help; politics.

Initial Contact. Query letter with synopsis/outline and book proposal.

Acceptance Policies. Unagented manuscripts: yes. Simultaneous submissions: yes. Disk submissions: no. Response time to initial inquiry: 2 weeks. Average time until publication: 1 year. **Advance:** none. **Royalty:** negotiable. First run: 5000. Subsidy basis: negotiable.

Marketing Channels. Distribution houses; independent reps; in-house staff. Subsidiary rights: all.

Additional Information. Catalog: SASE.

LIBRA PUBLISHERS, INC. 3089C Clairemont Dr., Ste. 383. San Diego, CA 92117. (619) 581-9449. Submissions Editor: William Kroll. Founded: 1960. Number of titles published: cumulative—230, 1990—15. Hardback 90%, softback 10%.

Subjects of Interest. Fiction—all categories. Recent publications: *The Long Wind* (novel of woman's self-realization); *Tarnished Hero.* **Nonfiction**—all categories. Recent publications: *Hidden Bedroom Partners* (needs and motives that destroy sexual pleasure); *Manual for Retirement Counselors; Sexual Friendship—A New Dynamics in Relationships.*

Initial Contact. Entire manuscript. Include author's background; previously published works.

Acceptance Policies. Unagented manuscripts: yes. Simultaneous submissions: yes; inform us. Disk submissions: no. First novels: yes. Response time to initial inquiry: 3 weeks. Average time until publication: 8-12 months. **Advance**: none. **Royalty**: 10-15%. First run: 1000-5000. Subsidy basis: on occasion if we like the book but feel it has limited sales potential, we offer assistance in self-publishing.

Marketing Channels. Direct mail; in-house staff; special sales. Subsidiary rights: all.

Light Wave Press *see* **HUNTER HOUSE, INC., PUBLISHERS.**

Philip E. Lilienthal Asian Studies *see* **UNIVERSITY OF CALIFORNIA PRESS.**

LINDEN PUBLISHERS. 1750 N. Sycamore, #305. Hollywood, CA 90028. Not accepting submissions.

LONE EAGLE PUBLISHING, INC. 9903 Santa Monica Blvd., Ste. 204. Beverly Hills, CA 90212. (213) 471-8066. Submissions Editor: Joan Singleton. Founded: 1982. Number of titles published: cumulative—50, 1991—11. Hardback and softback.

Subjects of Interest. Nonfiction—motion picture and video: self-help; technical; how-to; specialities. Recent publications: *The Film-Editing Room Handbook; Film Actor's Guide; Film Composer's Guide.* Do not want: biographies; anything unrelated.

Initial Contact. Outline; synopsis; sample chapters.

Acceptance Policies. Unagented manuscripts: yes. Simultaneous submissions: yes. Disk submissions: query. Response time to initial inquiry: 8 weeks. Average time until publication: 1 year. **Advance**: $250. **Royalty**: 5-10%. First run: n/i.

Marketing Channels. Distribution houses; in-house sales; direct mail. Subsidiary rights: all.

Additional Information. We are looking for professionals in the movie/video field with a specialty that has not been overworked. Tips: Expect to work hard on promotion. Catalog: #10 SASE, 2 first class stamps.

LONELY PLANET PUBLICATIONS. 112 Linden St. Oakland, CA 94607. (415) 893-8555. Submissions Editor: Eric Kettunen, Sales Manager. Founded: 1973. Number of titles published: cumulative—80, 1989—25. Softback 100%.

Subjects of Interest. Nonfiction—travel guides (series): Travel Survival Kits; On a Shoestring series; phrase books; trekking guides. Recent publications: *Eastern Europe on a Shoestring; Hawaii—A Travel Survival Kit; Samoa—A Travel Survival Kit; Islands of Australia's Great Barrier Reef; Trekking in Spain.* Do not want: anything outside of travel.

Initial Contact. Query letter; book proposal with cover letter.

Acceptance Policies. Unagented manuscripts: yes. Simultaneous submissions: n/i. Disk submissions: no. Response time to initial inquiry: varies; if promising, it must go to Australian office. Average time until publication: varies. **Advance**: depends. **Royalty**: negotiated with Australian office. First run: 10,000-30,000.

Marketing Channels. Direct mail; independent sales reps; in-house staff; special sales. Subsidiary rights: all.

Additional Information. We're the leading publisher of guides for the independent traveler. We cover the more exotic destinations. Tips: Look at our catalog before making submissions. Catalog: call or write.

LOS HOMBRES PRESS. PO Box 15428. San Diego, CA 92115. (619) 234-6710. Submissions Editors: Jim Kitchen; Marsh Cassady (gay and lesbian fiction and nonfiction, haiku). Founded: 1989. Number of titles published: cumulative—5, 1991—4. Softback 100%.

Subjects of Interest. Fiction—gay and lesbian novels and short story collections. Recent publications: *Love Theme with Variations* (mature man seeks lasting relationship). Nonfiction—gay and lesbian; haiku poetry. Recent publications: *Panels of Love—Paintings and Reflections by Artist with ARC*; *The Rise and Fall of Sparrows* (haiku anthology). Do not want: pornography; gay or lesbian "romance."

Initial Contact. Query letter with synopsis/outline. Include writing credits.

Acceptance Policies. Unagented manuscripts: yes. Simultaneous submissions: yes, inform us. Disk submissions: WordPerfect (preferred). First novels: yes. Response time to initial inquiry: 3-4 weeks. Average time until publication: 1 year. **Advance:** none. **Royalty:** 10% based on retail sales. First run: 1000-2000.

Marketing Channels. Distribution houses; direct mail. Subsidiary rights: all.

Additional Information. Tips: We are interested in good writing with strong character development portraying gays and lesbians in a positive light. Catalog: upon request. Writer's guidelines: upon request.

LUCENT BOOKS, INC. (Sister company to Greenhaven Press). PO Box 289011. San Diego, CA 92128-9011. (619) 485-7424. Submissions Editor: Carol O'Sullivan. Founded: 1987. Number of titles published: cumulative—16. Hardback 100%.

Subjects of Interest. Nonfiction—overview series on controversial topics written in an objective manner. Recent projects included endangered species; garbage; smoking. Also some fun books. Recent publications: Overview Series—*Aids, Dealing with Death; Endangered Species, Vietnam; Homeless Children; Smoking.* World Disasters—*Armenian Earthquake; Titanic; Chicago Fire; San Francisco Earthquake; Crash of 1929.* Do not want: fiction; anthologies; textbookish manuscripts.

Initial Contact. Query letter. In the initial contact, the idea will be sufficient. If we like the idea, we'll ask for a proposal, statement of purpose, and chapter outline. We also require a sample chapter. The initial contact should reflect a developed idea, i.e. slant or angle. Author should do some research to see what is already available in order to present a unique approach.

Acceptance Policies. Unagented manuscripts: yes. Simultaneous submissions: yes; inform us. Disk submissions: no. Response time to initial inquiry: 2 weeks. Average time until publication: 6 months. **Advance:** none. **Royalty:** flat fee, negotiable. First run: n/i.

Marketing Channels. Distribution houses; direct mail. Subsidiary rights: English language publication outside the United States and Canada.

Additional Information. We are a new company. We are interested in books for our Overview Series which will focus on issue-oriented books written at a 5-8 grade level. Tips: Request our guidelines and policies. Be familiar with our needs and requirements. Catalog: Write and request.

LURAMEDIA. 7060 Miramar Rd., Ste. 104. San Diego, CA 92121. (619) 578-1948. Submissions Editor: Lura Jane Geiger. Founded: 1962. Number of titles published: cumulative—23, 1991—6. Hardback 5%, softback 95%.

Subjects of Interest. Nonfiction—spiritual and religious growth; psychology; health; women; ministry. Recent publications: *Healing Your Habits* (controlling addictions). Do not want: poetry; children's stories.

Initial Contact. Query letter; book proposal with sample chapters; biography; annotated chapter outline; uniqueness of book; competition.

Acceptance Policies. Unagented manuscripts: yes. Simultaneous submissions: yes. Disk submissions: no. First novels: yes. Response time to initial inquiry: 3-4 weeks. Average time until publication: 9 months. **Advance:** None to $500. **Royalty:** 10% of sales; negotiable. First run: 2000-5000.

Marketing Channels. Distribution houses; direct mail; in-house staff; special sales. Subsidiary rights: all.

Additional Information. We select books that have a long shelf life, and we keep reprinting them. Tips: Tell me why you think your book will interest readers. Catalog: upon request. Writer's guidelines: upon request.

Mad Hatter *see* **SLAWSON COMMUNICATIONS, INC.**

MAGICAL MUSIC EXPRESS. PO Box 417. Palo Alto, CA 94302. (415) 856-0987. Submissions Editor: Greta Pedersen. Founded: 1983. Number of titles published: cumulative—2, 1991—1. Softback 100%.

Subjects of Interest. Nonfiction—music related areas; education and whole language via music. Recent publications: *Magical Music* (cassette and lyric book); *Whole Language Teacher's Guide*. Do not want: non-music related topics.

Initial Contact. Query letter with synopsis/outline.

Acceptance Policies. Unagented manuscripts: yes. Simultaneous submissions: yes. Disk submissions: IBM or Macintosh. Response time to initial inquiry: 4 weeks. Average time until publication: n/i. **Advance:** none. **Royalty:** none. First run: n/i.

Marketing Channels. Independent reps. Subsidiary rights: n/i.

Additional Information. Rarely accept outside material; willing to collaborate.

M AND T PUBLISHING, INC. 501 Galveston Dr. Redwood City, CA 94063. (415) 366-3600. Submissions Editor: Brenda McLaughlin, Editor-in-Chief. Founded: 1982. Number of titles published: cumulative—50. Softback 100%.

Subjects of Interest. Nonfiction—programming; computer books and software. Recent publications: *Netware User's Guide; C & T Techniques and Applications; Advanced Fractal Programming C; Using QuarkXPress*.

Initial Contact. Book proposal with sample chapters; or outline.

Acceptance Policies. Unagented manuscripts: yes. Simultaneous submissions: yes. Disk submissions: IBM PC (clone); MS-DOS. Response time to initial inquiry: 4 weeks. Average time until publication: 6 months. **Advance:** varies. **Royalty:** varies. First run: varies.

Marketing Channels. Wholesalers; direct mail; independent reps. Subsidiary rights: co-publishing agreement with Prentice-Hall International for overseas distribution and translation, except foreign rights to Germany, which is handled by Markt & Tecknik.

Additional Information. Catalog: call or write.

MANUAL 3, INC. 1150 S. Bascom Ave., Ste. 17. San Jose, CA 95128. (408) 293-9654. Submissions Editor: Phil Gold. Founded: 1981. Number of titles published: cumulative—300+, 1991—100. Hardback 15%; Softback 85%.

Subjects of Interest. Nonfiction—very technical programs directed to the electronics industry; documentation, telecommunications; hardware documentation.

Initial Contact. Query letter. Include previous experience.

Acceptance Policies. Unagented manuscripts: yes. Simultaneous submissions: yes. Disk submissions: Microsoft Word for Macintosh—3.01 or higher. Response time to initial inquiry: 30 days. Average time until publication: 4-5 months. **Advance:** negotiable. **Royalty:** negotiable. First run: 1000-2500.

Marketing Channels. Distribution houses. Subsidiary rights: none.

Additional Information. We publish for a variety of different companies: Apple, H-P, IBM, etc. Rarely does a book have our own company name on it. Tips: Manuscripts should be complete, accurate, and well written. Catalog: upon request.

MARKETING ARM, THE. PO Box 1994. Monterey, CA 93942. (408) 373-0592. Submissions Editor: n/i. Founded: 1988. Number of titles published: cumulative—3, 1991—5. Softback 100%.

Subjects of Interest. Nonfiction—cookbooks; travel.

Initial Contact. Query letter with synopsis/outline.

Acceptance Policies. Unagented manuscripts: yes. Simultaneous submissions: yes. Disk submissions: n/i. Response time to initial inquiry: 2 weeks. Average time until publication: n/i. **Advance:** n/i. **Royalty:** n/i. First run: n/i.

Marketing Channels. Distribution houses; direct mail; independent reps; special sales. Subsidiary rights: none.

Additional Information. Catalog: upon request.

MARKETSCOPE BOOKS. 119 Richard Ct. Aptos, CA 95003. (408) 688-7535. Submissions Editor: Ken Albert. Founded: 1985. Number of titles published: cumulative—9, 1991—3. Softback 100%.

Subjects of Interest. Nonfiction—fishing, outdoors. Recent publications: *Fishing in Northern California; Saltwater Fishing in California.* Do not want: fiction.

Initial Contact. Query letter.

Acceptance Policies. Unagented manuscripts: yes. Simultaneous submissions: yes. Disk submissions: no. Response time to initial inquiry: 1 week. Average time until publication: 6 months. **Advance:** varies. **Royalty:** varies. First run: 10,000.

Marketing Channels. Distribution houses; independent reps. Subsidiary rights: all.

Additional Information. Catalog: upon request.

MARKGRAF PUBLICATIONS GROUP. (Division of The Robots, Inc.). PO Box 936. Menlo Park, CA 94025. (415) 940-1299. Submissions Editor: Karin Hall. Founded: 1987. Number of titles published: cumulative—6, 1991—n/i. Hardback and softback, all books published in both formats.

Subjects of Interest. Fiction—historical fiction based on substantial research. Recent publications: *A Gathering at the River* (stories from a life in the Foreign Service). Nonfiction—history; government and current affairs; international relations; poetry; real estate. Recent publications: *America's Nazis, A Democratic Dilemma; They Don't Speak Russian in Sitka* (a new look at Alaskan history). Do not want: new age or how-to.

Initial Contact. Query letter with synopsis/outline. Include author bio.

Acceptance Policies. Unagented manuscripts: yes. Simultaneous submissions: yes. Disk submissions: no. Response time to initial inquiry: varies. Average time until publication: 8-10 months. **Advance:** usually not. **Royalty:** individual agreement. First run: n/i.

Marketing Channels. Distribution houses; direct mail. Subsidiary rights: all.

Additional Information. Catalog: n/i. Writer's guidelines: n/i.

MARK PUBLISHING, INC. 5400 Scotts Valley Dr. Scotts Valley, CA 95066. (408) 438-7668. Submissions Editor: Bill Myers. Founded: 1987. Number of titles published: cumulative—47, 1991—25. Softback 100%.

Subjects of Interest. Nonfiction—how-to books; arts and crafts. Recent publications: *Lillies and Orchids; Decorating Your Home for Christmas; Fashion Paisleys.*

Initial Contact. Query letter; book proposal; call Bill Myers and describe project.

Acceptance Policies. Unagented manuscripts: yes. Simultaneous submissions: yes. Disk submissions: yes. Response time to initial inquiry: 1 week. Average time until publication: varies. **Advance:** none. **Royalty:** varies. First run: 10,000.

Marketing Channels. Distribution houses. Subsidiary rights: yes.

Additional Information. Catalog: upon request.

MATURE LIFE PRESS. PO Box 90279. San Diego, CA 92109. Submissions Editor: Leonard J. Hansen. Founded: 1988. Number of titles published: cumulative—2, 1991—6. Softback 100%.

Subjects of Interest. Nonfiction—of interest to mature adults; business (concerning mature adults); directory of mature market media. Recent publications: *Successful Marketing to Mature Adults; Mature Market FinderBinder.* Do not want: poetry; inspiration; fiction; nostalgia.

Initial Contact. Query letter with synopsis/outline and book proposal. Include 3 sample chapters, background on the author, and the author's perspective of the reading public for the book.

Acceptance Policies. Unagented manuscripts: yes. Simultaneous submissions: yes; inform us. Disk submissions: IBM compatible; prefer WordPerfect 5.0. Response time to initial inquiry: 1 month. Average time until publication: varies on marketing plans. **Advance:** varies. **Royalty:** negotiable. First run: depends on book.

Marketing Channels. Distribution houses; cooperative distribution; direct mail. Subsidiary rights: varies; depends on book, author, and the "right deal" for all involved.

Additional Information. We are "evolving" now. Catalog: SASE, $.45 postage. Writer's guidelines: SASE, 1 first class stamp.

MAYFIELD PUBLISHING COMPANY. 1240 Villa St. Mountain View, CA 94041. (415) 960-3222. Submissions Editor: Thomas Broadbent. Founded: 1946. Number of titles published: cumulative—205 (in print), 1991—45. Hardback 40%, softback 60%.

Subjects of Interest. Nonfiction—college textbooks in English (composition and literature); education; dance; theater; art; music; health; physical education and recreation; psychology; anthropology; sociology; journalism; communication; speech. Do not want: books not intended for college courses.

Initial Contact. Query letter; or book proposal; tentative outline of contents.

Acceptance Policies. Unagented manuscripts: yes. Simultaneous submissions: yes; inform us. Disk submissions: yes; Wordstar for IBM compatibles; WordPerfect, Microsoft Word for IBM or Macintosh; Macwrite. Response time to initial inquiry: 2 weeks. Average time until publication: varies. **Advance:** varies. **Royalty:** varies. First run: varies.

Marketing Channels. Direct mail; full scale field sales force. Subsidiary rights: all.

Additional Information. Catalog: write to marketing director for materials pertinent to your subject.

MAZDA PUBLISHERS. 2991 Grace Lane. PO Box 2603. Costa Mesa, CA 92626. (714) 751-5252. Submissions Editor: Ahmad Jabbari. Founded: 1980. Number of titles published: cumulative—84, 1991—5. Hardback (mostly) and softback.

Subjects of Interest. **Fiction**—related to geographic specifications. **Nonfiction**—Middle East and North Africa in the areas of art, business, cooking and foods, history, politics, sociology, social sciences, informational books; emphasis on scholarly approach. **Poetry**—translations and works of Middle Eastern poets only.

Initial Contact. Outline; summary; sample chapters.

Acceptance Policies. Unagented manuscripts: yes. Simultaneous submissions: yes. Disk submissions: query. Response time to initial inquiry: 2-6 weeks. Average time until publication: 4 months. **Advance:** none. **Royalty:** standard on wholesale. First run: 2000.

Marketing Channels. Direct mail. Subsidiary rights: none.

Additional Information. Our audience is the academic and educated layperson. Tips: Use *Chicago Manual of Style.* Catalog: upon request. Writer's guidelines: SASE.

MCCUTCHAN PUBLISHING CORPORATION. 2940 San Pablo Ave. PO Box 774. Berkeley, CA 94701. (415) 841-8616 (outside of CA 800-227-1540). Submissions Editor: John McCutchan. Founded: 1963. Number of titles published: cumulative—73, 1991—10. Hardback 80%, softback 20%.

Subjects of Interest. **Nonfiction**—college texts: education; hotel and restaurant management; criminal justice. Recent publications: *Purchasing for Food Service Managers; Leaders for America's Schools; Introduction to Criminal Evidence Court Procedure.* Do not want: manuscripts.

Initial Contact. Prospectus on the topic; publishing plan.

Acceptance Policies. Unagented manuscripts: yes. Disk submissions: n/i. Response time to initial inquiry: 1 month. Average time until publication: 8-10 months. **Advance:** occasionally. **Royalty:** 12-15%. First run: 2500.

Marketing Channels. Direct mail. Subsidiary rights: none.

Additional Information. We publish for professionals in the field. We don't publish trade books. Catalog: upon written request.

MCKINZIE PUBLISHING COMPANY. (Subsidiary of Aaims Press). 11000 Wilshire Blvd., #241-777. Los Angeles, CA 90024-3602. (213) 934-7685. Submissions Editor: Janet Smith. Founded: 1969. Number of titles published: cumulative—15, 1991—7. Softback 100%.

Subjects of Interest. **Fiction**—romance. **Nonfiction**—family; poetry. Recent publications: *Family Reunions: How to Plan Yours; High School Reunions: How to Plan Yours; Names from East Africa; Women in Boxing.*

Initial Contact. Book proposal with sample chapters. Include resumé.

Acceptance Policies. Unagented manuscripts: yes. Multiple submissions: yes. Disk submissions: no. First novels: yes. Response time to initial inquiry: 90 days. Average time until publication: 1 year. **Advance:** none. **Royalty:** none. First run: 500. Subsidy basis: yes.

Marketing Channels. Cooperative distribution; direct mail. Subsidiary rights: first serialization; newspaper syndication; dramatization, motion picture, and broadcast; direct mail or direct sales; translation and foreign; computer and other magnetic and electronic media; commercial rights; English language publication outside the United States and Canada.

Additional Information. Catalog: SASE.

MERCURY HOUSE. 201 Filbert St., Ste. 400. San Francisco, CA 94133. (415) 433-7042. Submissions Editor: Alison Macondray. Founded: 1985. Number of titles published: cumulative—69, 1991—20. Hardback 90%, softback 10%.

Subjects of Interest. Fiction—quality in all subjects. Recent publications: *Carmon Dog.* **Nonfiction**—literary adult; translations; reprints. Recent publications: *Without Force or Lies: Voices from the Revolution in Europe in 1989-1990.* **Other**—Biography/Lively Arts Series, reprints of classic entertainment books. Recent publications: *Fun in a Chinese Laundry.* Do not want: genre fiction.

Initial Contact. Book proposal with 3 sample chapters. Include SASE.

Acceptance Policies. Unagented manuscripts: no. Simultaneous submissions: yes; inform us. Disk submissions: no. First novels: yes. Response time to initial inquiry: 3 months maximum. Average time until publication: 1 year. **Advance:** standard. **Royalty:** standard. First run: 4000 average.

Marketing Channels. Distribution houses; in-house staff. Subsidiary rights: all.

Additional Information. Catalog: request by mail, $.85 SASE.

Microtrend *see* **SLAWSON COMMUNICATIONS, INC.**

R AND E MILES PUBLISHERS. PO Box 1916. San Pedro, CA 90733. (213) 833-8856. Submissions Editor: Robert Miles. Founded: 1980. Number of titles published: cumulative—32, 1991—4. Hardback 30%, softback 70%.

Subjects of Interest. Nonfiction—ecology; quilts; politics; travel. Recent publications: *The Redesigned Forest; Ecophilosophy; Whatever Happened to the Hippies?* Do not want: fiction; poetry; coffee-table books.

Initial Contact. Book proposal.

Acceptance Policies. Unagented manuscripts: yes. Simultaneous submissions: no. Disk submissions: no. Response time to initial inquiry: 3 weeks. Average time until publication: 6 months. **Advance:** negotiable. **Royalty:** 10%. First run: 1000-7000.

Marketing Channels. Distribution houses; direct mail. Subsidiary rights: all.

Additional Information. Catalog: SASE.

MILLER BOOKS. 2908 W. Valley Blvd. Alhambra, CA 91803. (818) 284-7607. Submissions Editor: Joseph Miller. Number of titles published: cumulative—62, 1991—7. Hardback 66%, softback 34%.

Subjects of Interest. Fiction—western; historical; humor; mystery; adventure. **Nonfiction**—how-to; self-help; cookbooks; Americana; history; nature; philosophy; politics; emphasis on remedial. Recent publications: *Beds That Help You Sleep Better; The Life You Earn; Clothes Makes the Man.* Do not want: anything erotic.

Initial Contact. Complete manuscript.

Acceptance Policies. Unagented manuscripts: yes. Simultaneous submissions: yes. Disk submissions: no. Response time to initial inquiry: 2 months. Average time until publication: 1 year. **Advance:** no. **Royalty:** 10-15% on retail; some manuscripts bought outright. First run: n/i.

Marketing Channels. Distribution houses; direct dial; in-house staff. Subsidiary rights: all.

Additional Information. Approach subject in a positive vein; negativity doesn't sell. We need remedial texts in all areas. Catalog: upon request.

MINA PRESS PUBLISHERS. PO Box 854. Sebastopol, CA 95473. (707) 829-0854. Submissions Editors: Adam David Miller (poetry); Mei Nakano (all others). Founded: 1981. Number of titles published: cumulative—5, 1991—1. Softback 100%.

Subjects of Interest. Fiction—range of subjects and types of good literature (adult and children). Nonfiction—poetry. Do not want: any materials that glorify war, portray gratuitous violence, or demean a group of human beings.

Initial Contact. Query letter.

Acceptance Policies. Unagented manuscripts: yes. Simultaneous submissions: yes. Disk submissions: no. First novels: yes. Response time to initial inquiry: 2-3 months. Average time until publication: 12-18 months. **Advance:** none. **Royalty:** 10%. First run: 2000.

Marketing Channels. Distribution houses; direct mail; special sales. Subsidiary rights: all.

Additional Information. Our motto is "giving life to good books." We are a small press dedicated to the preservation and publication of good literature. We give particular attention to previously unpublished writers and non-mainstream writers, though we consider other works too. Tips: We like children's books of the variety that conveys some meaningful learning experience, which is not all fluff and prettiness. Catalog: none.

MONEYTREE PUBLISHING. (Subsidiary of LAWCO Ltd. Imprints: Moneytree Publications; Billiard Books). PO Box 2009. Manteca, CA 95336. (209) 239-6006. Submissions Editor: J.R. Lawson. Founded: 1980. Number of titles published: cumulative—25, 1991—2. Softback 100%.

Subjects of Interest. Nonfiction—career; directories. Recent publications: *Language of Success—Job Search for College Students.* Do not want: fiction.

Initial Contact. Book proposal with market analysis.

Acceptance Policies. Unagented manuscripts: yes. Simultaneous submissions: yes; inform us. Disk submissions: ASCII; WS 5.0. Response time to initial inquiry: 90 days. Average time until publication: varies. **Advance:** n/i. **Royalty:** n/i. First run: n/i.

Marketing Channels. Distribution houses; direct mail; special sales. Subsidiary rights: none.

Additional Information. We are focusing on books for billiard/pool players at this time. Tips: We have a well-defined market that is reachable. Catalog: n/i. Writer's guidelines: use *Chicago Manual of Style.*

MOON PUBLICATIONS. 722 Wall St. Chico, CA 95928. (916) 345-5473. Submissions Editors: Mark Morris or Deke Castleman. Founded: 1973. Number of titles published: cumulative—32, 1991—15. Softback 100%.

Subjects of Interest. Nonfiction—comprehensive travel guidebooks for independent travelers of all stripes. Recent publications: *Northern California Handbook* (a comprehensive resource—covers history, politics, culture, natural features, recreation, and all travel practicalities); *Cancun Handbook; Southeast Asia Handbook; Egypt Handbook*; etc. Do not want: fiction; travel narrative; how-to guides.

Initial Contact. Query letter; discussion of writer's previous experience and credentials.

Acceptance Policies. Unagented manuscripts: yes. Simultaneous submissions: yes; inform us. Disk submissions: IBM/DOS; Macintosh. Response time to initial inquiry: 2 weeks. Average time until publication: 18-24 months after signing contract. **Advance:** up to $5000. **Royalty:** standard. First run: 5000-20,000.

Marketing Channels. Distribution houses; direct mail; special sales. Subsidiary rights: all.

Additional Information. Tips: Study any of our guides first to find out what we do and do not publish. Catalog: SASE; legal-sized envelope with 2 first class stamps.

MUTUAL PUBLISHING. 2055 N. King St., #201. Honolulu, HI 96819. (808) 924-7732. Submissions Editor: Gay Wong. Founded: 1974. Number of titles published: cumulative—80, 1991—15. Hardback 50%, softback 50%.

Subjects of Interest. Fiction—Pacific; Hawaii. Recent publications: *A Dream of Islands.* **Nonfiction**—Hawaii. Recent publications: *From the Skies of Paradise.* Do not want: poetry; inspiration.

Initial Contact. Query letter only. Include credentials, sample of previously published writings.

Acceptance Policies. Unagented manuscripts: yes. Simultaneous submissions: yes. Disk submissions: only if accompanied by hard copy. Response time to initial inquiry: 30 days. Average time until publication: 1 year. **Advance:** $250. **Royalty:** 5% based on retail. First run: open. Subsidy basis: varies.

Marketing Channels. Distribution houses. Subsidiary rights: reprint; book club; translation and foreign; computer and other magnetic and electronic media; English language publication outside the United States and Canada.

Additional Information. Catalog: upon request. Writer's guidelines: only after we accept manuscript.

National Space Society *see* **UNIVELT, INC.**

NATUREGRAPH PUBLISHERS, INC. (Imprints: Prism Editions). 3543 Indian Creek Rd. PO Box 1075. Happy Camp, CA 96039. (916) 493-5353. Submissions Editor: Barbara Brown. Founded: 1946. Number of titles published: cumulative—100+, 1990—6. Hardback 5%, softback 95%.

Subjects of Interest. Nonfiction—natural history; Native American; health; crafts dealing with natural history or Native Americans. Recent publications: *Health Unlimited—Unleash Your Healing Power; Mystery Tracks in the Snow Karuk, the Upriver People.* Do not want: anything outside our category.

Initial Contact. Query letter; give reasons why book would sell; places to market it; a good sales pitch; how this book differs from other books on the subject.

Acceptance Policies. Unagented manuscripts: yes. Simultaneous submissions: yes; alert us; encourages quick publisher response. Disk submissions: no. Response time to initial inquiry: 1 week if not interested; 2 months if interested. Average time until publication: 18 months after contract. **Advance:** none. **Royalty:** 10% of net amount invoiced. First run: 2500. Subsidy basis: rarely; maybe 3-5%, and then we repay the investment at a rate of so much per book sold. Occurs when we want a book and can't afford to produce it without outside help.

Marketing Channels. Distribution houses; direct mail; independent reps; special sales. Subsidiary rights: reprint; dramatization, motion picture, and broadcast; direct mail or direct sales; book club; translation and foreign; commercial; English language publication outside United States and Canada.

Additional Information. We are both publishers and printers. Predominantly we print only our own publications, but we also produce books commercially. Tips: We appreciate neatly typed, double-spaced, properly margined pages with a black typewriter ribbon. Catalog: upon request.

NATURE'S DESIGN. (Imprints: Firehole Press). PO Box 255. Davenport, CA 95017. (408) 426-8205. Submissions Editor: Frank S. Balthis. Founded: 1980. Number of titles published: cumulative—6, 1991—2. Softback 100%.

Subjects of Interest. Nonfiction—natural history and travel; wildlife; guides to parks; children's guides to parks. Recent publications: *Mirounga: A Guide to Elephant Seals; Children's Guides to Yellowstone, Ano Nuevo, Pt. Reyes; Winter at Old Faithful.*

Initial Contact. Query letter. Include concise list of book, magazine, and newspaper credits; concise description of expertise. Include SASE.

Acceptance Policies. Unagented manuscripts: yes. Simultaneous submissions: yes. Disk submissions: no. Response time to initial inquiry: 1 week. Average time until publication: 1 year. **Advance:** varies. **Royalty:** varies. First run: 5000-10,000.

Marketing Channels. Independent reps; in-house staff; special sales. Subsidiary rights: n/a.

Additional Information. As photographers, we wish to "team up" with writers on natural history projects for books and periodicals. Tips: It is very helpful if the writer is familiar with the location and potential market for a book or periodical project. Catalog: SASE.

NETWORK PUBLICATIONS. PO Box 1830. Santa Cruz, CA 95061-1830. (408) 438-4060. Submissions Editor: Netha Thacker. Founded: 1981. Number of titles published: cumulative—200, 1991—50. Hardback 1%, softback 99%.

Subjects of Interest. Fiction—interactive books for young adults (ages 9-14) on substance abuse prevention. Recent publications: *Don't Let It Get Around* (taking chances with sex); *Serena's Secret* (alcohol); *Christy's Chance* (marijuana). **Nonfiction**—education: adolescent pregnancy; AIDS; sexuality; reproductive health; child sexual abuse; self-esteem. Recent publications: *Does Aids Hurt?* (Contemporary Health Series); *Smiling at Yourself.* **Other**—photo-novella; curricula; resource guides and pamphlets on family life education; sexuality education.

Initial Contact. Query letter.

Acceptance Policies. Unagented manuscripts: yes. Simultaneous submissions: yes. Disk submissions: n/i. Response time to initial inquiry: 1 month. Average time until publication: varies. **Advance:** sometimes. **Royalty:** varies. First run: 1000.

Marketing Channels. Distribution houses; direct mail; in-house staff; special sales. Subsidiary rights: split 50%.

Additional Information. Our primary audience is middle-school and secondary-level educators; our emphasis is prevention education within the context of comprehensive health education. Catalog: upon request.

NEWCASTLE PUBLISHING COMPANY, INC. 13419 Saticoy. North Hollywood, CA 91605. (213) 873-3191. Fax (818) 780-2007. Submissions Editor: Alfred Saunders. Number of titles published: cumulative—140, 1991—10. Softback 100%.

Subjects of Interest. Nonfiction—how-to; self-help; metaphysical; new age; fitness; holistic health; psychology; religion; titles for older adults. Recent publications: *Well Being Journal; Live Your Dream; Power of Your Other Hand.* Do not want: poetry; cookbooks; fiction.

Initial Contact. Query letter; or summary and sample chapters.

Acceptance Policies. Unagented manuscripts: yes. Simultaneous submissions: yes. Disk submissions: no. Response time to initial inquiry: 3-6 weeks. Average time until publication: n/i. **Advance:** none. **Royalty:** 5-10% on retail. First run: 3000-5000.

Marketing Channels. Distribution houses. Subsidiary rights: all.

Additional Information. Tips: Include something that will grab the reader. Know your market. Catalog: upon request; guidelines, SASE.

NEW HUMANITY PRESS. (Subsidiary of Independent). PO Box 215. Berkeley, CA 94701. (415) 644-1360. Submissions Editor: Doris Iberico, publisher's helper. Founded: 1986. Number of titles published: cumulative—1, 1991—3-6. Softback 100%.

Subjects of Interest. Fiction—all. **Nonfiction**—all. Recent publications: *Lab Animal Abuse: Vivisection Exposed!* (comprehensive case against research laboratories). Do not want: We aren't absolutists. Our minds are open to anything/everything.

Initial Contact. Query letter with synopsis/outline with book proposal and sample chapters. Include writer's background. Please never contact by phone first.

Acceptance Policies. Unagented manuscripts: yes. Simultaneous submissions: yes, at writer's discretion; it's their work. Disk submissions: no. First novels: yes. Response time to initial inquiry: 1 month or less. Average time until publication: 6-12 months. **Advance:** to be negotiated. **Royalty:** to be negotiated. First run: n/i. Subsidy basis: negotiable.

Marketing Channels. Direct mail; in-house staff; special sales. Subsidiary rights: all.

Additional Information. Our press is still in its early stages of development, though we aim to do away with exploitative middle people like agents, "publishers," and distributors. We will do direct marketing. Tips: Be honest in both writing and dealing. We are not snobs about these sacred SASEs. If a writer thinks enough of us to write, we think enough of him (or her) to answer. Catalog: ask. Writer's guidelines: ask.

NEW SAGE PRESS. PO Box 41029. Pasadena, CA 91104-8029. (818) 795-0266. Submissions Editor: Maureen Michelson. Founded: 1984. Number of titles published: cumulative—7, 1991—3. Hardback, softback, often published simultaneously.

Subjects of Interest. Nonfiction—photo essay books (primarily). Recent publications: *Women and Work; Portrait of American Mother and Daughters; The New Americans; Common Heroes; Exposures: Women and Their Art.* Do not want: fiction; how-to.

Initial Contact. Query letter; book proposal with 1 sample chapter. Include a strong sense of the author's conviction of the worthwhile nature of the project; markets.

Acceptance Policies. Unagented manuscripts: yes. Simultaneous submissions: no. Disk submissions: no. Response time to initial inquiry: 3 months. Average time until publication: 1 year. **Advance:** depends on project. **Royalty:** negotiable. First run: 5000-10,000.

Marketing Channels. Distribution houses; direct mail; independent reps; special sales. Subsidiary rights: all.

Additional Information. We are interested in quality, both production and content. Tips: Clearly delineate the market for your book in your query letter. We're not just interested in "good photos." Catalog: SASE.

NEW SEED PRESS. PO Box 9488. Berkeley, CA 94709. (415) 540-7576. Submissions Editor: Helen Chetin. Founded: 1971. Number of titles published: 1990—12. Softback 100%.

Subjects of Interest. Fiction—feminist press looking for nonsexist, nonracist stories for children which actively confront bigotry issues. Recent Publications: *The Girls of Summer; The Good Bad Wolf; My Mother and I Are Growing Strong* (Spanish/English).

Initial Contact. Query letter; brief summary; SASE.

Acceptance Policies. Unagented manuscripts: yes. Simultaneous submissions: yes. Disk submissions: no. First novels: yes. Response time to initial inquiry: 2 weeks. Average time until publication: 1 year. **Advance:** % of royalty. **Royalty:** 10%. First run: 2000-4000.

Marketing Channels. Distribution houses; direct mail. Subsidiary rights: none.

Additional Information. Tips: Your manuscript should be the best possible. Make sure who your market is. Catalog: upon request.

NEW SOCIETY PUBLISHERS. (Subsidiary of New Society Educational Foundation). PO Box 582. Santa Cruz, CA 95061. (408) 458-1191. Submissions Editor: David H. Albert, West Coast editorial coordinator. Founded: 1981. Number of titles published: cumulative—90, 1991—14. Hardback, softback, all dual editions.

Subjects of Interest. Nonfiction—books which help create a more peaceful and just world through nonviolent action. Do not want: poetry; plays; fiction; electoral politics; crystals.

Initial Contact. Request manuscript guidelines.

Acceptance Policies. Unagented manuscripts: yes. Simultaneous submissions: yes. Disk submissions: required; MS-DOS. Response time to initial inquiry: 1 month. Average time until publication: 8-12 months. **Advance:** negotiable. **Royalty:** negotiable. First run: 4000+.

Marketing Channels. Distribution houses; direct mail; independent reps; in-house staff; special sales. Subsidiary rights: all.

Additional Information. We publish books promoting fundamental social change through nonviolent action only. Tips: Ask yourself whether a world where trees are scarce and books are plentiful needs yours to add to the ecological burden. Catalog: SASE.

NEW WORLD LIBRARY. 58 Paul Dr. San Rafael, CA 94903. (415) 472-2100. Submissions Editor: Katherine Dieter. Founded: 1977. Number of titles published: cumulative—40, 1991—10. Hardback 20%, softback 80%.

Subjects of Interest. Nonfiction—self-improvement; new age; uplifting titles on a variety of subjects such as careers, prosperity, writing, psychology. Recent publications: *The Instant Millionaire; Reflections in the Light* (Shakti Gawain); *Embracing Our Selves; Maps to Ecstasy.* **Other**—audio and video cassettes. Do not want: poetry; military; books about specific gurus; crystals; channeling.

Initial Contact. Query letter; book proposal with 1 sample chapter. Include something about the author; SASE.

Acceptance Policies. Unagented manuscripts: yes. Simultaneous submissions: yes; inform us. Disk submissions: no. Response time to initial inquiry: 4-8 weeks. Average time until publication: 12 months. **Advance:** varies widely. **Royalty:** reasonable. First run: 3000-15,000.

Marketing Channels. Distribution houses; direct mail. Subsidiary rights: all.

Additional Information. We're a solid, profitable company with a distribution network in place that can sell as well as anybody. Tips: Be nice. Catalog: upon request.

Nitty Gritty Books *see* **BRISTOL PUBLISHING ENTERPRISES.**

NOLO PRESS-OCCIDENTAL. PO Box 722. Occidental, CA 95465. (707) 874-3105. Submissions Editor: Tracy H. Devine. Founded: 1971. Number of titles published: cumulative—7, 1991—1. Softback 100%.

Subjects of Interest. Nonfiction—how-to law books for laymen. Recent publications: *How to Get Restraining Orders to Stop Domestic Violence.* Do not want: fiction; poetry.

Initial Contact. Query letter with synopsis/outline.

Acceptance Policies. Unagented manuscripts: yes. Simultaneous submissions: no. Disk submissions: no. Response time to initial inquiry: 30 days. Average time until publication: 6-9 months, if manuscript complete. **Advance:** none. **Royalty:** 8%, based on retail. First run: 5000.

Marketing Channels. Distribution houses; direct mail. Subsidiary rights: all.

Additional Information. Tips: Be sure the subject fits our specialty. Catalog: call and ask.

NORTH ATLANTIC BOOKS. (Wholly owned, nonprofit; program of the Society for the Study of Native Arts and Sciences). 2800 Woolsey St. Berkeley, CA 94705. (415) 652-5309. Submissions Editor: Lindy Hough, associate publisher. Founded: 1974. Number of titles published: cumulative—300+, 1991—15. Hardback 30%, softback 70%.

Subjects of Interest. **Fiction**—avant-garde; contemporary; erotica; literary; new age; women's. **Nonfiction**—alternative medicine; biography (of well-known people); cooking and food; environmental and new science; film; internal martial arts; homeopathy; Peruvian/Brazilian studies; psychology; self-help; social implications of technology; sports; theater; visual arts; women of color; women's (autobiography, biography). Recent publications: *The Complete Book of Flowers.* Do not want: fiction; manuscripts from people unfamiliar with what we publish.

Initial Contact. Query letter. Include SASE; publishing history; academic/writing background.

Acceptance Policies. Unagented manuscripts: yes. Simultaneous submissions: no. Disk submissions: no. Response time to initial inquiry: 1 week. Average time until publication: 6 months. **Advance:** none. **Royalty:** 10%. First run: 1000-3000.

Marketing Channels. Distribution houses; cooperative distribution; direct mail; independent reps; special sales. Subsidiary rights: all.

Additional Information. We are a strong trade press with an eclectic but focused catalog. Tips: Be sure to query first. Catalog: SASE; $1.00 postage.

NORTH POINT PRESS. Box 6275. Albany, CA 94706. (415) 527-6260. Submissions Editor: Jack Shoemaker. Founded: 1978. Number of titles published: cumulative—300, 1991—30. Hardback and softback, depends on project.

Subjects of Interest. **Fiction**—serious and experimental; literary. Recent publications: *The Art Lover; The God of Nightmares.* **Nonfiction**—literary essays. Recent publications: *What Are People For?; The Island Within.* Do not want: Press absolutely does not accept unsolicited fiction or poetry.

Initial Contact. Write for manuscript guidelines. Include SASE.

Acceptance Policies. Unagented manuscripts: yes. Simultaneous submissions: yes. Disk submissions: no. Response time to initial inquiry: 2-6 months. Average time until publication: 1 year. **Advance:** yes. **Royalty:** standard. First run: 5000-10,000.

Marketing Channels. Distribution houses (Farrar, Straus and Giroux); in-house staff. Subsidiary rights: all.

Additional Information. We also publish a list of fiction and poetry and works in translation.

OAK TREE PUBLICATIONS. (Subsidiary of Vizcom, Inc.). 3870 Murphy Canyon Rd., Ste. 203. San Diego, CA 92123. (619) 560-5163. Submissions Editor: Linda Alioto. Number of titles published: 1988—10-15. Hardback 100%.

Subjects of Interest. Juvenile Fiction—picture books with toy tie-in. Recent publications: *I Wish I Had a Computer That Makes Waffles; Value Tales (an ongoing series).*

Initial Contact. Book proposal with sample chapters; full-color sample illustrations.

Acceptance Policies. Unagented manuscripts: yes. Simultaneous submissions: yes. Disk submissions: no. Response time to initial inquiry: 4-6 weeks. Average time until publication: 8 months. **Advance:** $500. **Royalty:** varies. First run: n/i.

Marketing Channels. Distribution houses; in-house staff; direct mail. Subsidiary rights: all.

Additional Information. We gear our books to ages 2-12. One of our subsidiaries is Value Tale Communications. Tips: Send request and SASE for manuscript guidelines. Catalog: 8 1/2 x 11 SASE, 3 first class stamps.

OAKWOOD PUBLICATIONS. 616 Knob Hill. Redondo Beach, CA 90277. (213) 378-9245. Submissions Editor: Philip Tamoush. Founded: 1987. Number of titles published: cumulative—6, 1991—2. Hardback 90%, softback 10%.

Subjects of Interest. Nonfiction—iconography, eastern Christian art; liturgical arts; Orthodox Christian materials. Recent publications: *The Icon; Dynamic Symmetry; Painter's Manual; Art of the Icon.*

Initial Contact. Query letter.

Acceptance Policies. Unagented manuscripts: yes. Disk submissions: any format. Response time to initial inquiry: 1 month. Average time until publication: 1 year. **Advance:** on royalties. **Royalty:** negotiable. First run: 2000. Subsidy basis: yes; percentage of sales.

Marketing Channels. Distribution houses; direct mail. Subsidiary rights: translation and foreign.

Additional Information. Catalog: upon request.

OCEAN VIEW BOOKS. Box 4148. Mountain View, CA 94040. (415) 965-3721. Submissions Editor: Lee Ballentine. Founded: 1981. Number of titles published: cumulative—16, 1989—3. Hardback and softback, we do two versions of each book.

Subjects of Interest. Fiction—science fiction; surrealist fiction. Recent publications: *Poly-New Speculative Writing* (anthology with Ray Bradbury, Tom Disch, William Stafford, et al.*)* **Nonfiction**—speculative and surrealist poetry. Recent publications: *Co-Orbital Moons* (poems of science and science fiction). Do not want: "mainstream" anything; we are a literary publisher.

Initial Contact. Query letter. Include clips of published works and evidence that the author has seen our books and understands our requirements.

Acceptance Policies. Unagented manuscripts: 90%. Simultaneous submissions: no. Disk submissions: after acceptance only. Response time to initial inquiry: 3 months. Average time until publication: 2 years. **Advance:** negotiable. **Royalty:** negotiable. First run: 500-5000.

Marketing Channels. Distribution houses; independent reps; in-house staff. Subsidiary rights: first serialization; reprint; book club; translation and foreign; English language publication outside United States and Canada.

Additional Information. Tips: Be familiar with our books and refer to our focus in cover letter. Catalog: 9x12 SASE.

OHARA PUBLICATIONS, INC. 1813 Victory Place. PO Box 7728. Burbank, CA 91510-7728. Submissions Editor: Mike Lee. Number of titles published: 1991—12. Softback 100%.

Subjects of Interest. Nonfiction—martial arts (systems, how-to, history, philosophy). Recent publications: *Small Circle Jujitsu.*

Initial Contact. Book proposal and entire manuscript. Include information about the author's martial arts background.

Acceptance Policies. Unagented manuscripts: yes. Simultaneous submissions: no. Disk submissions: no. Response time to initial inquiry: 3-8 weeks. Average time until publication: n/i. **Advance**: none. **Royalty**: yes. First run: n/i.

Marketing Channels. Distribution houses; direct mail; in-house staff. Subsidiary rights: all.

Additional Information. Tips: Write for guidelines. Catalog: written request. Writer's guidelines: written request.

C. OLSON AND COMPANY. PO Box 5100. Santa Cruz, CA 95063-5100. (408) 458-3365. Submissions Editor: Clay Olson. Founded: 1977. Number of titles published: cumulative—5, 1989—2. Softback 100%.

Subjects of Interest. Nonfiction—health; natural hygiene. Recent publications: *For the Vegetarian in You; The New Abolitionists: Animal Rights and Human Liberation.* Do not want: fiction; manuscripts without a query.

Initial Contact. Query letter. Include SASE (#10 window envelope).

Acceptance Policies. Unagented manuscripts: yes. Simultaneous submissions: yes. Disk submissions: MacWrite; MS Word; Writenow; WordPerfect for Macintosh or IBM; ASCII on 3 1/2" discs. Response time to initial inquiry: 2-3 weeks. Average time until publication: 6-9 months. **Advance**: negotiable. **Royalty**: negotiable. First run: 5000-10,000.

Marketing Channels. Distribution houses; direct mail; telemarketing. Subsidiary rights: negotiable; we work from our standard contract.

Additional Information. Looking for an author to take a series of newsletters on the subject of fruit trees to convert it to book form. Looking for overcoming AIDS stories. Tips: Query first with SASE. Keep it short. Catalog: SASE (#10 window envelope); $1.

101 Productions *see* **ORTHO INFORMATION SERVICES.**

ORTHO INFORMATION SERVICES. (Subsidiary of Chevron Chemical Co. Imprint: 101 Productions). 6001 Bollinger Canyon Road. San Ramon, CA 94583. (415) 842-5537. Submissions Editor: Christine L. Robertson. Number of titles published: cumulative—143, 1991—15. Hardback 5%, softback 95%.

Subjects of Interest. Nonfiction—cookbook; how-to; reference; pictorial; hobbies; nature; gardening; home repair. Recent publications: *Designing and Remodeling Bathrooms; Building Bird Houses and Feeders; Building Children's Wooden Toys.*

Initial Contact. Query first; outline and summary to follow on expressed interest of editors.

Acceptance Policies. Unsolicited manuscripts: we return them unopened. Unagented manuscripts: yes. Simultaneous submissions: yes. Disk submissions: query. Response time to initial inquiry: 2 months. Average time until publication: 2 years. **Advance**: purchase outright. **Royalty**: negotiable. First run: n/i.

Marketing Channels. Distribution houses; in-house staff; special sales. Subsidiary rights: all.

Additional Information. Also publishes quarterly *Chevron Travel Club Magazine*. Tips: We decide on total project, assign writers, photographers, etc., after viewing proposal. Check our catalog for topics not already covered. No first-person how-to. Catalog: 9x12 SASE, 2 first class stamps.

OYEZ. PO Box 5134. Berkeley, CA 94705. Submissions Editor: Robert Hawley. Not accepting manuscripts.

PACIFIC AERO PRESS. (Imprint: Fax-Files). PO Box 2643. Vista, CA 92084. (619) 724-5703. Submissions Editor: Chuck Banks. Founded: 1979. Number of titles published: cumulative—3, 1991—5. Hardback 34%, softback 66%.

Subjects of Interest. Fiction—aviation. **Nonfiction**—aviation. Recent publications: *Super Fax File No. 1* (contains *Fax-File #1-#4*). Do not want: n/i.

Initial Contact. Query letter with synopsis/outline.

Acceptance Policies. Unagented manuscripts: yes. Simultaneous submissions: yes. Disk submissions: yes. First novels: yes. Response time to initial inquiry: 2 weeks. Average time until publication: 6 months. **Advance:** negotiable. **Royalty:** negotiable. First run: based on sales potential.

Marketing Channels. Distribution houses; cooperative distribution; direct mail; independent reps; in-house staff; special sales. Subsidiary rights: all.

Additional Information. Catalog: upon request. Writer's guidelines: upon request.

PACIFIC BOOKS, PUBLISHERS. PO Box 558. Palo Alto, CA 94302-0558. (415) 965-1980. Submissions Editor: Henry Ponleithner. Founded: 1945. Number of titles published: cumulative—261, 1991—7. Hardback 65%, softback 35%.

Subjects of Interest. Nonfiction—general and scholarly; professional and technical reference; college level textbooks, including paperbacks. Recent publications: *Inventors and Their Inventions: A California Legacy; Heroes of the Golden Gate; Economic and Political Change in the Middle East*. Do not want: fiction; poetry.

Initial Contact. Query letter; description of manuscript; outline or table of contents. Include potential market(s).

Acceptance Policies. Unagented manuscripts: yes. Simultaneous submissions: yes. Disk submissions: yes. Response time to initial inquiry: 3-5 weeks. Average time until publication: 9-15 months. **Advance:** none. **Royalty:** standard. First run: 1500-10,000.

Marketing Channels. Direct mail; independent reps; in-house staff; special sales. Subsidiary rights: all.

Additional Information. Catalog: upon request.

PANJANDRUM BOOKS. 5428 Hermitage Ave. North Hollywood, CA 91607. (213) 477-8771. Submissions Editor: Dennis Koran. Founded: 1971. Number of titles published: cumulative—40+, 1988—6. Hardback and softback.

Subjects of Interest. Fiction—avant-garde; experimental. **Nonfiction**—biography; cooking; health; music; philosophy; poetry; theater; vegetarianism; childhood sexuality; juvenile. Do not want: religion; humor.

Initial Contact. Query letter; or outline and sample chapters. Include SASE.

Acceptance Policies. Unagented manuscripts: yes. Simultaneous submissions: yes. Disk submissions: no. Response time to initial inquiry: 2-4 weeks. Average time until publication: n/i. **Advance:** varies. **Royalty:** standard; varies. First run: n/i.

Marketing Channels. Distribution houses. Subsidiary rights: all.

Additional Information. Catalog: #10 SASE.

PANORAMA WEST PUBLISHING. 603 Fourth St. Davis, CA 95616.

(916) 756-7177. Submissions Editor: Karen Van Eppen. Founded: 1983. Number of titles published: cumulative—100, 1991—10. Hardback 60%, softback 40%.

Subjects of Interest. **Fiction**—fictionalized biographies of persons reflecting the history of the west. **Nonfiction**—California and Western American history; subjects relating to agriculture and rural living in the West; California ethnology. Recent publications: *Spanish in the Field; Bacon and Beans from a Gold Pan; Mineral King Country: Visalia to Mt. Whitney.*

Initial Contact. Book proposal with 3 sample chapters; book outline. Include description of potential market size; dates for completion of manuscript and book (if known).

Acceptance Policies. Unagented manuscripts: yes. Simultaneous submissions: yes; inform us. Disk submissions: yes; also send hard copy. Response time to initial inquiry: 3-4 weeks. Average time until publication: 4 months. **Advance**: none. **Royalty**: 10% of retail price. First run: 3000-5000. Subsidy basis: yes; we will publish for distribution by the author or distribute some of their books.

Marketing Channels. Direct mail; independent reps; in-house staff. Subsidiary rights: none.

Additional Information. We specialize in high-quality local histories written for general audiences. Catalog: 6x9 SASE.

PAPERWEIGHT PRESS. 761 Chestnut Street. Santa Cruz, CA 95060.

(408) 427-1177. Submissions Editor: Lizann Keyes. Founded: 1969. Number of titles published: cumulative—15, 1988—2. Hardback 90%, softback 10%.

Subjects of Interest. **Nonfiction**—paperweights. Recent publications: *Art of the Paperweight*. Do not want: anything else.

Initial Contact. Query letter.

Acceptance Policies. Unagented manuscripts: no. Disk submissions: Macintosh. Response time to initial inquiry: n/i. Average time until publication: n/i. **Advance**: n/i. **Royalty**: n/i. First run: n/i.

Marketing Channels. n/i. Subsidiary rights: n/i.

PAPIER-MACHÉ PRESS. 795 Via Manzana. Watsonville, CA 95076.

(408) 726-2933. Submissions Editor: Sandra Martz. Founded: 1984. Number of titles published: cumulative—11, 1991—3. Softback 100%.

Subjects of Interest. **Fiction**—women's issues; short story collections; anthologies. Recent publications: *When I Am an Old Woman I Shall Wear Purple* (anthology of poetry, short stories, and photographs about women and aging); *If I Had a Hammer: Women's Work in Poetry, Fiction and Photography.*

Initial Contact. Query.

Acceptance Policies. Unagented manuscripts: yes, preferred. Simultaneous submissions: yes; inform us. Disk submissions: Wordstar; ASCII; Symphony. First novels: yes. Response time to initial inquiry: 2-3 months. Average time until publication: 1 year. **Advance**: $300-$500 (single-author books). **Royalty**: 10-15% (single-author books). First run: 3000.

Marketing Channels. Distribution houses; direct mail; independent reps. Subsidiary rights: all.

Additional Information. We are a small (very) woman-owned publishing business specializing in books by, for, and about midlife and older women. Tips: It is absolutely essential to query before submitting material. We publish a very limited number of books and have a limited number of resources to review material. Writer's guidelines: SASE. Catalog: SASE.

PARA PUBLISHING. PO Box 4232-826. Santa Barbara, CA 93140-4232.
(805) 968-7277. Fax (805) 968-1379. Submissions Editor: Daniel Poynter. Founded: 1969. Number of titles published: cumulative—67, 1991—7. Hardback 10%, softback 90%.

Subjects of Interest. Nonfiction—parachutes/skydiving; book publishing and promotion. Recent publications: *new* editions of the following—*The Parachute Manual; Parachuting, the Skydiver's Handbook; The Self-Publishing Manual.* Do not want: anything other than parachutes/skydiving.

Initial Contact. Query letter. Include how many parachute jumps you have made.

Acceptance Policies. Unagented manuscripts: yes. Simultaneous submissions: yes. Disk submissions: IBM and Microsoft Word preferred; 3.5 or 5.25 disk. Response time to initial inquiry: 48 hours. Average time until publication: 90 days. **Advance:** $100. **Royalty:** 8%. First run: 2000-5000.

Marketing Channels. Cooperative distribution; direct mail; special sales. Subsidiary rights: all.

Additional Information. Catalog: upon request.

PARKER & SON PUBLICATIONS, INC. PO Box 9040. Carlsbad, CA
92008. (619) 931-5979. Submissions Editor: Margret O'Neil. Founded: 1898. Number of titles published: cumulative—50, 1991—5. Hardback 80%, softback 20%.

Subjects of Interest. Nonfiction—law books, especially on litigation topics, for the practicing attorney. Recent publications: *California Mechanics Lien Handbook; California Complex Litigation.*

Initial Contact. Query letter. Include author's resumé; author's publications; intended market; proposed length; jurisdiction of subject addressed.

Acceptance Policies. Unagented manuscripts: yes. Simultaneous submissions: no. Disk submissions: yes. Response time to initial inquiry: 3 weeks. Average time until publication: 4 months. **Advance:** n/i. **Royalty:** n/i. First run: n/i.

Marketing Channels. In-house staff; direct mail. Subsidiary rights: all.

Additional Information. Our editorial department is staffed with legal editors with law degrees. Tips: We are particularly interested in practical law handbooks which can be updated annually, books for legal assistants, litigators, office practitioners. Catalog: upon request.

PERIVALE PRESS. 13830 Erwin St. Van Nuys, CA 91401-2914.
(818) 785-4671. Submissions Editor: Lawrence P. Spingarn. Founded: 1968 (London, England). Number of titles published: cumulative—26, 1991—1. Hardback 10%, softback 90%.

Subjects of Interest. Fiction—novels; short story collections. Nonfiction—anthologies of poetry; translations of poetry; literary criticism. Recent publications: *Not-So-Simple Neil Simon; Moral Tales: Stories and Parables; Going Home.* Do not want: how-to manuals; romances; westerns.

Initial Contact. Query letter. Include publishing credits; willingness to promote book through readings.

Acceptance Policies. Unagented manuscripts: yes. Simultaneous submissions: yes; author must notify us of acceptance. Disk submissions: no. Response time to initial inquiry: 2 weeks.

Average time until publication: 9 months. **Advance**: $150 maximum. **Royalty**: 10% based on cover price. First run: 500+. Subsidy basis: money returnable from sales within two years.

Marketing Channels. Distribution houses; direct mail. Subsidiary rights: all.

Additional Information. No fiction at present. No poetry manuscripts outside of entries for occasional poetry chapbook contest (*Going Home* last winner, announced in *Poets & Writers*). We have acted as literary agents and sold short fiction for a few select clients who, though beginners, showed great promise. Contact: Barbara Rhys-Davies, this address. Tips: Be willing to help promote via readings, bookshop contacts, radio interviews, etc. Catalog: #10 SASE. Writer's guidelines: #10 SASE.

PERSEVERANCE PRESS. PO Box 384. Menlo Park, CA 94025.

Submissions Editor: Meredith Phillips. Founded: 1979. Number of titles published: cumulative—10, 1991—1. Trade softback 100%.

Subjects of Interest. **Fiction**—old-fashioned mystery without gratuitous violence, exploitive sex, or excessive gore. Recent publications: *The Last Page; Sea of Troubles*. Do not want: nonfiction; other genres.

Initial Contact. Book proposal with 3 sample chapters; cover letter with writing/publishing background.

Acceptance Policies. Unagented manuscripts: 85%. Simultaneous submissions: yes; inform us. Disk submissions: no. Response time to initial inquiry: 1 month. Average time until publication: 12 months. **Advance**: none. **Royalty**: 10% of net receipts. First run: 3000.

Marketing Channels. Distribution houses; cooperative distribution; direct mail; independent reps. Subsidiary rights: all.

Additional Information. Will not consider any material not meeting our guidelines. Tips: Characterization, background, plot, suspense, wit, humanity—all are essential. Catalog: upon request.

PILEATED PRESS. PO Box 4973. Santa Rosa, CA 95402. (707) 869-2704.

Submissions Editor: Tony Kendrew. Founded: 1989. Number of titles published: cumulative—1, 1991—2. Softback 100%.

Subjects of Interest. **Nonfiction**—consumer guides. Recent publications: *500 Best Wines of Sonoma County*. Do not want: fiction.

Initial Contact. Query letter only.

Additional Information. May in future consider publishing compilations/surveys of consumer products by others.

Plain Jane Books *see* **STRAWBERRY HILL PRESS.**

PLAYERS PRESS, INC. Box 1132. Studio City, CA 91604. (818) 789-4980. Submissions Editor: Robert W. Gordon. Founded: 1965. Number of titles published: cumulative—275. Hardback 1%, softback 99%.

Subjects of Interest. Nonfiction—plays; scenes; monologues; musicals, music, music how-to; theater; film; television. Recent publications: *Creative Drama in the Classroom; The Art of Stage Make-Up*. Adult plays. Recent Publications: *Conditioned Reflex; A Dusty Echo; Diary of a Mad Man*. Children's plays. Recent publications: *Peter N' The Wolf* (musical); *Frog King's Daughter* (musical); *Aladdin* (play).

Initial Contact. Query letter. Include SASE.

Acceptance Policies. Unsolicited manuscripts: plays and musicals only. Unagented manuscripts: yes. Simultaneous submissions: no. Disk submissions: no. Response time to initial inquiry: 90-180 days. Average time until publication: 6-24 months. **Advance:** optional. **Royalty:** varies. First run: 5000-20,000.

Marketing Channels. Distribution houses; direct mail; independent reps; in-house staff; special sales. Subsidiary rights: all.

Additional Information. For plays and musicals—submit only produced work. Catalog: send $1.00.

POPULAR MEDICINE PRESS. PO Box 1212. San Carlos, CA 94070. (415) 594-1855. Submissions Editor: Jack Yetiv, MD. Founded: 1986. Number of titles published: cumulative—1, 1991—1. Hardback 50%, softback 50%.

Subjects of Interest. Nonfiction—intelligent books on nutrition/health for lay public. Recent publications: *Popular Nutritional Practices* (deals with megavitamins, cholesterol, high blood pressure, diabetes, etc.). Do not want: alternative nutrition that is not scientifically-based.

Initial Contact. Query letter with synopsis/outline. Include author credentials and anticipated buyers.

Acceptance Policies. Unagented manuscripts: yes. Simultaneous submissions: yes. Disk submissions: Macintosh; prefer typed copy. Response time to initial inquiry: 4 weeks. Average time until publication: 12-18 months. **Advance:** depends on specific project. **Royalty:** depends on specific project. First run: 2500.

Marketing Channels. Distribution houses; direct mail; special sales. Subsidiary rights: all, through agent.

Additional Information. We are very small and part time right now; we are considering expanding. Catalog: none. Writer's guidelines: none.

PRESIDIO PRESS. 31 Pamaron Way. Novato, CA 94949. (415) 883-1373. Submissions Editor: Robert Tate. Number of titles published: cumulative—200, 1991—25. Hardback and softback.

Subjects of Interest. Fiction—military setting. Recent publications: *DEFCON One; Feast of Bones.* **Nonfiction**—military. Recent publications: *Encyclopedia of the Second World War; Into Cambodia.* Do not want: academic works.

Initial Contact. Query letter; or outline and 3 sample chapters.

Acceptance Policies. Unagented manuscripts: yes. Simultaneous submissions: n/i. Disk submissions: query. Response time to initial inquiry: 3 months. Average time until publication: 10 months. **Advance:** nominal. **Royalty:** 15% of net. First run: 5000+.

Marketing Channels. Distribution houses; special sales. Subsidiary rights: all.

Additional Information. Catalog: upon request.

PRICE STERN SLOAN, INC. (Imprints: The Body Press; Enrich; HP Books; Questron; Treasure Books; Troubador Press; Wonder Books). 360 N. La Cienega Blvd. Los Angeles, CA 90048. (213) 657-6100. Submissions Editors: Michael Gorter (photography); Gina Gross (adult, health and fitness, cooking); Michael Lutfy (automotive); Queta Moore (calendars); Wendy Vinitski (juvenile, humor); Jill Weisman (juvenile). Founded: 1964. Number of titles published: cumulative—1665, 1991—20. Hardback 2%, softback 98%.

Subjects of Interest. Fiction—juvenile original storybooks. Recent publications: *Camp Catastrophe* (humorous). **Nonfiction**—adult trade; automotive; cookery; game books; humor. Recent publications: *The Potent Male* (layperson's medical information). Do not want: religious books; novels; pornography.

Initial Contact. Query letter with synopsis/outline. Do not send original art. Include SASE.

Acceptance Policies. Unagented manuscripts: yes. Simultaneous submissions: yes. Disk submissions: no. Response time to initial inquiry: 4-8 weeks. Average time until publication: 12 months approximately. **Advance:** varies. **Royalty:** depends on project. First run: varies.

Marketing Channels. Distribution houses; direct mail; independent reps; in-house staff; special sales. Subsidiary rights: all.

Additional Information. We look for original ideas, not themes that have been done over and over again. We want children's books that teach as well as entertain. Catalog: SASE, $2.50 postage. Writer's guidelines: SASE.

PRIMA PUBLISHING AND COMMUNICATIONS. PO Box 1260. Rocklin, CA 95677. (916) 624-5718. Submissions Editor: Ben Dominitz. Founded: 1984. Number of titles published: cumulative—120, 1991—45.

Subjects of Interest. Nonfiction—business; cooking; general nonfiction; health; self help. Recent publications: *EarthRight: Every Citizen's Guide; The Insider's Guide to Book Editors and Publishers; More Lean and Luscious Cookbook; Raising Self Reliant Children in a Self Indulgent World.* Do not want: poetry; stories of people's vacations.

Initial Contact. Query letter. Include author's credentials; market for the book; name, publisher, sales history of previously published works; SASE.

Acceptance Policies. Unagented manuscripts: yes. Simultaneous submissions: yes. Disk submissions: no. Response time to initial inquiry: 3-4 weeks. Average time until publication: varies; seasonal. **Advance:** varies. **Royalty:** varies. First run: varies.

Marketing Channels. Distribution houses (St. Martin's Press). Subsidiary rights: all.

Additional Information. Tips: Be concise in your query. We want books with originality, written by highly qualified individuals. Catalog: 8 1/2 x 11 SASE, $1.65 postage.

Prism Editions *see* **NATUREGRAPH PUBLISHERS, INC.**

PROFESSIONAL PUBLICATIONS, INC. 1250 Fifth Ave. Belmont, CA 94002. (415) 593-9119. Submissions Editor: Wendy Nelson. Founded: 1975. Number of titles published: cumulative—60, 1990—6. Hardback 8%, softback 92%.

Subjects of Interest. Nonfiction—engineering and CPA exam review materials; other texts on engineering, business; architecture; professional exams; licensing review materials. Do not want: romance novels; cookbooks.

Initial Contact. Book proposal with sample chapters. Include curriculum vitae; proposed market.

Acceptance Policies. Unagented manuscripts: yes. Simultaneous submissions: yes. Disk submissions: IBM 5 1/4 format; must be accompanied by printout. Response time to initial inquiry: 2-4 weeks. Average time until publication: varies. **Advance:** varies. **Royalty:** varies. First run: depends on title, market.

Marketing Channels. Distribution houses; direct mail; independent reps; special sales. Subsidiary rights: first serialization; sound reproduction and recording; direct mail or direct sales; book club; translation and foreign rights; computer and magnetic and electronic media; English language publication outside United States and Canada.

Additional Information. Tips: Provide plenty of information on anticipated sales. Catalog: contact Wendy Nelson.

PROSTAR PUBLICATIONS, INC. (Subsidiary of Western Marine Enterprises, Inc.). P.O. Box 341688. Los Angeles, CA 90034. (213) 287-2833. Submissions Editor: Sue Artof. Founded: 1965. Number of titles published: cumulative—20, 1991—6. Hardback 15%, softback 85%.

Subjects of Interest. Nonfiction—marine how-to books. Recent publications: *Boat Cosmetics Made Simple.* Do not want: storytelling.

Initial Contact. Book proposal with sample chapters; or entire manuscript.

Acceptance Policies. Unagented manuscripts: yes. Disk submissions: MS-DOS; Wordstar. Response time to initial inquiry: 30 days. Average time until publication: 5-6 months. **Advance:** hardly ever. **Royalty:** 15% net sales price. First run: 2000-10,000.

Marketing Channels. Distribution houses; direct mail; independent reps, in-house staff. Subsidiary rights: all.

Additional Information. Tips: Should be marine-oriented subjects or fun books. Catalog: upon request.

PUBLITEC EDITIONS. 271 Lower Cliff Dr., Ste. A. Laguna Beach, CA 92652. (714) 497-6100. Submissions Editor: Maggie Rowe. Founded: 1984. Number of titles published: cumulative—6, 1991—2. Hardback 10%, softback 90%.

Subjects of Interest. Nonfiction—hang gliding; health and fitness; how-to. Recent publications: *Survival Kit for Those Who Sit: Simple Office Exercises to Boost Your Energy and Productivity.* Do not want: fiction; poetry.

Initial Contact. Query letter.

Acceptance Policies. Unagented manuscripts: yes. Simultaneous submissions: yes. Disk submissions: no. Response time to initial inquiry: 1 month. Average time until publication: varies. **Advance:** varies. **Royalty:** varies. First run: varies.

Marketing Channels. Distribution houses; cooperative distribution; direct mail; special sales. Subsidiary rights: all.

Additional Information. "We" are a one-person operation producing one or two titles per year on average. Catalog: upon request.

PUMA PUBLISHING. 1670 Coral Dr. Santa Maria, CA 93454. (805) 925-3216. Submissions Editor: John Baptiste. Founded: 1986. Number of titles published: cumulative—3, 1991—1. Softback 100%.

Subjects of Interest. Nonfiction—small business areas; housekeeping; defensive driving and traffic ticket avoidance. Recent publications: *Speedy Housekeeping; Free Help from Uncle Sam to Start Your Own Business; Money Sources for Small Business.* Do not want: fiction.

Initial Contact. Query letter.

Acceptance Policies. Unagented manuscripts: yes. Simultaneous submissions: yes. Disk submissions: not initially; can accept any format once manuscript is accepted. Response time to initial inquiry: 2 weeks. Average time until publication: 9 months. **Advance:** n/i. **Royalty:** 10% of retail. First run: 2000.

Marketing Channels. Distribution houses; cooperative distribution; direct mail; special sales. Subsidiary rights: direct mail or sales; book club; commercial; English language publication outside United States and Canada.

Additional Information. Need jokes, anecdotes, slogans, success stories of small businesses to be included in book in progress. Tips: No handwritten, no dot matrix.

QED PRESS. (Subsidiary of Comp-Type, Inc.). 155 Cypress St. Fort Bragg, CA 95437. (707) 964-9520. Fax (707) 964-9531. Submissions Editors: Cynthia Frank (poetry); John Fremont (prose). Founded: 1985. Number of titles published: cumulative—32, 1991—12. Hardback 25%, softback 75%.

Subjects of Interest. Fiction—historical; romance; science fiction. Recent publications: *Path of Many Windings; Red Zambesi; Coz.* Nonfiction—social sciences; religion. Recent publications: *To Leave This Port; Chronic Illness; Tashlas' Place.* Poetry. Recent publications: *Mendocino Portfolio.* Do not want: pornography; hate literature.

Initial Contact. Query letter. Include publishing history.

Acceptance Policies. Unagented manuscripts: yes. Simultaneous submissions: yes; inform us. Disk submissions: no. Response time to initial inquiry: 3 months. Average time until publication: 9 months. **Advance:** none. **Royalty:** 10%. First run: 3000. Subsidy basis: yes; 90% of our books are on a subsidy basis with author retaining all rights. Send for brochure.

Marketing Channels. Distribution houses; direct mail; in-house staff. Subsidiary rights: all.

Additional Information. Catalog: upon request.

Questron *see* **PRICE STERN SLOAN, INC.**

QUIKREF PUBLISHING. (Imprint: Dodo Bird Books, due out 1991). 4470-107 Sunset Blvd., Ste. 133. Hollywood, CA 90027. (213) 913-1430. Submissions Editor: Claudia O'Keefe. Founded: 1989. Number of titles published: cumulative—1, 1991—2. Softback 100%.

Subjects of Interest. Fiction—children's, grades 1-8 (Dodo Bird Books to focus on animal rights/endangered wildlife environment). Nonfiction—quick, handy references on all subjects. Recent publications: *Proper Noun Speller.* Do not want: adult fiction.

Initial Contact. Query letter with entire manuscript. Include list of published works and SASE.

Acceptance Policies. Unagented manuscripts: yes. Simultaneous submissions: yes, inform us. Disk submissions: Apple; Macintosh SE. First novels: yes, juvenile only. Response time to initial inquiry: immediately, if not for us; 6-8 weeks otherwise. Average time until publication: 12-18 months. **Advance**: no, our up-front money is spent on individual marketing for each book. **Royalty**: good. First run: 10,000-20,000.

Marketing Channels. Distribution houses; direct mail. Subsidiary rights: direct mail or direct sales; book club; translation and foreign; commercial.

Additional Information. Catalog: none. Writer's guidelines: SASE.

RAKHAMIM. PO Box 7. Berkeley, CA 94701. Submissions Editor: Dov Ben-Khayyim. Founded: 1983. Number of titles published: cumulative—1, 1991—unknown. Softback 100%.

Subjects of Interest. Nonfiction—Judeo-feminist; gay/lesbian; religion; women's issues. Recent publications: *The Telling: A Loving Hagadah for Passover*.

Initial Contact. Query letter only.

Acceptance Policies. Unagented manuscripts: yes. Simultaneous submissions: yes. Disk submissions: no. Response time to initial inquiry: n/i. Average time until publication: n/i. **Advance**: n/i. **Royalty**: n/i. First run: n/i.

Marketing Channels. Distribution houses; direct mail. Subsidiary rights: n/i.

Additional Information. Catalog: upon request.

R & E PUBLISHERS. PO Box 2008. Saratoga, CA 95070. (408) 866-6303. Submissions Editor: Bob Reed. Founded: 1967. Number of titles published: cumulative—1000+, 1989—26. Hardback 10%, softback 90%.

Subjects of Interest. Nonfiction—self-help; psychology; education; abuse; AIDS; health reference; how-to. Recent publications: *The Morning After: How to Manage Grief Wisely; Smooth Sailing in The Next Generation; Creating Well Being*. Do not want: poetry; fiction; computer; animal; gardening.

Initial Contact. Query letter; book proposal with 1 sample chapter. Include market; author's plans (seminars, classes, tours); when project complete.

Acceptance Policies. Unagented manuscripts: yes. Simultaneous submissions: yes. Disk submissions: ok, but want hard copy also. Response time to initial inquiry: 60 days. Average time until publication: 6 months. **Advance**: none. **Royalty**: 10%, 12 1/2%, 15%. First run: 2000-10,000. Subsidy basis: 10% of our books are with authors who market and sell their books along with our sales.

Marketing Channels. Distribution houses; direct mail; independent reps; special sales. Subsidiary rights: all.

Additional Information. We have published nearly 1000 titles and have been successful for 20 plus years. Tips: We want to work with authors who will work on efforts to make a book popular—a team effort. Catalog: upon request.

REBECCA HOUSE. 1550 California St. San Francisco, CA 94109. (415) 752-1453. Submissions Editor: David Waldman. Founded: 1985. Number of titles published: cumulative—1, 1991—2. Softback 100%.

Subjects of Interest. Fiction—children's books. Recent publications: *Crystal Moonlight*.

Initial Contact. Entire manuscript.

Acceptance Policies. Unagented manuscripts: yes. Simultaneous submissions: no. Disk submissions: no. First novels: yes. Response time to initial inquiry: 30 days. Average time until publication: 1 year. **Advance**: open. **Royalty**: to be negotiated. First run: open.

Marketing Channels. Direct mail; in-house staff; special sales. Subsidiary rights: all.

Additional Information. We are a new, small press looking for our growth to occur with innovative children's authors and illustrators. Tips: It is best to speak with us directly. Catalog: We are too new to have one yet.

REBIS PRESS. PO Box 2233. Berkeley, CA 94702. (415) 527-3845. Submissions Editor: Betsy Davids. Not accepting manuscripts.

RECREATION SALES PUBLISHING. 150 E. Olive Ave., Ste. 110. Burbank, CA 91502. (818) 843-3616. Submissions Editor: Diane Dirksen. Founded: 1974. Number of titles published: cumulative—15, 1991—3. Softback 100%.

Subjects of Interest. Nonfiction—guidebooks and maps on outdoor recreation. Recent publications: *Recreation Lakes of California* (9th edition); *Recreation on the Colorado River; Winter Recreation in California* (4th edition); *L.A. County Golf Courses.*

Additional Information. At this time we do not publish books by other authors.

RED ALDER BOOKS. Box 2992. Santa Cruz, CA 95063. (408) 426-7082. Submissions Editor: David Steinberg. Founded: 1977. Number of titles published: cumulative—6, 1991—1. Hardback 20%, softback 80%.

Subjects of Interest. **Fiction**—quality erotica. Recent publications: *Erotic by Nature* (a fine-quality hardcover collection of imaginative, provocative, non-pornographic photography, writing, and drawing). **Nonfiction**—fathering, changing men's roles; erotica. Recent publications: *Fatherjournal* (one man's experience during first 5 years of involved parenting). Poetry. Recent publications: *Beneath This Calm Exterior.* Do not want: pornography.

Initial Contact. Query letter; sample material.

Acceptance Policies. Unagented manuscripts: yes. Simultaneous submissions: yes. Disk submissions: Macintosh. Response time to initial inquiry: 4-8 weeks. Average time until publication: 1 year. **Advance**: none. **Royalty**: varies. First run: 1000-5000.

Marketing Channels. Distribution houses; direct mail. Subsidiary rights: all.

REDCLIFF PRESS. (Subsidiary of Los Angeles Urban Development). 4336 Kingswell Ave. Los Angeles, CA 90027-4502. (213) 661-0883. Fax (213) 660-4590. Submissions Editor: William R. Dowling. Founded: 1979. Number of titles published: cumulative—21, 1991—8. Hardback 5%, softback 95%.

Subjects of Interest. **Fiction**—humor; contemporary; erotica; folklore; literary; science fiction; short stories. **Nonfiction**—how-to books, any topic; cookbooks; poetry. Recent publications: *Easy Thai Recipes; SBA Loan Consultants Manual and Software.*

Initial Contact. Query letter with synopsis/outline with book proposal and sample chapters or entire manuscript. Advise us if software also available.

Acceptance Policies. Unagented manuscripts: yes. Simultaneous submissions: yes, advise us. Disk submissions: Macintosh, text files of Microsoft Word 3.01. First novels: yes. Response time to initial inquiry: 30-60 days. Average time until publication: 60-90 days. **Advance**: negotiable. **Royalty**: negotiable. First run: n/i. Subsidy basis: we haven't yet, but would consider it.

Marketing Channels. Cooperative distribution; direct mail; special sales. Subsidiary rights: all.

Additional Information. We will accept shorter works, even pamphlets. Tips: We like line drawings for our how-to books with explicit instructions—must be useful to reader. Catalog: write or Fax. Writer's guidelines: send query with outline.

REFERENCE SERVICE PRESS. 1100 Industrial Road, Ste. 9. San Carlos, CA 94070. (415) 594-0743. Fax (415) 594-0411. Submissions Editor: Stuart Hauser. Founded: 1976. Number of titles published: cumulative—22, 1991—3. Hardback 100%.

Subjects of Interest. Nonfiction—directories of financial aid for special groups or situations; careers; education. Recent publications: *Directory of Financial Aids for Women, 1989-1990; . . . for Minorities, 1989-1990.* Do not want: anything outside our area.

Initial Contact. Book proposal.

Acceptance Policies. Unagented manuscripts: yes. Simultaneous submissions: no. Disk submissions: no. Response time to initial inquiry: 30 days. Average time until publication: depends on project. **Advance:** n/i. **Royalty:** 10% and up, depending on sales. First run: 2000+.

Marketing Channels. Distribution houses; cooperative distribution; direct mail; special sales. Subsidiary rights: none.

Additional Information. We are the only publisher specializing solely in the development of directories of financial aid. Tips: Be sure your project matches our stated interests. Catalog: upon request.

REGAL BOOKS. (Division of Gospel Light Publications). 2300 Knoll Dr. Ventura, CA 93003. Submissions Editor: Linda Holland. Number of titles published: 1991—28. Hardback 15%, softback 85%.

Subjects of Interest. Nonfiction—Bible studies; marriage and family; inspirational; teaching enrichment; young adult; evangelism; personal growth; contemporary issues. Recent publications: *Always Daddy's Girl; Taking Hold of Tomorrow.*

Initial Contact. Query letter; or detailed outline and 2-3 sample chapters. No complete manuscripts.

Acceptance Policies. Unagented manuscripts: yes. Simultaneous submissions: yes. Disk submissions: no. Response time to initial inquiry: 3 months. Average time until publication: 11 months. **Advance:** negotiable. **Royalty:** negotiable. First run: 5000-7500.

Marketing Channels. Independent reps; telemarketing. Subsidiary rights: all.

Additional Information. Catalog: upon request.

RE/SEARCH PUBLISHING. 20 Romolo, #B. San Francisco, CA 94133. (415) 362-1465. Submissions Editors: V. Vale or A. Juno. Founded: 1980. Number of titles published: cumulative—10, 1989—5. Hardback 10%, softback 90%.

Subjects of Interest. Fiction—reprints of various out-of-print books varying from hard-boiled detective to literature. Recent publications: *Freaks; High Priest of California* ('50s detective); *Torture Garden* (turn of century decadence). **Nonfiction**—art; film; music; all books based on interviews with authors, directors, musicians, etc.; off-beat, unusual subjects with emphasis on philosophy behind art, music, and action. Recent publications: *Modern Primitives; Incredibly Strange Films* (forgotten gems of '50s, '60s); *Interviews of J.G. Ballard; Industrial Culture Handbook.* Do not want: poetry or fiction.

Initial Contact. book proposal.

Acceptance Policies. Unagented manuscripts: yes. Simultaneous submissions: yes. Disk submissions: PC compatible. Response time to initial inquiry: 1 month. Average time until publication: 1 year. **Advance:** none. **Royalty:** 8%. First run: 2000-3000.

Marketing Channels. Distribution houses; direct mail. Subsidiary rights: all.

Additional Information. Catalog: upon request.

RESOURCE PUBLICATIONS, INC. 160 E. Virginia St., Ste. 290. San Jose, CA 95112. (408) 286-8505. Submissions Editor: Kenneth Guentert. Founded: 1973. Number of titles published: cumulative—121, 1991—16. Hardback 10%, softback 90%.

Subjects of Interest. Nonfiction—resources for secular and liturgical celebrations; stories, parables, and fables; myth and symbol. Recent publications: *The Peer Counseling Training Course; The Topsy-Turvey Kingdom: Stories for the Faith Journey; Grief Ministry: Helping Others Mourn.* Do not want: inspirational fiction or poetry collections.

Initial Contact. Query letter; book proposal with sample chapters. Indicate willingness of author to promote book; phone.

Acceptance Policies. Unagented manuscripts: yes. Simultaneous submissions: yes; inform us. Disk submissions: IBM PC; CP/M; MS-DOS; Macintosh Wordstar; ASCII. Response time to initial inquiry: 6 weeks for query. Average time until publication: 18 months. **Advance:** books often offered at wholesale. **Royalty:** 8% of net. First run: 2000-4000. Subsidy basis: yes; some authors buy up to 500 copies at wholesale. However, the decision to publish the work is not based on the author providing a subsidy, and we do not print any book we do not believe will sell.

Marketing Channels. Distribution houses; cooperative distribution; direct mail; independent reps; special sales; foreign distributors. Subsidiary rights: all.

Additional Information. We are a communications company with editorial efforts in imaginative resources for celebrations, resources for professional pastoral ministry, liturgical art and environment, counseling and peer counseling. Tips: Call first. Write to fit our needs. Give us a book that represents your work so you have a stake in making it work. Catalog: SASE.

RIDGE TIMES PRESS. Box 90. Mendocino, CA 95460. (707) 964-8465. Submissions Editors: Jim and Judy Tarbell. Not accepting book manuscripts at this time. Major focus is on quarterly magazine.

RONIN PUBLISHING, INC. PO Box 1035. Berkeley, CA 94701. (415) 540-6278. Submissions Editor: Sebastian Orfal. Founded: 1983. Number of titles published: 1989—6-8. Softback 100%.

Subjects of Interest. Nonfiction—business: how-to, management psychology (major focus); visionary; new age; underground comics; psychedelic. Recent publications: *Drug Testing at Work.*

Initial Contact. Query letter.

Acceptance Policies. Unagented manuscripts: yes. Simultaneous submissions: n/i. Disk submissions: query. Response time to initial inquiry: 2-3 months. Average time until publication: 1 year. **Advance:** some. **Royalty:** 10% net. First run: 2000-10,000. Subsidy basis: some; inquire.

Marketing Channels. Distribution houses; direct mail. Subsidiary rights: all.

ROSS BOOKS. Box 4340. Berkeley, CA 94704. (415) 841-2474. Submissions Editor: Elizabeth Yerkes. Founded: 1977. Number of titles published: cumulative—32, 1989—3. Hardback 33%, softback 67%.

Subjects of Interest. Nonfiction—popular science; holography; desktop publishing. Recent publications: *Holography Handbook; Holography Marketplace, Second Edition* (sourcebook of the holography industry); *How to Plan and Book Meetings and Seminars; Build Your Own Database in Basic.* Do not want: dog or cat grooming; cosmetology; hairstyling.

Initial Contact. Query letter. Include SASE.

Acceptance Policies. Unagented manuscripts: yes. Simultaneous submissions: yes. Disk submissions: IBM; Macintosh. Response time to initial inquiry: 2-3 weeks. Average time until publication: 1-3 years. **Advance:** none. **Royalty:** 8-10%. First run: 3500-5000.

Marketing Channels. Distribution houses; direct mail. Subsidiary rights: first serialization; second serialization; newspaper syndication; reprint rights; direct mail or direct sale; book club; translation and foreign; computer and magnetic and electronic; commercial; English language publication outside United States and Canada.

Additional Information. Catalog: order (800) 367-0930.

ROXBURY PUBLISHING CO. Box 491044. Los Angeles, CA 90049. (213) 653-1068. Submissions Editor: Claude Teweles. Founded: 1979. Number of titles published: cumulative—20, 1991—6. Hardback 15%, softback 85%.

Subjects of Interest. Nonfiction—college texts in business, management, economics, English, speech, sociology, developmental studies. Recent publications: *Business Communication: Concepts, Applications and Strategies; The Answer Book; Speech Communication Workbook.*

Initial Contact. Query letter; book proposal with sample chapters.

Acceptance Policies. Unagented manuscripts: yes. Simultaneous submissions: yes. Disk submissions: no. Response time to initial inquiry: 2 months. Average time until publication: 6-12 months. **Advance:** negotiable. **Royalty:** varies. First run: 2000-5000.

Marketing Channels. Direct mail; independent reps; in-house staff. Subsidiary rights: all.

SAN DIEGO PUBLISHING COMPANY. Box 9222. San Diego, CA 92109-0060. (619) 495-8749. Submissions Editor: Thomas L. Thomson. Founded: 1981. Number of titles published: cumulative—4, 1989—1. Softback 100%.

Subjects of Interest. All. Do not want: incomplete manuscripts or manuscripts that aren't clean.

Initial Contact. Entire manuscript; $50,000 cashier's check.

Acceptance Policies. Unagented manuscripts: I do not deal with agents. Disk submissions: yes. Response time to initial inquiry: immediate. Average time until publication: 3 months maximum. Advance: n/a. Royalty: author keeps all revenues. First run: 10,000. Subsidy basis; $50,000 up-front fee. Publisher guarantees minimum $75,000 return from sales or $50,000 fee is returned prior to publication.

Marketing Channels. Distribution houses; direct mail; independent reps; in-house staff; special sales. Subsidiary rights: none; refer author to agent after publishing success as noted.

Additional Information. I subcontract all work and concentrate on promotion, distribution, and marketing. Author retains all rights and all profits. Tips: I guarantee sales or your money back. We'll rewrite or recompose manuscript for additional $25,000 and increase guaranteed return to $100,000.

SAN DIEGO STATE UNIVERSITY PRESS. San Diego State University.

San Diego, CA 92182. (619) 594-6220. Submissions Editor: Harry Polkinhorn. Founded: 1964. Number of titles published: cumulative—98, 1991—4. Hardback 12%, softback 88%.

Subjects of Interest. **Fiction**—Journals: *Fiction International* (fiction/literature); *Review of Latin American Studies* (scholarly articles). **Nonfiction**—Latin America; women's studies; gerontology; autobiography; history. Recent publications: *Eleanor Roosevelt: An American Journey; Chant the Names of God.*

Initial Contact. Query letter.

Acceptance Policies. Unagented manuscripts: yes. Simultaneous submissions: yes. Disk submissions: no. First novels: yes. Response time to initial inquiry: 1 month. Average time until publication: 6-18 months. **Advance**: none. **Royalty**: 5% of net; negotiable. First run: 1000. Subsidy basis: for monographs sponsored by departments or associations.

Marketing Channels. Distribution houses. Subsidiary rights: all.

Additional Information. Academic, generally. Tips: We are funded through the California State University System; therefore familiarity with state processes is helpful! Catalog: upon request.

SAND RIVER PRESS. 1319 14th St. Los Osos, CA 93402. (805) 543-3591.

Submissions Editor: Mary C. Donnelly. Founded: 1987. Number of titles published: cumulative—4, 1990—2. Softback 100%.

Subjects of Interest. **Fiction**—novels. **Nonfiction**—history; cookbooks; literature. Recent publications: *Rivers of the Heart* (essays); *Finding My Way* (essays).

Initial Contact. Query letter; book proposal with sample chapters. Include SASE.

Acceptance Policies. Unagented manuscripts: yes. Simultaneous submissions: yes. Disk submissions: yes. Response time to initial inquiry: 6 weeks. Average time until publication: 1 year. **Advance**: $1000. **Royalty**: standard. First run: 3000.

Marketing Channels. Distribution houses; independent reps. Subsidiary rights: first serialization; reprint rights; dramatization, motion picture, and broadcast; video; sound and recording; book club; translation and foreign; English language publication outside the United States and Canada.

Additional Information. We are small but qualified. Tips: Query first. Catalog: upon request.

SANTA CRUZ COUNTY HISTORICAL TRUST. (Santa Cruz Historical

Society). PO Box 246. Santa Cruz, CA 95061-0246. (408) 425-2450. Submissions Editor: Stanley D. Stevens. Founded: 1987. Number of titles published: cumulative—2, 1991—3. Hardback 34%, softback 66%.

Subjects of Interest. **Nonfiction**—Santa Cruz local history and related material. Recent publications: *Santa Cruz County Place Names: A Geographical Dictionary; Every Structure Tells a Story: How to Research the History of a Property in Santa Cruz County: Sources of Information and Locations of Research Material, with Examples of Research Results.* Do not want: fiction.

Initial Contact. Query letter; book proposal with sample chapters; abstract of central focus and table of contents. Material must not be under consideration by another publisher.

Acceptance Policies. Unagented manuscripts: yes. Simultaneous submissions: no. Disk submissions: Macintosh II; Microsoft Word; IBM; ASCII. Response time to initial inquiry: 30 days. Average time until publication: 12 months. **Advance**: none. **Royalty**: 10-12%. First run: varies.

Marketing Channels. Distribution houses; direct mail; special sales. Subsidiary rights: none.

Additional Information. This is a noncommercial operation by volunteers.

SANTA SUSANA PRESS. CSUN Library. 18111 Nordhoff St. Northridge, CA 91330. (818) 885-2271. Submissions Editor: Norman Tanis. Founded: 1973. Number of titles published: cumulative—46, 1989—2. Hardback 80%, softback 20%.

Subjects of Interest. Nonfiction—local history; history; biography. Recent publications: *Los Angeles: Dream of Reality; The Twilight of Orthodoxy in New England; The Last Good Kiss; Owensmouth Baby*.

Initial Contact. Query letter.

Acceptance Policies. Unagented manuscripts: yes. Simultaneous submissions: no. Disk submissions: no. Response time to initial inquiry: 1 month. Average time until publication: varies. **Advance**: 1/3 payment. **Royalty**: n/i. First run: 65-300.

Marketing Channels. Direct mail. Subsidiary rights: all.

Additional Information. We are a very specialized, limited-edition, artistic literary press. Tips: Send for catalog before submitting material. Catalog: upon request.

Saturday Press *see* **HUNTER HOUSE, INC., PUBLISHERS.**

SCHEHERAZADE BOOKS. PO Box 7573. Berkeley, CA 94707. (415) 526-8024. Submissions Editor: Mildred Messinger. Not accepting manuscripts at this time.

SCIENCE OF MIND COMMUNICATIONS. (Subsidiary of United Church of Religious Science). 3251 W. Sixth St. Los Angeles, CA 90020. (213) 388-2181. Submissions Editor: Kathleen Juline. Founded: 1930. Number of titles published: cumulative—85, 1991—n/i. Softback 100%.

Subjects of Interest. Nonfiction—self-help; metaphysical; Science of Mind philosophy. Recent publications: *Good for You, You Are the One*. Do not want: n/i.

Initial Contact. Query letter with synopsis/outline and sample chapters.

Acceptance Policies. Unagented manuscripts: yes. Simultaneous submissions: no. Disk submissions: no. Response time to initial inquiry: 6-8 weeks. Average time until publication: 6-12 months. **Advance**: none. **Royalty**: based on retail sales. First run: n/i.

Marketing Channels. Distribution houses; direct mail; in-house staff. Subsidiary rights: all.

Additional Information. Catalog: n/i. Writer's guidelines: n/i.

DALE SEYMOUR PUBLICATIONS. PO Box 10888. Palo Alto, CA 94303. (415) 324-2800. Submissions Editor: Dale Seymour, president. Founded: 1979. Number of titles published: cumulative—600+, 1989—30. Softback 100%.

Subjects of Interest. Nonfiction—supplementary educational materials, K-12, in areas of math, science, language arts, art education, gifted education. Recent publications: *Mental Math in the Middle Grades; Critical Thinking Activities; Teaching Characterization; Logic Number Problems; Science Around Me*. Do not want: fiction; children's storybooks; poetry.

Initial Contact. Query letter; author's teaching affiliation.

Acceptance Policies. Unagented manuscripts: yes. Simultaneous submissions: yes. Disk submissions: Macintosh in MacWrite or Microsoft Word. Response time to initial inquiry: 6

weeks. Average time until publication: 12 months. **Advance**: none. **Royalty**: 8%. First run: 1500.

Marketing Channels. Independent reps; direct mail. Subsidiary rights: none.

Additional Information. Catalog: call (800) 222-0766.

LI KUNG SHAW. PO Box 16427. San Francisco, CA 94116. (415) 731-0829.
Submissions Editor: Li Kung Shaw. Founded: 1982. Number of titles published: cumulative—10, 1987—1. Hardback 50%, softback 50%.

Subjects of Interest. Nonfiction—biology; Chinese input system. Recent publications: *Purposive Biology; Shell-Corner Method.* Do not want: fiction.

Initial Contact. Query letter.

Acceptance Policies. Unagented manuscripts: yes. Simultaneous submissions: yes. Disk submissions: Apple III. Response time to initial inquiry: 30 days. Average time until publication: varies. **Advance**: varies. **Royalty**: varies. First run: 1000+. Subsidy basis: yes; to be negotiated.

Marketing Channels. Direct mail; independent reps; special sales. Subsidiary rights: none.

Additional Information. Catalog: upon request.

G. MICHAEL SHORT, PUBLISHER. (Subsidiary of GMS Publication).
11659 Doverwood Dr. Riverside, CA 92505-3216. Submissions Editor: G. Michael Short. Founded: 1990. Number of titles published: 1991—4-6. Softback 100%.

Subjects of Interest. Nonfiction—business opportunity reports, manuals, booklets, and books; cookbooks. Do not want: "get-rich-quick" plans.

Initial Contact. Entire manuscript. Include resumé.

Acceptance Policies. Unagented manuscripts: yes. Simultaneous submissions: no. Disk submissions: no. Response time to initial inquiry: 2 weeks to 3 months, depending on size. Average time until publication: varies widely. **Advance**: none. **Royalty**: 5-10% based on retail price. First run: 500-1000. Subsidy basis: upon author request; author should inquire about co-op service.

Marketing Channels. Direct mail; independent sales; in-house staff. Subsidiary rights: all.

Additional Information. Books published by GMS Publications are not sold through book stores. They are usually sold via mail order. Tips: Know your subject. I do not consider books on theories. Catalog: not available. Writer's guidelines: not available.

SIERRA CLUB BOOKS. 730 Polk St. San Francisco, CA 94109. (415) 776-2211. Submissions Editor: Daniel Moses. Founded: 1892. Number of titles published: cumulative—500+, 1988—20. Hardback and softback.

Subjects of Interest. Fiction—rarely, and only if it fits our themes of environmental protection and appreciation of the wilderness. **Nonfiction**—natural history; environmental issues; animals; juveniles (ecology theme); philosophy; photography; recreation; travel; sports; science. Recent publications: *Adventuring in East Africa; Adventuring in the Chesapeake Bay Area; Lessons of the Rainforest; Reweaving the World; Orcas of the Gulf.* Do not want: "coffee-table" books with little text; personal experiences with the "great outdoors"; traveling by motorized vehicles; observations of wildlife.

Initial Contact. Query first; summary and sample chapters; availability of photographs or artwork.

Acceptance Policies. Unagented manuscripts: yes. Average time until publication: 12-18 months. **Advance**: $3000-$5000. **Royalty**: 7-12.5%. First run: n/i.

Marketing Channels. Distribution houses. Subsidiary rights: all.
Additional Information. Catalog: upon request.

SIERRA OAKS PUBLISHING COMPANY. PO Box 255354. Sacramento, CA 95865-5354. (916) 663-1474. Submissions Editor: Stephanie Morris. Founded: 1986. Number of titles published: cumulative—17, 1991—3. Softback 100%.

Subjects of Interest. Fiction—American Indian. Recent publications: *When Hopi Children Were Bad: A Monster Story.* Nonfiction—American Indian. Recent publications: *California's Indians and the Gold Rush.* Do not want: anything other than American Indian topics.

Initial Contact. Query letter with synopsis/outline.

Acceptance Policies. Unagented manuscripts: yes. Simultaneous submissions: yes. Disk submissions: Macintosh compatible. Response time to initial inquiry: 2 weeks. Average time until publication: 1 year. **Advance:** none. **Royalty:** 10% after first run and production costs. First run: 5000.

Marketing Channels. Distribution houses; direct mail; independent reps; in-house staff; special sales. Subsidiary rights: none.

Additional Information. We are a small, independent press specializing in American Indian children's literature. Tips: Patience! Catalog: upon request. Writer's guidelines: none available.

SILVERCAT PUBLICATIONS. 4070 Goldfinch St., Ste. C. San Diego, CA 92103-1865. (619) 299-6774. Submissions Editor: Robert Goodman. Founded: 1988. Number of titles published: cumulative—2, 1991—1-2. Softback 100%.

Subjects of Interest. Nonfiction—consumer and quality-of-life guides. Recent publications: *A Quick Guide to Food Additives* (2nd edition). **Other**—historical calendars. Recent publications: *The 1791-1991 Bill of Rights Bicentennial Calendar.* Do not want: poetry; fiction; children's; get-rich-quick; "woo-woo" new age.

Initial Contact. Query letter only.

Acceptance Policies. Unagented manuscripts: yes. Simultaneous submissions: no. Disk submissions: IBM; ASCII; XY-Write; WordPerfect 4.2. Response time to initial inquiry: 1 week. Average time until publication: depends. **Advance:** modest, at best. **Royalty:** 5-12% based on retail price. First run: 3000-5000.

Marketing Channels. Distribution houses; direct mail; independent reps; special sales. Subsidiary rights: all (negotiable).

Additional Information. Authors need to recognize that we are young and necessarily understaffed but looking to expand. Catalog: we don't have one; ask for press release or other literature. Writer's guidelines: call me.

SLAWSON COMMUNICATIONS, INC. (Imprints: Microtrend; Avant; Mad Hatter; Health Media). 165 Vallecitos de Oro. San Marcos, CA 92069. (619) 744-2299. Submissions Editor: Leslie Smith. Founded: 1981. Number of titles published: cumulative—386, 1991—26. Softback 100%.

Subjects of Interest. Fiction—children's. Recent publications: *Goldilocks; Ugly Duckling.* Nonfiction—computer; business; health; children's. Recent publications: *IBM PC Graphics Handbook; Talking Your Way to the Top; Inside Animals.* Do not want: children's books without finished art.

Initial Contact. Query letter only

Acceptance Policies. Unagented manuscripts: yes. Simultaneous submissions: yes. Disk submissions: no. Response time to initial inquiry: 2 weeks. Average time until publication: 4-6 months. **Advance:** varies. **Royalty:** varies. First run: n/i.

Marketing Channels. Direct mail; independent reps; in-house staff; special sales. Subsidiary rights: all.

Additional Information. Catalog: $3.

GENNY SMITH BOOKS. 1304 Pitman Ave. Palo Alto, CA 94301.

Submissions Editor: Genny Smith. Founded: 1976. Number of titles published: cumulative—6 (in print), 1991—1. Hardback and softback, most titles published in both.

Subjects of Interest. Nonfiction—natural history and history of the Eastern Sierra region of California. Recent publications: *The Mammoth Lakes Sierra; Mammoth Gold; Doctor Nellie: Autobiography of Helen MacKnight Doyle*. Do not want: anything other than the Eastern Sierra.

Initial Contact. Query letter; entire manuscript.

Acceptance Policies. Unagented manuscripts: n/i. Simultaneous submissions: no. Disk submissions: no. Response time to initial inquiry: 2 weeks. Average time until publication: varies. **Advance**: none. **Royalty**: 5-10%. First run: 5000+.

Marketing Channels. Direct mail; independent reps. Subsidiary rights: none.

Additional Information. Catalog: upon request.

SOCIAL JUSTICE. (Subsidiary of Global Options. Imprint: Crime and Social

Justice Associates). PO Box 40601. San Francisco, CA 94140. (415) 550-1703. Submissions Editor: Gregory Shank. Founded: 1974. Number of titles published: cumulative—44, 1991—4. Softback 100%.

Subjects of Interest. Nonfiction—racism; powerlessness; justice; contemporary issues; Hispanic; sociology. Recent publications: *The Iron Fist and the Velvet Glove; Punishment and Penal Discipline; Contragate and Counterterrorism*. Do not want: fiction; short stories.

Initial Contact. Query letter with synopsis/outline. Include author bio.

Acceptance Policies. Unagented manuscripts: yes. Simultaneous submissions: no. Disk submissions: yes. Response time to initial inquiry: 3 months. Average time until publication: 6 months. **Advance**: n/a. **Royalty**: n/a, unless reprinted elsewhere. First run: 3000.

Marketing Channels. Distribution houses; direct mail; independent reps. Subsidiary rights: all.

Additional Information. Catalog: upon request. Writer's guidelines: SASE.

SOFTWARE SUCCESS. PO Box 9006. San Jose, CA 95157-0006.

(408) 446-2504. Fax (408) 255-1098. Submissions Editor: David H. Bowen. Founded: 1987. Number of titles published: cumulative—n/i, 1991—n/i. Softback 100%.

Subjects of Interest. Nonfiction—software reference books; marketing. Recent publications: n/i.

Initial Contact. Query letter with synopsis/outline.

Acceptance Policies. Unagented manuscripts: yes. Simultaneous submissions: yes. Disk submissions: no. Response time to initial inquiry: 1 month. Average time until publication: varies. **Advance**: none. **Royalty**: 15% based on net. First run: n/i.

Marketing Channels. Direct mail. Subsidiary rights: direct mail or direct sales.

Additional Information. Catalog: n/i. Writer's guidelines: n/i.

SPINSTERS/AUNT LUTE BOOKS. PO Box 410687. San Francisco, CA 94141. (415) 558-9655. Submissions Editor: Lorraine Grassano. Founded: 1986. Number of titles published: cumulative—38, 1991—8. Softback 100%.

Subjects of Interest. Fiction—by and about women, mainly lesbian, women of color. Recent publications: *Tight Spaces* (short stories from three black women from Detroit). Nonfiction—themes directed towards a saner world; works by women. Recent publications: *Borderlands/La Frontera* (history of the Mestiza in prose, poetry); *Lesbian Passion: Loving Ourselves and Each Other*. Do not want: works supporting the status quo.

Initial Contact. Query letter. Include author information.

Acceptance Policies. Unagented manuscripts: yes. Simultaneous submissions: yes; inform us. Disk submissions: no. First novels: yes. Response time to initial inquiry: 2 weeks. Average time until publication: 1 year. **Advance:** none. **Royalty:** 7 1/2%. First run: 5000.

Marketing Channels. Distribution houses; cooperative distribution; direct mail; in-house staff; special sales. Subsidiary rights: all.

Additional Information. Tips: Be patient. Catalog: upon request.

SQUIBOB PRESS, INC. PO Box 4476. Walnut Creek, CA 94596. (415) 525-3982. Submissions Editor: Richard D. Reynolds. Founded: 1987. Number of titles published: cumulative—3, 1991—1. Softback 100%.

Subjects of Interest. Nonfiction—crime; photography; children's books. Recent publications: *Cry for War, The Story of Suzan and Michael Carson; The Ancient Art of Colima, Mexico; Squibob, an Early California Humorist.*

Initial Contact. Query letter.

Acceptance Policies. Unagented manuscripts: yes. Simultaneous submissions: yes. Disk submissions: yes. Response time to initial inquiry: 2 weeks. Average time until publication: n/i. **Advance:** $1000. **Royalty:** 10% net of retail. First run: 1000-3000. Subsidy basis: depends on cost estimates.

Marketing Channels. Distribution houses; in-house staff. Subsidiary rights: all.

Additional Information. We are a new press looking for product. Tips: We welcome your query letters. Catalog: write and request.

STAGE SCRIPTS. (Subsidiary of Dustbooks). PO Box 100. Paradise, CA 95967. Submissions Editor: Len Fulton. Founded: 1990. Number of titles published: cumulative—3; 1991—not yet determined. Softback 100%.

Subjects of Interest. Nonfiction—modern drama; plays.

Initial Contact. Query letter only.

Acceptance Policies. Unagented manuscripts: yes. Simultaneous submissions: yes. Disk submissions: query first, IBM compatible. Response time to initial inquiry: 2-3 weeks. Average time until publication: 9 months. **Advance:** none. **Royalty:** 15% of gross sales. First run: 1000.

Marketing Channels. Cooperative distribution; direct mail. Subsidiary rights: under contract—first serialization; reprint; dramatization, motion picture, and broadcast.

STANFORD UNIVERSITY PRESS. Stanford University. Stanford, CA 94305. (415) 723-9434. Submissions Editor: Norris Pope. Founded: 1925. Number of titles published: cumulative—1000+ (in print), 1991—65. Hardback and softback.

Subjects of Interest. Nonfiction—scholarly books in almost all academic fields; upper division texts; some for general audience.

Initial Contact. Query letter; prospectus; outline.

Acceptance Policies. Unagented manuscripts: yes. Disk submissions: query. Response time to initial inquiry: 3-5 weeks. Average time until publication: 1 year. **Advance**: sometimes. **Royalty**: none-15%. First run: varies enormously. Subsidy basis: 65% (nonauthor).

Marketing Channels. Distribution houses; direct sales. Subsidiary rights: all.

Additional Information. We are looking principally for works of academic scholarship with broad appeal. Catalog: upon request.

STAR PUBLISHING COMPANY. 940 Emmett Avenue. Belmont, CA 94002. (415) 591-3505. Submissions Editor: Stuart A. Hoffman. Founded: 1978. Number of titles published: cumulative—75. Hardback 5%, softback 95%.

Subjects of Interest. Nonfiction—textbooks for higher education and reference books; California regional history. Recent publications: *California: The Golden Shore by the Sundown Sea; Clinical Guide to Anaerobic Infections; Basic Microbiology Techniques*. Do not want: fiction; nontextbooks.

Initial Contact. Book proposal with sample chapters.

Acceptance Policies. Unagented manuscripts: yes. Simultaneous submissions: yes; with reservations. Disk submissions: no. Response time to initial inquiry: 30 days. Average time until publication: 1 year. **Advance**: none usually. **Royalty**: 5-15%. First run: varies greatly.

Marketing Channels. Distribution houses; cooperative distribution; direct mail; independent reps; special sales. Subsidiary rights: all.

Additional Information. Tips: Be sure subject of proposals are for higher education texts, or "Californiana." Catalog: upon request.

STAR ROVER HOUSE. 1914 Foothill Blvd. Oakland, CA 94606. (415) 532-8408. Submissions Editor: Robert Martens. Founded: 1978. Number of titles published: cumulative—40, 1991—5. Softback 100%.

Subjects of Interest. Fiction—reprints of Jack London, Mark Twain, Bret Harte.

STONE BRIDGE PRESS. PO Box 8208. Berkeley, CA 94707. (415) 524-8732. Fax (415) 524-8711. Submissions Editor: Peter Goodman. Founded: 1989. Number of titles published: 1991—3. Hardback 25%, softback 75%.

Subjects of Interest. Fiction—translations of Japanese literature. Recent publications: first book scheduled for 1991. Nonfiction—Japan-related subjects, especially language learning, design, culture, business. Recent publications: first book scheduled for 1991. Do not want: original haiku; travel diaries; mass-market fiction.

Initial Contact. Query letter with synopsis/outline; book proposal. Include sample chapters, author's resumé, and a demonstration of competence in Japan-related field.

Acceptance Policies. Unagented manuscripts: yes. Simultaneous submissions: yes, inform us. Disk submissions: no. Response time to initial inquiry: 1 month. Average time until publication: 12-18 months. **Advance**: yes. **Royalty**: yes. First run: varies.

Marketing Channels. Charles E. Tuttle Co., distributors; direct mail. Subsidiary rights: all.

Additional Information. Looking for competence and knowledge more than proven organizational ability. Tips: Go to Japanese bookstore like Kinokuniya (San Francisco, Los Angeles, New York) to see how Japanese books are done. Catalog: not available until 1991.

STRAWBERRY HILL PRESS. (Imprints: Walnut Hill Books; Plain Jane Books; Irio I O). 2594 15th Avenue. San Francisco, CA 94127. (415) 664-8112. Submissions Editors: Joseph M. Lubow; Mary Castiglione; Robin Witkin; Carolyn Soto; Anne Ingram (all work in all subject areas). Founded: 1973. Number of titles published: cumulative—135, 1991—15. Hardback 6%, softback 94%.

Subjects of Interest. Fiction—some, general. Recent publications: *Dogheaded Death* (historical mystery); *Wrong Man* (international intrigue/terrorism). **Nonfiction**—cookbooks; self-help; autobiography/biography; history; Third World; inspiration; health and nutrition; alternative lifestyles. Recent publications: *Diary of Courage* (cancer/inspirational); *Silent Menace* (health/nutrition). Do not want: poetry; plays; juveniles; short story collections; photography books.

Initial Contact. Query letter; book proposal. Include author's credentials. We neither read nor respond to anything not accompanied by a SASE.

Acceptance Policies. Unagented manuscripts: yes. Simultaneous submissions: never. Disk submissions: IBM compatible. First novels: sometimes. Response time to initial inquiry: 2-8 weeks. Average time until publication: 1-3 years. **Advance:** none at all—ever. **Royalty:** 10% of receipts. First run: 5000 +/-.

Marketing Channels. Distribution houses; direct mail; independent reps; in-house staff; special sales. Subsidiary rights: all; very active with same.

Additional Information. We are extremely active in the promotion of our authors and their books. Tips: We already see some 6000 unsolicited books projects each year. Catalog: appropriate SASE.

STUDIO PRESS. PO Box 1268. Twain Harte, CA 95383-1268. (209) 533-4222. Submissions Editor: Paul Castle. Founded: 1974. Number of titles published: cumulative—8 (in print), 1991—4. Hardback 40%, softback 60%.

Subjects of Interest. Nonfiction—books for professional studio photographers; books that tell how to take better pictures and sell more of them. Recent publications: *The Boudoir Portrait; Family Portraiture; Promoting Portraits; The Madonna Portrait; The Balloon Portrait; Publicity Photography.* Do not want: anything but above, especially not books of pretty photos for the coffee table.

Initial Contact. Best is a phone call and a quick pitch of the idea. I can give a go-ahead in two minutes for the written proposal and sample chapters. Be sure to mention expertise in photography.

Acceptance Policies. Unagented manuscripts: prefer them. Simultaneous submissions: no. Disk submissions: no; maybe later. Response time to initial inquiry: phone, 2 minutes; proposal, 3 days; proposal with chapters, 7 days. Average time until publication: 3 months. **Advance:** none; most authors are photographers who will write just one book with a lot of help from us. **Royalty:** up to 15%; depends on work needed and potential sales. First run: 3000+. Subsidy basis: we have in the past and may in the future; but we don't look for it.

Marketing Channels. Direct mail (95%). Subsidiary rights: all; we have worldwide distribution by mail and overseas distributors.

Additional Information. Please read very carefully and only send us what we want. Tips: We are very easy to work with if you send us what we want. We work very closely with the author until we get the manuscript we want. Catalog: upon request.

Sufi Publishing *see* **HUNTER HOUSE, INC., PUBLISHERS.**

SUN AND MOON PRESS. (Subsidiary of The Contemporary Arts Educational Project, Inc.). 6148 Wilshire Blvd. Gertrude Stein Plaza. Los Angeles, CA 90048. (213) 857-1115. Submissions Editor: Michael Anderson. Not accepting manuscripts at this time.

SUNBELT PUBLICATIONS. 8622 Argent St., Ste. A. Santee, CA 92071. (619) 448-0884. Fax (619) 449-3754. Submissions Editor: William G. Hample. Founded: 1984. Number of titles published: cumulative—5, 1991—1. Softback 100%.

Subjects of Interest. Nonfiction—regional guidebooks to Southern California or Southwest; Baja, California; bicycle books; tourist guides; hiking and nature guides. Recent publications: *Mountain Bicycling San Diego; Anza-Borrego Field Guide; Bicycling Baja; Southwest America Bicycle Route.* Do not want: fiction; self-help; new age.

Initial Contact. Query letter; book proposal with one sample chapter. Include author background.

Acceptance Policies. Unagented manuscripts: yes. Simultaneous submissions: no. Disk submissions: yes. Response time to initial inquiry: 2 weeks. Average time until publication: 1 year. **Advance:** negotiable. **Royalty:** 10%. First run: 3000-5000.

Marketing Channels. Distribution houses; in-house staff. Subsidiary rights: none.

Additional Information. We are a book wholesaler (95%) and publisher (5%). Tips: Check our catalog. Catalog: upon request.

SUNSET BOOKS. 80 Willow Rd. Menlo Park, CA 94025. (415) 321-3600. Does mostly in-house publication.

Sun West *see* **ELYSIUM GROWTH PRESS.**

SYBEX, INC. (Imprints: Sybex). 2021 Challenger Dr., #100. Alameda, CA 94501. (415) 523-8233. Submissions Editor: Dianne King. Founded: 1976. Number of titles published: cumulative—400, 1991—90. Softback 100%.

Subjects of Interest. Nonfiction—related to personal desktop or micro computer programs and equipment; mostly business and technical orientation. Recent publications: *Mastering Word Perfect 5.1; Mastering P.C. Tool Deluxe, 6.* Do not want: noncomputer subjects.

Initial Contact. Book proposal with sample chapters. Include author background.

Acceptance Policies. Unagented manuscripts: yes. Simultaneous submissions: yes; not too multiple. Disk submissions: 5 1/4 IBM PC; WordStar; WordPerfect; ASCII, etc. Response time to initial inquiry: 1 month. Average time until publication: 6 months. **Advance:** $3000. **Royalty:** 10%. First run: 5000-10,000.

Marketing Channels. Distribution houses; in-house staff. Subsidiary rights: translation and foreign; English language publication outside United States and Canada.

Additional Information. Tips: Call and talk to our acquisitions editor. Catalog: upon request.

JEREMY P. TARCHER, INC. 5858 Wilshire Blvd., Ste. 200. Los Angeles, CA 90036. (213) 935-9980. Submissions Editor: Donna Zerner. Founded: 1964. Number of titles published: cumulative—250, 1991—60. Hardback 50%, softback 50%.

Subjects of Interest. Nonfiction—human potential; personal and social transformation; health; creativity; self-help; relationships; spirituality; leading edge psychology. Recent publications: *Spiritual Emergency; Nontoxic and Natural; The Compass in Your Nose and Other Astonishing Facts About Humans; Age Wave; Personal Mythology; A Time to Heal.* Do not want: art; children's; astrology; textbooks; cookbooks; exposés; game books; fiction; channeled material.

Initial Contact. Outline; summary; sample chapters. Include author bio stressing expertise in field; market survey of competing books; uniqueness of this book; clear picture of audience. Include SASE.

Acceptance Policies. Unagented manuscripts: yes. Simultaneous submissions: yes. Disk submissions: no. Response time to initial inquiry: 6-8 weeks. Average time until publication: 1 year. **Advance:** variable. **Royalty:** standard. First run: 7500-100,000.

Marketing Channels. Distribution houses; special sales. Subsidiary rights: all.

Additional Information. Catalog: 6x9 SASE, $1.05 postage.

TECHNICAL COMMUNICATIONS ASSOCIATES. 1250 Oakmead Parkway, Ste. 210. Sunnyvale, CA 94088. (408) 737-2665. Submissions Editor: Steve J. Ayer. Founded: 1982. Number of titles published: cumulative—60, 1991—24. Hardback 10%, softback 90%.

Subjects of Interest. Nonfiction—technical/scientific books by professional computer scientists and documentation specialists. Recent publications: *Computer Systems Documentation Contents Development Handbook; Systems Development Documentation Series; Design Specifications for an Automated Documentation System; A Systems Development Methodology for a Small or Medium Size Data Processing Organization.*

Initial Contact. Query letter with synopsis/outline and sample chapters. Include information regarding experience.

Acceptance Policies. Unagented manuscripts: yes. Simultaneous submissions: yes. Disk submissions: yes. Response time to initial inquiry: 14 days. Average time until publication: 90 days. **Advance:** $1000-$1500. **Royalty:** 10% based on gross sales. First run: 100-2500. Subsidy basis: negotiated.

Marketing Channels. Distribution houses; cooperative distribution; direct mail; independent reps; in-house staff; special sales. Subsidiary rights: reprint rights; direct mail or direct sales; book club; translation and foreign; computer and other magnetic and electronic media; commercial; English language publication outside the United States and Canada.

Additional Information. Catalog: upon request. Writer's guidelines: upon request.

TECHNICAL INFORMATION SERVICES. 1263 Warner Ave. Los Angeles, CA 90024. (213) 821-4958. Submissions Editor: Ken Englert. Founded: 1972. Number of titles published: cumulative—3, 1991—2. Hardback 100%.

Subjects of Interest. Nonfiction—boating user's guides; educational guides. Recent publications: *Marine Radio User's Guide; Loran User's Guide; The Metric System.*

Initial Contact. Query letter only.

Acceptance Policies. Unagented manuscripts: yes. Simultaneous submissions: yes. Disk submissions: no. Response time to initial inquiry: 10 days. Average time until publication: 6 months. **Advance:** n/i. **Royalty:** n/i. First run: n/i.

Marketing Channels. Distribution houses; direct mail; in-house sales. Subsidiary rights: direct mail or direct sales; English language publication outside the United States and Canada.
Additional Information. Catalog: upon request.

TEN SPEED PRESS/CELESTIAL ARTS. Box 7123. Berkeley, CA 94707.
(415) 845-8414. Submissions Editor: Mariah Bear. Founded: 1971. Number of titles published: cumulative—600, 1991—70. Hardback 5%, softback 95%, published simultaneously, if hardback edition published.

Subjects of Interest. Nonfiction—careers; cookbooks; humor; general. Recent publications: *Coyote Cafe; Dynamic Cover Letters; Crazy Wizdom.* Do not want: poetry; fiction.

Initial Contact. Query letter. Tell briefly what the book is about, what makes it good, and who you are. Include SASE.

Acceptance Policies. Unagented manuscripts: yes. Simultaneous submissions: yes. Disk submissions: no. Response time to initial inquiry: 2 months. Average time until publication: 1 1/2-2 years. **Advance:** varies. **Royalty:** varies. First run: varies.

Marketing Channels. Distribution houses; direct mail; independent reps; in-house staff; special sales. Subsidiary rights: all.

Additional Information. Tips: Our books have a high level of integrity. There is no substitute for good, solid writing; it will always be the main reason for accepting a manuscript. Catalog: upon request.

TIOGA PUBLISHING COMPANY. 150 Coquito Way. Portola Valley, CA
94028. (415) 854-2445. Submissions Editor: Karen Nilsson. Founded: 1979. Number of titles published: cumulative—23, 1991—2. Hardback 20%, softback 80%.

Subjects of Interest. Nonfiction—Western Americana. Recent publications: *The Spirit of the Monterey Coast; Seasonal Expectations—Northern California.* Do not want: anything but Western nonfiction; no poetry.

Initial Contact. Query letter. Include experience of author, willingness to help market book, and funding ideas.

Acceptance Policies. Unagented manuscripts: yes. Simultaneous submissions: no. Disk submissions: yes. Response time to initial inquiry: 3 months. Average time until publication: 1 1/2 years. **Advance:** none. **Royalty:** 10% net amount received. First run: 2000-5000.

Marketing Channels. Distribution houses; direct mail; special sales. Subsidiary rights: all.

Additional Information. We work more through word of mouth. Tips: Explain why the world will be a better place if your book is published! Catalog: upon request.

TRAILER LIFE BOOKS. (Subsidiary of TL Enterprises). 29901 Agoura Rd.
Agoura, CA 91301. (818) 991-4980. Submissions Editor: Reno Copperman. Number of titles published: cumulative—15, 1991—2. Hardback 50%, softback 50%.

Subjects of Interest. Nonfiction—recreational vehicle-related subjects. Recent publications: *RV Repair and Maintenance Manual.*

Initial Contact. Query letter with synopsis/outline. Include author's background.

Acceptance Policies. Unagented manuscripts: yes. Simultaneous submissions: no. Disk submissions: IBM compatible. Response time to initial inquiry: 1-2 months. Average time until publication: 1 year. **Advance:** to be determined. **Royalty:** to be determined. First run: to be determined by project.

Marketing Channels. Distribution houses; direct mail. Subsidiary rights: all.

Additional Information. Catalog: upon request.

TRAVEL KEYS. PO Box 160691. Sacramento, CA 95816. (916) 452-5200. Submissions Editor: Peter Manston. Founded: 1984. Number of titles published: cumulative—16, 1991—5. Hardback 10%, softback 90%.

Subjects of Interest. Nonfiction—travel; home; antiques; how-to (travel related). Recent publications: *Before You Leave on Your Vacation; Manston's Europe '90; Manston's Italy.*

Initial Contact. Sample chapters or entire manuscript. Include enough of subject and book so we can determine if author is an authority in the field, if book topic and treatment fits our list.

Acceptance Policies. Unagented manuscripts: yes. Simultaneous submissions: yes; inform us. Disk submissions: IBM 5 1/4, 3 1/4; ASCII; Word; Wordstar. Response time to initial inquiry: 1 month. Average time until publication: 3-9 months. **Advance:** variable. **Royalty:** we estimate royalty and pay fee for book, usually as work for hire. First run: 4000-10,000.

Marketing Channels. Distribution houses; cooperative distribution; independent reps; direct mail; special sales. Subsidiary rights: all.

Additional Information. Catalog: SASE #10 envelope, postage for 3 ounces.

Treasure Books *see* **PRICE STERN SLOAN, INC.**

Troubador Press *see* **PRICE STERN SLOAN, INC.**

TURKEY PRESS. 6746 Sueno Rd. Isla Vista, CA 93117. Submissions Editor: Harry E. Reese. We publish hand-produced books in limited editions. We do not accept submissions of any kind.

ULYSSES PRESS. PO Box 4000-H. Berkeley, CA 94704. (415) 841-5271. Submissions Editor: Leslie Henriques. Founded: 1983. Number of titles published: cumulative—10, 1991—8. Softback 100%.

Subjects of Interest. Nonfiction—travel guide books. Recent publications: *Hidden New England; California: The Ultimate Guidebook; Hidden Miami; Hidden Florida Keys and Everglades.*

Initial Contact. Query letter; book proposal with sample chapters.

Acceptance Policies. Unagented manuscripts: yes. Simultaneous submissions: yes. Disk submissions: n/i. Response time to initial inquiry: 6 weeks. Average time until publication: 1 year. **Advance:** work for hire. **Royalty:** n/i. First run: 10,000-15,000.

Marketing Channels. Distribution houses; direct mail. Subsidiary rights: all.

Additional Information. Catalog: upon request.

UNITED RESOURCE PRESS. 4521 Campus Dr., #388. Irvine, CA 92715. Submissions Editor: Sally Marshall Corngold. Founded: 1986. Number of titles published: cumulative—9. Softback 100%.

Subjects of Interest. Nonfiction—"how-to" personal finance; small business. Recent publications: *Clearing Your Credit: Financial Strategies During Divorce.* Do not want: fiction.

Initial Contact. Entire manuscript. Include photo availability; disk availability.

Acceptance Policies. Unagented manuscripts: yes. Simultaneous submissions: yes. Disk submissions: Wordstar (IBM or other). Response time to initial inquiry: 2-3 months. Average time until publication: 2-3 months. **Advance:** none. **Royalty:** 5%. First run: varies.

Marketing Channels. Distribution houses; cooperative distribution; direct mail; independent sales. Subsidiary rights: varies; direct mail or direct sales.

Additional Information. Our primary focus is books. Tips: All information must be well documented. Send entire manuscript. Don't call. Catalog: 9x12 SASE, $1 postage.

UNIVELT, INC. (Imprints: American Astronautical Society; International Academy of Astronautics; associated organizations of the National Space Society). PO Box 28130. San Diego, CA 92128. (619) 746-4005. Submissions Editor: Horace Jacobs. Founded: 1970. Number of titles published: cumulative—160, 1989—12. Hardback 40%, softback 60%.

Subjects of Interest. Nonfiction—aerospace, especially space and related; astronomy; technical communications/writing, editing, etc; veterinary first aid. Recent publications: *The NASA Mars Conference; Soviet Space Programs; Low-Gravity Sciences; The Human Quest in Space; Realm of the Long Eyes; General First Aid for Dogs; To Catch a Flying Star, a Scientific Theory of UFOs.* Do not want: fiction.

Initial Contact. Query letter; book proposal with outline. Include biography.

Acceptance Policies. Unagented manuscripts: yes. Simultaneous submissions: yes; inform us. Disk submissions: after acceptance; IBM compatible. Response time to initial inquiry: 30-60 days. Average time until publication: 6-8 months. **Advance:** none. **Royalty:** 10%. First run: varies. Subsidy basis: yes; some organizations offer to buy a certain number of copies or provide funds to support editorial work or printing.

Marketing Channels. Distribution houses; cooperative distribution; direct mail. Subsidiary rights: all.

Additional Information. We are a small publisher but distribute worldwide—mostly technical books. Tips: Most of our titles deal with space or are space-related. We publish also in the field of technical communication. Catalog: upon request.

UNIVERSITY ASSOCIATES, INC. 8517 Production Ave. San Diego, CA 92121. (619) 578-5900. Submissions Editor: Richard L. Roe, Vice-President, Publications. Founded: 1968. Number of titles published: cumulative—240, 1991—17. Hardback 70%, softback 30%.

Subjects of Interest. Nonfiction—human resource development; management/leadership; consulting/training; strategic planning. Recent publications: *The Encyclopedia of Group Activities; Coaching for Commitment; The Complete Marketing Handbook for Consultants; The Team-Building Source Book.*

Initial Contact. Query letter; book proposal with 1 sample chapter.

Acceptance Policies. Unagented manuscripts: yes. Simultaneous submissions: yes. Disk submissions: WordPerfect 5.1. Response time to initial inquiry: 60 days. Average time until publication: 6 months. **Advance:** varies. **Royalty:** varies. First run: n/i.

Marketing Channels. Direct mail. Subsidiary rights: n/i.

Additional Information. Catalog: upon request.

UNIVERSITY OF CALIFORNIA PRESS. (Imprints: Philip E. Lilienthal Asian Studies Imprint). 2120 Berkeley Way. Berkeley, CA 94720. (415) 642-4247. Submissions Editor: send to attention of the subject editor. Founded: 1893. Number of titles published: cumulative—5000, 1991—300. Hardback 70%, softback 30%.

Subjects of Interest. Nonfiction—African studies; anthropology; art and architecture; Asian studies; biological sciences; classical studies; economics; film and theater; folklore and mythology; geography; history; labor relations; language and linguistics; Latin American studies; literature; medicine; music; natural history and ecology; Near Eastern studies; philosophy; political science; sociology; women's studies. Do not want: original fiction and poetry.

Initial Contact. Query letter. Include curriculum vitae.

Acceptance Policies. Unagented manuscripts: yes. Simultaneous submissions: preferably not. Disk submissions: no. Response time to initial inquiry: 2-6 weeks. Average time until publication: 1 year . **Advance:** n/i. **Royalty:** n/i. First run: n/i.

Marketing Channels. Cooperative distribution; direct mail; independent reps; in-house staff; special sales. Subsidiary rights: all.

Additional Information. Catalog: upon request.

VALLEY OF THE SUN PUBLISHING. (Subsidiary of Sutphen Corporation). Box 38. Malibu, CA 90265. (818) 889-1575. Submissions Editor: Sharon L. Boyd. Founded: 1972. Number of titles published: cumulative—15. Softback 100%.

Subjects of Interest. Nonfiction—metaphysical philosophy. Recent publications: *Master of Life Manual* (spiritual enlightenment principles); *Enlightenment Transcripts* (continues the spiritual enlightenment); *Lighting the Light Within* (collection of Dick Sutphen's writings). Do not want: fiction, metaphysical or otherwise; poetry; channeled information.

Initial Contact. Will only accept query letters. Unsolicited manuscripts returned unopened. Include SASE.

Acceptance Policies. Unagented manuscripts: yes. Simultaneous submissions: no. Disk submissions: PC compatible; Microsoft Word. If not MS Word, then sample chapter to show formatting, with rest of manuscript in unformatted ASCII. Response time to initial inquiry: 3-6 months. Average time until publication: 3 months. **Advance:** negotiable. **Royalty:** negotiable. First run: 30,000.

Marketing Channels. Direct mail. Subsidiary rights: first serialization.

Additional Information. Catalog: upon request.

VIEWPOINT PRESS. (Subsidiary of Boxwood Press). 183 Ocean View Blvd. Pacific Grove, CA 93950. (408) 375-9110. Submissions Editor: Dr. Buchsbaum.

Subjects of Interest. Nonfiction—scholarly controversial books. Recent publications: *Synocracy.* For details *see* Boxwood Press.

VINTAGE '45 PRESS. PO Box 266. Orinda, CA 94563. (415) 254-7266. Submissions Editor: Susan Aglietti. Number of titles published: cumulative—2, 1991—1.

Subjects of Interest. Publishes a literary anthology on specific themes related to women's issues by women writers only. Anthologies include poems, essays, or short stories. All submissions must be previously unpublished.

Initial Contact. Query before sending manuscript.

Additional Information. Tip: A sample issue of *Vintage '45,* the uniquely supportive quarterly journal for women, is available for $2.50. This is the best indicator of the type of writing sought for the anthology.

VOLCANO PRESS, INC. (Imprints: Kazan Books, on Pacific Rim subjects). PO Box 270. Volcano, CA 95689. (209) 296-3445. Fax: (209) 296-4515. Submissions Editor: Ruth Gottstein. Founded: 1969. Number of titles published: cumulative— 20, 1991—3. Hardback 10%, softback 90%.

Subjects of Interest. Fiction: children's. Nonfiction—women's health; family violence; children's books; health books in Spanish; art books. Recent publications: *Shingles; Mighty Mountain and the Three Strong Women; Berchick.* Do not want: poetry; adult fiction.

Initial Contact. Query letter. Include SASE.

Acceptance Policies. Unagented manuscripts: yes. Simultaneous submissions: yes; inform us. Disk submissions: no. Response time to initial inquiry: 4-6 weeks. Average time until publication: varies. **Advance**: none. **Royalty**: varies. First run: 5000-7000.

Marketing Channels. Distribution houses; cooperative distribution; direct mail; in-house staff; special sales. Subsidiary rights: all.

Additional Information. See our catalog. Tips: Inquire first; include SASE. Catalog: SASE.

Walnut Hill Books *see* **STRAWBERRY HILL PRESS.**

WAYFARER BOOKS. PO Box 5927. Concord, CA 94524. Submissions Editor: Michael Clark. Founded: 1989. Number of titles published: cumulative—3, 1991—4. Softback 100%.

Subjects of Interest. Nonfiction—travel; Buddhism. Recent publications: *The Meditation Temples of Thailand; Nibbana and Empty Mind.*

Initial Contact. Query letter with synopsis/outline.

Acceptance Policies. Unagented manuscripts: yes. Simultaneous submissions: no. Disk submissions: no. Response time to initial inquiry: 3 months. Average time until publication: 1 year. **Advance**: n/i. **Royalty**: negotiable. First run: n/i.

Marketing Channels. Cooperative distribution; direct mail. Subsidiary rights: all.

Additional Information. Catalog: n/i. Writer's guidelines: n/i.

WE PRESS. PO Box 1503. Santa Cruz, CA 95061. (408) 427-9711. Submissions Editor: Christopher Funkhouser. Founded: 1986. Number of titles published: cumulative—15, 1991—3. Softback 100%.

Subjects of Interest. Fiction—avant-garde; surrealism. Nonfiction—poetry only; some short fiction included in *We Magazine.* Recent publications: *Really Boomba.* Do not want: anything of the traditional variety.

Initial Contact. Query letter with sample chapters.

Acceptance Policies. Unagented manuscripts: yes. Simultaneous submissions: yes. Disk submissions: Microsoft Word for Macintosh. Response time to initial inquiry: varies. Average time until publication: varies. **Advance**: none. **Royalty**: n/i. First run: n/i.

Marketing Channels. Distribution houses; direct mail; special sales. Subsidiary rights: none.

Additional Information. We are dedicated to promotion of poetry. Writers should send small manuscripts of poems with SASE. Short story writers may send work with SASE for inclusion in our literary journal, *We Magazine.* Catalog: upon request.

WESTERN ASSOCIATION OF MAP LIBRARIES. Map and Imagery Laboratory. UC Santa Barbara. Santa Barbara, CA 93106. Founded: 1967. Number of titles published: cumulative—12, 1991—1. Softback 100%.

Subjects of Interest. Nonfiction—reference maps; bibliographies of maps; occasional papers. Recent publications: *Map Index to Topographic Quadrangles of the US, 1882-1940; A Cartobibliography of Separately Published U.S. Geological Survey Special Maps and River Surveys.*

Initial Contact. Book proposal. Include focus of the work; table of contents.

Acceptance Policies. Unagented manuscripts: no. Simultaneous submissions: no. Disk submissions: Microsoft Word for Macintosh. Response time to initial inquiry: 3 months. Average time until publication: 1 year. **Advance:** none. **Royalty:** none. First run: varies.

Marketing Channels. Special sales. Subsidiary rights: none.

Additional Information. Catalog: write and request.

WESTERN TANAGER PRESS. 1111 Pacific Ave. Santa Cruz, CA 95060. (408) 425-1111. Submissions Editor: Hal Morris. Founded: 1979. Number of titles published: cumulative—29, 1991—4. Hardback 25%, softback 75%.

Subjects of Interest. Fiction—*Miner's Christmas Carol* (a short story collection by Samuel Davis, 1886). Nonfiction—regional history and biography relating to California and the West; hiking and biking guides. Recent publications: *History of Steinbeck's Cannery Row; Mountain Biking in the Bay Area.*

Initial Contact. Query letter; book proposal. Include table of contents.

Acceptance Policies. Unagented manuscripts: yes. Simultaneous submissions: yes. Disk submissions: not yet. Response time to initial inquiry: 1 month. Average time until publication: 6 months. **Advance:** varies. **Royalty:** 10%. First run: 3000-7000. Subsidy basis: contract.

Marketing Channels. Distribution houses; in-house staff; special sales. Subsidiary rights: all.

Additional Information. Tips: Research us first. Do we already publish books similar to the one you have submitted? Catalog: upon request.

WILDERNESS PRESS. 2440 Bancroft Way. Berkeley, CA 94704. (415) 843-8080. Submissions Editor: Thomas Winnett. Founded: 1967. Number of titles published: cumulative—98, 1991—6. Hardback 5%, softback 95%.

Subjects of Interest. Nonfiction—guidebooks and how-to books for self-propelled outdoor recreations such as hiking, backpacking, cross-country skiing, rock climbing, cycling. Recent publications: *Ticks and What you Can Do About Them; Hawaii Naturally; Mountain Biking Around Los Angeles; Wilderness Cuisine; Stairway Walks in Los Angeles.* Do not want: fiction; poetry.

Initial Contact. Query letter; sample chapters; or entire manuscript. Include some photos if it is a guidebook; evidence that writer has personally covered all the places he writes about.

Acceptance Policies. Unagented manuscripts: yes. Simultaneous submissions: yes. Disk submissions: MS-DOS; any IBM compatible, except 1.44 megabyte high density. Response time to initial inquiry: 20 days. Average time until publication: 7-8 months. **Advance:** varies. **Royalty:** 8% if not previously published in our fields; 10% if so. First run: 5000.

Marketing Channels. Distribution houses; direct mail; independent sales reps. Subsidiary rights: all.

Additional Information. We seek to uphold a standard of English language that seems to be above most writers' abilities. Tips: Don't tell us the book is timely, well-written, or bound to sell well. Catalog: upon request.

WILSHIRE BOOK COMPANY. 12015 Sherman Rd. North Hollywood, CA 91605. (213) 875-1711. Submissions Editor: Melvin Powers. Founded: 1947. Number of titles published: cumulative—500, 1991—25. Softback 100%.

Subjects of Interest. Nonfiction—psychological; self-help; inspirational. Recent publications: *Psycho-Cybernetics; Magic of Thinking Big; Think and Grow Rich; Parent Survival Training; Magic of Thinking Success.* **Other**—adult fables. Recent publications: *The Knight in Rusty Armor.*

Initial Contact. Query letter; phone call.

Acceptance Policies. Unagented manuscripts: yes. Simultaneous submissions: yes. Disk submissions: no. Response time to initial inquiry: 1 month. Average time until publication: 7 months. **Advance:** varies. **Royalty:** 5%. First run: 5000.

Marketing Channels. Distribution houses; direct mail; independent reps; in-house staff; special sales. Subsidiary rights: all.

Additional Information. Call for immediate response about manuscript. I welcome such phone calls to discuss your book proposal. Catalog: SASE (legal size).

B. L. Winch and Assoc. *see* **JALMAR PRESS.**

WIZARDS BOOKSHELF. PO Box 6600. San Diego, CA 92106. (619) 297-9879. Submissions Editor: R. I. Robb. Founded: 1972. Number of titles published: cumulative—50, 1989—5. Hardback 95%, softback 5%.

Subjects of Interest. Nonfiction—Secret Doctrine references; philosophy; theosophy; antiquities. Recent publications: *Lost Fragments of Proclus, 1824; Surya Siddhanta; Life of Paracelsus; Gnostics and Their Remains; Zohar; Esoteric Buddhism; Sacred Mysteries Mayas.* Do not want: anything except translations, or S.D. studies.

Initial Contact. Query letter; synopsis of manuscript.

Acceptance Policies. Unagented manuscripts: yes. Simultaneous submissions: no. Disk submissions: no; unless preceded by typed manuscript. Response time to initial inquiry: 1 week. Average time until publication: 9-12 months. **Advance:** none. **Royalty:** 20%. First run: varies.

Marketing Channels. Distribution houses; cooperative distribution; direct mail. Subsidiary rights: all.

Additional Information. We don't fit the standard mold. Tips: Contact us first. Catalog: upon request.

ALAN WOFSY FINE ARTS. Box 2210. San Francisco, CA 94126. (415) 771-1252, 986-3030. Submissions Editor: Alan Wofsy. Founded: 1969. Number of titles published: cumulative—60. Hardback and softback.

Subjects of Interest. Nonfiction—art reference books; bibliographies related to art.

Initial Contact. Query.

Acceptance Policies. Unagented manuscripts: yes. Disk submissions: no. Response time to initial inquiry: 1 month. Average time until publication: 1 year. **Advance:** n/i. **Royalty:** negotiable. First run: n/i. Subsidy basis: about 15%.

Marketing Channels. Distribution houses; in-house reps; special sales.

Additional Information. Catalog: upon request.

WOLCOTTS, INC. 15124 Downey Ave. PO Box 467. Paramount, CA 90723. (213) 630-0911. Submissions Editor: Allen Hughes. Founded: 1893. Number of titles published—n/i. Hardback 5%, softback 95%.

Subjects of Interest. Nonfiction—mostly how-to legal books. Recent publications: *How To Evict a Tenant; Incorporation Made Easy; Divorce California Style; How To Deal With Contractors.* Do not want: fiction.

Initial Contact. Query letter.

Acceptance Policies. Unagented manuscripts: yes. Simultaneous submissions: no. Disk submissions: no. Response time to initial inquiry: 2 weeks. Average time until publication: n/i. **Advance:** n/i. **Royalty:** n/i. First run: n/i.

Marketing Channels. Distribution houses; direct mail. Subsidiary rights: n/i.

Wonder Books *see* **PRICE STERN SLOAN, INC.**

WOODBRIDGE PRESS. PO Box 6189. Santa Barbara, CA 93160. (805) 965-7039. Submissions Editor: Howard Weeks. Founded: 1971. Number of titles published: cumulative—120+, 1991—5. Hardback 10%, softback 90%.

Subjects of Interest. Nonfiction—general; some emphasis on health, nutrition, food, gardening, cooking. Recent publications: *Hydroponic Home Food Gardens; Hydroponic Gardening; Not Milk—Nut Milks.*

Initial Contact. Book proposal with sample chapters. Include author's credentials.

Acceptance Policies. Unagented manuscripts: yes. Simultaneous submissions: yes. Disk submissions: yes. Response time to initial inquiry: varies. Average time until publication: 6-8 months. **Advance:** usually none. **Royalty:** 10-15% of net receipts. First run: varies.

Marketing Channels. Distribution houses; direct mail; independent reps; special sales. Subsidiary rights: all (at our discretion).

Additional Information. Catalog: write and request.

WORMWOOD REVIEW PRESS. PO Box 8840. Stockton, CA 95208-0840. (209) 466-8231. Submissions Editor: Marvin Malone. Founded: 1959. Number of titles published: cumulative—15, 1991—1. Softback 100%.

Subjects of Interest. Nonfiction—contemporary poetry. Recent publications: *Bukowski's Beauti-ful and Other Long Poems; Locklin's Children of a Lesser Demagogue.* Do not want: fiction or nonfiction.

Initial Contact. Entire manuscript.

Acceptance Policies. Unagented manuscripts: yes. Simultaneous submissions: no. Disk submissions: no. Response time to initial inquiry: 4-8 weeks. Average time until publication: 4-8 months. **Advance:** none. **Royalty:** variable. First run: 700.

Marketing Channels. Direct mail. Subsidiary rights: all.

Additional Information. Concentration on the prose-poem and contemporary concerns. Catalog: SASE.

WRITERS CONNECTION PRESS. 1601 Saratoga-Sunnyvale Rd., Ste. 180. Cupertino, CA 95014. (408) 973-0227. Submissions Editor: Meera Lester. Founded: 1986. Number of titles published: cumulative—3, 1991—3. Softback 100%.

Subjects of Interest. Nonfiction—writing/publishing topics. Recent publications: *California Publishing Marketplace; Southwest Publishing Marketplace.* Do not want: fiction; poetry.

Initial Contact. Query letter; book proposal with 1 sample chapter. Include author's bio and identify target market for the project.

Acceptance Policies. Unagented manuscripts: yes. Simultaneous submissions: no. Disk submissions: IBM PC. Response time to initial inquiry: 4-6 weeks. Average time until publication: 1 year. **Advance**: none at present. **Royalty**: varies. First run: 3500-5000.

Marketing Channels. Direct mail; independent reps; distributors; special sales. Subsidiary rights: all (at our discretion).

Write to Sell *see* **COMMUNICATION UNLIMITED.**

Yes Press *see* **DOWN THERE PRESS.**

Magazines

A single issue of a magazine is constructed from many different manuscripts, including articles, interviews, fiction, columns, reviews, poetry, etc. Some of this material is produced in-house by the publisher's staff, and some is purchased from freelance writers. We collected and organized the following information to help you find and approach those publishers of periodicals in California and Hawaii most likely to accept your inquiry and your submission.

How to Use the Information in This Section

The first paragraph of each entry identifies the magazine, lists its location, provides the name of its submissions editor(s), and identifies its type. Also included is information on the frequency of publication, size of circulation, and percentage of freelance submissions used in each issue. If the publication buys freelance material, the number of manuscripts it buys each year is listed; if there is no payment, or if payment is made in the form of contributor's copies, that information is provided as well.

Editorial Needs

We divided editorial needs into two main fields: fiction and nonfiction, with information on suggested formats, word lengths, and payment offered. In the fiction field there is a growing market for short stories—literary, category, and mainstream. Payment varies and is often nominal in the case of small literary magazines. However, an added perk is that your published short stories provide portfolio clips that establish your credibility as a writer when you query other markets.

In the area of nonfiction you'll find markets for your poetry, columns, book reviews, feature articles, profiles/interviews, essays, and how-to and self-help pieces. An advantage of writing nonfiction is the option of selling your basic material several times over by slanting it to fit the themes of different publications.

The amount of payment offered for your writing is dependent on length, subject matter, timeliness, your writing skill, and the magazine's current rates. Some of the smaller magazines offer contributor's copies and publish your byline as payment.

Initial contact

This information indicates how the editor wants you to contact him or her. You increase your chances for selling to a particular editor if you follow the suggestions listed in this section. Whether stated or not, always include a SASE.

Acceptance Policies

Payment made: This information is crucial to the writer's budget, so we've listed it right after the notation of whether or not the magazine publishes the writer's byline. Payment is usually made either on acceptance or on publication, though occasionally it may be made several weeks after publication.

Simultaneous submissions: If the publisher information says "yes," you may submit your manuscript to several different publishers at the same time, but you must inform each publisher that the manuscript is being simultaneously submitted.

Response time to initial inquiry: Be patient and avoid phoning the editor unless you have an agreement with that individual to do so. Two to three weeks *after* the specified response time, you are entitled to send a written request for information concerning the status of your submission. As with any correspondence to a publisher or agent, remember to include your SASE.

Average time until publication: Always dependent upon a number of factors, this information provides an approximate idea of how long the publishing process takes after the editor has received and accepted the completed manuscript.

Writer's expenses on assignment: Magazine editors rarely authorize the payment of expenses incurred on assignment for authors unknown (and unproven) to them. Assignments are generally reserved for writers with proven ability and reliability.

Computer printouts: Most publishers will now accept computer printouts but will usually accept dot matrix only if it is of near letter quality. While the majority of magazine publishers want your material submitted in the form of manuscript pages, many will now accept your finished submission on a disk compatible with their computer systems.

Publishing rights: Most magazine editors purchase first North American serial rights, which means they buy the right to publish your material first in their periodical for distribution in United States and Canada.

For information concerning other rights purchased, we suggest that you consult one or more of the books listed in the Book Reference Section.

Photography Submissions

We've included the magazine's preference for film type and format (black-and-white or color prints or transparencies) and size. Requests for additional information (listed under "Photographs should include") may cover model releases, captions, and identification of subjects. Payment for photographs may be made separately or in conjunction with the article submitted. Photographic rights may also be handled in the same manner.

Additional Information

This section of the entry reflects additional comments by the editor aimed specifically at the writer. Tips are suggestions that can help ensure your success in placing an article with a particular magazine. The best first step toward approaching any magazine is to obtain its writer's guidelines and a sample copy.

Abbreviations

n/i means no information was given to us by the magazine.

n/a means that this particular question did not apply to the magazine.

ADOLESCENCE. (Subsidiary of Libra Publishers, Inc). 3089C Clairmont Dr., Ste. 383. San Diego, CA 92117. (619) 581-9449. Submissions Editor: William Kroll. Type: professional journal. Frequency of publication: quarterly. Circulation: 3000. Freelance submissions: all. No payment offered.

Editorial Needs. Nonfiction—articles dealing with adolescents (psychological, psychiatric, physiological, sociological, educational). Suggested word length—feature articles: 2400.

Initial Contact. Submission of abstract.

Acceptance Policies. Byline given: yes. Payment: none. Simultaneous submissions: no. Response time to initial inquiry: 3 weeks. Average time until publication: 1 year. Computer printouts: yes. Dot matrix: yes. Disk submissions: no. Publishing rights: all.

Additional Information. Writer's guidelines: upon request.

AFTER HOURS. 21541 Oakbrook. Mission Viejo, CA 92692-3044. Submissions Editor: William G. Raley. Type: fantasy and horror fiction. Frequency of publication: quarterly. Circulation: 750. Freelance submissions: 95%; number bought each year: 50.

Editorial Needs. Fiction—short stories: fantasy; horror; macabre humor. Suggested word length—6000 words maximum. Payment offered: $.01 per word and contributor's copy.

Initial Contact. Entire manuscript.

Acceptance Policies. Byline given: yes. Payment made: upon acceptance. Seasonal material: anytime. Simultaneous submissions: no. Response time to initial inquiry: 2-4 months. Average time until publication: 9 months. Computer printouts: yes. Dot matrix: yes. Disk submissions: IBM PC; ASCII; 5 1/4" disk. Publishing rights: first North American serial rights.

Additional Information. All stories must take place after dark. We publish fiction too weird or off-the-wall for other publications. Tips: No sexism, racism, or overdone plots. Nothing of a political, military, or religious nature. Sample copy: $4. Writer's guidelines: SASE.

ALL ABOUT BEER AND SUDS 'N STUFF. 4764 Galicia Way. Oceanside, CA 92058. (619) 724-4447. Submissions Editor: Michael Bosak. Type: for the beer consumer. Frequency of publication: 6 times per year. Circulation: 47,000. Freelance submissions: 60%; number of manuscripts bought each year: 120.

Editorial Needs. Fiction—short stories: beer related. Suggested word length—n/i. Payment offered: varies. **Nonfiction**—(all beer related) general interest; historical; how-to; humor; interview/profile; travel. Suggested word length—2000. Payment offered: $75 per page if photographs are in color; $50 per page if photographs are in black and white. Columns and fillers—beer related. Suggested word length—varies. Payment offered: varies.

Initial Contact. Query letter or article proposal with subject outline. Include SASE.

Acceptance Policies. Byline given: yes. Payment made: upon publication. Kill fee: no. Writer's expenses: yes, if on assignment. Simultaneous submissions: no. Response time to initial inquiry: as promptly as possible. Average time until publication: n/i. Computer printouts: yes. Dot matrix: yes. Disk submissions: Mac Write, 4.5; Microsoft Works, 1.1; Quark Xpress, 2.0; Pagemaker, 3.0. Publishing rights: first North American serial rights; first rights.

Photography Submissions. must accompany all articles. Format and film: prefer color prints; will accept black-and-white or color transparencies. Photographs should include: identity of author printed on each slide; captions; model release. **Payment**: included with article. Photographic rights: n/i.

Additional Information. Sample copy: $3.50. Writer's guidelines: upon request.

ALOHA, THE MAGAZINE OF HAWAII AND THE PACIFIC. 49 S. Hotel St., #309. Honolulu, HI 96813. (808) 523-9871. Submissions Editor: Cheryl Chee Tsutsumi. Type: Hawaii and Pacific area covering a wide range of topics, including the arts, business, destinations, food, people, sports, history, and flora and fauna. Frequency of publication: bimonthly. Circulation: 65,000. Freelance submissions: 80%; number bought each year: 30.

Editorial Needs. **Nonfiction**—historical; poetry; travel. Suggested word length—1500-2000. Payment offered: $150-$400; $25 (poetry).

Initial Contact. Query letter.

Acceptance Policies. Byline given: yes. Payment made: upon publication. Kill fee: 25-30%. Writer's expenses: with prior approval. Simultaneous submissions: no. Response time to initial inquiry: 2 months. Average time until publication: 4-12 months. Computer printouts: yes. Dot matrix: yes. Disk submissions: no. Publishing rights: first North American serial rights.

Photography Submissions. Format and film: color transparencies. Photographs should include: captions; model releases; identification of subjects. **Payment**: $60-$175. Photographic rights: one time.

Additional Information. Although most of our readers live outside of Hawaii, the magazine is directed primarily to residents of Hawaii. As a general statement, we welcome material reflecting the true Hawaiian experience. Sample copy: SASE, $2.95 postage. Writer's guidelines: upon request.

AMELIA. 329 E Street. Bakersfield, CA 93304. (805) 323-4064. Submissions Editor: Frederick A. Raborg, Jr. Type: literary. Frequency of publication: quarterly. Circulation: 1250 print run. Freelance submissions: 100%; number bought each year: 30-40 stories; 250-300 poems; 6-8 articles.

Editorial Needs. **Fiction**—literary; women's genre; mainstream. Short stories—number per issue: 6-8; per year: 24-40. Payment offered: $35 upon acceptance; $10 per 1000 words for fiction under 2000 words. **Nonfiction**—book excerpts; book reviews; general interest; historical; humor; interview/profile; opinion; photo feature; poetry; travel. Suggested word length—feature articles: 2500. Payment offered: $10 per 1000 words for nonfiction under 2000 words.

Initial Contact. Entire article; strong cover letter with bio or acknowledgments is helpful.

Acceptance Policies. Byline given: yes. Payment made: upon acceptance. Kill Fee: author keeps acceptance payment. Writer's expenses on assignment: no. Submit seasonal material 4 months in advance. Simultaneous submissions: yes; inform us. Response time to initial inquiry: 2 weeks to 3 months (latter for serious consideration). Average time until publication:

6 months. Computer printouts: yes. Dot matrix: yes; rarely. Disk submissions: no. Publishing rights: first North American serial rights.

Photography Submissions. Format and film: black-and-white prints, no smaller than 5x7; color, for cover only. Photographs should include: captions; model releases. **Payment:** $10-$50 (latter for b/w cover); $100 (color cover). Photographic rights: first rights.

Additional Information. We also publish two smaller magazines: *Cicada* (Japanese poetry, fiction, essays, art); *SPSM&H* (sonnets, fiction, essays, art). Tips: Be professional and submit your best, neat, clean, polished work. Writer's guidelines: SASE.

AMERICAN CINEMATOGRAPHER MAGAZINE. PO Box 2230.

Hollywood, CA 90078. (213) 876-5080. Submissions Editor: Jean Turn. Type: semi-technical entertainment. Frequency of publication: monthly. Circulation: 30,000. Freelance submissions 50%; number of manuscripts bought each year: 24-36.

Editorial Needs. Nonfiction—interview with cinematographers, art directors, production personnel, and technical articles on new equipment, process, or lighting procedures. Suggested word length—2000. Payment offered: $300 for first-time author.

Initial Contact. No letters. Pitch by phone.

Acceptance Policies. Byline given: yes. Payment made: upon publication. Kill fee: 50%. Writer's expenses: yes. Simultaneous submissions: no. Response time to initial inquiry: call for immediate response. Average time until publication: 2-3 months. Computer printouts: yes. Dot matrix: yes. Disk submissions: Microsoft Word. Publishing rights: first North American serial rights.

Photography Submissions. Yes. Format and film: n/i. Photographs should include: n/i. **Payment:** none. Photographic rights: n/i.

Additional Information. We cater to a knowledgeable audience of filmmakers all over the world. Sample copy: call Jean Turner. Writer's guidelines: call Jean Turner.

AMERICAN FITNESS MAGAZINE. 15250 Ventura Blvd., Ste. 310.

Sherman Oaks, CA 91403. (818) 905-0040. Submissions Editors: Editor-at-Large, Peg Jordan, RN; Managing Editor, Rhonda J. Wilson. Type: health and fitness. Frequency of publication: bimonthly. Circulation: 25,100. Freelance submissions: 75%; number bought each year: n/i.

Editorial Needs. Fiction—short stories—number per issue: 1; per year: 9. Payment offered: n/i. Nonfiction—general interest; health/fitness; how-to; inspiration; interviews/profile; opinion; photo feature; humor; nutrition; beauty; self-improvement; travel. Suggested word length—feature articles: 1500; columns: 1500. Payment offered: n/i.

Initial Contact. Query letter. Include writing samples.

Acceptance Policies. Byline given: yes. Payment made: 4-6 weeks after publication. Kill Fee: no. Writer's expenses on assignment: no. Submit seasonal material 4 months in advance. Simultaneous submissions: no. Response time to initial inquiry: 1 month. Average time until publication: varies. Computer printouts: yes. Dot matrix: yes. Disk submissions: yes. Publishing rights: first North American serial rights.

Additional Information. Writer's guidelines: upon request.

AMERICAN HANDGUNNER. 591 Camino de La Reina, Ste. 200.
San Diego, CA 92108. (619) 297-5352. Submissions Editor: Cameron Hopkins.
Type: handguns; handgun sports; accessories. Frequency of publication: bimonthly.
Circulation: 150,000. Freelance submissions: 90%; number bought each year: 50-70.

Editorial Needs. Nonfiction—how to; interview/profile; travel; photo feature; new products. Suggested word length—feature articles: 500-3000; columns: 600-800. Payment offered: $100-$400 for unsolicited; $175-$600 for assigned.

Initial Contact. Query letter (include availability of photographs).

Acceptance Policies. Byline given: yes. Payment made: upon publication. Kill Fee: $50. Writer's expenses on assignment: sometimes. Submit seasonal material 7 months in advance. Response time to initial inquiry: 1 week. Average time until publication: 5-9 months. Computer printouts: no. Dot matrix: no. Disk submissions: all copies must be submitted on disk. Publishing rights: first North American serial rights.

Photography Submissions. Format and film: slides; contact sheets; 4x5 transparencies; black-and-white or color prints, 5x7 . Photographs should include: captions; identification of subjects. **Payment**: none for black and white with article; $50-$250 for color. Photographic rights: first North American serial rights.

Additional Information. Tips: Writer must have technical knowledge of handguns as well as knowledge of the sport. Writer's guidelines: upon request.

ARTWEEK. 12 S. First St., Ste. 520. San Jose, CA 95113. (408) 279-2293.
Submissions Editor: Charlotte Moser. Type: contemporary art of the West Coast.
Frequency of publication: weekly. Circulation: 12,000. Freelance submissions: 95%; number bought each year: 500.

Editorial Needs. Nonfiction—art book reviews; art personalities interview/profile. Suggested word length—750. Payment offered: $45-$90. Columns—art related. Suggested word length—750. Payment offered: n/i.

Initial Contact. Query letter. Include resumé, clips.

Acceptance Policies. Byline given: yes. Payment made: upon publication. Kill fee: 50%. Writer's expenses: no. Simultaneous submissions: no. Response time to initial inquiry: 3-6 weeks. Average time until publication: 4 weeks. Computer printouts: yes. Dot matrix: yes. Disk submissions: Macintosh; Microsoft Word. Publishing rights: n/i.

Additional Information. Sample copy: call. Writer's guidelines: upon request.

AUTOMATED BUILDER. PO Box 120. Carpinteria, CA 93014.
(805) 684-7659. Submissions Editor: Don Carlson. Type: managing manufactured and volume home building. Frequency of publication: monthly. Circulation: 25,000.
Freelance submissions: 15%; number of manuscripts bought each year: 15.

Editorial Needs. Nonfiction—profile/interview; photo feature; technical aspects; in areas of large volume home builders, manufacturers of mobile homes, modular homes, prefabs, house components. Suggested word length—feature articles: 500-750. Payment offered: $300+.

Initial Contact. Query letter; or query by phone (preferred).

Acceptance Policies. Byline given: yes. Payment made: upon acceptance. Kill fee: n/i. Writer's expenses on assignment: n/i. Response time to initial inquiry: 2 weeks. Average time until publication: 3 months. Computer printouts: yes. Dot matrix: no. Disk submissions: no. Publishing rights: first North American serial rights.

Photography Submissions. Format and film: black-and-white glossy prints, 4x5, 5x7, 8x10; 35mm transparencies (color). Photographs should include: captions. **Payment**: included with article. Photographic rights: same as article.

Additional Information. Projects must be under construction or finished. Tips: Keep articles short and succinct. Writer's guidelines: upon request.

AXIOS. 806 S. Euclid St. Fullerton, CA 92632. (714) 526-4952. Submissions Editor: Daniel John Gorham. Type: literary. Frequency of publication: monthly. Circulation: 8587. Freelance submissions: 50%; number bought each year: 24-50.

Editorial Needs. Nonfiction—book excerpts; book reviews; historical; inspiration; interview/profile; opinion. Suggested word length—feature articles: 2000. Payment offered: $.05 a word, depending on quality of the work.

Initial Contact. Query letter.

Acceptance Policies. Byline given: yes. Payment made: upon acceptance. Kill fee: yes. Writer's expenses on assignment: no. Submit seasonal material 5 months in advance. Simultaneous submissions: yes. Response time to initial inquiry: 3-4 months. Average time until publication: 2 months. Computer printouts: yes. Dot matrix: yes. Disk submissions: Microsoft Word. Publishing rights: first North American serial rights; work-for-hire assignments.

Additional Information. We are an international publication of high quality for the serious reader, mostly religious minded. Tips: Be honest. Know the Orthodox Church.

BAY AND DELTA YACHTSMAN. 2019 Clement Ave. Alameda, CA 94501. (415) 865-7500. Submissions Editor: Bill Parks. Type: Northern California recreational boating for owners of small boats and yachts. Frequency of publication: monthly. Circulation: 22,000. Freelance submissions: 20%; number bought each year: 10-20.

Editorial Needs. Nonfiction—tips on boating. Suggested word length—feature articles: 1500. Payment offered: $1 per inch.

Initial Contact. Query letter. Include the type and general drift of the story.

Acceptance Policies. Byline given: yes. Payment made: by arrangement. Kill fee: no. Writer's expenses on assignment: no. Submit seasonal material 3 months in advance. Simultaneous submissions: sometimes, if to noncompetitive regional market. Response time to initial inquiry: 1 month. Average time until publication: 1-6 months. Computer printouts: yes. Dot matrix: yes. Disk submissions: Macintosh; Microsoft Word. Publishing rights: first rights.

Photography Submissions. Format and film: black-and-white glossy or matte prints, 8x10. Photographs should include: captions. **Payment:** $5 per photo. Photographic rights: same as article.

Additional Information. Tips: Our readers are knowledgeable about boating. Think of unique ways in which they could increase their knowledge and pleasure of the Northern California waterways and their boats. Sample copy: upon request. Writer's guidelines: upon request.

BAY AREA BABY NEWS MAGAZINE. BAY AREA PARENT NEWS MAGAZINE. 455 Los Gatos, #103. Los Gatos, CA 95032. (408) 356-4121. Submissions Editor: Lynn Berardo.

Bay Area Baby Magazine. Type: pregnancy. Frequency of publication: twice yearly. Circulation. 60,000 annually.

Bay Area Parent News Magazine. Type: parenting. Frequency of publication: monthly. Circulation: 60,000 monthly. Freelance submissions: 90%; number bought each year: 140 (most freelance articles by assignment).

Editorial Needs. Nonfiction—book excerpts; book reviews; general interest; health/fitness; how-to; humor; inspiration; interview/profile; photo feature; self-improvement; travel; local adventure trips for families, etc.; education issues. Suggested word length—feature articles: 1200-2000; columns: 800. Payment offered: $.05 per word.

Initial Contact. Query letter; article proposal or entire article. Include samples of previous work.

Acceptance Policies. Byline given: yes. Payment made: upon publication. Kill fee: no. Writer's expenses on assignment: phone expenses. Submit seasonal material 4 months in advance. Simultaneous submissions: yes; prefer first time local printing. Response time to initial inquiry: 3 months. Average time until publication: 3 months. Computer printouts: yes. Dot matrix: yes. Disk submissions: IBM or Macintosh; Microsoft Word. Publishing rights: first rights; simultaneous rights.

Photography Submissions. Format: prints (any size); contact sheets. Film: black and white; color. Photographs should include: model releases; identification of subjects. **Payment**: $10-$35. Photographic rights: one-time use.

BAY AREA HOMESTYLE RESOURCE MAGAZINE. 455 Los Gatos Blvd., #103. Los Gatos, CA 95032. (408) 356-7436. Submissions Editor: Lynn Berardo. Type: home and garden. Frequency of publication: monthly. Circulation: 50,000. Freelance submissions 90%; number of manuscripts bought each year: 90.

Editorial Needs. Nonfiction—book excerpts; book reviews; how-to; interview/profile. Suggested word length—1200-2000. Payment offered: $.05 per word. Columns—antiques; personality home profile; garden; craftsmen profiles. Fillers—home and garden. Suggested word length—n/i. Payment offered: $.05.

Initial Contact. Query letter; article proposal with subject outline; entire article.

Acceptance Policies. Byline given: yes. Payment made: upon publication. Kill fee: no. Writer's expenses: phone. Seasonal material: 4 months in advance. Simultaneous submissions: 2 months. Response time to initial inquiry: 2-4 months. Average time until publication: Computer printouts: yes. Dot matrix: yes. Disk submissions: IBM or Macintosh; Microsoft Word. Publishing rights: first North American serial rights; simultaneous rights.

Photography Submissions. Format and film: contact sheets; black-and-white or color prints, any size. Photographs should include: captions; model releases; identification of subjects. **Payment**: $10-$25. Photographic rights: one-time use.

Additional Information. We are a new publication as of June 1990.

BIRD TALK, Dedicated to Better Care for Pet Birds. PO Box 6050. Mission Viejo, CA 92690. (714) 855-8822. Submissions Editor: Karyn New. Type: care and training of cage birds. Frequency of publication: monthly. Circulation: 170,000. Freelance submissions: 85%; number bought each year: 300.

Editorial Needs. Fiction—pet birds in any genre (talking birds only if it's their vocabulary). Suggested word length—2000-3000 words. Payment offered: $.07+ per word. Nonfiction—general interest; historical; nostalgia; how-to; humor; interview/profile; photo feature; medical and legal information; personal experience. Suggested word length—feature articles: 500-3000. Payment offered: $.10-$.15 per word. Columns: editorial; short news items. Suggested word length—300-1200. Payment offered: $.07 per word.

Initial Contact. Query letter or complete manuscript (nonfiction); complete manuscript (fiction). Include availability of photos.

Acceptance Policies. Byline given: yes. Payment made: after publication. Kill fee: no. Writer's expenses on assignment: no. Submit seasonal material 7 months in advance. Simultaneous submissions: no. Response time to initial inquiry: 3 weeks. Average time until publication: 6 months. Computer printouts: yes. Dot matrix: letter quality. Disk submissions: yes. Publishing rights: first North American serial rights.

Photography Submissions. Format and film: black-and-white prints (preferred); transparencies (color). Photographs should include: model releases; identification of subjects. **Payment:** $15 (black and white); $50-$150 (color). Photographic rights: one-time rights.

Additional Information. We also need articles on building bird-related items; crafts; safe plants; health; nutrition; and human interest. Tips: Read back issues. Writer's guidelines: #10 SASE, 1 first class stamp.

BLITZ MAGAZINE. PO Box 48124. Los Angeles, CA 90048-0124.
(818) 761-5456. Submissions Editor: Mike McDowell. Type: music (emphasis on early rock and roll, country music). Frequency of publication: bimonthly. Circulation: 5000. Freelance submissions: 40%. Payment in copies.

Editorial Needs. Nonfiction—book reviews; entertainment reviews; historical; opinion; musician interviews. Suggested word length—feature articles: 8 double-spaced pages. Payment offered: copies.

Initial Contact. Query letter; entire article; proposed ideas.

Acceptance Policies. Byline given: yes. Payment made: in copies. Submit seasonal material 4 months in advance. Simultaneous submissions: yes. Response time to initial inquiry: 1 month. Average time until publication: 6-12 months. Computer printouts: yes. Dot matrix: yes. Disk submissions: no. Publishing rights: n/a.

Photography Submissions. Format and film: black-and-white prints, 8 1/2 x 11 or 5x8. Photographs should include: identification of subjects. **Payment:** cost of film or developing. Photographic rights: exclusive.

Additional Information. Journalistic slant is strictly academic—no sensationalism. We plan to start book publishing in the near future. Tips: Understand the subject matter; not interested in superficial stories. Writer's guidelines: upon request.

BLUE UNICORN. 22 Avon Rd. Kensington, CA 94707. (415) 526-8439.
Submissions Editor: Ruth G. Iodice; Robert L. Bradley (art editor). Type: literary; we publish only poetry and use a limited amount of art. Frequency of publication: 3 issues per year. Circulation. 500. Freelance submissions: 100%; number used each year: 250. Payment in copies.

Editorial Needs. Nonfiction—poetry. Payment offered: copy.

Initial Contact. The poem alone is sufficient, but we do not object to brief query or bio letters.

Acceptance Policies. Byline given: yes. Payment made: copy of issue in which work appears. Simultaneous submissions: no. Response time to initial inquiry: 3-4 months. Average time until publication: 1 year. Computer printouts: yes. Dot matrix: no. Disk submissions: no. Publishing rights: first North American serial rights; we hope poets will give credit to *BU* for first publication.

Additional Information. It is a good idea for poets to have read our magazine so they can see what we are looking for. Lacking that, they may send a SASE for brochure. Tips: Write good, well-crafted poetry. Writer's guidelines: SASE.

BOW AND ARROW HUNTING. PO Box HH. 34249 Camino Capistrano. Capistrano Beach, CA 92624. (714) 493-2101. Submissions Editor: Roger Combs. Type: bow hunters. Frequency of publication: bimonthly. Circulation: 140,000. Freelance submissions: 80%; number bought each year: n/i.

Editorial Needs. Nonfiction—how-to; techniques; first-person viewpoint. Suggested word length—feature articles: 1500-2500. Payment offered: $150-$350.

Initial Contact. Complete manuscript.

Acceptance Policies. Byline given: yes. Payment made: upon acceptance. Kill fee: no. Writer's expenses on assignment: no. Response time to initial inquiry: 2 months. Average time until publication: 6 months. Computer printouts: yes. Dot matrix: letter quality. Disk submissions: no. Publishing rights: all or first-time.

Photography Submissions. Good black and white photos are very important; no color. Format and film: black-and-white prints, 5x7 or larger. Photographs should include: captions; identification of subjects. **Payment:** included with article ($100 for cover transparencies, 35mm). Photographic rights: same as article.

Additional Information. Tips: Write with humor and know your archery terms and subject. We will help edit. Writer's guidelines: call or write.

CA CRAFT CONNECTION NEWSPAPER. PO Box 1280. Pine Grove, CA 95665-1280. (209) 295-4644. Submissions Editor: E. S. Matz. Type: professional crafters (not for hobbyists). Frequency of publication: bimonthly. Circulation: 8000. Freelance submissions: 90%; number bought each year: 12.

Editorial Needs. Nonfiction—how-to; interview/profile; marketing crafts; home-based crafts business. Suggested word length—feature articles: up to 1000. Payment offered: $.05 per word for original article; $.03 for reprint.

Initial Contact. Entire article.

Acceptance Policies. Byline given: yes. Payment made: upon publication. Kill fee: no. Writer's expenses on assignment: no. Submit seasonal material 2 months in advance. Simultaneous submissions: yes. Response time to initial inquiry: 1 week. Average time until publication: n/i. Computer printouts: yes. Dot matrix: yes. Disk submissions: no. Publishing rights: n/i.

Photography Submissions. Format and film. Film: black-and-white or color prints. Photographs should include: identification of subjects. **Payment:** n/i. Photographic rights: n/i.

Additional Information. We are a trade publication for professional craftspeople. We include a show calendar. Writer's guidelines: call or write.

CALIFORNIA. 11601 Wilshire Blvd., Ste. 1800. Los Angeles, CA 90025. (213) 479-6511. Submissions Editor: Rebecca Levy. Type: any subject with a California slant. Frequency of publication: monthly. Circulation: n/i. Freelance submissions: 90%; number bought each year: a large number.

Editorial Needs. Fiction—state of California tie-in. Short stories—per year: 2-3. Payment offered: varies. Nonfiction—book excerpts; book reviews; entertainment reviews; fillers; general interest; health/fitness; historical; how-to; humor; inspiration; interview/profile; photo feature; poetry; self-improvement; travel. Suggested word length—feature articles: we read anything, any length. Payment offered: varies.

Initial Contact. Query letter.

Acceptance Policies. Byline given: yes. Payment made: upon publication. Kill fee: 25%. Writer's expenses on assignment: sometimes. Submit seasonal material 2 months in advance. Simultaneous submissions: yes. Response time to initial inquiry: 6 weeks. Average time until publication: 3-5 months. Computer printouts: yes. Dot matrix: yes. Disk submissions: no. Publishing rights: first rights.

Photography submissions. Format and film: black-and-white prints; color transparencies. Photographs should include: captions; model releases; identification of subjects. **Payment:** varies. Photographic rights: first-time rights.

Additional Information. Tips: Be sure your article involves California, and read the magazine before making a submission. Writer's guidelines: none.

CALIFORNIA BUSINESS. 4221 Wilshire Blvd., Ste. 400. Los Angeles, CA 90010. (213) 937-5820. Submissions Editor: Michael Kolbenschlag. Type: business in California, Mexico, and the Pacific Rim. Frequency of publication: monthly. Circulation: 130,000. Freelance submissions: 50%; number bought each year: 45+/-.

Editorial Needs. Nonfiction—interview/profile; business exposé. Suggested word length—feature articles: 2000-4000. Payment offered: $1500-$4000 (assigned).

Initial Contact. Query letter. State availability of photos.

Acceptance Policies. Byline given: yes. Payment made: upon acceptance. Kill fee: 30%. Writer's expenses on assignment: yes. Submit seasonal material 6 months in advance. Response time to initial inquiry: 1 month. Average time until publication: 3 months. Computer printouts: yes. Dot matrix: letter quality. Disk submissions: modem only. Publishing rights: first North American serial rights.

Photography Submissions. Format and film: transparencies. Photographs should include: captions; model releases. **Payment:** n/i. Photographic rights: one-time rights.

Additional Information. Writer's guidelines: #10 SASE, 4 first class stamps.

CALIFORNIA FARMER. 731 Market St. San Francisco, CA 94103. (415) 495-3340. Submissions Editor: Ann Senuta. Type: agricultural (California only). Frequency of publication: semimonthly. Circulation: 53,000. Freelance submissions: 50%; number bought each year: 70.

Editorial Needs. Nonfiction—how-to. Suggested word length—feature articles: 1500-2000. Payment offered: $400 plus expenses.

Initial Contact. Query letter. Include resumé and published clips.

Acceptance Policies. Byline given: yes. Payment made: upon acceptance. Kill fee: only for assigned stories. Writer's expenses on assignment: yes. Simultaneous submissions: no. Response time to initial inquiry: 4 weeks. Average time until publication: 1-3 months. Computer printouts: yes. Dot matrix: yes. Disk submissions: ASCII. Publishing rights: first North American serial rights.

Photography Submissions. Format and film: color transparencies; black-and-white proof sheets. Photographs should include: captions; identification of subjects. **Payment:** $50-125 for color (depending upon size used in magazine); $35-$100 for black-and-white. Photographic rights: first rights.

CALIFORNIA HIGHWAY PATROLMAN. 2030 V Street. Sacramento, CA 95818. (916) 452-6751. Submissions Editor: Carol Perri. Type: general interest. Frequency of publication: monthly. Circulation: 19,000. Freelance submissions: 80%; number bought each year: 100-150.

Editorial Needs. Fiction—short stories. Payment offered: $.025 per word. **Nonfiction**—automobiles; general interest; health/fitness; historical; humor; photo feature; self-improvement; travel; safety. Suggested word length—feature articles: as long as necessary. Payment offered: $.025 per word.

Initial Contact. Query letter; outline. Include author's expertise in area; SASE.

Acceptance Policies. Byline given: yes. Payment made: upon publication. Kill fee: no. Writer's expenses on assignment: no. Submit seasonal material 3-6 months in advance. Simultaneous submissions: yes; inform us where else submitted or previously published. Response time to initial inquiry: 2 months. Average time until publication: varies. Computer printouts: yes. Dot matrix: yes. Disk submissions: Macintosh. Publishing rights: one-time use.

Photography Submissions. Format and film: black-and-white prints, any size, but very clear. Photographs should include: captions; identification of subjects; credit line. **Payment:** $5 each. Photographic rights: one-time use, all photos returned.

Additional Information. We are a two-person staff, so rejects are sent back immediately, but patience is requested for others. Tips: Good writing! Writer's guidelines and sample copy: SASE.

CALIFORNIA HORSE REVIEW. PO Box 2437. Fair Oaks, CA 95628.
(916) 638-1519. Submissions Editor: Jennifer F. Meyer. Type: all breeds horse magazine. Frequency of publication: monthly. Circulation: 6500. Freelance submissions: 70%; number bought each year: 24.

Editorial Needs. Nonfiction—book reviews; fillers; how-to; humor; interview/profile; video reviews. Suggested word length—feature articles: 500-1500. Payment offered: $25-$125.

Initial Contact. Entire article.

Acceptance Policies. Byline given: yes. Payment made: upon publication. Kill fee: no. Writer's expenses on assignment: no. Simultaneous submissions: yes; inform us, specific details. Response time to initial inquiry: 6-8 weeks. Average time until publication: 2-3 months. Dot matrix: no. Disk submissions: no. Computer printouts: yes. Publishing rights: first North American serial rights.

Photography Submissions. Format and prints: black-and-white prints, 5x7. Photographs should include: captions; identification of subjects. **Payment:** purchased with article only. Photographic rights: first-time rights.

Additional Information. Writer's guidelines: SASE.

CALIFORNIA JOURNAL. 1714 Capitol Ave. Sacramento, CA 95814.
(916) 444-2840. Submissions Editor: Richard Zeiger. Type: politics and government. Frequency of publication: monthly. Circulation: 19,000. Freelance submissions: 75%; number bought each year: 50+.

Editorial Needs. Nonfiction—politics and government. Suggested word length—feature articles: open. Payment offered: payment negotiable.

Initial Contact. Query letter; entire article. Include background of author; clips.

Acceptance Policies. Byline given: yes. Payment made: upon publication. Kill fee: no. Writer's expenses on assignment: no. Simultaneous submissions: no. Response time to initial inquiry: 1 month. Average time until publication: 1-2 months. Computer printouts: yes. Dot matrix: yes. Disk submissions: IBM PC. Publishing rights: all.

Additional Information. Writer's guidelines: upon request.

CALIFORNIA LAWYER. 1390 Market St., Ste. 1016. San Francisco, CA 94102. (415) 558-9888. Submissions Editors: Thomas K. Brom; Gordon Smith (illustrations). Type: trade. Frequency of publication: monthly. Circulation: 125,000. Freelance submissions: 80%; number bought each year: 60.

Editorial Needs. Nonfiction—current legal affairs; in-depth legal features and profiles; book reviews; interview/profile; current legal affairs reporting. Suggested word length—feature articles: 3000; news articles: 750-1000; columns: 2000. Payment offered: news section to $200; departments $300-$400; features $600-$1000.

Initial Contact. Query letter; article proposal with subject outline; entire article. Include previously published work.

Acceptance Policies. Byline given: yes. Payment made: upon acceptance. Kill fee: 1/3 article fee. Writer's expenses on assignment: yes. Simultaneous submissions: no. Response time to initial inquiry: 2 weeks. Average time until publication: 2 months. Computer printouts: yes. Dot matrix: yes. Disk submissions: 3 1/2" IBM. Publishing rights: first North American serial rights; reprints by nonprofit, educational organizations.

Photography Submissions. Format and film: slides; black-and-white prints; contact sheets. Photographs should include: model releases; identification of subjects. **Payment:** varies by assignment.

Additional Information. Tips: Knowledge of the law and legal practice vital. Writer's guidelines: SASE.

CALIFORNIANS: THE MAGAZINE OF CALIFORNIA HISTORY, THE. 5720 Ross Branch Rd. Sebastopol, CA 95472. (707) 887-9834. Submissions Editor: Jean Sherrell. Type: historic California's development, life, and literature. Frequency of publication: 6 times per year. Circulation: 19,000. Freelance submissions: 66%; number bought each year: 30-40+.

Editorial Needs. Fiction—short stories—illuminating some aspect of California history. Suggested word length—3000-5000. Payment offered: $.01 per word plus 10 author's copies. Nonfiction—historical; historical opinion. Suggested word length—6000-8000. Payment offered: $.01 per word plus 10 author's copies.

Initial Contact. Entire article, if already written. Otherwise request writer's guidelines and read them before submitting material.

Acceptance Policies. Byline given: yes. Payment made: upon publication. Kill fee: no. Writer's expenses: no. Seasonal material: 1 year in advance (we often schedule 2-3 years in advance). Simultaneous submissions: no. Response time to initial inquiry: 1-2 months. Average time until publication: 6 months to 3 years. Computer printouts: yes. Dot matrix: yes. Disk submissions: IBM compatible. Publishing rights: n/i.

Photography Submissions. Format and film: black-and-white prints, any size. Photographs should include: historical documentation, full source credits. **Payment:** author's expenses. Photographic rights: n/i.

Additional Information. We are deluged with manuscripts, but we give each a fair reading which is why our response is so delayed. Tips: We are a reference publications. Quality and depth of research is a first concern; writing style is secondary only. As our name implies, our focus is on people. We look for good biographical-quality character development, motivation, and as many quotes from the person as possible. This makes the very best history. Sample copy: Buy one from us or the newsstand. Writer's guidelines: SASE.

CALIFORNIA NURSING REVIEW. 1470 Halford Ave. Santa Clara, CA 95051. (408) 249-5877. Submissions Editor: Jeroo Captain. Type: nursing. Frequency of publication: every 2 months. Circulation: 210,000 California RNs. Freelance submissions: n/i; number bought each year: n/i.

Editorial Needs. Nonfiction—articles related to nursing. Suggested word length—feature articles: 2000. Payment offered: varies.

Initial Contact. Article proposal with subject outline. Include resumé of writer.

Acceptance Policies. Byline given: n/i. Payment made: upon publication. Kill fee: no. Writer's expenses on assignment: no. Submit seasonal material 4 months in advance. Simultaneous submissions: no. Response time to initial inquiry: 6 weeks. Average time until publication: 2-4 months. Computer printouts: yes. Dot matrix: no. Disk submissions: yes. Publishing rights: all rights.

Photography Submissions. Format and film: color prints. Photographs should include: captions; model releases; identification of subjects. **Payment:** n/i. Photographic rights: n/i.

Additional Information. Writer's guidelines: upon request.

CALIFORNIA STATE POETRY QUARTERLY (CQ). 1200 E. Ocean Blvd., #64. Long Beach, CA 90802. (213) 495-0925. Submissions Editor: John M. Brander. Type: poetry. Frequency of publication: 3 times per year. Circulation: 700. Freelance submissions: 65%. Payment in copies.

Editorial Needs. Nonfiction—poetry. Payment offered: copies.

Initial Contact. Entire submission.

Acceptance Policies. Byline given: no. Payment made: in copies. Simultaneous submissions: okay, but not preferred. Response time to initial inquiry: 4-5 months. Average time until publication: 3-6 months. Computer printouts: yes. Dot matrix: no. Disk submissions: no. Publishing rights: n/i.

Additional Information. Tips: Submitting at least six poems with only one being longer than a page is preferred and gives the writer a better chance of being read. Writer's guidelines: upon request.

CAR CRAFT. 8490 Sunset Blvd. Los Angeles, CA 90069. (213) 657-5100, ext 345. Submissions Editor: Jim McGowan. Type: audience 18-34, owners of 1955 and newer muscle cars. Frequency of publication: monthly. Circulation: 450,000. Freelance submissions: n/i; number bought each year: 2-10.

Editorial Needs. Nonfiction—how-to; drag features; do-it-yourself. Suggested word length—feature articles: any. Payment offered: $100-$200 per page; rate higher for complete submissions (photos, captions, titles, etc.).

Initial Contact. Query letter.

Acceptance Policies. Byline given: yes. Payment made: upon publication. Kill fee: n/i. Writer's expenses on assignment: n/i. Response time to initial inquiry: n/i. Average time until publication: n/i. Computer printouts: yes. Dot matrix: n/i. Disk submissions: no. Publishing rights: all rights.

Photography Submissions. Will purchase separate photos. Format and film: black-and-white glossy prints, 8x10; color, 35mm or 2 1/4 x 2 1/4. Photographs should include: caption. **Payment:** $30, black-and-white; color, negotiable. Photographic rights: n/i.

Additional Information. Tips: Review past issues before coming up with ideas or making submissions.

CAT FANCY. PO Box 6050. Mission Viejo, CA 92690. (714) 855-8822. Submissions Editor: K. E. Segnar. Type: for cat owners. Frequency of publication: monthly. Circulation: 332,000. Freelance submissions: 80-90%; number bought each year: 80.

Editorial Needs. Fiction—cats in any genre (none that speak). Payment offered: $.05 per word (more for complete story/photo submission). **Nonfiction**—historical; how-to; photo feature; personal experience; medical; technical. Suggested word length—feature articles: 500-3000. Payment offered: $.05 per word (more for complete story/photo submission). Columns; fillers; unique items; cartoons. Suggested word length—100-500 words. Payment offered: $25-$30.

Initial Contact. Query letter or complete manuscript (nonfiction); complete manuscript (fiction).

Acceptance Policies. Byline given: yes. Payment made: after publication. Kill fee: n/i. Writer's expenses on assignment: n/i. Submit seasonal material 4 months in advance. Response time to initial inquiry: 6 weeks. Average time until publication: n/i. Computer printouts: yes. Dot matrix: n/i. Disk submissions: no. Publishing rights: first North American serial rights.

Photography Submissions. Will also purchase separate photos. Format and film: black-and-white glossy prints, 8x10; color transparencies, 35mm or 2 1/4 x 2 1/4. Photographs should include: model release. **Payment:** $15 (black and white); $50-$150 (color). Photographic rights: n/i.

Additional Information. Tips: We need the longer well-researched article rather than fillers. Writer's guidelines: SASE.

CHIPS OFF THE WRITER'S BLOCK and FICTION FORUM. PO Box

83371. Los Angeles, CA 90083. Submissions Editor: Wanda Windham. Type: *Chips* is on the craft of writing, and *Fiction Forum* is a showcase for short stories. Frequency of publication: *Chips*, 6 times per year; *Fiction Forum*, 4 times per year. Circulation: 500+. Freelance submissions: 100%; number used each year: 100. Payment in copies.

Editorial Needs. Fiction—open to all genres. Suggested word length—1200. Payment offered: 1 copy with byline. Short Stories—all genres. Suggested word length—1200. Payment offered: 1 copy and byline. **Nonfiction**—articles related to craft of writing, short stories; some poetry. Suggested word length—500-1200. Payment offered: 1 copy and byline. Columns—anything of interest to writers. Suggested word length—500 words. Payment offered: 1 copy and byline. Fillers—writing related.

Initial Contact. Query letter or entire article.

Acceptance Policies. Byline given: yes. Payment made: in copies. Seasonal material: 6 months in advance. Simultaneous submissions: yes, advise us. Response time to initial inquiry: 2-4 weeks. Average time until publication: 3-6 months. Computer printouts: yes. Dot matrix: yes, but not preferred. Disk submissions: no. Publishing rights: first North American serial rights; second serial rights.

Additional Information. *Chips Off the Writer's Block* provides how-to inspiration for writers. *Fiction Forum* encourages beginning short story writers. Tips: Submit an article of interest to writers with direct how-to information. Personal experience also related to first sale, etc. Sample copy: $3. Writer's guidelines: SASE.

CHURCH EDUCATOR. 2861-C Saturn St. Brea, CA 92621. (714) 961-0622. Submissions Editors: Robert G. Davidson (youth and adult); Linda Davidson (children's). Type: Christian education. Frequency of publication: monthly. Circulation: 4000. Freelance submissions: 60%; number bought each year: 120.

Editorial Needs. Fiction—children's. Payment offered: $.03 per word. **Nonfiction**—book reviews; how-to's on church educator programs. Suggested word length—feature articles: 700-2000. Payment offered: $.03 per word.

Initial Contact. Entire article.

Acceptance Policies. Byline given: yes. Payment made: upon publication. Kill fee: no. Writer's expenses on assignment: no. Submit seasonal material 6 months in advance. Simultaneous submissions: yes. Response time to initial inquiry: 2-3 months. Average time until publication: 4-5 months. Computer printouts: yes. Dot matrix: yes. Disk submissions: no. Publishing rights: all rights.

Photography Submissions. Format and film: 3 1/2 x 5 black-and-white prints. Photographs should include: captions; model releases; identification of subjects. **Payment:** $5-$10. Photographic rights: n/i.

Additional Information. Our readers are mostly main-line Christian protestants, so do not submit conservative, fundamental type articles. Writer's guidelines: upon request to Linda Davidson.

CRAZY QUILT LITERARY QUARTERLY. 3341 Adams Ave. San Diego, CA 92116. (619) 576-0104. Submissions Editors: Marsh Cassady, Steve Smith, Scott Byrom (fiction); Nancy Churnin (drama); Jackie Cicchetti (poetry); Edee Suslick (art); Leif Fearn (nonfiction). Type: literary. Frequency of publication: quarterly. Circulation: 200. Freelance submissions: 100%. Payment in copies.

Editorial Needs. Fiction—literary; science fiction. Short stories—number per issue: 3-4; per year: 12-15. Payment offered: 2 copies per accepted submission. **Nonfiction**—about writers; literary criticism. Drama (one act plays): 1-4. Poetry: 15-60. Payment offered: 2 copies per accepted submission.

Initial Contact. Entire article.

Acceptance Policies. Byline given: yes. Payment made: upon publication. Simultaneous submissions: yes. Response time to initial inquiry: 8-10 weeks. Average time until publication: 12-15 months. Computer printouts: yes. Dot matrix: yes. Disk submissions: no. Publishing rights: first North American serial rights.

Photography Submissions. Format and film: black-and-white prints. Photographs should include: n/i. **Payment:** 2 copies per photo. Photographic rights: first North American serial rights.

Additional Information. Annual fiction/poetry contest; annual chapbook contest with publication. Writer's guidelines: SASE.

CREATIVE WITH WORDS PUBLICATIONS. PO Box 223226. Carmel, CA 93922. (408) 649-1862. Submissions Editor: Brigitta Geltrich. Type: general interest; children (for and by); senior citizens (for and by); folklore; poetry and prose. Frequency of publication: 2-3 times yearly. Circulation: varies. Freelance submissions: 100%. Payment in reduction of cost of copies.

Editorial Needs. Fiction—children's; folklore. Short stories—number per issue: depends on topic; publish according to theme. Payment offered: 20% reduction in cost of copies. **Nonfiction**—varies. Suggested word length—feature articles: 1000. Payment offered: 20% reduction in cost of copies.

Initial Contact. Query letter. Writer should state his/her age if child.

Acceptance Policies. Byline given: yes. Payment made: in copies. Submit seasonal material 2-6 months in advance. Simultaneous submissions: no. Response time to initial inquiry: 2 months. Average time until publication: depends on theme and deadline. Computer printouts: yes. Dot matrix: yes. Disk submissions: TR-80 (TRSDOS: Radio Shack). Publishing rights: first rights.

Additional Information. Tips: Be proficient, yet brief. Include SASE. Accept set rules. Writer's guidelines: SASE.

CURRENT WORLD LEADERS. 800 Garden St., Ste. D. Santa Barbara, CA 93101. (805) 965-5010. Fax (805) 965-6071. Submissions Editor: Thomas S. Garrison, editorial director. Type: international relations; comparative politics. Frequency of publication: 6 issues per year. Circulation: 1000. Freelance submissions: 25-50%. Number of articles reprinted each year: 10-15.

Editorial Needs. Nonfiction—historical; political, especially international politics; photo feature. Suggested word length—feature articles: 4500-13,500. Payment offered: $25-$100. Columns: international relations and comparative politics. Suggested word length: 450-2250. Payment offered: yes.

Initial Contact. Article proposal with subject outline. Include evidence of author's expertise in subject area.

Acceptance Policies. Byline given: yes. Payment made: upon publication. Kill fee: no. Writer's expenses on assignment: no. Simultaneous submissions: no. Response time to initial inquiry: 2 weeks. Average time until publication: 6 months. Computer printouts: yes. Dot matrix: yes. Disk submissions: Word Perfect 4.2 or 5.0. Publishing rights: first rights.

Photography Submissions. Format and film: black-and-white 4x6 prints. Photographs should include: captions; model releases; identification of subjects. **Payment:** $10-$25. Photographic rights: first rights.

Additional Information. Writer's guidelines and sample copy: upon request.

DANCE TEACHER NOW. 3020 Beacon Blvd. West Sacramento, CA 95691-3436. (916) 373-0201. Submission Editor: K. C. Patrick. Type: trade publication for dance. Frequency of publication: 9 times per year. Circulation: 7000. Freelance submissions: n/i; number bought each year: 40.

Editorial Needs. Nonfiction—book reviews; health/fitness; how-to; humor; inspiration; interview/profile; self-improvement; travel. Suggested word length—feature articles: 2500-3000. Payment offered: $150-$400; varies with length, complexity.

Initial Contact. Query letter; article proposal with subject outline; entire article.

Acceptance Policies. Byline given: yes. Payment made: upon publication. Kill fee: no. Writer's expenses on assignment: some; usually telephone. Submit seasonal material 4-6 months in advance. Simultaneous submissions: yes, if not being submitted in dance industry. Response time to initial inquiry: 4 weeks. Average time until publication: 4-6 months. Computer printouts: yes. Dot matrix: letter quality. Disk submissions: IBM compatible; Word Star, Word Perfect; ASCII. Publishing rights: all rights; released back to author, on request, in most cases.

Photography Submissions. Format and film: black-and-white or color contact sheets, prints, slides, or color transparencies. Photographs should include: captions; model releases; identification of subjects; credits. **Payment:** negotiable. Photographic rights: negotiable.

Additional Information. Tips: Prefer written queries. Writer's guidelines and sample copy: upon request.

DOG FANCY. PO Box 6050. Mission Viejo, CA 92690. Submissions Editor: K. E. Segnar. See information under **CAT FANCY.**

DOLPHIN LOG, THE. (The Cousteau Society). 8440 Santa Monica Blvd. Los Angeles, CA 90069. (213) 656-4422. Submissions Editor: Beth Kneeland. Type: (for children) ecology; marine biology; environment; natural history. Frequency of publication: bimonthly. Circulation: 100,000. Freelance submissions: 25%.

Editorial Needs. Nonfiction—any area (including games, experiments, humor, jokes, crafts, and articles) that directly relates to the ecological global water system and that will encourage young people to understand and respect the environment. Suggested word length—feature articles: 500-1000. Payment offered: $25-$150.

Initial Contact. Query letter; or complete manuscript.

Acceptance Policies. Byline given: yes. Payment made: upon publication. Kill fee: no. Writer's expenses on assignment: no. Submit seasonal material 4 months in advance. Response time to initial inquiry: 1 month. Average time until publication: n/i. Computer printouts: yes. Dot matrix: letter quality. Disk submissions: no. Publishing rights: one-time; translation.

Photography Submissions. Send with manuscript. Only duplicates accepted, no originals. Format and film: n/i. Photographs should include: identification of subject. **Payment:** $25-$100 per photo. Photographic rights: one-time.

Additional Information. Writers should be current in their knowledge and able to write in a lively style appropriate for an audience ages 7-15. Tips: Make sure material is accurate. Feature an interesting marine animal, and make it interesting. No fiction or talking animals. Writer's guidelines: SASE; sample copy $2, SASE.

DR. DOBB'S JOURNAL. 501 Galveston Dr. Redwood City, CA 94061. (415) 366-3600. Submissions Editors: Jon Erickson, Ray Valdes, or Michael Floyd (proposals); Janna Custer (manuscripts). Type: for computer programmers. Frequency of publication: monthly; plus 2 special issues a year. Circulation: 87,000. Freelance submissions: 90%; number bought each year: 100+/-.

Editorial Needs. Nonfiction—book reviews; product reviews; opinion; articles for programers, often including listings. Suggested word length—feature articles: 2500+/-; reviews: 500-1000. Payment offered: varies, depending on length of article, completeness, and author skill and knowledge.

Initial Contact. Article proposal with outline. Include author's address, home and work phone; social security number.

Acceptance Policies. Byline given: yes. Payment made: $50 on acceptance; remainder upon publication. Kill fee: $50. Writer's expenses on assignment: depends. Submit seasonal material 3 months in advance. Simultaneous submissions: only in proposal form rather than full manuscript. Response time to initial inquiry: 1 month. Average time until publication: 6 months. Computer printouts: yes; double spaced. Dot matrix: yes. Disk submissions: pure ASCII unformatted with control codes on either PC compatible (5 1/4 DS/DD) or Macintosh disk. Publishing rights: all.

Photography Submissions. We encourage charts, listings, etc.

Additional Information. *DDJ* readers are advanced programmers, and *DDJ* is primarily a software magazine. Tips: If you submit an article but don't hear from us for a while, call us. Writer's guidelines: write or call Janna Custer.

DUNE BUGGIES AND HOT VWS. PO Box 2260. Costa Mesa, CA 92628. (714) 548-6250. Submissions Editor: Bruce Simurda. Type: automotive enthusiasts. Frequency of publication: monthly. Circulation: 110,000. Freelance submissions 10%; number of manuscripts bought each year: 20.

Editorial Needs. Nonfiction—how-to; photo feature. All articles must be Volkswagen related. Suggested word length—1200. Payment offered: n/i. Columns: by prior arrangement only.

Initial Contact. Query letter.

Acceptance Policies. Byline given: yes. Payment made: upon publication. Kill fee: no. Writer's expenses: yes. Seasonal material: 3 months in advance. Simultaneous submissions: no. Response time to initial inquiry: 1 month. Average time until publication: 3 months. Computer printouts: yes. Dot matrix: yes. Disk submissions: Macintosh; Macwrite. Publishing rights: first rights.

Photography Submissions. Format and film: black-and-white or color prints, 5x7; contact sheets; transparencies. Photographs should include: captions; model releases; identification of subjects. **Payment:** varies. Photographic rights: first rights.

Additional Information. Writer's guidelines: upon request.

EASYRIDERS MAGAZINE. 28210 Dorothy Dr. Agoura Hills, CA 91301. (818) 889-8740. Submissions Editor: Keith Ball. Type: men's magazine for riders of Harley-Davidsons. Frequency of publication: monthly. Circulation: 300,000. Freelance submissions: 40%; number bought each year: 24-30.

Editorial Needs. Fiction—motorcycle (Harley-Davidson) related. Short stories—number per issue: 2; per year: 24. Payment offered: $.10-$.15 per word. Nonfiction—how-to; humor; interview/profile; opinion; photo feature. Suggested word length—feature articles: 3000-5000. Payment offered: $.10-$.15 per word.

Initial Contact. Query letter; article proposal with subject outline.

Acceptance Policies. Byline given: yes. Payment made: upon publication. Kill fee: n/i. Writer's expenses on assignment: yes. Submit seasonal material 4 months in advance. Simultaneous submissions: yes. Response time to initial inquiry: 4-6 weeks. Average time until publication: 3-4 months. Kill fee: n/i. Computer printouts: yes. Dot matrix: yes. Disk submissions: ASCII; IBM or Macintosh. Publishing rights: all rights; work-for-hire assignments.

Photography Submissions. Format and film: black-and-white or color prints; slides; transparencies. Photographs should include: identification of subjects. **Payment:** $40 (color); $30 (black and white). Photographic rights: first rights.

Additional Information. Our magazine has a macho male audience who rides Harley-Davidson motorcycles only. Writer's guidelines: upon request.

ECPHORIZER. 481 Century Dr. Campbell, CA 95008. (408) 378-8820. Submissions Editor: Michael J. Eager. Type: Literary and idea oriented. The name means to take a concept from a latent form to a real state. Frequency of publication: 6 times per year. Circulation: 350. Freelance submissions: 85%. Payment in copies.

Editorial Needs. Fiction—literary; women's; genre. Short stories—number per issue: 5. Payment offered: copies. Nonfiction—book excerpts; book reviews; fillers; general interest; historical; humor; interview/profile; opinion; poetry; travel. Suggested word length—feature articles: 1000-5000. Payment offered: copies.

Initial Contact. Query letter; article proposal with subject outline; entire article.

Acceptance Policies. Byline given: yes. Payment made: in copies. Submit seasonal material 4 months in advance. Simultaneous submissions: yes. Response time to initial inquiry: 4 weeks. Average time until publication: 3-6 months. Computer printouts: yes. Dot matrix: yes. Disk submissions: IBM PC; ASCII; Macintosh MacWrite. Publishing rights: n/i.

Photography Submissions. Format and film: black-and-white prints, 5x7 or larger. Photographs should include: captions; model releases; identification of subjects. **Payment:** none. Photographic rights: n/i.

Additional Information. Ecphorize means to evoke ideas. We are a non-profit magazine oriented toward the Mensa community, with interest in articles which are provocative or humorous. Complementary copies only.

ELLIPSIS. 1176 E. Campbell Ave. Campbell, CA 95008. (408) 559-7283, 354-1481. Submissions Editor: Jonathan Ther. Type: literary. Frequency of publication: biannual. Circulation: 300 and growing. Freelance submissions: 100%; number bought each year: 30-40.

Editorial Needs. Fiction—avant-garde; fantasy; humor; literary; women's. Short stories—number per issue: 12; per year: 24. Payment offered: $5 minimum; $.01 per word; 2 copies of issue and discount for additional copies. **Nonfiction**—poetry; opinion section is open to essays of a philosophical bent. Suggested word length—feature articles: 1500-5000. Payment offered: $5 minimum; $.01 per word; 2 copies of issue and discount for additional copies.

Initial Contact. Query letter; entire article.

Acceptance Policies. Byline given: yes. Payment made: upon publication. Kill fee: $5 minimum or 50%. Writer's expenses on assignment: no. Simultaneous submissions: yes; inform us. Response time to initial inquiry: 3 months. Average time until publication: 6 months. Computer printouts: yes. Dot matrix: yes. Disk submissions: Macintosh. Publishing rights: first North American serial rights; second serial rights (on occasion).

Additional Information. We are interested in unpublished writers. We are looking for unique use of language—stories and poetry that reflect the human condition with sensitivity, grace, depth, and humor. Tips: Do not send personally cathartic writing unless it is prize-winning material! Writer's guidelines: SASE.

EMMY MAGAZINE. (Academy of Television Arts & Sciences). 3500 W. Olive, Ste. 700. Burbank, CA 91505-4628. Editor/Publisher: Hank Rieger. Type: focus on thoughtful analysis of television's impact on society. Magazine is read by TV industry as well as general subscribers, so articles must be appropriate for both. Frequency of publication: bimonthly. Circulation: 15,000. Freelance submissions: 100%; number bought each year: 40.

Editorial Needs. Nonfiction—interview/profile; opinion; current topics; humor; nostalgia. Suggested word length—feature articles: n/i. Payment offered: $450-$1000. Columns—opinion. Suggested word length—800-1500 words. Payment offered: $450-$650.

Initial Contact. Query. Include clips.

Acceptance Policies. Byline given: yes. Payment made: upon publication. Kill fee: 20%. Writer's expenses on assignment: sometimes. Response time to initial inquiry: 3-4 weeks. Average time until publication: 3 months. Computer printouts: yes. Dot matrix: letter quality. Disk submissions: no. Publishing rights: first North American serial rights.

Additional Information. *Emmy* is not a fan magazine; do not send these types of articles. Tips: Make sure your query letter accurately describes your article. Do not call. Read the magazine first (9x12 SASE, 5 first class stamps).

ENTREPRENEUR. 2392 Morse Ave. Irvine, CA 92714. (714) 261-2325. Submissions Editor: Maria Anton. Type: business. Frequency of publication: monthly. Circulation: 250,000. Freelance submissions: 10-20%; number bought each year: 30-40.

Editorial Needs. Nonfiction—how-to; interview/profile. Suggested word length—feature articles: 500-750; 1750-2000. Payment offered: $200-$400.

Initial Contact. Query letter; article proposal with subject outline; outline specifically who/what you plan to write about and why. Get to the point immediately in the submission.

Acceptance Policies. Byline given: yes. Payment made: upon acceptance. Kill fee: yes; 20%. Writer's expenses on assignment: varies. Submit seasonal material 6-7 months in advance. Simultaneous submissions: no. Response time to initial inquiry: 6-8 weeks. Average time until publication: varies. Computer printouts: yes. Dot matrix: yes. Disk submissions: no. Publishing rights: all rights.

Photography Submissions. Format and film: color transparencies. Photographs should include: model releases; identification of subjects. **Payment:** n/i. Photographic rights: n/i.

Additional Information. We are a national magazine, aimed at the person wanting to start a business or already in business and seeking additional guidance and assistance. Tips: Read the magazine before querying. Put address and phone on every page of query. Writer's guidelines: SASE. For sample of magazine send $3.

FAMILY MAGAZINE. PO Box 4993. Walnut Creek, CA 94596. (415) 284-9093. Submissions Editor: Janet A. Venturino. Type: military. Frequency of publication: monthly. Circulation: 550,000. Freelance submissions 99%; number of manuscripts bought each year: 10.

Editorial Needs. Fiction—women's. Suggested word length—1500-2000. Payment offered: $100-$300. Short Stories—of interest to military wives. Suggested word length—1500-2000. Payment offered: $100-$300. Nonfiction—general interest; health/fitness; how-to; humor; self-improvement. Suggested word length—1500. Payment offered: $100-$300.

Initial Contact. Query letter; article proposal with subject outline; entire article.

Acceptance Policies. Byline given: yes. Payment made: upon publication. Kill fee: 25%. Writer's expenses: no. Seasonal material: 6 months in advance. Simultaneous submissions: yes, if they are not to competing magazines in the military market. Response time to initial inquiry: 4-6 weeks. Average time until publication: 6-12 months. Computer printouts: yes. Dot matrix: yes. Disk submissions: no. Publishing rights: first North American serial rights.

Photography Submissions. Format and film: black-and-white or color prints, 8x10; transparencies. Photographs should include: captions; model releases; identification of subjects. **Payment:** $25 black and white; $50 color; $150 cover. Photographic rights: n/i.

Additional Information. We do not want poetry or cartoons. Sample copy: $1.25. Writer's guidelines: SASE.

FAMILY THERAPY. (Subsidiary of Libra Publishers, Inc.) 3089C Clairemont Dr., Ste. 383. San Diego, CA 92117. (619) 581-9449. Submissions Editor: Martin Blinder, M.D. Type: professional journal. Frequency of publication: 3 times per year. Circulation: 1000. Freelance submissions: 100%. No payment offered.

Editorial Needs. Nonfiction—articles on marital and family therapy. Suggested word length—feature articles: 2400. Payment offered: none.

Initial Contact. Submission of abstract.

Acceptance Policies. Byline given: yes. Payment made: none. Simultaneous submissions: no. Response time to initial inquiry: 3 weeks. Average time until publication: 6-12 months. Computer printouts: yes. Dot matrix: yes. Disk submissions: no. Publishing rights: all.

Additional Information. Writer's guidelines: upon request.

FAMILY TRAVEL GUIDES CATALOGUE, THE. PO Box 6061. Albany, CA 94706. (415) 527-5849. Submissions Editor: Carole T. Meyers. Type: family travel. Frequency of publication: annual. Circulation: 30,000. Freelance submissions: sell reprinted articles; number bought each year: 5-10.

Editorial Needs. Nonfiction—travel; columns (family travel). Suggested word length—feature articles: 750-1500; columns: 750-1500. Payment offered: 10% commission on each reprint copy of article sold through catalog; usually $3-$5 each sale.

Initial Contact. Outline. Reprints are preferred.

Acceptance Policies. Byline given: yes. Payment made: at end of year. Simultaneous submissions: yes. Response time to initial inquiry: 1 month. Average time until publication: next annual catalog. Computer printouts: yes. Dot matrix: yes. Disk submissions: no. Publishing rights: second serial rights.

Additional Information. Writer's guidelines and sample catalog: #10 SASE; $.45 postage.

FEMINIST BOOKSTORE NEWS. PO Box 882554. San Francisco, CA 94188. (415) 626-1556. Submissions Editor: Carol Seajay. Type: feminist publishing and bookselling. Frequency of publication: bimonthly. Circulation: 500. Freelance submissions: n/i. Payment in subscription or issues.

Editorial Needs. Nonfiction—book excerpts; book reviews; interview/profile. Suggested word length—feature articles: 500. Payment offered: subscription or issues.

Initial Contact. Query letter. Include your experience in the book trade.

Acceptance Policies. Byline given: yes. Payment made: subscription or issues. Simultaneous submissions: no. Response time to initial inquiry: 6 weeks. Average time until publication: 3 months. Computer printouts: yes. Dot matrix: yes. Disk submissions: yes; must be accompanied by hard copy. Publishing rights: n/i.

Photography Submissions. Format and film: 4x6 black-and-white prints. Photographs should include: captions; model releases; identification of subjects. Payment: copies. Photographic rights: n/i.

Additional Information. We publish only nonfiction articles about the feminist book trade. Ninety-five percent of our articles are written by women working in the book trade.

FESSENDEN REVIEW. PO Box 7272. San Diego, CA 92107. (619) 488-4991. Submissions Editor: Mike Jennings. Type: literary book review. Frequency of publication: quarterly. Circulation: Freelance submissions: 20%; number of manuscripts bought per year: 50.

Editorial Needs. Nonfiction—book reviews, most with illustrations. Suggested word length—feature articles: 200-2000. Payment offered: $30. Columns—brief reviews, nontraditional, humorous. Suggested word length—200-500. Payment offered: $15.

Initial Contact. Complete manuscript. Include availability of photos.

Acceptance Policies. Byline given: no. Payment made: upon publication. Kill fee: no. Writer's expenses on assignment: no. Simultaneous submissions: n/i. Response time to initial inquiry: 3 months. Average time until publication: 3-6 months. Computer printouts: yes. Dot matrix: no. Disk submissions: query. Publishing rights: one-time.

Photography Submissions. State availability with manuscript submission.

Additional Information. Tips: Know your subject; send for sample copy, 9x12 SASE, 9 first class stamps.

Fiction Forum *see* **CHIPS OFF THE WRITER'S BLOCK.**

FILM QUARTERLY. University of California Press. 2120 Berkeley Way. Berkeley, CA 94720. (415) 642-6333. Submissions Editor: Ernest Callenbach. Type: film criticism. Frequency of publication: quarterly. Circulation: 6700. Freelance submissions: 100%; number bought each year: 50.

Editorial Needs. Nonfiction—book reviews; film reviews; critical articles; some history and theory; columns: film reviews. Suggested word length—feature articles: 5000-6000; columns: 1500. Payment offered: $.02+ per word; two gratis copies.

Initial Contact. Query letter; entire article or sample page for proposed or another article.

Acceptance Policies. Byline given: yes. Payment made: upon publication. Kill fee: no. Writer's expenses on assignment: no. Simultaneous submissions: yes; inform us. Response time to initial inquiry: 2 weeks. Average time until publication: 2 months. Computer printouts: yes. Dot matrix: a real handicap. Disk submissions: no. Publishing rights: all rights; we then split subsidiary (reprint) payments 50/50.

Photography Submissions. Only if free with article. Format and film: black-and-white prints, 4x5. Photographs should include: captions.

Additional Information. We are extremely specialized, and writers must have a serious knowledge of film to have much chance of acceptance. We don't have a substantial backlog like many other scholarly journals. Tips: Would-be contributors must study back issues carefully and have a good film background.

FITNESS MANAGEMENT, THE MAGAZINE FOR PROFESSIONALS IN ADULT PHYSICAL FITNESS. PO Box 1198. Solana Beach, CA 92075. (619) 481-4155. Submissions Editor: Edward H. Pitts. Type: fitness centers. Frequency of publication: monthly. Circulation: 21,000. Freelance submissions: 50%; number bought each year: 30.

Editorial Needs. Nonfiction—book excerpts; how-to; new product; photo feature; technical; health and research in industry. Suggested word length—feature articles: 750-2000. Payment offered: $60-$300 (assigned); $160 (unsolicited).

Initial Contact. Query letter.

Acceptance Policies. Byline given: yes. Payment made: upon publication. Kill fee: 50%. Writer's expenses on assignment: yes. Submit seasonal material 6 months in advance. Simultaneous submissions: no. Response time to initial inquiry: 1 month. Average time until publication: 5 months. Computer printouts: yes. Dot matrix: letter quality. Disk submissions: query. Publishing rights: all.

Photography Submissions. Send with manuscript. Format and film: black-and-white and color contact sheets; 5x7 prints; 2x2, 4x5 transparencies. Photographs should include: captions; model releases. **Payment:** $10. Photographic rights: same as article.

Additional Information. Helps owners, managers, and program directors to better run their establishment. Tips: Author should be current with new happenings in the field; include quotes from people concerned with your subject. Writer's guidelines: #10 SASE; sample copy $5.

FLOWERS&, THE BEAUTIFUL MAGAZINE ABOUT THE BUSINESS OF FLOWERS. 12233 W. Olympic Blvd., Ste. 260. Los Angeles, CA 90064. (213) 826-5253. Submissions Editor: Marie Monysmith. Type: retail florist industry. Frequency of publication: monthly. Circulation: 33,000+. Freelance submissions: 40%; number bought each year: 20.

Editorial Needs. Nonfiction—book excerpts; historical; nostalgia; how-to; interview/profile; new product; technical. Suggested word length—feature articles: 1000-3000. Payment offered: $250-$500.

Initial Contact. Query. Include clips.

Acceptance Policies. Byline given: yes. Payment made: upon acceptance. Kill fee: 20%. Writer's expenses on assignment: sometimes. Submit seasonal material 4 months in advance. Simultaneous submissions: yes. Response time to initial inquiry: 1 month. Average time until publication: 4 months. Computer printouts: yes. Dot matrix: letter quality. Disk submissions: query. Publishing rights: first North American serial rights; second serial rights.

Photography Submissions. Format and film: black-and-white or color contact sheets; 4x5 transparencies. Photographs should include: captions; model releases; identification of subjects. **Payment:** $25-$100 per photo. Photographic rights: one-time rights.

Additional Information. Geared to the small business owner's daily problems and solutions as they apply to the floral industry. Tips: Make sure query letter is direct and covers both your approach to the problem and the solution. Writer's guidelines: #10 SASE; sample copy 9 1/2 x 11 SASE.

FOUR WHEELER. 6728 Eton Ave. Canoga Park, CA 91306. (818) 992-4777. Submissions Editor: John Stewart. Type: hobbyist-enthusiasts for 4x4 vehicles. Frequency of publication: monthly. Circulation: 275,000. Freelance submissions: 30%; number bought each year: 12-15.

Editorial Needs. Nonfiction—how-to; humor; photo feature; travel; truck features. Suggested word length—feature articles: 2000; columns: 750. Payment offered: $100-$1000.

Initial Contact. Query first. If requested, send entire article. Must be accompanied by photos. Include SASE. Read guidelines.

Acceptance Policies. Byline given: yes. Payment made: upon acceptance. Kill fee: yes. Writer's expenses on assignment: no. Submit seasonal material 4 months in advance. Simultaneous submissions: no. Response time to initial inquiry: 3-4 weeks. Average time until publication: n/i. Computer printouts: yes. Dot matrix: yes. Disk submissions: yes. Publishing rights: n/i.

Photography Submissions. We are very particular as to type of film. Format and prints: 35mm color slides; 2 1/2" transparencies; 8x10 black-and-white glossy prints. Photographs should include: captions; model releases; identification of subjects. **Payment:** n/i. Photographic rights: n/i.

Additional Information. Tips: Be sure to read at least six months of current back issues. Writer's guidelines: SASE.

GARGOYLE. 4953 Desmond. Oakland, CA 94618. (415) 658-4645. Submissions Editor: Toby Barlow. Type: literary. Frequency of publication: biannually. Circulation: n/i. Freelance submissions: 100%; number used each year: varies. Payment in copies.

Editorial Needs. Fiction—avant-garde/experimental; contemporary; erotica; general; modern. Suggested word length—n/i. Payment offered: 1 copy. Short Stories—general. Suggested word length—n/i. Payment offered: 1 copy.

Initial Contact. Entire article. Include SASE.

Acceptance Policies. Byline given: yes. Payment made: in copies. Simultaneous submissions: no. Response time to initial inquiry: 2 weeks. Average time until publication: 2-6 months. Computer printouts: yes. Dot matrix: yes. Disk submissions: no. Publishing rights: n/i.

Photography Submissions. Format and film: black-and-white prints. Photographs should include: n/i. **Payment**: in copies. Photographic rights: n/i.

Additional Information. Sample copy: n/i. Writer's guidelines: n/i.

GAS: JOURNAL OF THE GROSS AMERICANS' SOCIETY. PO Box 397. Marina, CA 93933. Submissions Editor: Jeannette M. Hopper. Type: humorous horror, horrible humor, and a touch of the serious to keep you regular. Frequency of publication: twice yearly. Circulation: 250. Freelance submissions: 100%; number bought each year: 50.

Editorial Needs. **Fiction**—women's; mystery; humorous horror (serious considered, if very strong). Short stories—number per issue: 4+; per year: 20+/-. No fiction over 1500 words considered. Payment offered: $.025 cents per word, with $2 minimum (may be credited toward next issue). Willing to consider any form of barter trade. **Nonfiction**—book reviews; entertainment reviews; fillers; how-to; humor; interview/profile; opinion; poetry; puzzles; quizzes (with answers); cartoons; classified advertising; columns. Suggested word length—feature articles: as needed; columns: 1500. Payment offered: $.025 cents per word, with $2 minimum (may be credited toward next issue). $1 per poem. Willing to consider any form of barter trade.

Initial Contact. Query letter; entire article. Include brief personal information; past publications if applicable; indication you have read the magazine.

Acceptance Policies. Byline given: yes. Payment made: upon publication. Kill fee: same as payment. Writer's expenses on assignment: no. Submit seasonal material 6 months in advance. Simultaneous submissions: no. Response time to initial inquiry: 4-6 weeks. Average time until publication: 1 year. Computer printouts: yes. Dot matrix: if dark and clearly readable. Disk submissions: no. Publishing rights: first rights.

Photography Submissions. Format and film: black-and-white (screened) prints. Photographs should include: model releases; identification of subjects. **Payment**: $3 per full-page; $1.50 per half page; $1 per quarter page or spot; cover pays $5 plus 3 copies. (Art work is acceptable according to guidelines and pays the same). Photographic rights: one-time use.

Additional Information. Potential submitters must be familiar with *GAS*, due to its unique slant on the horror/humor genres. Tips: Write well. Do not assume that because *GAS* dwells on the strange and forbidden, inferior writing is acceptable. Writer's guidelines: #10 SASE; sample copy $3.50.

GREEN FUSE. 3365 Holland Dr. Santa Rosa, CA 95404. (707) 544-8303. Submissions Editor: Brian Boldt. Type: dedicated to pursuit of peace and preservation of the planet. Frequency of publication: twice yearly. Circulation: 300. Freelance submissions: 100%. Payment in copies.

Editorial Needs. **Nonfiction**—poetry. Suggested word length—60 lines of poetry maximum. Payment offered: 1 copy.

Initial Contact. No more than three submissions.

Acceptance Policies. Byline given: yes. Payment made: in copies. Submit seasonal material 4 months in advance. Response time to initial inquiry: 2-3 months. Average time until publication: 2 months. Computer printouts: yes. Dot matrix: no. Disk submissions: no. Publishing rights: n/i.

Additional Information. Deadlines are July 15 and January 15. Writer's guidelines: SASE.

GUITAR PLAYER MAGAZINE. 20085 Stevens Creek Blvd. Cupertino, CA 95014. (408) 446-1105. Submissions Editor: Tom Wheeler. Type: all aspects of guitar (for musicians). Frequency of publication: monthly. Circulation: 180,000. Freelance submissions: 50%; number bought each year: 35+/-.

Editorial Needs. Nonfiction—how-to; interview/profile; techniques. Suggested word length—feature articles: open. Payment offered: $100-$300.

Initial Contact. Query letter.

Acceptance Policies. Byline given: yes. Payment made: upon acceptance. Kill fee: yes. Writer's expenses on assignment: sometimes. Response time to initial inquiry: 6 weeks. Average time until publication: 3 months. Computer printouts: yes. Dot matrix: letter quality. Disk submissions: Macintosh; Microsoft Word. Publishing rights: first North American serial rights; second serial rights (limited).

Photography Submissions. Format and film: black-and-white glossy prints; color transparencies. Photographs should include: captions. **Payment:** $35-$50 (black and white); $75-$250 (color transparencies, cover shot). Photographic rights: one-time rights.

Additional Information. Writer's guidelines: #10 SASE.

HAWAII HOTEL NETWORK. 513 Uluhala St. Kailua, HI 96734. (808) 262-4636. Submissions Editor: Camie Foster. Type: in-room magazine for visitors to Hawaii. Frequency of publication: 3 times per year. Circulation: free in more than 17,000 hotel rooms—1.7 million per year. Freelance submissions: 75%; number bought each year: 10-16.

Editorial Needs. Fiction—just beginning to publish fiction. "Pitch" us. Suggested word length—2000-2500. Payment offered: $600 minimum. Short Stories—contemporary. Suggested word length—2000. Payment offered: $600. Nonfiction—historical; interview/profile; travel; Hawaii. Suggested word length—2000. Payment offered: $.30 per word.

Initial Contact. Query letter; article proposal with subject outline. Include tear sheets of previously published works.

Acceptance Policies. Byline given: yes. Payment made: upon acceptance. Kill fee: n/i. Writer's expenses: n/i. Seasonal material: at least 8 months in advance. Simultaneous submissions: no. Response time to initial inquiry: 2-4 weeks. Average time until publication: 6 months. Computer printouts: yes. Dot matrix: yes. Disk submissions: yes, if accompanied by printout. Publishing rights: first North American serial rights; work-for-hire assignments.

Photography Submissions. Format and film: color transparencies. Photographs should include: captions; model releases; identification of subjects. **Payment:** depends on size and placement. Photographic rights: one time, with provision for reuse and payment for each.

Additional Information. Quality is the key. The Hawaii Hotel Network wins visitor writing awards each year from the Hawaii Publishers Association. Tip: Know your subject. Keep in mind that these are visitor magazines, but be aware that we don't treat Hawaii superficially as a paradise where the sun continually sets just beyond the palm trees. Sample copy: upon request, postage required. Writer's guidelines: upon request.

HAWAII MAGAZINE. PO Box 6050. Mission Viejo, CA 92690. (714) 855-8822. Submissions Editor: Dennis Shattuck. Type: general interest for residents and travelers to the Hawaiian Islands. Frequency of publication: bimonthly. Circulation: 60,000. Freelance submissions n/i.; number of manuscripts bought each year: n/i.

Editorial Needs. Nonfiction—book reviews; entertainment reviews; health/fitness; historical; how-to; interview/profile; photo feature; travel. Suggested word length—500-3000.

Payment offered: $100-$300. Columns—*Hopping the Islands* (news items). Suggested word length—50-150. Payment offered: $50-$75.

Initial Contact. Query letter. Include writer's credentials and clips.

Acceptance Policies. Byline given: yes. Payment made: upon publication. Kill fee: no. Writer's expenses: no. Seasonal material: 6 months in advance. Simultaneous submissions: no. Response time to initial inquiry: 90 days. Average time until publication: 90 days. Computer printouts: yes. Dot matrix: yes. Disk submissions: any DOS-based system. Publishing rights: first North American serial rights.

Photography Submissions. Format and film: black-and-white or color prints, 4x5, 8x10; contact sheets; transparencies. Photographs should include: model releases; identification of subjects. **Payment**: $25-$150. Photographic rights: one-time use.

Additional Information. Sample copy: $3.95. Writer's guidelines: SASE.

HAWAII REVIEW. Department of English. University of Hawaii. 1733 Donaghalo Rd. Honolulu, HI 96822. (808) 998-8548. Submissions Editors: Tracy Ellig (nonfiction); Stewart Anderson (fiction). Type: literary. Frequency of publication: quarterly. Circulation: 2000. Freelance submissions: 90%; number bought each year: 100.

Editorial Needs. Fiction—literary. Suggested word length—7000. Payment offered: $5 per page. **Nonfiction**—book excerpts; book reviews; interviews/profile; opinion; poetry. Suggested word length—8000; 500 lines (poetry).

Initial Contact. Entire article. Include SASE.

Acceptance Policies. Byline given: yes. Payment made: upon publication. Kill fee: no. Writer's expenses: no. Simultaneous submissions: yes. Response time to initial inquiry: 2-3 months. Average time until publication: 2-3 months. Computer printouts: yes. Dot matrix: no. Disk submissions: no. Publishing rights: first rights.

Additional Information. Sample copy: $4 plus $1 postage. Writer's guidelines: SASE.

HIBISCUS MAGAZINE. PO Box 22248. Sacramento, CA 95822. Submissions Editors: Margaret Wensrich (fiction, art); Joyce Odam (poetry). Type: literary. Frequency of publication: 3 times per year. Circulation: 1000. Freelance submissions: 100%+/-; number used each year: 10-12 short stories; 40-60 poems; art on commission. Payment in subscription.

Editorial Needs. Fiction—mystery; romance; western; science fiction; fantasy; slice of life. Short stories—number per issue: 2-3; per year: 6-10. Payment offered: one-year subscription ($9.97 value). **Nonfiction**—poetry. Payment offered: one-year subscription ($9.97 value).

Initial Contact. n/i.

Acceptance Policies. Byline given: yes. Payment made: subscription begins with next issue. Submit seasonal material 12 months in advance. Simultaneous submissions: yes. Response time to initial inquiry: 2-4 months. Average time until publication: 1-2 years. Computer printouts: yes. Dot matrix: new black ribbon, double strike. Disk submissions: no. Publishing rights: first North American serial rights.

Additional Information. We do not answer any letter unless accompanied by a SASE. We often cannot return Canadian or overseas manuscripts because author does not include sufficient IRC. Writer's guidelines: SASE with first class postage. Two IRC for each 4 pages of Canadian or foreign manuscripts to pay for return postage. Sample copy $4.

HIGH TECHNOLOGY CAREERS. also *Professional Careers*. c/o Writers Connection. 1601 Saratoga-Sunnyvale Rd., Ste. 180. Cupertino, CA 95014. (408) 973-0227. Submissions Editor: Meera Lester. *High Technology Careers* is circulated in the Sunday edition of the *San Jose Mercury News*. *Professional Careers* is circulated in Southern California. Type: high technology breakthroughs, products, and issues (biotechnology, computers, space, robotics) and their impact on our lives. Directed to engineers and electronic, aerospace, and defense professionals. Frequency of publication: monthly. Circulation: 348,000. Freelance submissions: 100%; number bought each year: 36.

Editorial Needs. Nonfiction—biotechnology; computers; electronics; aerospace; defense; technology; transportation; science; marketing; management; futuristic high technology; new technology applications. Suggested word length—feature articles: 1000-1500; sidebar for article: 500. Payment offered: $.175 per word based on edited, final count.

Initial Contact. Query letter; completed manuscript.

Acceptance Policies. Byline given: yes. Payment made: upon publication. Kill fee: 25%. Writer's expenses on assignment: sometimes. Simultaneous submissions: no. Response time to initial inquiry: 2-4 weeks. Average time until publication: 3 months. Computer printouts: yes. Dot matrix: letter quality. Disk submissions: query for electronic submissions. Publishing rights: all rights.

Additional Information. Our audience includes managers, engineers, and other professionals working in high technology industries. Writer's guidelines: SASE. Sample copy $3.

HINDUISM TODAY. PO Box 157. Hanamaulu, HI 96715. (808) 822-7032. Submissions Editor: Rev. Swami Arumugam Katir. Type: Hindu religion. Frequency of publication: monthly. Circulation: 20,000. Freelance submissions: 20%; number bought each year: 40+.

Editorial Needs. Nonfiction—interview/profile; photo feature. Suggested word length—500-2500. Payment offered: $.05 per word. Column—"My Turn," personal and practical experiences of the writer. Suggested word length—800 words. Payment offered: none.

Initial Contact. Query letter. Include published writings.

Acceptance Policies. Byline given: yes. Payment made: upon publication. Kill fee: $25. Writer's expenses: by arrangement only. Simultaneous submissions: no. Response time to initial inquiry: 1 month. Average time until publication: 1-3 months. Computer printouts: yes. Dot matrix: yes. Disk submissions: ASCII; Macintosh preferred. Publishing rights: all rights.

Photography Submissions. Format and film: 8x10 black and white prints. Photographs should include: identification of subjects. **Payment:** $10. Photographic rights: all.

Additional Information. All articles need to be related to the Hindu religion. Sample copy: upon request. Writer's guidelines: upon request.

HIPPO. 28834 Boniface Dr. Malibu, CA 90255. Submissions Editor: Karl Heiss. Type: literary, social commentary, and artwork. Frequency of publication: biannually. Circulation: 200. Freelance submissions: 100%; number used each year: 26+. Payment in copies.

Editorial Needs. Fiction—surreal, hyper-real; avant-garde/experimental; science fiction; erotica; fantasy; horror; humor; mystery. Suggested word length—100-2000. Payment offered: copy. Short Stories—all subject areas. Suggested word length—100-2000. Payment offered: copy. Nonfiction—interview/profile; opinion; poetry; black-and-white artwork. Suggested word length—3000 maximum. Payment offered: copy.

Initial Contact. Query letter; article proposal with subject outline; entire article.

Acceptance Policies. Byline given: yes. Payment made: in copies. Seasonal material: 6 months in advance. Simultaneous submissions: no. Response time to initial inquiry: 1-2 months. Average time until publication: next issue. Computer printouts: yes. Dot matrix: yes. Disk submissions: no. Publishing rights: first North American serial rights; second serial rights.

Photography Submissions. Format and film: black-and-white prints, 5x7; transparencies. Photographs should include: facts of authorial pertinence. **Payment:** copy. Photographic rights: first rights only, all others revert.

Additional Information. *Hippo* is nonsexist as well as environmentally conscious. Tips: Submit only your best material and leave all pretensions behind you. Sample copy: $2.50 United States; $3.50 foreign. Writer's guidelines: pester me.

HONOLULU. 36 Merchant St. Honolulu, HI 96813. (808) 524-7400. Submissions Editor: Brian Nicol. Type: city and regional. Frequency of publication: monthly. Circulation: 75,000. Freelance submissions: 25%; number bought each year: 15-20.

Editorial Needs. Nonfiction—general interest; historical. Suggested word length—2000-4000. Payment offered: $500.

Initial Contact. Query letter.

Acceptance Policies. Byline given: yes. Payment made: upon acceptance. Kill fee: $100. Writer's expenses: no. Seasonal material: 3 months in advance. Simultaneous submissions: yes, if not submitted to other Hawaii publications. Response time to initial inquiry: 2-3 weeks. Average time until publication: 3-6 months. Computer printouts: yes. Dot matrix: yes. Disk submissions: no. Publishing rights: first rights.

Photography Submissions. Format and film: black-and-white contact sheets; color transparencies. Photographs should include: captions; model releases. **Payment:** $25-$200, depending on use. Photographic rights: first rights.

Additional Information. Sample copy: SASE, $2.40 postage plus $2. Writer's guidelines: SASE.

HOUSEWIFE-WRITER'S FORUM. Drawer 1518. Lafayette, CA 94549. (415) 932-1143. Submissions Editor: Deborah Haeseler. Type: literary; for and by women running a house and writing. Frequency of publication: quarterly. Circulation: 800+. Freelance submissions: 100%; number bought each year: 300.

Editorial Needs. Fiction—humorous; experimental; mainstream; mystery; etc. Suggested word length—2000 maximum. Payment offered: $.08-$.25 per word. Nonfiction—(all related to writing) excerpts; essays; how-to; humor; interview/profile; opinion; personal experience; poetry; fillers. Suggested word length—feature articles: 1500. Columns—Confession of Housewife-Writers (lifestyle, reminiscences); suggested word length—25-800. Book reviews; suggested word length—25-800. Payment offered: $.08-$.25 per word.

Initial Contact. Query letter or complete manuscript for nonfiction; complete manuscript for fiction, poetry, (maximum of 10 poems), and columns.

Acceptance Policies. Byline given: yes. Payment made: on acceptance. Submit seasonal material 6 months in advance. Simultaneous submissions: yes. Response time to initial inquiry: 2-3 months. Average time until publication: 6-12 months. Computer printouts: yes. Dot matrix: yes. Disk submissions: no. Publishing rights: one-time rights.

Additional Information. We encourage beginning writers; we try to get to know you and help you be the best writer you can be.   Sample copy $4. Writer's guidelines: #10 SASE.

HUSTLER. 9171 Wilshire Blvd., Ste. 300. Beverly Hills, CA 90210. (213) 858-7100. Submissions Editors: Allan MacDonell (articles, nonfiction feature articles); Tim Power (fiction, columns). Type: men's. Frequency of publication: monthly. Circulation: 800,000. Freelance submissions: 2 features, 2 columns monthly; number bought each year: 30-35.

Editorial Needs. Fiction—strong adventure/mystery story with sex scenes. Short stories—number per year: 6. Payment offered: $1000. **Nonfiction**—adventure; real male recreation; how-to; general interest; interview/profile; work must have sex angle related to current sexual topic or strong political angle. Suggested word length—feature articles: 4000. Payment offered: $1500. Columns—sex play. Suggested word length—1500-2000. Payment offered: $500.

Initial Contact. Article proposal with subject outline. State how the article fits our specific approach.

Acceptance Policies. Byline given: yes. Payment made: upon acceptance. Kill fee: 20% of commissioned fee. Writer's expenses on assignment: yes. Simultaneous submissions: no. Response time to initial inquiry: 2-3 weeks. Average time until publication: varies. Computer printouts: yes. Dot matrix: no. Disk submissions: ASCII (MS-DOS/APPLE); Macintosh. Publishing rights: all rights.

Additional Information. We expect articles that take a deeper look at sex/politics/social issues than other media. Writer's guidelines: write "Guidelines" in care of above address.

IL CAFFE, THE INTERNATIONAL JOURNAL OF THE ITALIAN EXPERIENCE. 900 Bush, #418. San Francisco, CA 94109. (415) 928-4886.
Submissions Editor: R.T. Loverso. Type: Italian and Italian-American experience. Frequency of publication: bimonthly. Circulation: 20,000. Freelance submissions 100%.; number of manuscripts used. each year: n/i. Payment in copies.

Editorial Needs. Fiction—short stories: literary; historical; genre. Suggested word length—3000. Payment offered: copies. **Nonfiction**—book reviews; entertainment reviews; general interest; historical; interview/profile; opinion; photo feature; poetry; self-improvement; travel; politics; economy. Suggested word length—1500. Payment offered: copies. Columns—Italian and Italian-American culture. Suggested word length—n/i. Payment offered: n/i. Fillers—Italian, Italian-American.

Initial Contact. Article proposal with subject outline; entire article.

Acceptance Policies. Byline given: yes. Payment made: in copies. Seasonal material: 1 month in advance. Simultaneous submissions: yes, with credit to our publication if we publish it before the other publication. Response time to initial inquiry: 3 months. Average time until publication: 1-6 months. Computer printouts: yes. Dot matrix: n/i. Disk submissions: yes. Publishing rights: n/i.

Photography Submissions. Format and film: black-and-white or color prints, any size. Photographs should include: captions; model releases; identification of subjects. **Payment:** none. Photographic rights: none.

Additional Information. Writer's guidelines: write or call.

INTERNATIONAL GYMNAST MAGAZINE. PO Box 2450. Oceanside, CA
92051. (619) 722-0030. Submissions Editor: Dwight T. Normile. Type: sports consumer. Frequency of publication: monthly. Circulation: 25,000. Freelance submissions 10%; number of manuscripts used each year: 4-5. Payment in copies.

Editorial Needs. Fiction—relating to gymnastics appropriate for ages 9-14. Suggested word length—1000-1500. Payment offered: copies. **Nonfiction**—health/fitness; how-to; interview/profile; photo feature; news; competition reports. Suggested word length—1000-

1500. Payment offered: copies. Columns—nutrition; psychology; coaching and training tips. Suggested word length—750-1000. Payment offered: copies.

Initial Contact. Entire article. Include bio indicating writer's connection to the sport.

Acceptance Policies. Byline given: yes. Payment made: in copies. Simultaneous submissions: yes, inform us. Response time to initial inquiry: 1 month. Average time until publication: 3 months. Computer printouts: yes. Dot matrix: yes. Disk submissions: no. Publishing rights: n/i.

Photography Submissions. Format and film: black-and-white prints, 8x10, 5x7; color transparencies. Photographs should include: captions; identification of subjects. **Payment:** $5-$50. Photographic rights: one time.

Additional Information. We serve hard-core gymnastic types. Outsiders rarely produce what we need. Tips: Knowledge of gymnastics is essential! If your don't know this sport, don't bother. Sample copy: $3.25. Writer's guidelines: SASE.

INTERNATIONAL OLYMPIC LIFTER.

PO Box 65855. Los Angeles, CA 90065. (213) 257-8762. Submissions Editor: Bob Hise. Type: Olympic sport of weight lifting. Frequency of publication: 6 issues per year. Circulation: 10,000. Freelance submissions: 5%; number bought each year: 4.

Editorial Needs. Nonfiction—training; diet; contest reports; poetry. Suggested word length—feature articles: 250-2000. Payment offered: variable.

Initial Contact. Query letter. State availability of photos.

Acceptance Policies. Byline given: yes. Payment made: upon publication. Kill fee: $25. Writer's expenses on assignment: no. Submit seasonal material 5 months in advance. Simultaneous submissions: no. Response time to initial inquiry: 6 weeks. Average time until publication: 2 months. Computer printouts: yes. Dot matrix: letter quality. Disk submissions: no. Publishing rights: one-time rights; negotiable.

Photography Submissions. action; training. Format and film: black-and-white prints. 5x7. Photographs should include: identification of subjects. **Payment:** $5. Photographic rights: all.

Additional Information. Writing must be apolitical. Writer's guidelines: 9x12 SASE, 5 first class stamps; sample copy $4.

IN TOUCH FOR MEN.

7216 Varna Ave. North Hollywood, CA 91605-4186. (818) 764-2288. Submissions Editor: Tom Quinn. Type: gay men's. Frequency of publication: monthly. Circulation: 300,000. Freelance submissions 80%; number of manuscripts bought each year: 48.

Editorial Needs. Fiction—short stories: gay men. Suggested word length—3000. Payment offered: $75. Nonfiction—humor; interview/profile; travel. Suggested word length—3000. Payment offered: $75, negotiable.

Initial Contact. Entire article. Include social security number, real name, and SASE.

Acceptance Policies. Byline given: yes. Payment made: upon publication. Kill fee: no. Writer's expenses: no. Seasonal material: 4-5 months in advance. Simultaneous submissions: yes, notify us. Response time to initial inquiry: 2 weeks. Average time until publication: 3-4 months. Computer printouts: yes. Dot matrix: yes. Disk submissions: Word Perfect. Publishing rights: first North American serial rights.

Photography Submissions. Format and film: black-and-white or color prints, any size; transparencies. Photographs should include: captions; model releases; identification of subjects; 2 pieces of identification with age, name, and picture. **Payment:** $35 per use. Photographic rights: one-time use.

Additional Information. All fictional characters need to be over 18 years old. Erotic and sexual okay, but no bondage. Tips: Send for copy of the magazine. Sample copy: $4.95. Writer's guidelines: upon request.

ISLANDS. 3886 State Street. Santa Barbara, CA 93105. (805) 682-7177.
Submissions Editor: Joan Tapper (manuscript and story idea queries); Zorah Kruger (photo stock lists). Type: travel. Frequency of publication: 6 times per year. Circulation: 15,000. Freelance submissions: 100%; number bought each year: 25.

Editorial Needs. Nonfiction—features; departments; short items; interview/profile; historical; nature; sports; art; travel; columns. Suggested word length—feature articles: 2000-3000; columns: 1200-1700. Payment offered: $.25 per word and up.

Initial Contact. Query letter; article proposal with subject outline. Include tear sheets of previously published manuscripts; support materials, and tear sheets for photographers.

Acceptance Policies. Byline given: yes. Payment made: on acceptance. Kill fee: 1/4. Writer's expenses on assignment: yes. Submit seasonal material 6+ months in advance. Simultaneous submissions: no. Response time to initial inquiry: 4-6 weeks. Average time until publication: 3-6 months. Computer printouts: yes. Dot matrix: yes. Disk submissions: ASCII; modem. Publishing rights: first rights.

Photography Submissions. Format and film: color transparencies. Photographs should include: captions; model releases; identification of subjects. **Payment:** $75-$300 depending on usage. Photographic rights: one-time use.

Additional Information. Writer's guidelines: SASE.

JOTS (JOURNAL OF THE SENSES). (Subsidiary of Elysium Growth Press).
814 Robinson Rd. Topanga, CA 90290. (213) 455-1000. Submissions Editor: Ed Lange. Type: clothing optional lifestyle; body self-esteem. Frequency of publication: quarterly. Circulation: 14,000. Freelance submissions: 10%; number bought each year: 4.

Editorial Needs. Fiction—short stories (1 per year). Nonfiction—book reviews; inspiration; photo feature; self-improvement. Suggested word length—feature articles: 700. Payment offered: $100.

Initial Contact. Query letter.

Acceptance Policies. Byline given: yes. Payment made: upon publication. Kill fee: no. Writer's expenses on assignment: no. Simultaneous submissions: yes. Response time to initial inquiry: 6 weeks. Average time until publication: 6 months. Computer printouts: yes. Dot matrix: yes. Disk submissions: Macintosh. Publishing rights: all.

Photography Submissions. Format and film: 8x10 35mm transparencies; black-and-white or color prints; contact sheets. Photographs should include: captions; model releases; identification of subjects. **Payment:** $25. Photographic rights: all.

Additional Information. Writer's guidelines: upon request.

JOURNAL OF WISDOM. (Subsidiary of Li Kung Shaw). PO Box 16427.
San Francisco, CA 94116. (415) 731-0829. Submissions Editor: Li Kung Shaw. Type: philosophy. Frequency of publication: monthly. Circulation: 100. Freelance submissions: 50%; number bought each year: 1-2.

Editorial Needs. Nonfiction—philosophy. Suggested word length—feature articles: 3000. Payment offered: yes.

Initial Contact. Query letter.

Acceptance Policies. Byline given: n/i. Payment made: upon publication. Kill fee: no. Writer's expenses on assignment: no. Simultaneous submissions: yes; we negotiate. Response time to initial inquiry: 30 days. Average time until publication: 6 months. Computer printouts: yes. Dot matrix: no. Disk submissions: Apple 3 (Three Easy Pieces). Publishing rights: first rights.

KEYBOARD MAGAZINE. 20085 Stevens Creek Blvd. Cupertino, CA 95014. (408) 446-1105. Submissions Editor: Dominic Milano. Type: keyboard players, all styles, all abilities. Frequency of publication: monthly. Circulation: 82,000. Freelance submissions: 25%; number bought each year: 20.

Editorial Needs. Nonfiction—interviews; historical; how-to. Suggested word length—feature articles: 1000-5000. Payment offered: $150-$500.

Initial Contact. Query letter.

Acceptance Policies. Byline given: yes. Payment made: upon acceptance. Kill fee: under special circumstances only. Writer's expenses on assignment: sometimes. Response time to initial inquiry: 2 weeks. Average time until publication: 6 months. Computer printouts: yes. Dot matrix: letter quality. Disk submissions: query. Publishing rights: first serial rights; second serial rights.

Additional Information. We are looking for anything that amateur or professional keyboard players and computer musicians would find helpful, new, or interesting. Writer's guidelines: upon request.

KINGFISHER. PO Box 9783. North Berkeley, CA 94709. (415) 893-2425. Submissions Editor: c/o Editor. Type: literary magazine focusing on short fiction. Frequency of publication: twice yearly. Circulation: 1000. Freelance submissions: 100%. Payment in copies.

Editorial Needs. Fiction—literary. Short stories—number per year: 20. Payment offered: 2 copies. **Nonfiction**—occasional essays. Payment offered: 2 copies.

Initial Contact. Cover letter with fiction or poetry. Include previous publication credits and SASE.

Acceptance Policies. Byline given: yes. Payment made: in copies. Simultaneous submissions: yes (if previously published or translated, include release from original publisher or author). Response time to initial inquiry: 2-3 months. Average time until publication: 6-12 months. Computer printouts: yes. Dot matrix: no. Disk submissions: n/i. Publishing rights: first North American serial rights.

Additional Information. Writer's guidelines: upon request; SASE.

KITPLANES. PO Box 6050. Mission Viejo, CA 92690. (714) 855-8822. Submissions Editor: Dave Martin. Type: for designers, builders, and pilots of experimental aircraft. Frequency of publication: monthly. Circulation: 63,000. Freelance submissions: 70%; number bought each year: 100.

Editorial Needs. Nonfiction—how to; interview/profile; new product; personal experience; photo feature; technical; general interest. Suggested word length—feature articles: 500-5000. Payment offered: $60 per page.

Initial Contact. Query letter; availability of photos.

Acceptance Policies. Byline given: yes. Payment made: upon publication. Kill fee: negotiable. Writer's expenses on assignment: no. Submit seasonal material 6 months in advance. Simultaneous submissions: no. Response time to initial inquiry: 2 weeks. Average time until publication: 3 months. Computer printouts: yes. Dot matrix: caps and lower case. Disk submissions: query. Publishing rights: first North American serial rights.

Photography Submissions. Format and film: prints; transparencies. Film: black-and-white; color. Photographs should include: captions; identification of subjects. **Payment**: $10-$75 (black-and-white); $20-$150 (color); $250 for cover photo. Photographic rights: one-time rights.

Additional Information. Tips: Article must be directed to the individual craftsperson. We are looking for photo features. Writer's guidelines: #10 SASE; sample copy $3.

LA BELLA FIGURA. PO Box 411223. San Francisco, CA 94141-1223.
Submissions Editor: Rose Romano. Type: Italian-American. Frequency of publication: quarterly. Circulation: 100. Freelance submissions: 100%; number used each year: 45-50. Payment in copies.

Editorial Needs. **Fiction**—literary; women's; Italian-American history and culture. Suggested word length—3000. Payment offered: 2 copies. Short Stories—Italian-American culture. Suggested word length—3000. Payment offered: 2 copies. **Nonfiction**—book reviews; poetry. Suggested word length—3000. Payment offered: 2 copies.

Initial Contact. Entire articles; friendly cover letters; include anything a writer thinks the editor should know.

Acceptance Policies. Byline given: yes. Payment made: in copies. Seasonal material: 3-6 months in advance. Simultaneous submissions: yes, inform me. Response time to initial inquiry: 1-2 months. Average time until publication: 3-6 months. Computer printouts: yes. Dot matrix: yes. Disk submissions: no. Publishing rights: first rights.

Additional Information. We print only work written by Italian-Americans. But we hope to be appreciated by others as well. Tips: I don't like work that treats Italian-American culture in a negative way (complaints can be positive). Sample copy: $2. Writer's guidelines: not available.

LA GENTE de AZTLAN. (Chicano student newspaper published at UCLA).
112D Kerchoff Hall. 308 Westwood Plaza. Los Angeles, CA 90024. (213) 825-9836, 206-3757. Submissions Editor: Teresa Magno. Type: Chicano student newspaper. Frequency of publication: 6 times during the academic year. Circulation: 10,000. Freelance submissions: 10%. No payment offered.

Editorial Needs. **Fiction**—literary; women's; Chicano/Latino issues, etc. Short stories—number per year: 2. Payment offered: none. **Nonfiction**—book reviews; entertainment reviews; fillers; general interest; health/fitness; historical; how-to; humor; interview/profile; opinion; photo feature; poetry; self-improvement. Suggested word length—feature articles: 1000; columns: 500. Payment offered: none.

Initial Contact. Query letter; article proposal; entire article. Include background of the author.

Acceptance Policies. Byline given: yes. Payment made: none. Submit seasonal material 1 month in advance. Simultaneous submissions: yes. Response time to initial inquiry: 2 weeks. Average time until publication: 3 weeks. Computer printouts: yes. Dot Matrix: yes. Disk submissions: Macintosh 3.5 disk; Macwrite or Microsoft Word (preferred). Publishing rights: n/i.

Photography Submissions. Format and film: black-and-white prints, 8x10; contact sheets. Photographs should include: captions; identification of subjects; place, time, and event. **Payment**: none. Photographic rights: all.

Additional Information. We deal with issues of relevance to the Latino community. If possible, send a Spanish version also. Writer's guidelines: call or write.

L.A. WEST. 919 Santa Monica Blvd., #245. Santa Monica, CA 90401. (213) 458-3376. Submissions Editor: Mary Daily. Type: service/lifestyle for West Los Angeles. Frequency of publication: monthly. Circulation: 50,000. Freelance submissions: 95%; number bought each year: 45.

Editorial Needs. Nonfiction—general interest; health/fitness; historical; how-to; humor; interview/profile; opinion; travel. Suggested word length—feature articles: 800-1000; columns: 550. Payment offered: $75-$1000.

Initial Contact. Query letter; entire article; clips.

Acceptance Policies. Byline given: yes. Payment made: upon acceptance. Kill fee: no. Writer's expenses on assignment: no. Simultaneous submissions: no. Response time to initial inquiry: 6-8 weeks. Average time until publication: 6-8 months. Computer printouts: yes. Dot matrix: yes. Disk submissions: yes. Publishing rights: all.

Photography Submissions. Format and film: color transparencies. Photographs should include: captions; model releases; identification of subjects. **Payment:** $45. Photographic rights: all.

Additional Information. Writer's guidelines: SASE.

LECTOR. 16161 Ventura Blvd., Ste. 830. Encino, CA 91436. (818) 990-1885. Submissions Editor: Roberto Cabello-Argandona. Type: Hispanic book review media. Frequency of publication: biannual. Circulation: 3000. Freelance submissions: 90%; number bought each year: 4.

Editorial Needs. Fiction—Hispanic literary and women's. Short stories—number per issue: 2; per year: 4. **Nonfiction**—book excerpts; book reviews; entertainment reviews; humor; interview/profile; literary opinion; photo feature; poetry. Suggested word length—feature articles: 2000; columns: 1000. Payment offered: $50, negotiable.

Initial Contact. Query letter; article proposal with written subject outline. Include resumé and clips.

Acceptance Policies. Byline given: yes. Payment made: within 90 days after publication. Kill fee: no. Expenses of writers on assignment: no. Submit seasonal material 12 months in advance. Simultaneous submissions: yes. Response time to initial inquiry: 60-90 days. Average time until publication: 60-90 days. Computer printouts: yes. Dot matrix: yes. Disk submissions: prefer MS-DOS with hard copy; other accepted. Publishing rights: all.

Photography Submissions. Call about color submissions. Format and film: transparencies, call about size; black-and-white or color prints. Photographs should include: caption. **Payment:** photographic essay paid separately. Photographic rights: one-time rights.

Additional Information. Publication provides literary articles with Hispanic cultural and humanistic focus. Tips: Writing should be in a creative, literary style. Writer's guidelines: SASE, include $5.

LEFT CURVE. PO Box 472. Oakland, CA 94604. (415) 763-7193. Submissions Editor: CSABA Polony. Type: progressive art and culture. Frequency of publication: irregular. Circulation: 1000. Freelance submissions: 50%. Payment in copies.

Editorial Needs. Fiction—literary; science-fiction; avant-garde; progressive culture; minority; activist; experimental. Short stories—number per year: 1. Payment offered: 5 copies of issue. **Nonfiction**—art reviews; book reviews; historical; interview/profile; opinion; photo feature; poetry; progressive culture. Suggested word length—feature articles: 2500. Payment offered: 5 copies of issue.

Initial Contact. Article proposal with subject outline. State author's purpose. Include SASE.

Acceptance Policies. Byline given: yes. Payment made: copies. Simultaneous submissions: no. Response time to initial inquiry: 3 months. Average time until publication: 6 months. Computer printouts: yes. Dot matrix: yes. Disk submissions: no. Publishing rights: rights revert to author with written permission.

Photography Submissions. Format and film: black-and-white prints, 5x7 or less. Photographs should include: captions as necessary for story. **Payment:** none. Photographic rights: none.

Additional Information. Writer's guidelines: no.

LET'S LIVE MAGAZINE. 444 N. Larchmont Blvd. PO Box 74908.

Los Angeles, CA 90004. (213) 469-8379. Submissions Editors: Debra Jenkins Robinson (print editor); Victoria Clayton (photo editor). Type: health and fitness. Frequency of publication: monthly. Circulation: 140,000. Freelance submissions: 10%; number bought each year: 12-30.

Editorial Needs. Nonfiction—book excerpts; book reviews; health/fitness; interview/profile; self-improvement. Suggested word length—feature articles: 1000-1200. Payment offered: $150 per article.

Initial Contact. Query letter. State photo availability.

Acceptance Policies. Byline given: yes. Payment made: upon publication. Kill fee: no. Writer's expenses on assignment: no; some exceptions. Submit seasonal material 9 months in advance. Simultaneous submissions: no. Response time to initial inquiry: 6 weeks. Average time until publication: 4-6 months. Computer printouts: yes. Dot matrix: letter quality. Disk submissions: IBM PC. Publishing rights: first North American serial rights.

Photography Submissions. Format and film: black and white; color transparencies. Photographs should include: model releases; identification of subjects. **Payment:** $35 per photo. Photographic rights: one-time use.

Additional Information. Writer's guidelines: SASE.

LLAMAS. PO Box 100. Herald, CA 95638. (916) 448-1668. Submissions Editor:

Assistant Editor, Susan Jones-Ley. Type: livestock. Frequency of publication: 8 times per year. Circulation: 5500. Freelance submissions: 40% and growing; number bought each year: 30.

Editorial Needs. Nonfiction—book excerpts; fillers; general interest; photo feature; travel. Suggested word length—feature articles: 1000-4000. Fiction—llamas or camelids tie-in a must. Short stories—number per issue: 4; per year: 24-30. Payment offered: $50-$400.

Initial Contact. Query letter; article proposal with subject outline; entire article. Include sample work.

Acceptance Policies. Byline given: yes. Payment made: upon publication. Kill fee: per contract agreement. Writer's expenses on assignment: on occasion. Submit seasonal material 5 months in advance. Simultaneous submissions: yes. Response time to initial inquiry: 30 days. Average time until publication: varies. Computer printouts: yes. Dot matrix: no. Disk submissions: no. Publishing rights: first and second North American serial rights; first rights.

Photography Submissions. Format and film: black-and-white or color prints, any size. Photographs should include: captions; model releases; identification of subjects. **Payment:** $25-$50 color; $10-$15 black-and-white. Photographic rights: varies. Please do not write on photograph!

Additional Information. Sample magazine sent upon request.   Tips: Know our magazine and its needs. Writer's guidelines: SASE.

LOS ANGELES LAWYER. PO Box 55020. Los Angeles, CA 90055. (213) 627-2727. Submissions Editor: Susan Pettit. Type: Law. Directed to the membership of the Los Angeles County Bar Association. Consists of scholarly legal articles, legal features, and profiles; practice tips and tax tips. Frequency of publication: monthly. Circulation: 25,000. Freelance submissions: 20%; number bought each year: 8-10.

Editorial Needs. Nonfiction—book reviews; historical; interviews/profile; legal education. Suggested word length—feature articles: 4000. Payment offered: $300-$800.

Initial Contact. Query letter. Include brief biography of writer; clips.

Acceptance Policies. Byline given: yes. Payment made: upon acceptance. Kill fee: yes. Writer's expenses on assignment: no. Simultaneous submissions: yes; if manuscript is accepted by another publication, we must be notified immediately. Response time to initial inquiry: 8 weeks. Average time until publication: varies. Computer printouts: yes. Dot matrix: yes. Disk submissions: Macintosh. Publishing rights: first North American serial rights; work-for-hire assignments.

Photography Submissions. Format and film: black-and-white or color prints. Photographs should include: captions; model releases; identification of subjects. **Payment:** varies. Photographic rights: one-time use; work for hire.

Additional Information. Emphasis on scholarly legal articles of interest to Southern California attorneys. Tips: Footnotes must be typed double-spaced on separate pages at the end of article. Writer's guidelines: upon request; sample copies $2.

LOS ANGELES MAGAZINE. 1888 Century Park East, Ste. 920. Los Angeles, CA 90067. (213) 557-7569. Submissions Editors: Rodger Claire, Executive Editor; Lew Harris, Editor. Type: articles of general interest pertaining to the Los Angeles and Southern California area. Frequency of publication: monthly. Circulation: 172,000. Freelance submissions: 90%.

Editorial Needs. Nonfiction—book excerpts; book reviews; historical; interview/profile; travel; business; politics. Suggested word length—feature articles: 1500. Payment offered: individually based.

Initial Contact. Query letter. Include clips.

Acceptance Policies. Byline given: yes. Payment made: upon acceptance. Kill fee: 30%. Writer's expenses on assignment: mostly. Submit seasonal material 2-3 months in advance. Simultaneous submissions: yes. Response time to initial inquiry: 3-4 weeks. Average time until publication: varies. Computer printouts: yes. Dot matrix: yes. Disk submissions: no. Publishing rights: first North American serial rights.

Additional Information. All articles should have a local angle. Tips: Research the magazine and be sure to address our audience, which is sophisticated and upscale. Writer's guidelines: request by mail with SASE.

LOS ANGELES READER. 5550 Wilshire Blvd., Ste. 307. Los Angeles, CA 90036. (213) 933-1061; (818) 763-3555. Submissions Editors: Heidi Dvorak (cityside); James Vowell (features). Type: general interest; arts and entertainment (especially reviews and listings). Frequency of publication: weekly. Circulation: 701,000. Freelance submissions: 100%; number bought each year: 300.

Editorial Needs. Fiction—literary (rarely use fiction). Nonfiction—book excerpts; book reviews; entertainment reviews; general interest; humor; interview/profile. Suggested word length—feature articles: 3500; columns: 1000. Payment offered: $300 for major features of 3500 words or more; graduated down for shorter pieces.

Initial Contact. Query letter.

Acceptance Policies. Byline given: yes. Payment made: upon publication. Kill fee: no. Writer's expenses on assignment: no. Simultaneous submissions: no. Response time to initial inquiry: 1 month. Average time until publication: a few weeks. Computer printouts: yes. Dot matrix: yes. Disk submissions: MS-DOS; IBM. Publishing rights: first North American serial rights.

Photography Submissions. Format and film: 8x10 prints. Photographs should include: captions. **Payment**: $30 per published photo. Photographic rights: first.

Additional Information. Writer's guidelines: upon request.

LOS ANGELES TIMES BOOK REVIEW. Times Mirror. Times Mirror
Square. Los Angeles, CA 90053. (213) 237-7777. Submissions Editor: Jack Miles. Type: review of current books. Frequency of publication: weekly. Circulation: 1.5 million. Freelance submissions: 70%; number bought each year: 650.

Editorial Needs. Nonfiction—book reviews. Suggested word length—feature articles: 200-1500. Payment offered: $75-$500.

Initial Contact. Query letter. Include published samples of pertinent works.

Acceptance Policies. Byline given: yes. Payment made: upon publication. Kill fee: variable. Writer's expenses on assignment: n/a. Simultaneous submissions: no. Response time to initial inquiry: immediate. Average time until publication: 3 weeks. Computer printouts: yes. Dot matrix: letter quality. Disk submissions: no. Publishing rights: first North American serial rights.

Additional Information. We will not accept requests for specific titles to review or unsolicited reviews without query first.

LOS ANGELES TIMES MAGAZINE. Times Mirror Square. Los Angeles, CA
90053. (213) 237-5000. Submissions Editors: Leslie Allyson Ware (freelance and excerpts); John Lindsay (projects editor). Type: Sunday magazine. Frequency of publication: weekly. Circulation: 1,421,711. Freelance submissions: 70-80%; number bought each year: 260.

Editorial Needs. Nonfiction—book excerpts; general interest; health/fitness; historical; interview/profile; photo feature. Suggested word length—feature articles: 1500-4000. Payment offered: $1 per word, on average.

Initial Contact. Query letter for each article to be submitted. Include clips and resumé.

Acceptance Policies. Byline given: yes. Payment made: upon acceptance. Kill fee: yes. Writer's expenses on assignment: yes. Submit seasonal material 2 months in advance. Simultaneous submissions: yes. Response time to initial inquiry: 6 weeks. Average time until publication: 1 month. Computer printouts: yes. Dot matrix: n/i. Disk submissions: no. Publishing rights: first North American serial rights; first rights.

Additional Information. Looking for Los Angeles, Southern California, Pacific Rim-oriented stories. Tips: Have a concise query letter. Include writing samples if no clips. Writer's guidelines: SASE.

MACWEEK. 301 Howard St., 15th Floor. San Francisco, CA 94105. (415) 243-3500. Submissions Editors: Henry Norr (news); Bernard Ohanian (opinions and features); Anita Malnig (graphic arts); Rochelle Garner (Window On, product overviews); Rebecca Waring (reviews). Type: computer. Frequency of publication: weekly. Circulation: n/i. Freelance submissions: most features, some news; number bought each year: hundreds.

Editorial Needs. Nonfiction—opinion; computer industry news; profiles of Macintosh users in big business. Suggested word length—feature articles: 300-1200; columns: variable. Payment offered: $.40 per word is typical.

Initial Contact. Query letter. State computer expertise of writer.

Acceptance Policies. Byline given: yes. Payment made: upon acceptance. Kill fee: varies according to contract. Writer's expenses on assignment: yes. Simultaneous submissions: no. Response time to initial inquiry: 4 weeks. Average time until publication: 1 month. Computer printouts: We want all submissions on disk or electronic file via MCI or other e-mail services. Disk submissions: Macintosh (3.5) only; Word format. Publishing rights: all rights.

Photography Submissions. Photographers wishing assignments should contact Photo Editor John Hornstein.

Additional Information. We are the preeminent service publication for "volume buyers" of Apple Macintosh computers and accompanying software and peripherals. Tips: Don't call us; send query. Writer's guidelines: written request.

MAGICAL BLEND, A TRANSFORMATIVE JOURNEY. PO Box 11303.
San Francisco, CA 94101. (415) 673-1001. Submissions Editor: Jerry Snider. Type: new age spirituality. Frequency of publication: quarterly. Circulation: 45,000. Freelance submissions: 30%; number bought each year: 5.

Editorial Needs. Fiction—adventure; book selections; erotica; experimental; fantasy; science fiction; novels (condensed and serialized). Suggested word length—100-3000. Payment offered: $1-$100. Nonfiction—book excerpts; essays; general interest; how-to; humor; interview/profile; photo feature; new product; religious; technical; travel; columns (crystals; Magic In Your Life; astrology; spiritual travel). Suggested word length—feature articles: 900-4000; columns: 100-3000. Payment offered: $1-$100.

Initial Contact. Complete manuscript. Send photos.

Acceptance Policies. Byline given: yes. Payment made: upon publication. Kill fee: no. Writer's expenses on assignment: no. Submit seasonal material 6 months in advance. Response time to initial inquiry: 5 months. Average time until publication: 6 months. Computer printouts: yes. Dot matrix: letter quality. Disk submissions: query first. Publishing rights: first-time rights.

Photography Submissions. Format and film: n/i. Photographs should include: captions; model releases; identification of subjects. **Payment:** $1-100. Photographic rights: first-time rights.

Additional Information. Tips: Be positive in your approach. Read the journal before submitting material. Writer's guidelines: #10 SASE; sample copy $4.

MAINSTREAM, MAGAZINE OF THE ABLE-DISABLED.
2973 Beech St. San Diego, CA 92102. (619) 234-3138. Submissions Editor: Cyndi Jones. Type: audience is disabled consumers. Frequency of publication: 10 times yearly. Circulation: 15,500. Freelance submissions: 100%; number bought each year: 50.

Editorial Needs. Fiction—humor. Suggested word length—800-1200 words. Payment offered: $100. Nonfiction—book excerpts; how-to; humor; interview/profile; photo feature;

travel; legislation; personal experience. Suggested word length—feature articles: 8 pages. Payment offered: $100. Columns: Creative Solutions; Personal Page. Suggested word length—500-800. Payment offered: $50.

Initial Contact. Query letter and complete manuscript.

Acceptance Policies. Byline given: yes. Payment made: upon publication. Kill fee: no. Writer's expenses on assignment: no. Submit seasonal material 4 months in advance. Response time to initial inquiry: 2 months. Average time until publication: 3 months. Computer printouts: yes. Dot matrix: letter quality. Disk submissions: call. Publishing rights: all.

Photography Submissions. Format and film: black-and-white or color contact sheets; transparencies, 1 1/2 x 3/4; black-and-white or color prints, 5x7+. Photographs should include: captions; identification of subjects. **Payment:** $35 (black and white). Photographic rights: all.

Additional Information. Sample copy: $4.25. Writer's guidelines: #10 SASE or 9x12 envelope.

MANOA: A PACIFIC JOURNAL OF INTERNATIONAL WRITING.

University of Hawaii Press. 2840 Kolawalu St. Honolulu, HI 96822. (808) 948-8833. Submissions Editors: Roger Whitlock, Jeffrey Carroll (fiction); Frank Stewart (poetry); Alan MacGregor (reviews); Darlaine Dudoit (all other). Type: literary. Frequency of publication: twice yearly. Circulation: 1800. Freelance submissions: 90%; number bought each year: 500.

Editorial Needs. Fiction—contemporary, literary. Short Stories—any subject area. Suggested word length—no set limit. Payment offered: competitive. **Nonfiction**—poetry; general interest; book excerpts; book reviews. Suggested word length—no set limit. Payment offered: competitive.

Initial Contact. Entire article.

Acceptance Policies. Byline given: yes. Payment made: upon acceptance. Kill fee: no. Writer's expenses: no. Simultaneous submissions: no. Response time to initial inquiry: 6-12 weeks. Average time until publication: 3 months. Computer printouts: yes. Dot matrix: no. Disk submissions: no. Publishing rights: first North American serial rights.

Additional Information. We publish highest quality literary work only. Work must have relevance to the Pacific Rim countries, including Asia and Latin America. Sample copy: upon request. Writer's guidelines: SASE.

MASSAGE MAGAZINE. PO Box 1389. Kailua-Kona, HI 96745. (808) 329-

2433. Submissions Editor: Helen C. Morgan. Type: massage, body work, and allied healing arts. Frequency of publication: bimonthly. Circulation: 45,000. Freelance submissions: 20%; number bought each year: 25.

Editorial Needs. Fiction—related to magazine theme. Short Stories—massage/body work. Suggested word length—n/i. Payment offered: $25-$50. **Nonfiction**—book excerpts; health/fitness; how-to; humor; inspiration; interview/profile; self-improvement; travel; massage and body work. Suggested word length—300-2000. Payment offered: $25-$60. Fillers—massage/body work. Suggested word length—n/i. Payment offered: yes.

Initial Contact. Query letter; article proposal with subject outline, or entire article.

Acceptance Policies. Byline given: yes. Payment made: 30 days after publication. Kill fee: no. Writer's expenses: no. Seasonal material: 3 months in advance. Simultaneous submissions: yes, if we are notified immediately of its acceptance elsewhere. Response time to initial inquiry: 2 weeks. Average time until publication: 2-12 months. Computer printouts: yes. Dot matrix: yes. Disk submissions: Macintosh, AT-Microsoft Word. Publishing rights: first North American serial rights.

Additional Information. Sample copy: $4. Writer's guidelines: upon request.

MERCURY. (Astronomical Society of the Pacific). 390 Ashton Ave. San Francisco, CA 94112. Submissions Editor: Andrew Fraknoi. Type: astronomy. Frequency of publication: every two months. Circulation: 7500. No payment offered.

Editorial Needs. Nonfiction—book excerpts; book reviews; general interest; historical; interview/profile; opinion; photo feature. Suggested word length—feature articles: varies. Payment offered: none. All are written by scientists or science writers who believe in our international program of science education.

Initial Contact. Query letter.

Acceptance Policies. Byline given: yes. Payment made: none. Submit seasonal material 5-6 months in advance. Simultaneous submissions: no. Response time to initial inquiry: 2-5 months. Average time until publication: 2 months. Computer printouts: yes. Dot matrix: yes. Disk submissions: IBM or Macintosh. Publishing rights: first North American serial rights.

Photography Submissions. Format and film: black-and-white prints. Photographs should include: captions.

Additional Information. *Mercury* is a popular-level (nontechnical) magazine on popular astronomy, published by the nonprofit Astronomical Society of the Pacific, founded in 1889.

METRO. 410 S. First St. San Jose, CA 95113. (408) 298-8000. Submissions Editor: Sharan Street. Type: general interest regional weekly magazine. Frequency of publication: weekly. Circulation: 55,000. Freelance submissions 30%; number of manuscripts bought weekly: 5-7.

Editorial Needs. Nonfiction—book reviews; entertainment reviews; general interest; interview/profile. Suggested word length—1000. Payment offered: n/i.

Initial Contact. Query letter. Clips are most helpful.

Acceptance Policies. Byline given: yes. Payment made: upon publication. Kill fee: 50%. Writer's expenses: only by prearrangement. Seasonal material: 2 months in advance. Simultaneous submissions: yes, if it's not in the same state. Response time to initial inquiry: 4 weeks. Average time until publication: 3 weeks. Computer printouts: yes. Dot matrix: yes. Disk submissions: MS-DOS; Wordstar 4.0 preferred. Publishing rights: first rights.

Photography Submissions. Format and film: black-and-white prints, 5x7. Photographs should include: captions; model releases; identification of subjects. **Payment:** $25; $10 reprint rate. Photographic rights: first-time rights.

Additional Information. Sample copy: SASE (manila envelope). Writer's guidelines: SASE.

MEXICO WEST. PO Box 1646. Bonita, CA 92002. (619) 585-3033. Submissions Editor: Shirley Miller. Type: Baja (Mexico) travel information. Frequency of publication: monthly. Circulation: 3500. Freelance submissions: 100%; number bought each year: 60.

Editorial Needs. Nonfiction—book reviews; travel. Suggested word length—feature articles: 900-1200. Payment offered: $50.

Initial Contact. Article proposal with subject outline; story as information.

Acceptance Policies. Byline given: yes. Payment made: upon publication. Kill fee: yes. Writer's expenses on assignment: n/i. Simultaneous submissions: yes. Response time to initial inquiry: 2 weeks. Average time until publication: 1 month. Computer printouts: yes. Dot matrix: yes. Disk submissions: Microsoft Word; Macintosh Plus. Publishing rights: first North American serial rights.

Photography Submissions. Format and film: black-and-white or color prints, 3x5. Photographs should include: captions. **Payment**: included with story. Photographic rights: one-time use.

Additional Information. We are very specialized. Informational material only; no "Me and Joe went . . . ." Tips: Know something about area. Writer's guidelines: write and request.

MIND IN MOTION, A MAGAZINE OF POETRY AND SHORT PROSE. PO Box 1118. Apple Valley, CA 92307. (619) 248-6512. Submissions Editor: Celeste Goyer. Type: literary. Frequency of publication: quarterly. Circulation: 250. Freelance submissions: 100%; number bought each year: 160. Payment in copies.

Editorial Needs. **Fiction**—literary; science fiction; fantasy; avant-garde; satire; philosophy; surrealism. Short stories—number per issue: 10; per year: 40. Suggested word length—250-3000. Payment offered: 1 copy, when feasible. **Nonfiction**—might consider essays. Suggested word length—250-3000. Poetry which appeals to the intellect and expresses thoughts through images. Free verse or free association preferred. Suggested word length—25-45 lines. Payment offered: 1 copy, when feasible.

Initial Contact. Entire manuscript; cover letter or bio with published credits not necessary.

Acceptance Policies. Byline given: initials follow piece; full name appears in index in back of each issue. Payment made: in copies. Simultaneous submissions: yes; inform us. Response time to initial inquiry: 1 week to 3 months. Average time until publication: 1 week to 3 months. Computer printouts: yes. Dot matrix: yes. Disk submissions: no. Publishing rights: first North American serial rights; or first rights.

Additional Information. Tips: Send your works of inspired brilliance. Please include dates of composition (if available) for all works. Sample copy: $2.50 payable to *Mind in Motion*. Writer's guidelines: #10 SASE.

MINORITY BUSINESS ENTREPRENEUR. 924 N. Market St. Inglewood, CA 90302. (213) 673-9398. Submissions Editors: Jeanie Barnett (general editor); Barbara Daley (circulation, classifieds, and calendar). Type: for minority and women business owners. Frequency of publication: bimonthly. Circulation: 27,000. Freelance submissions 50%; number of manuscripts used each year: 12. Payment in copies.

Editorial Needs. **Fiction**—short stories: business (women and minority owned). Suggested word length—1500. Payment offered: copies. **Nonfiction**—how-to; interview/profile. Suggested word length—2000. Payment offered: copies.

Initial Contact. Article proposal with subject outline. Include bio and photos.

Acceptance Policies. Byline given: depends on how much editing is needed. Payment made: in copies. Seasonal material: 3 months in advance. Simultaneous submissions: yes, if not direct competitors or we get first rights. Response time to initial inquiry: 1 month. Average time until publication: 1 month. Computer printouts: yes. Dot matrix: yes. Disk submissions: ASCII. Publishing rights: first rights.

Photography Submissions. Format and film: black-and-white or color prints, 8x10. Photographs should include: captions; identification of subjects. **Payment**: none. Photographic rights: none.

Additional Information. Focus is strictly on minority and women business owners. Sample copy: call or write. Writer's guidelines: not available.

MODERN CARTOONING AND GAGWRITING. PO Box 1142. Novato, CA 94947. (415) 382-1963. Submissions Editors: Raymond Moore; J. Moore (managing editor). Type: trade journal for the professional cartoonist. Frequency of publication: monthly. Circulation: 375+. Freelance submissions: 40%; number bought each year: 24+.

Editorial Needs. Nonfiction—inspiration; cartoons; cartoon covers; illustrations; spots. Suggested word length—query. Payment offered: according to assignments. Columns and fillers: humor, gagwriting. Suggested word length—query. Payment offered: according to assignment.

Initial Contact. Query letter. Include name, address, phone number, and sample of work. SASE a must!

Acceptance Policies. Byline given: yes. Payment made: upon acceptance. Kill fee: negotiable. Writer's expenses: no. Seasonal material: 3 months in advance. Simultaneous submissions: yes, ask us. Response time to initial inquiry: 1 month. Average time until publication: 1 month. Computer printouts: no. Dot matrix: no. Disk submissions: no. Publishing rights: second serial rights; simultaneous rights; work-for-hire assignments.

Additional Information. Tips: Obtain sample copy of publication to grasp slant. Sample copy: $5. Writer's guidelines: SASE.

MODERN MATURITY. (American Association of Retired Persons). 3200 E. Carson. Lakewood, CA 90712. Submissions Editor: Ian Ledgerwood. Type: for persons aged 50 and over. Frequency of publication: bimonthly. Circulation: 20 million. Freelance submissions: 50%; number bought each year: n/i.

Editorial Needs. Fiction—write for information. Nonfiction—practical information; health; legal; consumer; profiles. Suggested word length—feature articles: up to 2000. Payment offered: up to $3000. Fillers: jokes, short anecdotes, and humor; word-search puzzles. Payment offered: $50.

Initial Contact. Query first.

Acceptance Policies. Byline given: yes. Payment made: upon acceptance. Kill fee: yes. Writer's expenses on assignment: sometimes. Submit seasonal material 6 months in advance. Response time to initial inquiry: 6-8 weeks. Average time until publication: 4-6 months. Computer printouts: yes. Dot matrix: no. Disk submissions: query first. Publishing rights: first North American serial rights.

Additional Information. Writer's guidelines: upon request.

MOTHER JONES MAGAZINE. 1663 Mission Street. San Francisco, CA 94103. (415) 558-8881. Submissions Editors: Peggy Orenstein (general submissions); David Beers (profiles; shorter articles). Type: political. Frequency of publication: bimonthly. Circulation: 190,000. Freelance submissions: 100%.

Editorial Needs. Fiction—political. Short stories—number per year: 2-3. Payment offered: per text. Nonfiction—book excerpts; general interest. Suggested word length—feature articles: 3500; columns: 1000. Payment offered: per text.

Initial Contact. Query letter. Include clips.

Acceptance Policies. Byline given: yes. Payment made: upon publication. Kill fee: 1/4. Writer's expenses on assignment: yes. Submit seasonal material 3 months in advance. Simultaneous submissions: no. Response time to initial inquiry: 4-6 weeks. Average time until publication: 3 months. Computer printouts: yes. Disk submissions: yes. Publishing rights: all rights.

Additional Information. Politically to the left. Writer's guidelines: request by mail.

MOTORCYCLIST. 8490 Sunset Blvd. Los Angeles, CA 90069. (213) 854-2230. Submissions Editor: Art Friedman. Type: motorcycle enthusiasts. Frequency of publication: monthly. Circulation: n/i. Freelance submissions: n/i.

Editorial Needs. Fiction—only the best humorous, philosophical, suspenseful, or science fiction-type pieces involving motorcycles. Suggested word length—1500-2000. Payment offered: $75-$100 per published page. **Nonfiction**—how-to; interview/profile; travel; timely news items; humor. Suggested word length—feature articles: 2000-2500. Payment offered: $75-$100 per published page.

Initial Contact. Entire article. Include SASE.

Acceptance Policies. Byline given: yes. Payment made: upon publication. Kill fee: varies. Writer's expenses on assignment: varies. Submit seasonal material 3-4 months in advance. Simultaneous submissions: no. Response time to initial inquiry: 4-6 weeks. Average time until publication: varies. Computer printouts: yes. Dot matrix: okay. Disk submissions: yes. Publishing rights: all rights.

Photography Submissions. Format and film: color, 35mm or 2 1/4 x 2 1/4 transparencies; black-and-white glossy or matte prints, 8x10 . Photographs should include: captions. **Payment**: according to quality and published size. Photographic rights: n/i.

Additional Information. Our audience is young, affluent, and educated. Tips: Typed, double-spaced, single side only. Material is subject to condensation or editing. Writer's guidelines: upon request.

MOTORHOME. 29901 Agoura Rd. Agoura, CA 91301. (818) 991-4980. Submissions Editors: Gail Harrington; Barbara Leonard. Type: travel and technical publication for motorhome owners. Frequency of publication: monthly. Circulation: 130,000. Freelance submissions: 75%; number bought each year: 75.

Editorial Needs. Nonfiction—general interest; historical; how-to; humor; interview/profile; photo feature; travel. Payment offered: $200-$500.

Initial Contact. Query letter.

Acceptance Policies. Byline given: yes. Payment made: upon acceptance. Kill fee: 1/3 of payment. Writer's expenses on assignment: yes. Submit seasonal material 6-9 months in advance. Simultaneous submissions: no. Response time to initial inquiry: 30 days. Average time until publication: 6-12 months. Computer printouts: yes. Dot matrix: letter quality. Disk submissions: yes. Publishing rights: first North American serial rights.

Photography Submissions. Format and film: Kodachrome 64; 35mm. Photographs should include: captions; model releases; identification of subjects. **Payment**: $75-$250. Photographic rights: one-time rights.

Additional Information. Tips: Understand our subject and travel needs and the interests of motorhome travelers. Writer's guidelines: send letter to reader correspondent.

MOTORLAND. Not accepting manuscripts.

MOTOR TREND. 8490 Sunset Blvd. Los Angeles, CA 90069. (213) 854-2222. Submissions Editor: Jack Nerad. Type: automotive and related subjects of national interest. Frequency of publication: monthly. Circulation: 75,000. Freelance submissions: 20%; number bought each year: n/i.

Editorial Needs. Nonfiction—new products; impressions; domestic and imported cars; classics; travel; racing. Payment offered: n/i.

Initial Contact. Query letter (be specific).

Acceptance Policies. Byline given: yes. Payment made: n/i. Simultaneous submissions: no. Response time to initial inquiry: 1-6 months. Average time until publication: 3 months. Computer printouts: yes. Dot matrix: letter quality. Disk submissions: no. Publishing rights: all.

Photography Submissions. Format and film: black-and-white glossy prints; color transparencies. Photographs should include: n/i. **Payment**: $25. Photographic rights: n/i.

Additional Information. Tips: Concentrate on the facts.

MYSTERY READERS JOURNAL. PO Box 8116. Berkeley, CA 94707.

(415) 548-5799, 339-2800. Submissions Editor: Janet A. Rudolph. Type: literary/mystery review. Frequency of publication: quarterly. Circulation: 1000. Freelance submissions: 100%. Payment in copies.

Editorial Needs. Nonfiction—book reviews; entertainment reviews; interview/profile. Suggested word length—feature articles: 500-2500; columns: 500. Payment offered: issue of journal.

Initial Contact. Article proposal with subject outline. Include background of writer.

Acceptance Policies. Byline given: yes. Payment made: copy. Submit seasonal material 2 months in advance. Simultaneous submissions: yes. Response time to initial inquiry: 2-3 weeks. Average time until publication: 1-2 months (depending on theme). Computer printouts: yes. Dot matrix: yes. Disk submissions: yes. Publishing rights: negotiable.

Additional Information. Each issue is thematic; articles pertaining to that issue only, i.e. 1991 *Murder on the Big Screen; Murder in the Plot* (garden); *Holiday Mysteries; Murder on the Menu* (food). Writer's guidelines: upon request.

NATIONAL MASTERS NEWS. PO Box 2372. Van Nuys, CA 91404.

(818) 785-1895. Submissions Editors: Al Sheahen (stories, photos); Jerry Wojcik (all track and field). Type: running, racewalking; track and field for age 40+. Frequency of publication: monthly. Circulation: 5400. Freelance submissions: 60%. No payment offered.

Editorial Needs. Nonfiction—general interest; health/fitness; interview/profile; opinion; coverage of races or meets. Suggested word length—feature articles: 1000; columns: 1000. Payment offered: none.

Initial Contact. Query letter.

Acceptance Policies. Byline given: yes. Payment made: none. Submit seasonal material 1 month in advance. Simultaneous submissions: yes. Response time to initial inquiry: 2 weeks. Average time until publication: 2-4 weeks. Computer printouts: yes. Dot matrix: no. Disk submissions: no. Publishing rights: n/i.

Photography Submissions. Format and film: black-and-white prints, any size. Photographs should include: identification of subjects; age of runner; event; finishing time. **Payment**: $7.50. Photographic rights: we keep photos, or return if requested.

Additional Information. Tips: Brevity is appreciated. Writer's guidelines: write and request.

NATURE'S IMAGE. PO Box 255. Davenport, CA 95017. (408) 426-8205. Submissions Editor: Frank S. Balthis. As photographers we seek science, history, and travel writers for joint submissions to magazine and book publishers, mainly in the areas of natural history and travel with a California emphasis.

NEW BLOOD MAGAZINE. 540 W. Foothill Blvd., Ste. 3730. Glendora, CA 91740. Submissions Editor: Chris Lacher. Type: horror/dark fantasy; science fiction; publishes fiction and other considered too strong by other periodicals. Frequency of publication: quarterly. Circulation: 10,000. Freelance submissions: 90%; number bought each year: 100-150.

Editorial Needs. Fiction—no restrictions, as long as themes are strong or bizarre. Short stories—number per issue: 8-12; per year: 48-50. Payment offered: $.03-$.06 per word; higher for special. **Nonfiction**—fillers; general interest; historical; humor; interview/profile; opinion. Suggested word length—feature articles: 3000. Payment offered: $.03-$.06 per word; higher for special.

Initial Contact. Any method is acceptable. Include publishing background, if any; brief bio.

Acceptance Policies. Byline given: yes. Payment made: 1/2 upon acceptance; 1/2 upon publication. Kill fee: 1/2 of offered payment. Writer's expenses on assignment: no. Submit seasonal material 6 months in advance. Simultaneous submissions: no. Response time to initial inquiry: average of 3 weeks, or less, on dated correspondence. Average time until publication: 3-6 months. Computer printouts: yes. Dot matrix: yes (all submissions with faded ribbon returned unread). Disk submissions: no. Publishing rights: all rights revert back to author upon publication.

Photography Submissions. Format and film: black-and-white prints, any size. Photographs should include: n/i. Payment: negotiable. Photographic rights: all rights revert back to photographer on publication.

Additional Information. As a writer myself, I treat all contributors as family; I support you, and I ask you to support your magazine. Tips: Becoming familiar with the unique type of fiction and features before submitting by purchasing a subscription is crucial (1 year, $14). Writer's guidelines: SASE; I always respond personally.

NEW METHODS, JOURNAL OF ANIMAL HEALTH TECHNOLOGY. PO Box 22605. San Francisco, CA 94122-0605. (415) 664-3469. Submissions Editor: Ronald S. Lippert. Type: animal professional's industry journal. Frequency of publication: irregular. Circulation: 5400+. Freelance submissions: 25%; number bought each year: 2.

Editorial Needs. Nonfiction—book reviews; fillers; how-to; interview/profile; photo feature; animal field on an information level. Suggested word length—feature articles: varies; columns: varies. Payment offered: varies, but low.

Initial Contact. Query letter. Include name, address, phone. State minimum acceptable fee and turnaround for specific work submitted.

Acceptance Policies. Byline given: yes. Payment made: upon publication. Kill fee: no. Writer's expenses on assignment: yes. Submit seasonal material 2 months in advance. Response time to initial inquiry: 1 month or less. Average time until publication: 2 months +/-. Computer printouts: yes. Dot matrix: yes. Disk submissions: no. Publishing rights: author retains all rights.

Photography Submissions. Don't submit unless we request. Format and film: black-and-white prints, 3x5. Photographs should include: whatever you think is necessary. **Payment:** low. Photographic rights: photographer retains rights.

Additional Information. Tips: Write first please; include SASE. Writer's guidelines: write; enclose SASE.

NEW WORLD TRAVELER; WEST COAST TRAVELER; EASY TRAVELER. 1449 Grant St. Berkeley, CA 94703. (415) 524-8383. Submissions Editors: Selma Exton; Peter Von Blum. All writing is done in-house at this time.

NOCTURNAL LYRIC, THE. PO Box 2602. Pasadena, CA 91102-2602.
Submissions Editors: Susan Ackerman (editor); Robin (coeditor); Lisa (art editor). Type: horror/fantasy story and poetry journal for new writers. Frequency of publication: bimonthly. Circulation: 250. Freelance submissions: 100%; number used each year: 50 stories, 50 poems. No payment offered.

Editorial Needs. Fiction—short stories: horror/fantasy. Suggested word length—2000. Payment offered: none. Fillers: bizarre things.

Initial Contact. Entire article.

Acceptance Policies. Byline given: yes. Payment made: none. Seasonal material: 3 months in advance. Simultaneous submissions: yes. Response time to initial inquiry: 1 week on queries; 6 months on manuscripts. Average time until publication: 6-8 months. Computer printouts: yes. Dot matrix: yes. Disk submissions: no. Publishing rights: up to the author.

Additional Information. No one gets paid. Not us. Not the authors. It is a nonprofit, communal effort and all money earned goes straight back into the expenses of the magazine. Our purpose is to get new writers read by others, not to make money off of them or let them make money off of us. Tips: Give us something unusual and original—different than that commercial junk. Sample copy: $1.25 (check made out to Susan). Writer's guidelines: SASE.

NORTHCOAST VIEW. PO Box 1374. Eureka, CA 95502. (707) 443-4887.
Submissions Editors: Scott K. Ryan and Damon Maguire (general); Stephen P. Miller (poetry). Type: regional Humboldt County, CA. Frequency of publication: monthly. Circulation: 22,500. Freelance submissions: 80%; number bought each year: 100.

Editorial Needs. Fiction—literary; genre. Short stories—number per issue: 1; per year: 8. Payment offered: $.02-$.10 per word. **Nonfiction**—book reviews; general interest; health/fitness; historical; interview/profile; opinion; photo feature; poetry. Suggested word length—feature articles: 2250; columns: 600. Payment offered: $.02-$.10 per word.

Initial Contact. Query letter; entire article. Include author bio.

Acceptance Policies. Byline given: yes. Payment made: upon publication. Kill fee: no. Writer's expenses on assignment: no. Submit seasonal material 6 months in advance. Simultaneous submissions: no. Response time to initial inquiry: 4-6 months. Average time until publication: 2 months. Computer printouts: yes. Dot matrix: no. Disk submissions: no. Publishing rights: all rights.

Photography Submissions. Format and film: black-and-white prints, 5x7. Photographs should include: model releases; identification of subjects. **Payment:** $20. Photographic rights: all.

Additional Information. Tips: Most submissions must have Humboldt County angle. Writer's guidelines: SASE. Sample copy $1.

NURSEWEEK. 1470 Halford Ave. Santa Clara, CA 95051. (408) 249-5877. Submissions Editor: Lydia Selling. Type: nursing, trade. Frequency of publication: biweekly. Circulation: 70,000 Southern California; 43,000 Northern California. Freelance submissions 50%; number of manuscripts bought each year: 300+.

Editorial Needs. Nonfiction—health/fitness; opinion. Suggested word length—n/i. Payment offered: n/i.

Initial Contact. Article proposal with subject outline.

Acceptance Policies. Byline given: yes. Payment made: upon publication. Kill fee: no. Writer's expenses: no. Seasonal material: 4 months in advance. Simultaneous submissions: no. Response time to initial inquiry: 4-6 weeks. Average time until publication: 2-4 months. Computer printouts: yes. Dot matrix: no. Disk submissions: IBM compatible. Publishing rights: first North American serial rights.

Photography Submissions. Format and film: color prints. Photographs should include: n/i. **Payment:** varies. Photographic rights: all rights.

Additional Information. Sample copy: call.

OFF DUTY MAGAZINE. 3303 Harbor Blvd., Ste. C-2. Costa Mesa, CA 92626. (714) 549-7172. Submissions Editors: Gary Birch (photo; audio/video; home computers); Joy Vandenberg (food; finance; lifestyle; home). Type: general interest for active duty military and their families. Frequency of publication: bimonthly. Circulation: 525,000. Freelance submissions: 40% +/-; number bought each year: 25-30.

Editorial Needs. Fiction—We use one piece of fiction a year. It must be military and holiday themes. Query first. Payment offered: $.20 per word; or by arrangement. **Nonfiction**—general interest; health/fitness; interview/profile; photo feature; self-improvement; travel (often, we like to deal with the how of travel rather than the where); off-duty concerns of today's military people. Suggested word length—feature articles: 800, 1400, 1800 words. Payment offered: $.20 per word; or by arrangement.

Initial Contact. Query letter (first); article proposal with subject outline.

Acceptance Policies. Byline given: yes. Payment made: upon acceptance. Kill fee: no. Writer's expenses on assignment: sometimes phone and mileage. Submit seasonal material 6 months in advance. Simultaneous submissions: yes; if they aren't offered elsewhere to our special audience. Response time to initial inquiry: varies; we're flooded. Average time until publication: n/i. Computer printouts: yes. Dot matrix: yes. Disk submissions: IBM PC; Wordstar. Publishing rights: first rights.

Photography Submissions. Format and film: black-and-white prints (depends on subject); slides; transparencies. Photographs should include: model releases; identification of subjects. **Payment:** depends on use. Photographic rights: first rights.

Additional Information. We're in California, but not *of* it. Our "beat" is 50 states. We are national. We assign half our stories to freelancers who work with us constantly. "On spec" stories are rarely for us. Tips: Query first. Writer's guidelines: $1; SASE.

OPERA COMPANION. 40 Museum Way. San Francisco, CA 94114. (415) 626-2741. Submissions Editor: James Keolker. Type: opera; music. Frequency of publication: 14 times yearly. Circulation: 8000. Freelance submissions: 25%; number bought each year: 10.

Editorial Needs. Nonfiction—essay; historical; nostalgia; humor; interview/profile; fillers (humor; anecdotes). Suggested word length—feature articles: 500-5000; fillers: 150-500. Payment offered: $50-$250.

Initial Contact. Query. Include clips.

Acceptance Policies. Byline given: yes. Payment made: upon acceptance. Kill fee: no. Writer's expenses on assignment: no. Response time to initial inquiry: 1-4 weeks. Average time until publication: 2 months. Computer printouts: yes. Dot matrix: letter quality. Disk submissions: no. Publishing rights: first rights.

Additional Information. Each issue highlights a specific opera and composer. Contact us for which composers and operas will be featured in upcoming issues. Writer's guidelines: 8 1/2 x 11 SASE, 3 first class stamps.

OUT OF THE CLOSET. Excellence Enterprises. 15831 Olden St., #71.
Sylmar, CA 91342-1254. Submissions Editor: LaVonne Taylor-Pickell. Type: literary. Frequency of publication: quarterly. Circulation: n/i. Freelance submissions: 100%; number used each year: varies. Payment in copies.

Editorial Needs. Fiction—science fiction; fantasy; avant-garde; general. Suggested word length—1500 maximum. Payment offered: copies. Short Stories—all. Suggested word length—1500. Payment offered: copies. **Nonfiction**—book excerpts; book reviews; entertainment reviews; interview/profile; poetry. Suggested word length—500-1000. Payment offered: copies. Columns—writing; arts. Suggested word length—500-1000. Payment offered: copies. Fillers—writing; arts.

Initial Contact. Entire article, short story, and poem. Include author bio, writing credits, and credentials.

Acceptance Policies. Byline given: yes. Payment made: in copies. Seasonal material: 6 months in advance. Simultaneous submissions: no. Response time to initial inquiry: 1 month. Average time until publication: 3 months. Computer printouts: yes. Dot matrix: letter quality. Disk submissions: no. Publishing rights: first North American serial rights.

Additional Information. A new, small literary journal, good for new writers. Tips: Be professional. Sample copy: $3. Writer's guidelines: SASE, plus $.25.

OUT WEST. 10522 Brunswick Rd. Grass Valley, CA 95945. (916) 477-9378.
Submissions Editor: Chuck Woodbury. Type: American West, general interest. Frequency of publication: quarterly. Circulation: 8000 and growing fast. Freelance submissions: 15%; number bought each year: 20.

Editorial Needs. Nonfiction—book reviews; fillers; general interest; historical; interview/profile; photo feature; travel. Suggested word length—feature articles: 400-900; columns and fillers: 350-600. Payment offered: $.04-$.06 per word; more on occasion.

Initial Contact. Query letter; entire article.

Acceptance Policies. Byline given: yes. Payment made: upon acceptance; or upon publication. Kill fee: 50%. Writer's expenses on assignment: no. Submit seasonal material 3 months in advance. Simultaneous submissions: yes. Response time to initial inquiry: 1-7 weeks. Average time until publication: 1-4 months. Computer printouts: yes. Dot matrix: yes. Disk submissions: no. Publishing rights: second serial rights; usually one-time rights.

Photography Submissions. Format and film: black-and-white prints, 5x7, 8x10. Photographs should include: captions; identification of subjects. **Payment:** $6-$15. Photographic rights: one-time.

Additional Information. We are looking for the offbeat "little" story; out-of-the-way travel places; humor always a plus. Tips: Be sure to read the publication first; $6 for yearly subscription. Writer's guidelines: #10 SASE.

OWLFLIGHT. 1025 55th St. Oakland, CA 94608. (415) 655-3024. Submissions Editor: Millea Kenin. Type: science fiction and fantasy. Frequency of publication: 1-3 per year. Circulation: 1000. Freelance submissions: 100%; number bought each year: 10-45.

Editorial Needs. Fiction—science fiction; fantasy. Suggested word length—3000-8000. Short stories—number per issue: 10-15; per year: 10-45. Payment offered: $.01 per word, $1 minimum up to $10. **Nonfiction**—no unsolicited nonfiction other than poetry (same genre as fiction); line art. Payment offered: $.01 per word, $1 minimum up to $10.

Initial Contact. Query letter with SASE (only to learn if we're still overstocked and to receive guidelines if we're open). No descriptions of story or lengthy author credit sheet. Send only 1 story, up to 6 poems or art samples per submission.

Acceptance Policies. Byline given: yes. Payment made: 1/2 on acceptance; 1/2 on publication. Kill fee: all or $10, whichever is smaller. Writer's expenses on assignment: no. Simultaneous submissions: yes; must be identified; will only take second options on them. Response time to initial inquiry: 1 week to 2 months. Average time until publication: 1-2 years. Computer printouts: yes. Dot matrix: black, letter quality. Disk submissions: only after acceptance of hard copy; Macintosh or IBM compatible text format. Publishing rights: first North American serial rights; second serial rights (send for reprint guidelines, SASE, 1 first class stamp).

Photography Submissions. Query first.

Additional Information. We have won Small Press Writers and Artists Association award twice. Tips: Get guidelines first. They are detailed and let you know what lengths, what themes are overstocked. Writer's guidelines: #10 SASE with postage to cover 2 ounces.

PAN-EROTIC REVIEW. PO Box 2992. Santa Cruz, CA 95063. (408) 426-7082. Submissions Editor: David Steinberg. Type: erotica—high quality, provocative, non-pornographic erotic fiction, poetry, and photography. Frequency of publication: quarterly. Circulation: n/i. Freelance submissions: most; number bought each year: varies.

Editorial Needs. Fiction—quality erotica, sexually explicit is fine. Short stories—number per issue: varies. Payment offered: varies. **Nonfiction**—poems; photo feature. Payment offered: varies.

Initial Contact. Query letter. Include samples of work.

Acceptance Policies. Byline given: yes. Payment made: varies. Kill fee: no. Writer's expenses on assignment: no. Simultaneous submissions: yes. Response time to initial inquiry: 6-8 weeks. Average time until publication: varies. Computer printouts: yes. Dot matrix: yes. Disk submissions: Macintosh. Publishing rights: first North American serial rights; first rights; second serial rights.

Photography Submissions. Format and film: black-and-white or color prints, 8x10; slides. Photographs should include: n/i. **Payment:** varies. Photographic rights: one-time.

PENINSULA MAGAZINE. 656 Bair Island Road, 2nd Floor. Redwood City, CA 94063. (415) 368-8800. Submissions Editor: David Gorn, Dale Conour. Type: general interest local magazine covering San Francisco Peninsula (not including San Francisco). Frequency of publication: monthly. Circulation: 40,000. Freelance submissions: 50%; number bought each year: 100.

Editorial Needs. Nonfiction—general interest; health/fitness; historical; interview/profile; photo feature; investigative pieces; environment. Suggested word length—feature articles: 2500-4000; columns: 750. Payment offered: varies.

Initial Contact. Query letter.

Acceptance Policies. Byline given: yes. Payment made: 1 month following acceptance. Kill fee: 30% of purchase price. Writer's expenses on assignment: yes. Submit seasonal material 4-5 months in advance. Simultaneous submissions: no. Response time to initial inquiry: 1 month. Average time until publication: 4 months. Computer printouts: yes. Dot matrix: yes. Disk submissions: ASCII. Publishing rights: first rights; rights of reuse without further compensation.

Photography Submissions. Format and film: black-and-white or color contact sheets; transparencies. Photographs should include: captions; model releases; identification of subjects. **Payment**: varies. Photographic rights: first rights.

Additional Information. Tips: Use local angle. Writer's guidelines: write and request.

PETERSEN'S PHOTOGRAPHIC MAGAZINE. 8490 Sunset Blvd.
Los Angeles, CA 90069. (213) 854-2200. Submissions Editor: Bill Hurter. Type: how-to photography. Frequency of publication: monthly. Circulation: 275,000. Freelance submissions: 40%; number bought each year: 50+.

Editorial Needs. Nonfiction—how-to. Suggested word length—feature articles: 2000+. Payment offered: $60 per printed page.

Initial Contact. Complete manuscript. Include captioned photos.

Acceptance Policies. Byline given: n/i. Payment made: upon publication. Kill fee: no. Writer's expenses on assignment: no. Submit seasonal material 5 months in advance. Response time to initial inquiry: 2 months. Average time until publication: 9 months. Computer printouts: yes. Dot matrix: okay. Disk submissions: IBM PC compatible only. Publishing rights: all.

Photography Submissions. Cover shots purchased separately. Format and film: black and white or color; all formats from 35mm to 8x10. Photographs should include: model releases; technical details. **Payment**: $25-$35; cover, negotiable. Photographic rights: all. Writer's guidelines: #10 SASE; sample copy $3.

PINEHURST JOURNAL. PO Box 360747. Milpitas, CA 95036. (408) 945-
0986. Submissions Editors: Michael K. McNamara (fiction, poetry); Kathleen M. McNamara (nonfiction). Type: literary. Frequency of publication: quarterly. Circulation: n/i. Freelance submissions: 100%; number bought each year: 60.

Editorial Needs. Fiction—literary; women's; mystery; historic; gay/lesbian; mild erotica; suspense. Suggested word length—1000-2500. Payment offered: $5 and a one-year subscription. Short Stories—anything tasteful. Suggested word length—50-1500. Payment offered: $5 and a one-year subscription. Nonfiction—book excerpts; book reviews; general interest; health/fitness; historical; humor; interview/profile; opinion; poetry. Suggested word length—1500-3000. Payment offered: $5 and a one-year subscription. Fillers: anything tasteful.

Initial Contact. Entire article. Query first on literary reviews. Include 25-word bio with each submission.

Acceptance Policies. Byline given: yes. Payment made: upon publication. Kill fee: no. Writer's expenses: no. Seasonal material: 7 months in advance. Simultaneous submissions: yes, inform us. Response time to initial inquiry: queries in 4 weeks; manuscripts in 8 weeks or less. Average time until publication: 6 months. Computer printouts: yes. Dot matrix: yes. Disk submissions: no. Publishing rights: one-time rights (publication is copyrighted).

Additional Information. Copies are sent to selected libraries and agents to broaden writer's exposure. Tips: We prefer a human, emotional stake, not technological approaches from our writers. Sample copy: $4.50 (including postage; SAE. Writer's guidelines: upon request.

PLAYERS PRESS, INC. PO Box 1132. Studio City, CA 91604. (818) 789-4980. Submissions Editor: Robert W. Gordon. Type: publishes plays, scripts, musicals, and performing arts books. Send for writer's guidelines; has very specific and unusual requirements.

POETRY/LA. PO Box 84271. Los Angeles, CA 90073. (213) 472-6171. Submissions Editor: Helen Friedland. Type: literary, poetry only. Frequency of publication: twice yearly. Circulation: 500. Freelance submissions: 100%; number used each year: about 200 poems. Payment in copies.

Editorial Needs. Nonfiction—poetry. Suggested word length—any. Payment offered: 1-5 copies depending on length and number of poems.

Initial Contact. Submit poems.

Acceptance Policies. Byline given: yes. Payment made: copies. Simultaneous submissions: no. Response time to initial inquiry: n/i. Average time until publication: 6 months. Computer printouts: yes. Dot matrix: no. Disk submissions: no. Publishing rights: all rights; will release on request for reprint.

Additional Information. We publish only Los Angeles area poets (Santa Barbara to Irvine). Tips: Send a SASE for writer's guidelines; or $3.50 for sample copy.

POLICE. 6300 Yarrow Dr. Carlsbad, CA 92009. (619) 438-2511. Submissions Editor: Sean T. Hilferty. Type: professional trade journal for law enforcement officers. Frequency of publication: monthly. Circulation: 54,000. Freelance submissions: 90%; number bought each year: 100.

Editorial Needs. Nonfiction—book excerpts; how-to; interview/profile; photo feature; columns. Suggested word length—feature articles: 2500: columns: 2000. Payment offered: varies with type of article.

Initial Contact. Article proposal with subject outline.

Acceptance Policies. Byline given: yes. Payment made: upon acceptance. Kill fee: no. Writer's expenses on assignment: no. Submit seasonal material 3 months in advance. Simultaneous submissions: no. Response time to initial inquiry: 2 weeks. Average time until publication: 3-6 months. Computer printouts: yes. Dot matrix: yes. Disk submissions: Macintosh compatible. Publishing rights: first North American serial rights.

Photography Submissions. Format and film: color transparencies. Photographs should include: captions; identification of subjects. **Payment**: $30 per photo. Photographic rights: first rights.

Additional Information. Tips: All material must have a strong law enforcement slant. Writer's guidelines: SASE. Sample copy: $2.

POWDER, THE SKIERS' MAGAZINE. PO Box 1028. Dana Point, CA 92629. (714) 496-5922. Submissions Editor: Steve Casimiro. Type: skiing. Frequency of publication: 7 times per year. Circulation: 150,000. Freelance submissions: 90%; number bought each year: 30.

Editorial Needs. Fiction—short stories—number per year: 30. Nonfiction—book excerpts; book reviews; entertainment reviews; general interest; health/fitness; historical; humor; interview/profile; photo feature; travel. Suggested word length—feature articles: 1500-2000. Payment offered: $.40 per word.

Initial Contact. Query letter; article proposal with subject outline; entire article. Any okay, just no phone queries.

Acceptance Policies. Byline given: yes. Payment made: on publication if article on spec; on acceptance if assigned. Kill fee: 25% for assigned articles only. Writer's expenses on assignment: if approved in advance. Submit seasonal material 5 months in advance. Simultaneous submissions: no. Response time to initial inquiry: 6-8 weeks. Average time until publication: 2-3 months. Computer printouts: yes. Dot matrix: no. Disk submissions: Macintosh. Publishing rights: first rights.

Photography Submissions. Format and film: color transparencies. Photographs should include: captions; model releases; identification of subjects. **Payment:** $50-$500 depending on size used. Photographic rights: first rights only.

Additional Information. Articles should be directed to advanced to expert skiers only! Tips: Read back issues for style. Writer's guidelines: write and request.

POWERBOAT MAGAZINE. 15917 Strathern St. Van Nuys, CA 91406.
Submissions Editor: Lisa Nordskog. Type: recreational power boating (high performance); water skiing. Frequency of publication: monthly (November/December combined). Circulation: 82,000. Freelance submissions: 60%; number bought each year: n/i.

Editorial Needs. Nonfiction—how-to photo essays; competition coverage; interviews/profiles; new products. Suggested word length—feature articles: 1500-2000. Payment offered: $150-500.

Initial Contact. Query letter required.

Acceptance Policies. Byline given: yes. Payment made: upon publication. Kill fee: no. Writer's expenses on assignment: sometimes. Response time to initial inquiry: 2 weeks. Average time until publication: 3 months. Computer printouts: yes. Dot matrix: letter quality. Disk submissions: query. Publishing rights: all; first North American serial rights.

Photography Submissions. Format and film: 35mm Kodachrome slides.

Additional Information. We are interested in how our readers can maximize their high-performance boating experiences. Writer's guidelines: upon request. Sample copy: $4.

PRIVATE PILOT. PO Box 6050. Mission Viejo, CA 92690. (714) 855-8822.
Submissions Editor: Mary F. Silitch. Type: for owner/pilots of private planes. Frequency of publication: n/i. Circulation: 100,000. Freelance submissions: 75%; number bought each year: 75+/-.

Editorial Needs. Nonfiction—general aviation field; flying techniques; new products; test reports; columns. Suggested word length—feature articles: 1000-4000; columns: 1000. Payment offered: features $75-$300; columns $50-$125.

Initial Contact. query letter.

Acceptance Policies. Byline given: n/i. Payment made: upon publication. Kill fee: no. Writer's expenses on assignment: no. Simultaneous submissions: no. Response time to initial inquiry: 8 weeks. Average time until publication: 6 months. Computer printouts: yes. Dot matrix: double-spaced; upper and lower case. Disk submissions: query. Publishing rights: first North American serial rights.

Photography Submissions. Format and film: black-and-white glossy prints, 8x10; color transparencies (cover). Photographs should include: n/i. **Payment:** $15 (black and white); $150 (cover). Photographic rights: same as article.

Additional Information. Our audience is particularly knowledgeable; articles should be well researched and written to that level. Writer's guidelines: SASE.

PROFESSIONAL CAREERS. c/o Writers Connection. 1601 Saratoga-Sunnyvale Rd., Ste. 180. Cupertino, CA 95014. (408) 973-0227. Submissions Editor: Meera Lester. *See* **HIGH TECHNOLOGY CAREERS.**

PROPHETIC VOICES. 94 Santa Maria Dr. Novato, CA 94947. (415) 897-5679. Submissions Editors: Ruth Wildes Schuler; Goldie L. Morales; Jeanne Leigh Schuler-Farrell. Type: literary, poetry. Frequency of publication: twice yearly. Circulation: 400. Freelance submissions: most. Payment in copies.

Editorial Needs. Fiction—short stories—rarely. **Nonfiction**—poetry; art. Payment offered: contributor's copy.

Initial Contact. Submit complete material.

Acceptance Policies. Byline given: n/i. Payment made: in copies. Simultaneous submissions: prefer exclusive. Response time to initial inquiry: 2 weeks. Average time until publication: varies. Computer printouts: yes. Dot matrix: n/i. Disk submissions: no. Publishing rights: n/i.

Additional Information. Tips: No religious poetry. Prefer poetry of social significance.

PUBLISH!, THE HOW-TO MAGAZINE OF DESKTOP PUBLISHING. 501 Second St. San Francisco, CA 94107. (415) 546-7722. Submissions Editor: c/o Managing Editor. Type: desktop publishing. Frequency of publication: monthly. Circulation: 100,000. Freelance submissions: 80%; number bought each year: 120.

Editorial Needs. Nonfiction—book excerpts; new products; interview/profile; technical information. Suggested word length—feature articles: 300-2500. Payment offered: $300-$2000.

Initial Contact. Query. Include clips; photo availability.

Acceptance Policies. Byline given: yes. Payment made: upon acceptance. Kill fee: no. Writer's expenses on assignment: sometimes. Response time to initial inquiry: 3 weeks. Average time until publication: n/i. Computer printouts: yes. Dot matrix: letter quality. Disk submissions: query. Publishing rights: first international.

Photography Submissions. Format and film: black-and-white contact sheets. Photographs should include: captions; identification of subjects. **Payment:** n/i. Photographic rights: same as article.

Additional Information. Writer's guidelines: upon request.

RADIANCE, THE MAGAZINE FOR LARGE WOMEN. PO Box 31703. Oakland, CA 94604. (415) 482-0680. Submissions Editor: Alice Ansfield. Type: women's; health; psychology; fashion. Frequency of publication: quarterly. Circulation: 40,000. Freelance submissions: 100%; number bought each year: 70-80.

Editorial Needs. Fiction—women's (prefer if stories are related to large women). Short stories—number per year: 10. Payment offered: $50-$100 per article at this point, plus issue in which article appears. **Nonfiction**—book excerpts; book reviews; entertainment reviews; general interest; health/fitness; historical; how-to; humor; inspiration; interview/profile; opinion; photo feature; poetry; self-improvement. Suggested word length—feature articles: 2000; columns: 1500. Payment offered: $50-$100 per article at this point, plus issue in which article appears.

Initial Contact. Article proposal with subject outline; entire article (would be nice). Include clips.

Acceptance Policies. Byline given: yes. Payment made: upon publication. Kill fee: $25, only if we requested article. Writer's expenses on assignment: most of the time. Submit seasonal material 6 months in advance. Simultaneous submissions: yes. Response time to initial inquiry: 2 1/2 months. Average time until publication: varies—our issues have themes (1-6 months). Computer printouts: yes. Dot matrix: letter quality only. Disk submissions: not at this time. Publishing rights: we're negotiable and open.

Photography Submissions. Format and film: black-and-white prints, 5x7; contact sheets; color slides. Cover in color, inside black and white. Photographs should include: captions; identification of subjects; photo credit. **Payment**: $20 per inside photo used; $50-$100 for cover. Photographic rights: n/i.

Additional Information. We're an upbeat, supportive magazine for the larger woman. We like good, strong profiles, interviews. We cover health, fashion, cultural/social views of body size, and more. Our focus is self-esteem. Tips: Send for sample copy at $2 to get the flavor of our magazine first. Writer's guidelines: SASE.

RAINBOW CITY EXPRESS. PO Box 8447. Berkeley, CA 94707-8447.
Submissions Editor: Helen B. Harvey. Type: spirituality, women's issues, psychology. Frequency of publication: quarterly. Circulation: 900 (and growing daily). Freelance submissions: 75-80%; number bought each year: 50-80. Money and/or copies.

Editorial Needs. Fiction—women's (we use very little fiction). Suggested word length—500-1000. Payment offered: copies. **Nonfiction**—book reviews; inspiration; true spiritual experiences; insights; archetypal and Kundalini activation. Suggested word length—500-1000. Payment offered: $5-$50, negotiated individually. Short features: nonfiction accounts of spiritual experiences. Columns: regular features each issue, *True Spiritual Experiences and Awakenings*. Suggested word length—n/i. Payment offered: n/i. Fillers: spiritual experiences.

Initial Contact. Obtain and read 1-2 issues of *RCE* prior to submitting anything at all.

Acceptance Policies. Byline given: yes. Payment made: upon publication. Kill fee: no. Writer's expenses: no. Seasonal material: 5-6 months in advance. Simultaneous submissions: no. Response time to initial inquiry: 1-3 months. Average time until publication: 1-5 months. Computer printouts: yes. Dot matrix: no. Disk submissions: no. Publishing rights: first North American serial rights; second serial rights.

Additional Information. *RCE* is unique, and it is essential to obtain and read one or two issues prior to writing for us. Sample copy: $6 (payable to Rainbow City). Writer's guidelines: $1 plus SASE.

RIDER. 29901 Agoura Rd. Agoura, CA 91301. Submissions Editor: Mark Tuttle,
Jr. Type: motorcycle commuting, touring, and sport riding. Frequency of publication: monthly. Circulation: 150,000. Freelance submissions: 50%; number bought each year: varies.

Editorial Needs. Nonfiction—general interest; historical; humor; inspiration; interview/profile; travel. Suggested word length—feature articles: 1000-3000. Payment offered: $100 (short feature); $350-$500 (major articles).

Initial Contact. Query first.

Acceptance Policies. Byline given: yes. Payment made: upon publication. Kill fee: no. Writer's expenses on assignment: sometimes. Submit seasonal material 4 months in advance. Response time to initial inquiry: 1 month. Average time until publication: 6 months. Computer printouts: yes. Dot matrix: no. Disk submissions: no. Publishing rights: first North American serial rights.

Photography Submissions. Format and film: black-and-white prints, 8x10; contact sheets; color transparencies. Photographs should include: captions. **Payment**: included with manuscript. Photographic rights: same as article.

Additional Information. Any submissions must be motorcycle related. Tips: Feature travel stories and favorite rides are needed. Photo quality is stressed and very important. Writer's guidelines: SASE. Sample copy: SASE, include $2.

ROAD & TRACK. 1499 Monrovia Ave. Newport Beach, CA 92663.
(714) 720-5300. Submissions Editor: Thos L. Bryant. Type: for car enthusiasts. Frequency of publication: monthly. Circulation: 700,000. We do not accept freelance submissions.

RV BUSINESS. 29901 Agoura Rd. Agoura, CA 91301. (818) 991-4980.
Submissions Editor: Katherine Sharma. Type: RV industry. Frequency of publication: semimonthly. Circulation: 25,000. Freelance submissions: 60%; number bought each year: 75; columns: 100-120.

Editorial Needs. Nonfiction—directed toward dealership owners, manufacturers, suppliers: articles on marketing; how-to; business; interview/profile; legal; verifiable statistics. Suggested word length—feature articles: 1000-1500. Payment offered: $500. Columns: guest editorial; RV people. Suggested word length—50-500. Payment offered: $10-$200.

Initial Contact. Query letter (send one or more ideas with outline of article). State photo availability; or send complete manuscript (include photos). Include clips.

Acceptance Policies. Byline given: yes. Payment made: upon acceptance. Kill fee: 50%. Writer's expenses on assignment: sometimes. Submit seasonal material 6 months in advance. Response time to initial inquiry: 3-6 weeks. Average time until publication: 2 months. Computer printouts: yes. Dot matrix: letter quality. Disk submissions: query. Publishing rights: first North American serial rights.

Photography Submissions. Required. Format and film: 35mm transparencies; black-and-white prints, 8x10. Photographs should include: captions; model releases; identification of subjects. **Payment:** included with article. Photographic rights: buys one-time or all rights. (Unused photos returned.)

Additional Information. Writer's guidelines: #10 SASE; sample copy 9x12 SASE, 3 first class stamps.

SACRAMENTO MAGAZINE. PO Box 2424. Sacramento, CA 95812-2424.
Submissions Editor: Jan Hoag. Type: regional. Frequency of publication: monthly. Circulation: 25,000. Freelance submissions: 60%; number bought each year: 15.

Editorial Needs. Nonfiction—local issues pertinent to Sacramento region. Suggested word length—feature articles: 2000-3000. Payment offered: $65-$300. Columns: business; home and garden; parenting; politics; travel; sports; arts. Suggested word length—1000-1500. Payment offered: $65-$300.

Initial Contact. Query letter. Include photo availability.

Acceptance Policies. Byline given: yes. Payment made: upon publication. Kill fee: no. Writer's expenses on assignment: sometimes. Response time to initial inquiry: 8 weeks. Average time until publication: 3 months. Computer printouts: yes. Dot matrix: letter quality. Disk submissions: no. Publishing rights: first North American serial rights; second serial rights (rarely).

Photography Submissions. Format and film: n/i. Photographs should include: captions (identification, location, and date). **Payment:** varies. Photographic rights: one-time rights.

Additional Information. Writer's guidelines: SASE; sample copy $4.50.

SAN DIEGO HOME/GARDEN. PO Box 1471. San Diego, CA 92112. (619) 233-4567. Submissions Editor: Peter Jensen. Type: regional. Frequency of publication: monthly. Circulation: 33,000. Freelance submissions: 50%; number bought each year: 60+\-.

Editorial Needs. Nonfiction—homes; gardens; home entertainment; food; local travel; architecture; interior design; arts; environment. Suggested word length—feature articles: 700-2000. Payment offered: $50-$400.

Initial Contact. Query letter. Include clips.

Acceptance Policies. Byline given: yes. Payment made: upon acceptance. Kill fee: no. Writer's expenses on assignment: sometimes. Submit seasonal material 3 months in advance. Response time to initial inquiry: 2 month. Average time until publication: 6 months. Computer printouts: yes. Dot matrix: yes. Disk submissions: Macintosh. Publishing rights: first North American serial rights.

Additional Information. Regional, unique to San Diego area only. Writer's guidelines: SASE.

SAN DIEGO READER. PO Box 80803. San Diego, CA 92138. (619) 235-3000. Submissions Editor: James E. Holman. Type: general interest for the San Diego area only. Frequency of publication: weekly. Circulation: 131,000. Freelance submissions: 15%; number bought each year: 50.

Editorial Needs. Nonfiction—general interest. Short features—number per issue: 2 3. Payment offered: $500-$1500, shorter features; $1500-$2000, longer features.

Initial Contact. Query letter.

Acceptance Policies. Byline given: yes. Payment made: upon publication. Kill fee: no. Writer's expenses on assignment: only extraordinary. Simultaneous submissions: yes. Response time to initial inquiry: 10 days. Average time until publication: 15-30 days. Computer printouts: yes. Dot matrix: yes. Disk submissions: CPM or MS-DOS. Publishing rights: first rights.

Additional Information. Only local San Diego items. Tips: Don't call us. Writer's guidelines: write and request.

SAN FERNANDO POETRY JOURNAL. 18301 Halsted St. Northridge, CA 91325. (818) 349-2080. Submissions Editor: Richard Cloke. Type: social protest poetry; women's liberation; minority rights; peace issues; environmental concerns. Frequency of publication: quarterly. Circulation: 500. Freelance submissions: 100%. Payment in copies.

Editorial Needs. Nonfiction—poetry which urges or implies struggle to alter our system. Payment offered: copies.

Initial Contact. Send poetry.

Acceptance Policies. Byline given: yes. Payment made: in copies. Submit seasonal material 12 months in advance. Simultaneous submissions: yes. Response time to initial inquiry: 1 week. Average time until publication: 1 year. Computer printouts: yes. Dot matrix: yes. Disk submissions: no. Publishing rights: one-time rights only.

Additional Information. Tips: We like to see work with energy, well thought out and with compelling ideas. See our guidelines first. Writer's guidelines: SASE.

SAN FRANCISCO BAY GUARDIAN. 520 Hampshire. San Francisco, CA 94110. (415) 824-7660. Submissions Editors: Eileen Ecklund (arts, entertainment, lifestyles, books); Vince Bielski (news); John Schmitz (illustrations, photos). Type: alternative newsweekly, with an emphasis on news, entertainment, consumer and lifestyle features. Frequency of publication: weekly. Circulation: 80,000. Freelance submissions: 80%; number bought each year: 60-200.

Editorial Needs. Nonfiction—book reviews; entertainment reviews; general interest; health/fitness; interview/profile; travel; news on local and statewide issues. Suggested word length—feature articles: 2500; columns: 800-1000. Payment offered: $40-$250, depending on length and scope.

Initial Contact. Article proposal with subject outline; entire article. Include resumé, clips.

Acceptance Policies. Byline given: yes. Payment made: upon acceptance. Kill fee: no. Writer's expenses on assignment: yes. Submit seasonal material 2 months in advance. Simultaneous submissions: no. Response time to initial inquiry: 1 month. Average time until publication: varies. Computer printouts: yes. Dot matrix: yes. Disk submissions: CPM or MS-DOS; please include printout. Publishing rights: first rights.

Photography Submissions. Format and film: black-and-white prints, 8x10. Photographs should include: captions; model releases; identification of subjects. **Payment:** $40. Photographic rights: one-time.

Additional Information. We only print high-quality individual features. Tips: Read the paper to learn our style and types of features. Write queries, don't call! Sample copy: call or write and request. There is a small fee.

SAN FRANCISCO BUSINESS TIMES. 325 Fifth St. San Francisco, CA 94107. (415) 777-9355. Submissions Editors: Delbert Schafer, Chris Rauber. Type: local business. Frequency of publication: weekly. Circulation: 20,000. Freelance submissions: 15-25%; number bought each year: 25.

Editorial Needs. Nonfiction—interview/profile; opinion. Suggested word length—feature articles: 800-1000; columns: 800. Payment offered: $100-$150.

Initial Contact. Query letter.

Acceptance Policies. Byline given: yes. Payment made: upon publication. Kill fee: no. Writer's expenses on assignment: yes. Simultaneous submissions: inform us; not to publication in our area. Response time to initial inquiry: 2-3 weeks. Average time until publication: 3 months. Computer printouts: yes. Dot matrix: yes. Disk submissions: ASCII, no control characters. Publishing rights: first North American serial rights; second serial rights.

Photography Submissions. Format and film: black-and-white prints, 5x7. Photographs should include: captions; identification of subjects. **Payment:** $35. Photographic rights: first rights.

Additional Information. Stress Bay Area business language. Tips: No puff pieces. Writer's guidelines: upon request.

SAN FRANCISCO FOCUS. 680 Eighth Ave. San Francisco, CA 94103. (415) 553-2800. Submissions Editors: Mark Powelson (features); Amy Rennert (entertainment; fashion); Rick Clogner (fiction); Karen Croft (events). Type: general interest. Frequency of publication: monthly. Circulation: 250,000. Freelance submissions: n/i; number bought each year: 5-10.

Editorial Needs. Fiction—short stories—literary. Nonfiction—entertainment reviews; fillers; general interest; health/fitness; historical; humor; interview/profile; travel. Suggested word length—feature articles: 1500. Payment offered: $50-$150 (50-500 words); $300-$750 (departments and features of 1500-3000 words).

Initial Contact. Query letter. Include resumé; clips.

Acceptance Policies. Byline given: yes. Payment made: upon acceptance. Kill fee: 25% of publication payment. Writer's expenses on assignment: yes. Submit seasonal material 2 months in advance. Simultaneous submissions: no. Response time to initial inquiry: 2-3 weeks. Average time until publication: 2-3 months. Computer printouts: yes. Dot matrix: no. Disk submissions: no. Publishing rights: first North American serial rights.

Additional Information. Writer's guidelines: SASE.

SAN JOSE STUDIES. San Jose State University. San Jose, CA 95192. (408) 924-4476. Submissions Editors: Fauneil J. Rinn (general); O.C. Williams (poetry). Type: interdisciplinary—sciences, humanities and arts, social sciences, business, and technology. Frequency of publication: winter; spring; fall. Circulation: 500+/-. Freelance submissions: 100%. Payment in copies.

Editorial Needs. Fiction—literary. Short stories—number per issue: 1-3; per year: 6-8. Payment offered: 2 copies of issue in which article appears. **Nonfiction**—articles that will provoke intellectual pleasure; poetry. Suggested word length—feature articles: 5000. Payment offered: 2 copies of issue in which article appears.

Initial Contact. Entire article (double-spaced, normal margins).

Acceptance Policies. Byline given: yes. Payment made: in copies. Simultaneous submissions: no. Response time to initial inquiry: 6-8 weeks. Average time until publication: 1 year. Computer printouts: yes. Dot matrix: no. Disk submissions: no. Publishing rights: first North American serial rights.

Additional Information. Each February a $100 award, along with a year's subscription, is given to the author of the best essay, short story, or poem appearing in the previous volume. Writer's guidelines: SASE.

SEA MAGAZINE. PO Box 1579. Newport Beach, CA 92663. (714) 660-6150. Submissions Editor: Linda Yuskaitis. Type: recreational boating; sportfishing; boating sports; cruising. Frequency of publication: monthly. Circulation: 60,000. Freelance submissions: 70%; number bought each year: 300.

Editorial Needs. Nonfiction—general interest; historical; how-to; humor; interview/profile; short news stories; photo feature; travel. Suggested word length—feature articles: 1500-2000. Payment offered: depends on length, content, and topic.

Initial Contact. Complete query letter including description of proposed story. Include brief bio; clips. State availability of photos.

Acceptance Policies. Byline given: yes. Payment made: upon publication. Kill fee: up to 50%. Writer's expenses on assignment: sometimes. Submit seasonal material 6-8 months in advance. Simultaneous submissions: no. Response time to initial inquiry: 4-6 weeks. Average time until publication: 3-6 months. Computer printouts: yes. Dot matrix: yes; letter quality. Disk submissions: IBM compatible; Word Star. Publishing rights: first North American serial rights; second serial rights (sometimes).

Photography Submissions. Format and film: color transparencies or slides. Photographs should include: captions; identification of subjects. **Payment:** $50-$250, depending on size. Photographic rights: n/i.

Additional Information. We are *the* magazine of Western boating, and our audience is made up of experienced boat owners. They seek well-informed, lively articles about the sport and its participants. Tips: A well-written, concise query letter accompanied by writing samples and, if possible, some photographs depicting your subject will be received and read with interest. Writer's guidelines: SASE (includes sample copy).

SENIOR. 3565 S. Higuera. San Luis Obispo, CA 93401. (805) 544-8711. Submissions Editors: George Brand, Herb Kamm. Type: general interest for senior citizens. Frequency of publication: monthly. Circulation: 340,000. Freelance submissions 85%; number of manuscripts bought each year: 70-80.

Editorial Needs. Nonfiction—book reviews; general interest; historical; self-improvement; travel. Suggested word length—600-900. Payment offered: $1.50 per inch.

Initial Contact. Entire article.

Acceptance Policies. Byline given: yes. Payment made: upon publication. Kill fee: no. Writer's expenses: no. Seasonal material: 2 months in advance. Simultaneous submissions: yes. Response time to initial inquiry: n/i. Average time until publication: 4-8 weeks. Computer printouts: yes. Dot matrix: no. Disk submissions: no. Publishing rights: simultaneous.

Photography Submissions. Format and film: black-and-white prints, 5x7, 8x10. Photographs should include: captions; identification of subjects. **Payment:** $15-$25. Photographic rights: n/i.

Additional Information. Sample copy: $1.50 in postage. Writer's guidelines: SAE.

SENIOR WORLD NEWSMAGAZINE. 1000 Pioneer Way. El Cajon, CA 92020. (619) 442-4404. Submissions Editors: Arlene Holmes (health); Sandy Pasqua (lifestyle); Gerald Goodrum (travel). Type: senior adults 55 years and older. Frequency of publication: monthly. Circulation: 700,000 in 7 Southern California counties. Freelance submissions: 10%; number bought each year: 15-20.

Editorial Needs. Nonfiction—News: local, state, national; Living: celebrities, remarkable seniors; also consumer, finance and investment, innovative approaches to housing, sports, hobbies, etc. Travel: destinations, how-to. Health: health and medicine emphasizing wellness and preventive care; latest medical updates. Suggested word length—feature articles: 1000-1200; columns: 800 (will consider query and sample column). Payment offered: $50-$100.

Initial Contact. Query letter. State article availability, photo availability.

Acceptance Policies. Byline given: yes. Payment made: upon publication. Kill fee: no. Writer's expenses on assignment: no. Submit seasonal material 4 months in advance. Simultaneous submissions: yes; exclusive one-time rights in our circulation area. Response time to initial inquiry: 60 days. Average time until publication: 3 months. Computer printouts: yes. Dot matrix: yes. Disk submissions: no. Publishing rights: first rights.

Photography Submissions. Format and film: black-and-white prints, 5x7, 8x10. Photographs should include: captions; model releases; identification of subjects. **Payment:** $10-$15. Photographic rights: same as written material.

Additional Information. All accepted material will be made available to all of our publications. Tips: Read the publication. Adhere to guidelines. Do not make telephone inquiries. Include your phone on all submissions. Poor spelling and presentation will automatically disqualify submissions. Writer's guidelines: upon request; sample copy $2.

SIERRA. 730 Polk Street. San Francisco, CA 94109. (415) 923-5656. Submissions Editor: Johnithon King. Type: environmental protection; outdoor recreation. Frequency of publication: every 2 months. Circulation: 350,000. Freelance submissions: 90%; number bought each year: 100.

Editorial Needs. Nonfiction—book reviews; interview/profile; travel; environmental protection and politics; outdoor adventure. Suggested word length—feature articles: 2000-3000; columns: 500-1000. Payment offered: $75-$350 (departments); $500-$1000 (features).

Initial Contact. Query letter. Include clips and SASE for reply.

Acceptance Policies. Byline given: yes. Payment made: upon acceptance. Kill fee: no. Writer's expenses on assignment: phone only; no travel. Submit seasonal material 6 months in advance. Simultaneous submissions: no. Response time to initial inquiry: 4-6 weeks. Average time until publication: 2-4 months. Computer printouts: yes. Dot matrix: yes. Disk submissions: We make arrangements with author. Publishing rights: first North American serial rights.

Photography Submissions. Photo research is conducted separately.

Additional Information. Tips: Get to know the magazine so that you are familiar with the departments and what we've published recently. Writer's guidelines: SASE.

SILVER WINGS. PO Box 1000. Pearblossom, CA 93553-1000. (805) 264-3726.
Submissions Editor: Jackson Wilcox. Type: inspirational poetry; affirmatively Christian and ecumenical in nature. Frequency of publication: quarterly. Circulation: 400+. Freelance submissions: 100%; number used each year: 200. Payment in subscription and copies.

Editorial Needs. **Nonfiction**—inspiration; poetry. Suggested word length—no more than 20 lines. Payment offered: $7 subscription plus $2 copy of issue ($9 per poem in value).

Initial Contact. Entire article; cover letter listing poet's credentials. Include SASE for return.

Acceptance Policies. Byline given: yes. Payment made: in subscription and copies. Submit seasonal material 9 months in advance. Simultaneous submissions: yes; first rights. Response time to initial inquiry: 10-30 days. Average time until publication: 3-18 months. Computer printouts: yes. Dot matrix: yes. Disk submissions: no. Publishing rights: first rights.

Additional Information. Our purpose is to encourage poetry to lift the spirit of humankind to God. Tips: We also sponsor contests which result in chapbooks, as *Thanatopsis Wings*, *Wings of Wonder*, and *New Life Wings*. Writer's guidelines: SASE.

SINISTER WISDOM. PO Box 3252. Berkeley, CA 94703. Submissions Editor:
Elana Dykewomon. Type: lesbian literary, art and political journal (since 1976). Frequency of publication: quarterly. Circulation: 3000. Freelance submissions: 90%. Payment in copies.

Editorial Needs. **Fiction**—theme issues on lesbian subjects. Short stories—number per issue: 4-9; per year: 20-40. Payment offered: in copies. **Nonfiction**—book reviews; historical; opinion; poetry. Suggested word length—feature articles: under 3000 words preferred. Payment offered: in copies.

Initial Contact. n/i.

Acceptance Policies. Byline given: yes. Payment made: in copies. Simultaneous submissions: no. Response time to initial inquiry: 2 weeks for inquiry; up to 9 months for acceptance or rejection decision. Average time until publication: 2-4 months. Computer printouts: yes. Dot matrix: yes. Disk submissions: Macintosh Word or Write. Publishing rights: all rights remain with author.

Photography Submissions. Format and film: black-and-white prints, 5x7. Photographs should include: captions; model releases. **Payment**: 2 copies. Photographic rights: none.

Additional Information. Send 2 copies, SASE, and postcard for acceptance notification. Tips: Read *Sinister Wisdom* first. Writer's guidelines: SASE. Sample copy: $6.

SKIN DIVER MAGAZINE. 8490 Sunset Blvd. Los Angeles, CA 90069.
(213) 854-2960. Submissions Editor: Bill Gleason. Type: broad coverage of topics related to scuba diving. Frequency of publication: monthly. Circulation: 225,000. Freelance submissions: 85%; number bought each year: 200.

Editorial Needs. Nonfiction—how-to; interview/profile; personal experience (no "how I learned to . . ."); travel (no Caribbean); photo feature; fillers; cartoons. Suggested word length—feature articles: 1200 preferred. Payment offered: $50 per published page; $25 (cartoon).

Initial Contact. Complete manuscript. Include photos.

Acceptance Policies. Byline given: yes. Payment made: upon publication. Kill fee: no. Writer's expenses on assignment: no. Submit seasonal material 6 months in advance. Simultaneous submissions: no. Response time to initial inquiry: 3 months. Average time until publication: 9 months. Computer printouts: yes. Dot matrix: letter quality. Disk submissions: query. Publishing rights: one-time rights.

Photography Submissions. Format and film: 35mm transparencies. Photographs should include: captions; identification of subjects. **Payment:** n/i. Photographic rights: one-time rights.

Additional Information. Tips: Write for areas of interest. Writer's guidelines: upon request.

SOCCER AMERICA MAGAZINE. PO Box 23704. Oakland, CA 94623.
(415) 528-5000. Submissions Editor: Lynn Berling-Manuel. Type: for soccer fans. Frequency of publication: weekly. Circulation: 25,000. Freelance submissions: 10%; number bought each year: 35.

Editorial Needs. Nonfiction—interview/profile; photo feature; technical; historical; expose; special issues (query for subject). Suggested word length—feature articles: 200-1500. Payment offered: $.50 per inch minimum.

Initial Contact. Query letter.

Acceptance Policies. Byline given: yes. Payment made: upon publication. Kill fee: no. Writer's expenses on assignment: on a case-by-case basis. Submit seasonal material 3 months in advance. Response time to initial inquiry: 2 months. Average time until publication: 2 months. Computer printouts: yes. Dot matrix: letter quality. Disk submissions: query. Publishing rights: all.

Photography Submissions. With or without manuscript; query. Format and film: black-and-white glossy prints, 5x7+. Photographs should include: captions. **Payment:** $12. Photographic rights: one time.

Additional Information. Tips: Read the publication! Writer's guidelines: $1.

SONOMA MANDALA. Department of English. Sonoma State University.
1801 E. Cotati Ave. Rohnert Park, CA 94928. (707) 664-2140. Submissions Editor: Elizabeth Herron, Faculty Advisor. Type: literary magazine. Frequency of publication: annual. Circulation: 700. Freelance submissions: 100%. Payment in copies.

Editorial Needs. Fiction—literary; general. Short stories—number per year: 5-8. Payment offered: 2 copies. Nonfiction—humor; poetry. Payment offered: 2 copies.

Initial Contact. Send 10 pages of fiction; 3-5 poems.

Acceptance Policies. Byline given: yes. Payment made: in copies. Simultaneous submissions: inform us. Response time to initial inquiry: 3-6 months. Average time until publication: 6 months. Computer printouts: yes. Dot matrix: yes. Disk submissions: no. Publishing rights: first North American serial rights.

Photography Submissions. Our art does not illustrate text, but stands on its own. Art is reviewed in May. Format and film: black-and-white prints, 8x10 high contrast. Photographs should include: artist's name, address, and phone on back; with title. **Payment**: contributor's copy. Photographic rights: all rights revert to artist.

Additional Information. We accept submissions between August 1 and November 15 only. Writer's guidelines: SASE.

SPECIALTY RETAILER. 7628 Densmore. Van Nuys, CA 91406. (818) 782-7328. Submissions Editor: Barbara Feiner. Type: hospital gift shops, hotel gift shops, and college bookstores. Frequency of publication: monthly. Circulation: 11,555. Freelance submissions: 40%; number bought each year: 12-25.

Editorial Needs. Nonfiction—how-to; interview/profile; photo feature; cartoons; management. Suggested word length—feature articles: 750-2500. Payment offered: $10-$100; $20 (cartoons).

Initial Contact. Query first; double-spaced submissions. State availability of photos.

Acceptance Policies. Byline given: yes. Payment made: upon acceptance. Kill fee: no. Writer's expenses on assignment: no. Submit seasonal material 8 months in advance. Simultaneous submissions: no. Response time to initial inquiry: 1 month. Average time until publication: 4 months. Computer printouts: yes. Dot matrix: must be readable. Disk submissions: yes. Publishing rights: first North American serial rights.

Photography Submissions. Format and film: black-and-white or color prints, 5x7. Photographs should include: captions; model release; identification of subjects. **Payment**: varies. Photographic rights: n/i.

Additional Information. Tips: Make sure your query is direct and exciting. That will help convince me your story will be also. Writer's guidelines: and sample copy $4 postage.

STARRY NIGHTS. 274 Roanoke Rd. El Cajon, CA 92020. (619) 546-2130. Submissions Editor: Robin Hood. Type: science fiction erotica. Frequency of publication: yearly. Circulation: 1000. Freelance submissions: 75; number bought each year: 12.

Editorial Needs. Fiction—science fiction; fantasy; erotica. Suggested word length—open. Payment offered: $.01 per word. Short Stories—science fiction; fantasy; erotica. Suggested word length—open. Payment offered: $.01 per word.

Initial Contact. Entire article.

Acceptance Policies. Byline given: yes. Payment made: upon acceptance. Kill fee: no. Writer's expenses: no. Simultaneous submissions: no. Response time to initial inquiry: 2 weeks. Average time until publication: next issue. Computer printouts: yes. Dot matrix: yes. Disk submissions: IBM compatible; ASCII or Word Perfect. Publishing rights: first North American serial rights.

Additional Information. We pay $5 per art piece (halftones are okay). Sample copy: upon request. Writer's guidelines: upon request.

STONE SOUP, THE MAGAZINE BY CHILDREN. PO Box 83. Santa Cruz, CA 95063. (408) 426-5557. Submissions Editor: Gerry Mandel. Type: literary magazine of work by children through age 13. Frequency of publication: every other month. Circulation: 12,000. Freelance submissions: 100%; number bought each year: 60.

Editorial Needs. Fiction—literary. Short stories—number per issue: 7; per year: 35. Payment offered: schedule available upon request. **Nonfiction**—book reviews; poetry. Payment offered: schedule available upon request.

Initial Contact. Entire article.

Acceptance Policies. Byline given: yes. Payment made: n/i. Submit seasonal material 6 months in advance. Simultaneous submissions: no. Response time to initial inquiry: 4 weeks. Average time until publication: 10 weeks. Computer printouts: yes. Dot matrix: yes. Disk submissions: no. Publishing rights: all rights.

Additional Information. Please note that all the writing we publish is by children. We have a preference for work based on real-life experiences. Tips: Read a couple of issues of our magazine to get a sense of the kind of work we like. Sample copy: $4. Writer's guidelines: SASE.

SUNSET MAGAZINE. 80 Willow Rd. Menlo Park, CA 94025. (415) 321-3600. Does not accept freelance submissions.

SURFER MAGAZINE. PO Box 1028. Dana Point, CA 92629. (714) 496-5922. Submissions Editors: Matt Warshaw (features); Ben Marcus (columns); Jeff Divine (photography). Type: surf specialty. Frequency of publication: monthly. Circulation: 112,000. Freelance submissions: 40%; number bought each year: 50-60.

Editorial Needs. **Fiction**—surf related. Short stories—number per issue: 1. Payment offered: $.10-$.15 per word as published. **Nonfiction**—book reviews; health/fitness; historical; how-to; humor; inspiration; interview/profile; opinion; photo feature; travel. Suggested word length—feature articles: 1500-3500; columns: 500-1200. Payment offered: $.10-$.15 per word as published.

Initial Contact. Query letter; or article proposal with subject outline.

Acceptance Policies. Byline given: yes. Payment made: upon publication. Kill fee: no. Writer's expenses on assignment: yes. Submit seasonal material 3 months in advance. Simultaneous submissions: yes; no responsibility, no obligation. Response time to initial inquiry: 60-90 days. Average time until publication: 90 days. Computer printouts: yes. Dot matrix: yes. Disk submissions: no. Publishing rights: first North American serial rights.

Photography Submissions. Format and film: transparencies only; K64 color. Photographs should include: identification of subjects; photographer identification. **Payment**: $30-200. Photographic rights: first rights.

Additional Information. Articles should be aimed at intermediate to advance surfers. Writer's guidelines: SASE.

THIS WORLD. (*San Francisco Chronicle* Sunday Feature Magazine). 901 Mission St. San Francisco, CA 94103. (415) 777-7050. Submissions Editor: Lyle York. Type: features, columns, analysis. Frequency of publication: weekly. Circulation: 750,000. Freelance submissions: 20%; number bought each year: 100.

Editorial Needs. **Fiction**—literary. Short stories—number per issue: 1; per year: 5. Very rarely used. Payment offered: $75-$300 per piece. **Nonfiction**—book excerpts; general interest; health/fitness; historical; humor; interview/profile; opinion; photo feature; science; psychology; technology. Suggested word length—feature articles: up to 4000 words; columns: up to 2000 words. Payment offered: $75-$300 per piece.

Initial Contact. Query letter; or entire article. State author's qualifications if appropriate.

Acceptance Policies. Byline given: yes. Payment made: upon publication. Kill fee: no. Writer's expenses on assignment: no. Submit seasonal material 1 month in advance. Simultaneous submissions: yes. Response time to initial inquiry: 4 weeks. Average time until publication: 10 weeks. Computer printouts: yes. Dot matrix: no. Disk submissions: no. Publishing rights: first rights; second serial rights.

Photography Submissions. Format and film: black-and-white prints. Photographs should include: identification of subjects. **Payment:** $40 or less. Photographic rights: one-time use.

Additional Information. Phone queries not acceptable. All articles must be submitted on spec. Tips: Send finished manuscript with SASE. Don't call.

THRASHER MAGAZINE. PO Box 884570. San Francisco, CA 94188-4570.
(415) 822-3083. Submissions Editors: Kevin J. Thatcher, Kurt Carlson. Type: skateboarding and snowboarding. Frequency of publication: monthly. Circulation: n/i. Freelance submissions 10%.; number of manuscripts bought each year: 6.

Editorial Needs. Fiction—rock 'n roll; "gonzo." Suggested word length—1500-2000. Payment offered: $.15 per word. Short Stories—skateboarding. Suggested word length—1000-1500. Payment offered: $.15 per word. **Nonfiction**—humor; interview/profile; photo feature; poetry; music reviews. Suggested word length—1000-1500. Payment offered: $.15 per word.

Initial Contact. Query letter; article proposal with subject outline; entire article. Include social security number.

Acceptance Policies. Byline given: yes. Payment made: upon publication. Kill fee: no. Writer's expenses: yes. Simultaneous submissions: no. Response time to initial inquiry: immediate, if we like it. Average time until publication: 3-6 months. Computer printouts: yes. Dot matrix: yes. Disk submissions: IBM or Macintosh. Publishing rights: all rights.

Photography Submissions. Format and film: black-and-white or color prints, 8x10. Photographs should include: captions; model releases; identification of subjects; location. **Payment:** $35-$250 (by published size). Photographic rights: all or part.

Additional Information. Tips: Use a fresh approach. Talk to a youth audience, not to their parents. Sample copy: upon request. Writer's guidelines: not available.

THREEPENNY REVIEW. PO Box 9131. Berkeley, CA 94709.
(415) 849-4545. Submissions Editor: Wendy Lesser. Type: literary magazine in the areas of politics and the arts. Frequency of publication: quarterly. Circulation: 8,000. Freelance submissions: 100%; number bought each year: 40.

Editorial Needs. Fiction—literary. Suggested word length—800-4000. Payment offered: $50. **Nonfiction**—(best area for freelancers) reviews (book, film, theater, dance, music, art); interview/profile; personal experience; historical; essays; exposes; poetry (free verse, traditional). Suggested word length—feature articles: 1500-4000. Payment offered: $50.

Initial Contact. Query. Include clips.

Acceptance Policies. Byline given: yes. Payment made: upon acceptance. Kill fee: no. Writer's expenses on assignment: no. Response time to initial inquiry: 1-2 months. Average time until publication: 1 year. Computer printouts: yes. Dot matrix: letter quality. Disk submissions: no. Publishing rights: first North American serial rights.

Additional Information. Writer's guidelines: SASE.

TOTAL HEALTH. 6001 Topanga Canyon Blvd., Ste. 300. Woodland Hills, CA
91367. (818) 887-6484. Submissions Editor: Robert L. Smith. Type: health and fitness. Frequency of publication: every other month. Circulation: 85,000. Freelance submissions: 80%; number bought each year: 40.

Editorial Needs. Nonfiction—health/fitness; inspiration; self-improvement. Suggested word length—feature articles: 1600-1800. Payment offered: $50-$75 depending on length and professional experience.

Initial Contact. Outline of article (send on spec).

Acceptance Policies. Byline given: yes. Payment made: upon publication. Kill fee: no. Writer's expenses on assignment: no. Submit seasonal material 3 months in advance. Simultaneous submissions: yes. Response time to initial inquiry: 4 weeks. Average time until publication: 6-8 weeks. Computer printouts: no. Dot matrix: no. Disk submissions: no. Publishing rights: first rights.

Photography Submissions. Format and film: black-and-white or color glossy prints, 5x7 or 8x10. Photographs should include: captions; model releases. **Payment:** $45. Photographic rights: n/i.

Additional Information. We look for the holistic approach: body, mind, and spirit. Writer's guidelines: $1 plus postage for sample copy and guidelines.

TRADESWOMEN. PO Box 40664. San Francisco, CA 94140. (415) 821-7334. Submissions Editor: Molly Martin. Type: for blue-collar working women. Frequency of publication: quarterly. Circulation: 900. Freelance submissions: 75%. No payment offered.

Editorial Needs. **Fiction**—women's (related to work in the trades). Short stories—number per issue: 2. Payment offered: sorry, none. **Nonfiction**—book excerpts; book reviews; general interest; health/fitness; inspiration; interview/profile; photo feature; fillers. Suggested word length—feature articles: 1000-2000. Payment offered: sorry, none.

Initial Contact. Query letter; article proposal with subject outline. Include phone.

Acceptance Policies. Byline given: yes. Payment made: none. Submit seasonal material: write or call for next deadline. Simultaneous submissions: yes. Response time to initial inquiry: 4-6 weeks. Average time until publication: 4-8 weeks. Computer printouts: yes. Dot matrix: yes. Disk submissions: Macintosh. Publishing rights: share rights with author.

Photography Submissions. Format and film: black-and-white prints; contact sheets. Photographs should include: captions; identification of subjects. **Payment:** up to $25. Photographic rights: none.

Additional Information. Looking for articles by or about women in blue-collar occupations.

TRAILER BOATS. 20700 Belshaw Ave. Carson, CA 90746. (213) 537-6322. Submissions Editor: Willey Poole. Type: boating for people who own powerboats 26 feet and less. Frequency of publication: monthly. Circulation: 83,000. Freelance submissions: 20%; number bought each year: 10.

Editorial Needs. **Nonfiction**—fillers; historical; how-to; humor; photo feature; travel. Suggested word length—feature articles: 1000-1500. Payment offered: $.07-$.10 per word.

Initial Contact. Query letter. Include samples of published work if available.

Acceptance Policies. Byline given: yes. Payment made: upon publication. Kill fee: no. Writer's expenses on assignment: no. Submit seasonal material 4 months in advance. Simultaneous submissions: yes. Response time to initial inquiry: 30 days. Average time until publication: 3-6 months. Computer printouts: yes. Dot matrix: yes. Disk submissions: ASCII. Publishing rights: first rights.

Photography Submissions. Format and film: black-and-white prints or color, 8x10; (color preferred, depending on story). Photographs should include: captions; model releases; identification of subjects. **Payment:** $10-50 per photo. Photographic rights: first rights.

Additional Information. No articles on sailboats; powerboats only. Tips: Read our magazine and be familiar with our format. Writer's guidelines: SASE.

TRAILER LIFE. 29901 Agoura Rd. Agoura, CA 91301. (213) 991-4980. Submissions Editors: Barbara Leonard (features, travel); Bob Livingston (technical). Type: for the dedicated RV owner. Frequency of publication: monthly. Circulation: 340,000. Freelance submissions: 60%; number bought each year: 100.

Editorial Needs. Nonfiction—health/fitness; lifestyle; photo feature; travel. Suggested word length—feature articles: 1000-2000. Payment offered: $50-$500.

Initial Contact. Query letter; article proposal with subject outline.

Acceptance Policies. Byline given: yes. Payment made: upon acceptance. Kill fee: yes, if assigned article. Writer's expenses on assignment: sometimes. Submit seasonal material 4 months in advance. Response time to initial inquiry: 2-4 weeks. Average time until publication: 6 months. Computer printouts: yes. Dot matrix: no. Disk submissions: IBM compatible. Publishing rights: first rights.

Photography Submissions. Buys some supplemental photography. Format and film: contact sheets; transparencies; black-and-white prints, 8x10. Photographs should include: captions. **Payment:** $75-$250. Photographic rights: first North American.

Additional Information. Tips: Guidelines will help determine areas most open to freelancers. Make sure you have the expertise to write about RV life. Writer's guidelines: upon request.

TUCUMCARI LITERARY REVIEW. 3108 W. Bellevue Ave. Los Angeles, CA 90026. (213) 413-0789. Submissions Editor: Troxey Kemper. Type: literary; poetry; fiction. Frequency of publication: bimonthly. Circulation: 125+. Freelance submissions: 100%; number used each year: 500. Payment in copies.

Editorial Needs. Fiction—short stories: anything interesting. Suggested word length—1200. Payment offered: 1 copy. **Nonfiction**—general interest; historical; humor; opinion; poetry. Suggested word length—1200. Payment offered: 1 copy. Fillers: writing, authorship.

Initial Contact. Entire article. Include SASE.

Acceptance Policies. Byline given: yes. Payment made: in copies. Seasonal material: 4 months in advance. Simultaneous submissions: yes. Response time to initial inquiry: 1 day to 1 month. Average time until publication: 2 months. Computer printouts: yes. Dot matrix: no. Disk submissions: no. Publishing rights: one-time rights (copyright remains with author).

Additional Information. No Japanese poetry forms here; we use old-fashioned, standard forms of poems here, no disjointed fragments. Sample copy: $1.50, $.50 postage. Writer's guidelines: SASE.

UNIX WORLD, MCGRAW-HILL'S MAGAZINE OF OPEN SYSTEMS COMPUTING. McGraw-Hill Publishing. 444 Castro St., 2nd Floor. Mountain View, CA 94041. (415) 940-1500. Submissions Editors: Diane Jacob, Executive Editor; Howard Baldwin (new products); Dr. Becca Thomas (tutorial); Alan Southerton (products review editor); Frank Hayes (features); Gary Andrew Pool (features). Type: trade. Frequency of publication: monthly. Circulation: 55,000. Freelance submissions: less than 15-20%.

Editorial Needs. Nonfiction—book reviews; how-to; interview/profile; technical relating to UNIX. Suggested word length—feature articles: 2400; columns: 1500-1800 (varies). Payment offered: features, $700-$800; columns, varies.

Initial Contact. Query letter; article proposal with subject outline.

Acceptance Policies. Byline given: yes. Payment made: upon publication; when the story is sent to be typeset. Kill fee: yes. Writer's expenses on assignment: yes. Submit seasonal material 3-4 months in advance. Simultaneous submissions: no. Response time to initial inquiry: 1-3 months. Average time until publication: 3-4 months. Computer printouts: yes. Dot matrix: yes. Disk submissions: ASCII; 5 1/4" IBM. Publishing rights: first North American serial rights.

Photography Submissions. Format and film: color transparencies; black-and-white proof sheets. Photographs should include: captions; identification of subjects. **Payment:** included in text transaction. Photographic rights: first run.

Additional Information. This is a magazine for networked and multitasking systems. Writer's guidelines: upon request from the editorial assistant. Sample copy: upon request from the circulation department.

VALLEY MAGAZINE. 16800 Devonshire, Ste. 275. Granada Hills, CA 91344. (818) 368-3353. Submissions Editor: Barbara Wernik. Type: issues and concerns related to residents of the San Fernando Valley and Southern California. Frequency of publication: monthly. Circulation: 35,000. Freelance submissions: 70%; number bought each year: 100.

Editorial Needs. Nonfiction—adventure; agriculture; art; book reviews; business opportunities; career; child care; children; economics; entertainment reviews; general interest; health/fitness; interview/profile; photo feature; self-improvement; travel. Suggested word length—feature articles: 1200-1800; columns: 800-1000. Payment offered: $150-$350 depending on length and topic.

Initial Contact. Query letter; or article proposal with subject outline; or entire article. Include bio; clips.

Acceptance Policies. Byline given: yes. Payment made: upon acceptance. Kill fee: 20%. Writer's expenses on assignment: no. Submit seasonal material 3 months in advance. Simultaneous submissions: yes; we want first rights. Response time to initial inquiry: 4 weeks. Average time until publication: 8 weeks. Computer printouts: yes. Dot matrix: yes. Disk submissions: no. Publishing rights: first rights.

Photography Submissions. Format and film: black and white; color transparencies. Photographs should include: identification of subjects. **Payment:** depends on assignment. Photographic rights: n/i.

Additional Information. Everything we do, except travel, somehow relates to the San Fernando Valley. Tips: Articles should be upbeat, positive, and geared to enhancing the quality of our readers' lives. Writer's guidelines: SASE.

VERVE. PO Box 3205. Simi Valley, CA 93093. (805) 527-8824. Submissions Editors: Ron Reichick; Mona Locke; Marilyn Hochheiser. Type: literary. Frequency of publication: quarterly. Circulation: 300. Freelance submissions 100; number of manuscripts used each year: 140. Payment in copies.

Editorial Needs. Fiction—literary. Suggested word length—1000. Payment offered: 1 copy. Short Stories—each issue has a theme. Suggested word length—1000. Payment offered: 1 copy. **Nonfiction**—general interest; humor; opinion. Poetry. Suggested length—36 lines. Payment offered: 1 copy.

Initial Contact. Entire article.

Acceptance Policies. Byline given: yes. Payment made: upon publication and in copies. Seasonal material: 3 months in advance. Simultaneous submissions: yes, inform us. Response time to initial inquiry: 4 weeks after issue deadline. Average time until publication: 6 weeks after issue deadline. Computer printouts: yes. Dot matrix: yes. Disk submissions: no. Publishing rights: first North American serial rights.

Additional Information. Each issue has a theme. Tips: Be familiar with our writing style. Sample copy: $3.50. Writer's guidelines: SASE.

VISION. 561 Dalton Way, A. Goleta, CA 93117. Submissions Editor: Roy Smith. Type: science fiction. Frequency of publication: bimonthly. Circulation: n/i. Freelance submissions: 90%; number bought each year: 30. Payment in money and copies.

Editorial Needs. Fiction—science fiction. Suggested word length—2000. Payment offered: 6 issue subscription. Short Stories—science fiction. Suggested word length—2000. Payment offered: 10 copies of that issue. **Nonfiction**—high-tech breakthrough; science; poetry. Suggested word length—2000 or less. Payment offered: $.005 per word.

Initial Contact. Entire article. Include SASE for return of manuscript.

Acceptance Policies. Byline given: yes. Payment made: upon publication and in copies. Kill fee: no. Writer's expenses: no. Seasonal material: 3 months in advance. Simultaneous submissions: no. Response time to initial inquiry: 2 weeks for rejection, longer if accepted. Average time until publication: 3-4 months. Computer printouts: yes. Dot matrix: yes. Disk submissions: IBM or Macintosh; TRS 80 M3. Publishing rights: first rights.

Additional Information. We use only 12 poems per year. Sample copy: $1.75. Writer's guidelines: SASE.

WEST. 750 Ridder Park Dr. San Jose, CA 95190. (408) 920-5000. Submissions Editor: Charles Matthews. Type: general interest with a Bay Area focus. Frequency of publication: weekly. Circulation: 320,000. Freelance submissions: 33%; number bought each year: 50.

Editorial Needs. Fiction—rarely accept any. Payment offered: $150 and up per text. **Nonfiction**—book excerpts; general interest; health/fitness; how-to; humor; interview; profile; photo feature; travel. Payment offered: $150 and up per text.

Initial Contact. Query letter. Include clips.

Acceptance Policies. Byline given: yes. Payment made: upon acceptance. Kill fee: 25%. Writer's expenses on assignment: no. Submit seasonal material 2 months in advance. Simultaneous submissions: no. Response time to initial inquiry: 3 weeks. Average time until publication: 2 months. Computer printouts: yes. Dot matrix: yes. Disk submissions: yes. Publishing rights: first North American serial rights.

Additional Information. Tips: We expect authors to familiarize themselves with our magazine. Writer's guidelines: none.

WESTART. PO Box 6868. Auburn, CA 95604. (916) 885-0969. Submissions Editor: Martha Garcia. Type: current reviews of art for the artist/craftsman and people who enjoy art. Frequency of publication: semimonthly tabloid. Circulation: 6000. Freelance submissions: yes; number bought each year: 6-8.

Editorial Needs. Nonfiction—information; photo feature; interview/profile. Suggested word length—feature articles: 700-800. Payment offered: $.50 per column inch.

Initial Contact. Query letter; or complete manuscript. Phone queries accepted.

Acceptance Policies. Byline given: yes. Payment made: upon publication. Kill fee: no. Writer's expenses on assignment: no. Response time to initial inquiry: 1 month. Average time until publication: 1 month. Computer printouts: yes. Publishing rights: all.

Photography Submissions. Purchase with or without article. Format and film: black-and-white prints. Photographs should include: n/i. **Payment:** $.50 per column inch. Photographic rights: yes.

Additional Information. Tips: deadlines critical. Writer's guidelines: upon request; sample copy $1.

WESTERN AND EASTERN TREASURES. 5440 Ericson Way.
PO Box 1095. Arcata, CA 95521. (707) 822-8442. Submissions Editor: Rosemary Anderson. Type: treasure hunting as hobby and sport. Frequency of publication: monthly. Circulation: 100,000. Freelance submissions: 100%; number bought each year: 300+/-.

Editorial Needs. Nonfiction—book reviews; fillers; how-to; interview/profile; opinion; travel. Suggested word length—feature articles: 1500. Payment offered: $.02 per word.

Initial Contact. Entire article; cover letter listing amount of experience in the hobby/sport of treasure hunting.

Acceptance Policies. Byline given: yes. Payment made: upon publication. Kill fee: n/i. Writer's expenses on assignment: no. Submit seasonal material 6 months in advance. Simultaneous submissions: no. Response time to initial inquiry: 4 weeks. Average time until publication: 3-12 months. Computer printouts: yes. Dot matrix: no. Disk submissions: no. Publishing rights: all.

Photography Submissions. Format and film: black-and-white prints, 3x5. Photographs should include: captions; model releases; identification of subjects. **Payment:** $5 per photo; more for cover. Photographic rights: all.

Additional Information. Tips: Read guidelines first; follow them. I'm especially looking for how-to material. Writer's guidelines: upon request.

WESTERN OUTDOORS. PO Box 2027. Newport Beach, CA 92559-1027.
(714) 546-4370. Submissions Editor: Jack Brown. Type: fishing, hunting. Frequency of publication: 9 times per year. Circulation: 138,000. Freelance submissions: 70%; number bought each year: 70+/-.

Editorial Needs. Nonfiction—interviews/profile; how-to; where-to. Suggested word length—feature articles: 1100-1200. Payment offered: $400+/-.

Initial Contact. Query letter. Include published credits.

Acceptance Policies. Byline given: yes. Payment made: upon acceptance. Kill fee: no. Writer's expenses on assignment: no. Submit seasonal material 6 months in advance. Simultaneous submissions: no. Response time to initial inquiry: 4 weeks. Average time until publication: 4-6 months. Computer printouts: yes. Dot matrix: no. Disk submissions: no. Publishing rights: first North American serial rights.

Photography Submissions. Format and film: color transparencies. Photographs should include: captions; model releases. **Payment:** included in package. Photographic rights: included.

Additional Information. Tips: Avoid first-person writing. Writer's guidelines: SASE.

WESTWAYS. (Automobile Club of Southern California). PO Box 2890. Los
Angeles, CA 90051. Submissions Editor: Eric Seyforth. Type: regional publication with emphasis on Western and world travel. Frequency of publication: monthly. Circulation: 450,000. Freelance submissions: 90%; number bought each year: 125.

Editorial Needs. Nonfiction—foreign and domestic travel; general interest; history; humor; photo feature. Payment offered: $150-$350. Suggested word length—feature articles: 1500. Columns: *Wit and Wisdom*; 750-900 words.

Initial Contact. Query; or complete manuscript. Include clips.

Acceptance Policies. Byline given: yes. Payment made: 30 days before publication. Kill fee: $75. Writer's expenses on assignment: sometimes. Submit seasonal material 6 months in advance. Response time to initial inquiry: 2 weeks. Average time until publication: 6 months.

Computer printouts: yes. Dot matrix: letter quality. Disk submissions: no. Publishing rights: first North American serial rights.

Photography Submissions. Send with queries or manuscripts. Format and film: color transparencies. Photographs should include: captions; model releases; identification of subjects. **Payment:** $50; $400 (full color cover). Photographic rights: one-time rights.

Additional Information. Writer's guidelines: freelancer newsletter upon request. Sample copy: 9x12 SASE plus $1.

WIDE OPEN MAGAZINE. 116 Lincoln St. Santa Rosa, CA 95401.

(707) 545-3821. Submissions Editor: Clif Simms, Lynn Simms. Type: works with viable solutions to widespread problems. Frequency of publication: quarterly. Circulation: 500. Freelance submissions: 99%; number bought each year: 8-12.

Editorial Needs. Fiction—problems that people face in the world today with a realistic, purposeful solution; no blind luck or the intervention of the fates. Suggested (required) word length: 500-2500. Short stories—number per issue: 1-3; per year: 4-12. Payment offered: $5-$25; 1 copy. **Nonfiction**—opinions on world problems expressed logically. Suggested (required) word length—feature articles: 500-2500. Payment offered: $5-$25; 1 copy.

Initial Contact. Entire article (Do not send bio or clips). Include SASE.

Acceptance Policies. Byline given: yes. Payment made: upon publication. Kill fee: no. Writer's expenses on assignment: no. Simultaneous submissions: no. Response time to initial inquiry: 1-6 months. Average time until publication: 2 months. Computer printouts: yes. Dot matrix: yes. Disk submissions: no. Publishing rights: one-time rights only.

Additional Information. Our prose requirements are very strict. We also charge a $5 reading fee for prose, refundable if we accept your manuscript. Tips: Study our guidelines and copies of our magazines. Sample copy: $7. Writer's guidelines: #10 SASE.

WINES AND VINES. 1800 Lincoln Ave. San Rafael, CA 94901. (415) 453-

9700. Submissions Editor: Philip E. Hiaring. Type: professionals in all phases of the wine industry. Frequency of publication: monthly. Circulation: 4500. Freelance submissions: 20%; number bought each year: 4.

Editorial Needs. Nonfiction—general interest to the trade; how-to; history; technical; interview/profile; new products. Suggested word length—feature articles: 1000-2500. Payment offered: $.05 per word.

Initial Contact. Query letter.

Acceptance Policies. Byline given: yes. Payment made: upon acceptance. Kill fee: no. Writer's expenses on assignment: sometimes. Submit seasonal material 3 months in advance. Response time to initial inquiry: 2 weeks. Average time until publication: 3 months. Computer printouts: yes. Dot matrix: yes. Disk submissions: no. Publishing rights: first North American serial rights; simultaneous rights.

Photography Submissions. Format and film: black-and-white prints, 4x5, 8x10. Photographs should include: captions. **Payment:** $10. Photographic rights: same as article.

Additional Information. Contact us for special subject each month. Writer's guidelines: 10x12 SASE.

WINE SPECTATOR. Opera Plaza, Suite 2014. 601 Van Ness Ave.
San Francisco, CA 94102. (415) 673-2040. Submissions Editor: Jim Gordon. Type:
for the wine consumer. Frequency of publication: twice monthly. Circulation: 80,000.
Freelance submissions: 10%; number bought each year: n/i.

Editorial Needs. Nonfiction—general interest; humor; interview/profile; opinion; photo
feature. Suggested word length—feature articles: 100-2000. Payment offered: $50-$300.

Initial Contact. Query letter.

Acceptance Policies. Byline given: yes. Payment made: upon publication. Kill fee: no.
Writer's expenses on assignment: no. Submit seasonal material 3 months in advance. Response
time to initial inquiry: 3 weeks. Average time until publication: 2 months. Computer printouts:
yes. Dot matrix: legible. Disk submissions: query. Publishing rights: first-time rights; work for
hire.

Photography Submissions. Format and film: color transparencies. Photographs should
include: captions; model releases; identification of subjects. **Payment:** $25+. Photographic
rights: all.

Additional Information. Tips: Succinct query letter detailing the article is a must. Writer's
guidelines: upon request; sample copy $2.

WISE WOMAN, THE. 2441 Cordova St. Oakland, CA 94602. (415) 536-3174.
Submissions Editor: Ann Forfreedom. Type: women's, feminist issues; feminist
spirituality; feminist witchcraft. Frequency of publication: quarterly. Circulation: small
but influential. Freelance submissions: almost all. Payment in copies.

Editorial Needs. Fiction—generally no; maybe, if brief, clearly feminist, and relevant to
feminism and feminist spirituality. Payment offered: 1 copy of the issue in which submission
appears. Nonfiction—book reviews; entertainment reviews; fillers; general interest;
health/fitness; historical; how-to; humor; inspiration; interview/profile; opinion; photo feature;
poetry; self-improvement; travel; news analysis; annotated songs; spiritual rituals; Goddess
lore; political cartoons on feminist issues. Suggested word length—keep it brief. Payment
offered: 1 copy of the issue in which submission appears.

Initial Contact. Query letter; entire manuscript. State whether article has been submitted
elsewhere. Include SASE.

Acceptance Policies. Byline given: yes. Payment made: in copies. Submit seasonal
material at least 3-6 months in advance. Simultaneous submissions: yes; include where the
material has been submitted. Response time to initial query: usually within several months.
Average time until publication: varies. Computer printouts: yes. Dot matrix: letter quality.
Disk submissions: no. Publishing rights: first rights; second serial rights.

Photography Submissions: Format and film: black-and-white prints, any size.
Photographs should include: captions; identification of subjects; model releases. Include name
and address on each photo. **Payment:** copies. Photographic rights: n/i.

Additional Information. Since the publication is a quarterly, articles should be timely
within 3-6 months and appropriate for *The Wise Woman.* We have been publishing quarterly
since February 1980 and are listed in feminist and new age directories. Tips: Keep materials as
short as possible—space is always tight. Editorial revisions may be necessary; I usually check
with the author. Writer's guidelines: SASE; sample copy $4.

WOMAN IN THE MOON PUBLICATIONS (WIM). 2215 R Market St.,
Box 137-Dept CPM. San Francisco, CA 94114. (209) 667-0966. Submissions
Editor: SDiane Bogus. Type: women's; African-American; gay poetry; prisoners. We
accept chapbook manuscripts April-August each year. Frequency of publication:
yearly (2-4 books). Circulation: n/i. Freelance submissions: 100%; number used
each year: 2-4. We give half the press run to author.

Editorial Needs. Fiction—literary. Payment offered: 1/2 of press run.

Initial Contact. Query letter.

Acceptance Policies. Byline given: yes. Payment made: 1/2 press run. Simultaneous
submissions: yes; inform us. Response time to initial inquiry: 2-6 weeks. Average time until
publication: one year. Computer printouts: yes. Dot matrix: no. Disk submissions: 3 1/2"
diskettes; ASCII; Word Perfect. Publishing rights: second serial rights.

Additional Information. We offer a poetry test for practicing and novice poets; useful for
marketing analysis, to check skills, and for fun. Tips: Writing must have a real voice and come
from human experience. Writer's guidelines: free upon request. Catalog: SASE, $.45 postage.

WOODWORK. 42 Digital Dr., #5. Novato, CA 94949. (415) 382-0580.
Submissions Editor: Jeff Greef. Type: hobby. Frequency of publication: quarterly.
Circulation: 70,000. Freelance submissions 80%; number of manuscripts bought
each year: 40.

Editorial Needs. Nonfiction—how-to; interview/profile; photo feature. Suggested word
length—1000-4000. Payment offered: $150 per published page. Fillers—woodworking.

Initial Contact. Query letter. Include photographs and drawings.

Acceptance Policies. Byline given: yes. Payment made: upon publication. Kill fee: no.
Writer's expenses: sometimes. Simultaneous submissions: yes, inform us. Response time to
initial inquiry: 6-8 weeks. Average time until publication: 6-12 months or more. Computer
printouts: yes. Dot matrix: yes, reluctantly. Disk submissions: IBM; ASCII. Publishing rights:
first North American serial rights; reprint for books and promo.

Photography Submissions. Format and film: color transparencies. Photographs should
include: captions. **Payment**: page rate. Photographic rights: same as article rights.

Additional Information. Tips: If you have no woodworking experience, try an
interview/profile of an accomplished woodworker. Good photos are essential. Sample copy:
$2. Writer's guidelines: upon request.

WORKING CLASSICS. 298 Ninth Ave. San Francisco, CA 94118.
(415) 387-3412. Submissions Editor: David Joseph. Type: literary and general
interest creative work of working people. Frequency of publication: occasional.
Circulation: 2000. Freelance submissions: 95%. Payment in copies.

Editorial Needs. Fiction—literary workers' stories. Short stories—number per issue: 2; per
year: 4. Payment offered: copies. **Nonfiction**—book excerpts and book reviews; entertainment
reviews; general interest; historical; how-to; humor; interview/profile; opinion; photo feature;
poetry. Suggested word length—feature articles: 1000-3700. Payment offered: copies.

Initial Contact. Query letter. Include work background.

Acceptance Policies. Byline given: yes. Payment made: in copies. Simultaneous
submissions: yes; let us know if accepted elsewhere. Response time to initial inquiry: 1-4
weeks. Average time until publication: varies. Computer printouts: yes. Dot matrix: yes. Disk
submissions: query. Publishing rights: first rights.

Photography Submissions. Format and film: black-and-white prints. Photographs should
include: captions. **Payment**: copies. Photographic rights: first rights.

Additional Information. This magazine showcases the lives of working people, the creativity involved, and the innovative methods used to juggle a busy life, which includes the work place and a place for creativity. Writer's guidelines: upon request.

WORMWOOD REVIEW. PO Box 8840. Stockton, CA 95208-0840.
(209) 466-8231. Submissions Editor: Marvin Malone. Type: contemporary poetry. Frequency of publication: quarterly. Circulation: 700. Freelance submissions: 100%. Payment in copies.

Editorial Needs. Nonfiction—prose-poetry; poetry. Payment offered: 2-35 copies or cash equivalent.

Initial Contact. Entire article.

Acceptance Policies. Byline given: yes. Payment made: upon publication. Simultaneous submissions: no. Response time to initial inquiry: 4-8 weeks. Average time until publication: 4-8 months. Computer printouts: no. Dot matrix: no. Disk submissions: no. Publishing rights: all rights.

Additional Information. We have been operating since 1959. We concentrate on the Prose-Poem and contemporary concerns. Writer's guidelines: SASE.

WRITERS CONNECTION. 1601 Saratoga-Sunnyvale Rd, Ste. 180. Cupertino, CA 95014. (408) 973-0227. Submissions Editor: Jan Stiles. Type: how-to for writers.
Editorial content covers writing, publishing, technical writing, business writing, and related topics. Frequency of publication: monthly. Circulation: 2700. Freelance submissions: 50%.

Editorial Needs. Nonfiction—writing-related strategies; how-to. Suggested word length—feature: 1800-2000; secondary articles: 1000-1400. Columns: staff written. Payment offered: trade out for Writers Connection membership, subscription, seminars, or classified ad.

Initial Contact. Query letter; or entire article. Include brief bio; no clips.

Acceptance Policies. Byline given: yes. Submit seasonal material 4 months in advance. Simultaneous submissions: no. Response time to initial inquiry: 1 month, sometimes less. Average time until publication: 4-8 months. Computer printouts: yes. Dot matrix: letter quality. Disk submissions: ASCII or Microsoft Word; disk must be accompanied by formatted manuscript. Publishing rights: first North American serial rights.

Additional Information. We like to see articles stress nuts-and-bolts information and present the information in a logical, concise, and easy-to-read style. Tips: Study our publication and request the guidelines. Writer's guidelines: SASE. Sample copy: $.45 or first class stamps for 2 ounces.

YELLOW SILK, JOURNAL OF EROTIC ARTS. PO Box 6374. Albany, CA 94706. (415) 644-4188. Submissions Editor: Lily Pond. Type: erotica.
Frequency of publication: quarterly. Circulation: 14,000. Freelance submissions: 90%; number bought each year: 5 (nonfiction); 16 (fiction).

Editorial Needs. Fiction—erotica; fantasy; humor; mainstream; novel excerpts; science fiction. Payment offered: $10 minimum, copies. Nonfiction—book excerpts; humor; reviews; poetry; columns (reviews, emphasis on erotic content). Suggested word length—feature articles: any. Payment offered: $10 minimum, 3 copies; $5 minimum, copies (poetry).

Initial Contact. Complete manuscript.

Acceptance Policies. Byline given: yes. Payment made: upon publication. Kill fee: no. Writer's expenses on assignment: no. Response time to initial inquiry: 3 months. Average time until publication: 1 month to 3 years. Computer printouts: yes. Dot matrix: letter quality. Disk submissions: no. Publishing rights: all (revert to author after 1 year).

Photography Submissions. May be submitted without manuscript. Also, 4-color or black-and-white artwork. Format and film: photocopies; transparencies; contact sheets; black-and-white or color prints. Photographs should include: n/i. **Payment**: varies. Photographic rights: one-time; reprint.

Additional Information. Our policy is to emphasize the erotic through well-crafted literature; no brutality or minute descriptions or personal accounts. Tips: Sample copy $6.

YOGA JOURNAL. 2054 University Ave. Berkeley, CA 94704. (415) 841-9200. Submissions Editor: Stephan Bodian. Type: new age. Frequency of publication: bimonthly. Circulation: 50,000. Freelance submissions: 75%; number bought each year: 40.

Editorial Needs. **Nonfiction**—book excerpts; how-to; interview/profile; opinion; photo feature; travel; inspirational; columns (book and music reviews); cooking; psychology; interviews. Suggested word length—feature articles: 750-3500. Payment offered: $75-$250 (nonfiction); $25-$100 (columns).

Initial Contact. Query letter.

Acceptance Policies. Byline given: yes. Payment made: upon publication. Kill fee: $50. Writer's expenses on assignment: no. Submit seasonal material 4 months in advance. Simultaneous submissions: yes. Response time to initial inquiry: 6-8 weeks. Average time until publication: 6 months. Computer printouts: yes. Dot matrix: yes. Disk submissions: Macintosh. Publishing rights: first North American serial rights.

Photography Submissions. Format and film: black-and-white prints. Photographs should include: model release; identification of subjects. **Payment**: $15-$25; $200-$300 (color transparencies, cover). Photographic rights: one-time.

Additional Information. While our focus is on yoga, we feature a monthly subject or personality in the broader new age field. Tips: We read all manuscripts and encourage submissions. Writer's guidelines: upon request.

ZYZZYVA. 41 Sutter St., Ste. 1400. San Francisco, CA 94104. (415) 982-3440. Submissions Editor: Howard Junker. Type: literary. Frequency of publication: quarterly. Circulation: 3500. Freelance submissions: 100%; number bought each year: 80.

Editorial Needs. **Fiction**—literary. Short stories—number per issue: 2. Payment offered: $50-$250.

Initial Contact. Entire story.

Acceptance Policies. Byline given: yes. Payment made: upon acceptance. Kill fee: no. Writer's expenses on assignment: no. Simultaneous submissions: no. Response time to initial inquiry: prompt. Average time until publication: varies. Computer printouts: yes. Dot matrix: no. Disk submissions: no. Publishing rights: first North American serial rights.

Additional Information. Writer's guidelines: SASE.

Newspapers

Many writers first break into print with a published column in a local newspaper. While the pay may be nominal, writing for a newspaper provides an opportunity to learn about writing within editorial requirements, targeting specific markets, and meeting deadlines.

How to Use the Information in This Section

Our listings are alphabetized by the name of the newspaper or by the area serviced. There are also several newspaper publishing groups that are listed alphabetically by the name of the group. We felt it would be more useful to do it this way since writers are often writing for a specific audience in a specific area. If the name of the area is in parenthesis, do not include it when sending material to the newspaper; it is for your use in determining the geographical area served by that publication.

The initial entry identifies the name of the publication, its location, and phone number.

Submissions Editor: Direct your initial contact to the appropriate editor.

Book Review Editor: Send review copies and press releases about your book to this individual.

Travel Editor: Most newspapers use travel material in the form of articles or columns. We have included the names of travel editors for this updated edition.

Freelance submissions: If the text indicates that the newspaper accepts freelance submissions, write to the editor requesting writer's guidelines and information about the editorial needs of the newspaper's special sections.

Circulation: This number helps you judge the size of your market.

Abbreviations

n/i means no information was given to us by the newspaper.

California

AGOURA ACORN. 960 S. Westlake Blvd., Ste. 207. Westlake Village, CA 91361. (818) 706-0266. Freelance submissions: rarely. Submissions Editor: Steve Holt. Circulation: 33,000.

ALAMEDA COUNTY/BAY AREA OBSERVER. PO Box 817. San Leandro, CA 94577. (415) 483-7119. Freelance submissions: no. Submissions Editor: Ad Fried (general, book review, and travel). Circulation: 135,000.

(ANTIOCH) DAILY LEDGER/PITTSBURGH POST DISPATCH. 1650 Cavallo Rd. PO Box 2299. Antioch, CA 94531-2299. (415) 757-2525. Freelance submissions: yes. Submissions Editors: Mark Stafforini (general); Clay Kallam (lifestyles and book review); Carol Gardner (travel). Circulation: 24,834.

AZUSA HERALD PRESS. 568 E. Foothill Blvd., Ste 105. Azusa, CA 91702. (818) 969-1711. Freelance submissions: rarely. Submissions Editor: Jannlee Watson. Circulation: 300,000.

BAKERSFIELD CALIFORNIAN. PO Box 440. Bakersfield, CA 93301. (805) 395-7384. Freelance Submissions: yes. Submissions Editors: Bob Bentley (general); Rick Heredia (book review); Pete Tittl (travel). Circulation: 88,000 daily, 98,000 Sunday.

BERKELEY DAILY CALIFORNIAN, THE. 2150 Dwight Way. Berkeley, CA 94704. (415) 849-2482. Freelance submissions: no. Submissions Editors: Patrizia Jacobus (general); Jason Sine (book review). Circulation: 25,000.

BERKELEY EAST BAY EXPRESS. PO Box 3198. Berkeley, CA 94703. (415) 652-4610. Freelance submissions: yes. Submissions Editors: John Raeside (general); Michael Covino, Rob Hurwitt (book review). Circulation: 60,000.

BLYTHE PALO VERDE VALLEY TIMES. PO Box 1159. Blythe, CA 92226. (619) 922-3181. Freelance submissions: yes, but generally local. Submissions Editor: Donna James (general and book review). Circulation: 4,000.

(BURLINGAME) BOUTIQUE AND VILLAGER. 1755 Rollins Rd. Burlingame, CA 94010. (415) 692-9406. Freelance submissions: yes. Submissions Editor: Stephan Kech (general, book review, and travel). Circulation: 15,000.

CALISTOGAN, THE. PO Box 385. Calistoga, CA 94515. (707) 942-6242. Freelance submissions: no. Submissions Editors: Pat Hampton (general and book review); Marjorie Brandon (travel). Circulation: 2,000.

CAMARILLO DAILY NEWS. PO Box 107. Camarillo, CA 93011. (805) 987-5001. Freelance submissions: no. Submissions Editors: Harold Kinsch (general); Donna DiPaolo (book review and travel). Circulation: 11,500.

CAPISTRANO VALLEY NEWS. 23811 Via Fabricante. Mission Viejo, CA 92691. (714) 768-3631. Freelance submissions: yes. Submissions Editor: Chris Meyers (general and book review). Circulation: 150,000.

CARLSBAD JOURNAL. PO Box 878. Encinitas, CA 92024. (619) 729-2345. Freelance submissions: possible. Submissions Editor: Steve Dreyer (general, book review, and travel). Circulation: 4,000.

CARMEL AND MONTEREY/KEY MAGAZINE. PO Box 223859. Carmel, CA 93922. (408) 624-3411. Freelance submissions: no. Submissions Editor: Penny Green. Circulation: 37,000.

CENTRAL NEWS-WAVE PUBLICATIONS. 2621 W. 54th St. Los Angeles, CA 90043. (213) 290-3000. Freelance submissions: no. Submissions Editors: Alice Marshall (general and travel); Tomas Lewis (book review). Circulation: 283,000.

CERES COURIER. 2940 Fourth St. PO Box 7. Ceres, CA 95307. (209) 537-5032. Freelance submissions: no. Submissions Editor: Jeff Benziger (general, book review, and travel). Circulation: 16,000.

CHICO NEWS AND REVIEW. 353 East Second St. Chico, CA 95928. (916) 894-2300. Freelance submissions: some. Submissions Editors: George Thurlow (general); Bob Speer (book review and travel). Circulation: 44,000.

CHINO VALLEY NEWS. 13179 9th St. PO Box 607. Chino, CA 91708-0607. (714) 628-5501. Freelance submissions: seldom. Submissions Editor: Charles Ferrell (general, book review, and travel). Circulation: 40,000.

CHULA VISTA STAR NEWS. 835 Third Ave. Chula Vista, CA 92010. (619) 427-3000. Freelance submissions: no. Submissions Editor: Charles Walker (general and travel). Circulation: 84,000.

CLAREMONT COURIER. PO Box 820. Claremont, CA 91711-0820. (714) 621-4761. Freelance submissions: yes. Submissions Editor: Martin Weinberger (general, book review, and travel). Circulation: 6,000.

CLOVIS INDEPENDENT. PO Box 189. Clovis, CA 93613. (209) 298-8081. Freelance submissions: yes. Submissions Editor: Curtis Tuck (general, book review, and travel). Circulation: 7,500.

COAST DISPATCH GROUP. PO Box 878. Encinitas, CA 92024. (619) 753-6543. Freelance submissions: rarely. Submissions Editors: Dennis Lhota (general); Patricia Morris (book review); Lorin Hallinan (travel). Circulation: 24,000.

COAST MEDIA NEWSPAPER GROUP. 4034 Irving Place. Culver City, CA 90232. (213) 839-5271. Freelance submissions: yes. Submissions Editors: John Hartmire (general and book review); Ruby Elbogen (travel). Circulation: 17,000.

CONTRA COSTA TIMES. PO Box 5088. Walnut Creek, CA 94596. (415) 935-2525. Freelance submissions: sometimes. Submissions Editors: Michael Laumiere (features); Carol Fowler (book review); John Dengel (travel). Circulation: 120,000.

COPLEY LOS ANGELES NEWSPAPERS. 5215 Torrance Blvd. Torrance, CA 90509. (213) 540-5511. Freelance submissions: no. Submissions Editors: Jean Adelsman (general); Don Lechman (book review); Don Chapman (travel). Circulation: 130,000.

CORONADO JOURNAL. PO Box 8. Coronado, CA 92118. (619) 435-3141. Freelance submissions: local only. Submissions Editor: Shannon Quinn-Langley (general, book review, and travel). Circulation: 6,500.

(CORTE MADERA) TWIN CITIES TIMES. PO Box 186. Corte Madera, CA 94925. (415) 924-8552. Freelance submissions: local only. Submissions Editor: Beth Galetto (general, book review, and travel). Circulation: 5,500.

COVINA INTER-CITY EXPRESS. PO Box 1259. Covina, CA 91722. (818) 962-8811. Freelance submissions: no. Submissions Editors: Art Kuhn (general and book review); Bob Christiansen (travel). Circulation: 62,000.

CRESCENT CITY DEL NORTE TRIPLICATE. PO Box 277. Crescent City, CA 95531. (707) 464-2141. Freelance submissions: local only. Submissions Editor: Larry Wills (general, book review, and travel). Circulation: 8,700.

CUPERTINO COURIER. 10950 N. Blaney Ave. Cupertino, CA 95014. (408) 255-7500. Freelance Submissions: yes. Submissions Editor: Mike Betz (general, book review, and travel). Circulation: 14,000.

DAILY VARIETY. 5700 Wilshire Blvd., Ste. 120. Los Angeles, CA 90036. (213) 857-6000. Freelance submissions: no. Submissions Editors: Rick Bozanich (general); Marie Marich (book review); Woody Wilson (travel). Circulation: 25,000.

DAVIS ENTERPRISE, THE. PO Box 1470. Davis, CA 95617. (916) 756-0800. Freelance submissions: very rarely. Submissions Editors: Debbie Davis (general); Judy Dufty (book review and travel). Circulation: 10,000.

DESERT SENTINEL. PO Box 338. Desert Hot Springs, CA 92240. (619) 329-1411. Freelance submissions: accepts, but no payment. Submissions Editor: Rick McLaughlin (general, book review, and travel) Circulation: 10,000.

DRAMA-LOGUE. PO Box 38771. Los Angeles, CA 90038. (213) 464-5079. Freelance submissions: yes. Submissions Editor: Faye Vordy (general and book review). Circulation: 18,000.

(EL CAJON) DAILY CALIFORNIA, THE. PO Box 1565. El Cajon, CA 92022. (619) 442-4404. Freelance submissions: yes. Submissions Editors: Ray Bordner (general and travel); Karen Barnett (book review). Circulation: 23,000.

EL SEGUNDO HERALD. PO Box 188. El Segundo, CA 90245. (213) 322-1830. Freelance submissions: no. Submissions Editor: Linda Collins (general, book review, and travel). Circulation: 14,000.

(EUREKA) TIMES-STANDARD. PO Box 3580. Eureka, CA 95501. (707) 442-1711. Freelance submissions: sometimes. Submissions Editors: Rhonda Parker (general); Kathy Dillon (book review and travel). Circulation: 25,000.

(FAIRFIELD) DAILY REPUBLIC. 1250 Texas St. PO Box 47. Fairfield, CA 94533. (707) 425-4646. Freelance submissions: rarely. Submissions Editors: Rick Jensen (general); Ian Thompson (book review and travel). Circulation: 20,000.

FOLSOM TELEGRAPH. 825 Sutter St. PO Box 157. Folsom, CA 95630. (916) 985-2581. Freelance submissions: no. Submissions Editor: Cris Angell (general, book review, and travel). Circulation: 26,000.

FOSTER CITY PROGRESS. 969 Edgewater Blvd., Ste. N. Foster City, CA 94404. (415) 574-9293. Freelance submissions: yes. Submissions Editor: Barbara Vogt (general, book review, and travel). Circulation 9,700.

FREMONT ARGUS. 3850 Decoto Rd. Fremont, CA 94555. (415) 794-0111. Freelance submissions: seldom. Submissions Editors: Helen Saltz (general); John Boudreau (book review). Circulation: 34,000.

FRESNO BEE. 1626 "E" St. Fresno, CA 93786. (209) 441-6111. Freelance submissions: yes. Submissions Editors: Dana Heupel (general); Eddie Lopez (book review and travel). Circulation: 180,000.

FULLERTON NEWS TRIBUNE. 701 W. Commonwealth. Fullerton, CA 92632. (714) 871-2345. Freelance submissions: no. Submissions Editor: John Kane (general, book review, and travel). Circulation: 33,000.

GARDENA VALLEY NEWS. PO Box 219. Gardena, CA 90247. (213) 329-6351. Freelance submissions: generally, no. Submissions Editor: n/i. Circulation: 14,000.

GILROY DISPATCH. 6400 Monterey Rd. PO Box 22365. Gilroy, CA 95021-2365. (408) 842-6411. Freelance submissions: rarely. Submissions Editors: Mark Derry (general); Kathy Gillespie (travel). Circulation: 8,000.

GLENDALE NEWS PRESS. 111 N. Isabel St. Glendale, CA 91206. (818) 241-4141. Freelance submissions: yes. Submissions Editor: Phil Drake (general, book review, and travel). Circulation: 39,500.

GOLETA SUN. PO Box 1670. Goleta, CA 93116. (805) 683-1587. Freelance submissions: no. Submissions Editor: Steve Humphries (general, book review, and travel). Circulation: 20,000.

GRASS VALLEY UNION. PO Box 1025. Grass Valley, CA 95945. (916) 273-9561. Freelance submissions: no. Submissions Editors: Judy Mooers (general and book review); Paul Harrar (travel). Circulation: 16,000.

HALF MOON BAY REVIEW. PO Box 68. Half Moon Bay, CA 94019. (415) 726-4424. Freelance submissions: no. Submissions Editor: Kimberly Stein (general, book review, and travel). Circulation: 7,500.

(HAYWARD) DAILY REVIEW. 116 W. Winton Ave. Hayward, CA 94544. (415) 783-6111. Freelance submissions: yes. Submissions Editors: Bob Wynne (general); Barry Caine (book review); Jerry Gengler (travel). Circulation: 48,000 daily, 53,000 Sunday.

HEALDSBURG TRIBUNE. PO Box 518. Healdsburg, CA 95448. (707) 433-4451. Freelance submissions: no payment. Submissions Editor: Barry Dugan (general, book review, and travel). Circulation: 10,000.

(HOLLISTER) PINNACLE. 341 Tres Pinos Rd., Ste. 201. Hollister, CA 95023. (408) 637-6300. Freelance submissions: yes. Submissions Editor: Herman Wrede (general, book review, and travel). Circulation: 13,700.

HOLLYWOOD REPORTER, THE. 6715 Sunset Blvd. Hollywood, CA 90028. (213) 464-7411. Freelance submissions: no. Submissions Editor: Glen Abel. Circulation: 22,000.

HUMBOLDT BEACON. PO Box 310. Fortuna, CA 95540. (707) 725-6166. Freelance submissions: no. Submissions Editor: Glen Simmons (general, book review, and travel). Circulation: 4,200.

HUNTINGTON BEACH NEWS. PO Box 31. Huntington Beach, CA 92648. (714) 969-4335. Freelance submissions: rarely. Submissions Editor: Gray Hernandez (general and book review). Circulation: 20,000.

IMPERIAL VALLEY PRESS & BRAWLY NEWS.
205 N. 8th St. (92243). PO Box 2770. El Centro, CA 92244. (619) 352-2211. Freelance submissions: rarely. Submissions Editors: J. R. Fitch (general); Don Quinn (book review); Shali Dore (travel). Circulation: 19,200 (both papers combined).

LA JOLLA LIGHT & LA JOLLA UNIVERSITY CITY LIGHT.
450 Pearl St. PO Box 1927. La Jolla, CA 92038. (619) 459-4201. Freelance submissions: yes. Submissions Editors: Rod Presley (general and travel); Chuck Border (book review). Circulation: 10,000 & 12,500.

(LIVERMORE) DAILY REVIEW (& LIVERMORE TRI-VALLEY HERALD). PO Box 5050. Hayward, CA 94540. (415) 783-6111. Freelance submissions: yes. Submissions Editors: Bob Wynne (general); Shary Betz (book review); Dianne Dawson (travel). Circulation: 135,000.

LODI NEWS SENTINEL. PO Box 1360. Lodi, CA 95241. (209) 369-2761. Freelance Submissions: yes. Submissions Editor: Michelle Drier (general, book review, and travel). Circulation: 18,000.

LOMPOC RECORD. PO Box 578. Lompoc, CA 93438. (805) 736-2313. Freelance submissions: sometimes. Submissions Editors: Rita Henning (general); Mike Hugen (book review and travel). Circulation: 10,500 daily, 10,900 Sunday.

(LONG BEACH) PRESS TELEGRAM. 604 Pine Ave. Long Beach, CA 90844-0001. (213) 435-1161. Freelance submissions: sometimes. Submissions Editors: Mike Schwartz (general); Tim Grobaty (book review); Harold Glicken (travel). Circulation: 136,000 daily, 158,000 Sunday.

LOS ALTOS TOWN CRIER. 138 Main St. Los Altos, CA 94022. (415) 948-4489. Freelance submissions: yes. Submissions Editor: Ann Chappel (general, book review, and travel). Circulation: 20,000.

(LOS ANGELES) ADVOCATE, THE. 6922 Hollywood Blvd., 10th Fl. Los Angeles, CA 90028. (213) 871-1225. Freelance submissions: yes. Submissions Editors: Gerry Kroll (general); Mark Thompson (book review); Devon Clayton (travel). Circulation: 70,000.

(Los Angeles) Copley Newspapers *see* **COPLEY LOS ANGELES NEWSPAPERS**.

(LOS ANGELES COUNTY, NORTH) DAILY NEWS. PO Box 4200. Woodland Hills, CA 91365. (818) 713-3000. Freelance submissions: travel & book reviews only. Submissions Editors: Bob Burdick (general); Bruce Cook (book review); Sean Fisher (travel). Circulation: 300,000.

(Los Angeles) Northeast Newspaper Group *see* **NORTHEAST NEWSPAPER GROUP**.

LOS ANGELES SENTINEL. 1112 East 43rd St. Los Angeles, CA 90011. (213) 232-3261. Freelance submissions: sometimes. Submissions Editors: Andrea Smith (general and book review); Tim Lester (travel). Circulation: 40,000.

LOS ANGELES TIMES. Times Mirror Square. Los Angeles, CA 90053. (213) 237-5000. Freelance submissions: yes. Submissions Editors: Ceci Vandervoort (general); Jack Miles (book review); Jerry Hulse (travel). Circulation: 1,225,000 daily, 1,515,000 Sunday.

LOS GATOS TIMES OBSERVER. 236 N. Santa Cruz Ave., Ste. 105A. Los Gatos, CA 95030. (408) 354-3900. Freelance submissions: yes. Submissions Editor: Caroline Leal (general, book review, and travel). Circulation: 13,500.

LOS GATOS WEEKLY. PO Box 65. Los Gatos, CA 95031. (408) 354-3110. Freelance submissions: yes. Submissions Editor: Irving Shear (general, book review, and travel). Circulation: 16,000.

(MAMMOTH LAKES) REVIEW HERALD, THE. PO Box 110. Mammoth Lakes, CA 93546. (619) 934-8544. Freelance submissions: yes, generally local. Submissions Editor: Kevin Gartland (general, book review, and travel). Circulation: 5,600.

MARIN INDEPENDENT JOURNAL. PO Box 151790. San Rafael, CA 94915-1790. (415) 883-8600. Freelance submissions: yes. Submissions Editors: Joe Konte (general and travel); Rebecca Larsen (book review). Circulation: 40,000.

(MARYSVILLE) YUBA-SUTTER APPEAL-DEMOCRAT. 1530 Ellis Lake Dr. Marysville, CA 95901. (916) 741-2345. Freelance submissions: yes. Submissions Editors: Larry Badger (general); Bob Curry (book review and travel). Circulation: 26,000.

MERCED SUN STAR. 3033 N. G St. PO Box 739. Merced, CA 95341-0739. (209) 722-1511. Freelance submissions: seldom. Submissions Editors: Randy Brandt (general); Rick Albright (book review); Colleen Bondy (travel). Circulation: 23,000.

MILLBRAE SUN/LEADER. 475 El Camino Real, Ste. 418. Millbrae, CA 94030. (415) 697-5336. Freelance Submissions: yes. Submissions Editor: Tim Donohue (general, book review, and travel). Circulation: 20,000.

MILL VALLEY RECORD. PO Box 848. Mill Valley, CA 94941. (415) 388-3211. Freelance submissions: yes. Submissions Editor: Peter Seidman (general, book review, and travel). Circulation: 22,000.

MODESTO BEE. 1325 H St. Modesto, CA 95354. (209) 578-2000. Freelance submissions: sometimes. Submissions Editors: Larry McSwain (general); Lorie Wickenhauser (book review); Walt Williams (travel). Circulation: 80,000.

MONTEREY HERALD. #8 Upper Ragsdale. Monterey, CA 93940. (408) 372-3311. Freelance submissions: sometimes. Submissions Editors: Reg Henry (general); Dennis Sharp (book review and travel). Circulation: 37,000.

NAPA REGISTER. 1615 Second St. PO Box 150. Napa, CA 94559. (707) 226-3711. Freelance submissions: no. Submissions Editors: Doug Ernst (general); Mary Wallace (book review and travel). Circulation: 22,000.

NORTHEAST NEWSPAPER GROUP. 5420 N. Figueroa. Los Angeles, CA 90042. (213) 259-6200. Freelance submissions: yes. Submissions Editors: Roger Swanson (general); Charles Cooper (book review and travel). Circulation: 92,000.

OAKLAND PRESS PUBLICATIONS. PO Box 10151. Oakland, CA 94610. (415) 547-4000. Freelance submissions: no. Submissions Editors: Ray Epstein (general); Jan Miller (book review and travel). Circulation: 27,000.

(OAKLAND) TRIBUNE, THE. 409 13th St. Oakland, CA 94612. (415) 645-2000. Freelance submissions: sometimes. Submissions Editors: Robert Maynard (general); Diana Ketchum (book review); Roger Rapaport (travel). Circulation: 135,000.

OCEANSIDE BLADE/CITIZEN. 1722 S. Hill St. PO Box 90. Oceanside, CA 92054. (619) 433-7333. Freelance submissions: yes. Submissions Editors: William Missett (general); Joseph Taylor (book review); Lucille Thomas (travel). Circulation: 45,000.

(ONTARIO) INLAND VALLEY DAILY. PO Box 4000. Ontario, CA 91761. (714) 622-1201. Freelance submissions: sometimes. Submissions Editors: Paul McAfee (general and book review); Doug Arnold (travel). Circulation: 100,000.

ORANGE COAST DAILY PILOT. PO Box 1560. Costa Mesa, CA 92626. (714) 642-4321. Freelance submissions: yes. Submissions Editors: William Lobdell (general and book review); Donna & Ray Ott (travel). Circulation: 30,000.

ORANGE COUNTY NEWS. 9872 Chapman, Ste. 8. Garden Grove, CA 92641. (714) 530-7622. Freelance submissions: sometimes. Submissions Editor: Al Kolber (general, book review, and travel). Circulation: 37,000.

OROVILLE MERCURY-REGISTER. PO Box 651. Oroville, CA 95965. (916) 533-3131. Freelance submissions: no. Submissions Editor: John Seelmyer. Circulation: 9,000.

OXNARD PRESS COURIER. 300 W. Ninth St. Oxnard, CA 93030. (805) 483-1101. Freelance submissions: no. Submissions Editors: Ed Smith (general); Georgeann Plank (book review and travel). Circulation: 20,000.

PACIFICA TRIBUNE. 59 Aura Vista. PO Box 1188. Pacifica, CA 94044. (415) 359-6666. Freelance submissions: rarely. Submissions Editor: Nancy DeBolt (general, book review, and travel). Circulation: 8,600.

(PALM DESERT) PUBLIC RECORD. PO Drawer J. Palm Desert, CA 92261. (619) 346-8177. Freelance submissions: sometimes. Submissions Editor: Jane Curtis (general, book review, and travel). Circulation: 1,000.

PALM SPRINGS DESERT SUN. 750 N. Gene Autry Trail. Palm Springs, CA 92262. (619) 322-8889. Freelance submissions: no. Submissions Editor: Rick Martinez. Circulation: 50,000.

(PALO ALTO) TIMES. 245 Lytton Ave. Palo Alto, CA 94301. (415) 853-1200. Freelance submissions: yes. Submissions Editor: Paul Salvoni (general, book review, and travel). Circulation: 28,000.

PALO ALTO WEEKLY. 703 High St. Palo Alto, CA 94301. (415) 326-8210. Freelance submissions: yes. Submissions Editors: Becky Bartindale (general); Don Kazak (book review and travel). Circulation: 45,000.

PALOS VERDES PENINSULA NEWS. 900 Silver Spur Rd. Palos Verdes, CA 90274. (213) 377-6877. Freelance submissions: yes. Submissions Editors: Ann LaJaunesse (general); David Knoles (book review and travel). Circulation: 19,000.

PASADENA/ALTADENA WEEKLY, THE. 155 S. El Molino., Ste. 101. Pasadena, CA 91101. (818) 584-1500. Freelance submissions: yes. Submissions Editors: Lizanne Fleming (general and travel); Dan O'Heron (book review). Circulation: 40,000.

PASADENA STAR-NEWS. 525 E. Colorado Blvd. Pasadena, CA 91109. (818) 578-6300. Freelance submissions: yes (mostly features). Submissions Editors: Jerrianne Hayslett (general); Kathy Register (book review); Jackie Knowles (travel). Circulation: 50,000.

PENINSULA TIMES TRIBUNE. 245 Lytton Ave. Palo Alto, CA 94301. (408) 245-2990. Freelance Submissions: yes. Submissions Editor: Bill Harkey (general, book review, and travel). Circulation: 50,000 daily.

PETALUMA ARGUS-COURIER. 830 Petaluma Blvd. N. PO Box 1091. Petaluma, CA 94953. (707) 762-4541. Freelance submissions: no. Submissions Editors: Chris Samson (general); Richard Bammer (book review and travel). Circulation: 22,000.

(PINOLE) WEST COUNTY TIMES. 4301 Lakeside Dr. Richmond, CA 94806. (415) 758-8400. Freelance submissions: yes. Submissions Editor: Al Pacciorini (general, book review, and travel). Circulation: 35,000.

(PLACERVILLE) MOUNTAIN DEMOCRAT. PO Box 1088. Placerville, CA 95667. (916) 622-1255. Freelance submissions: sometimes. Submissions Editors: Mike Raffety (general); Rosemary Moore (book review and travel). Circulation: 16,000.

(PLEASANTON) VALLEY TIMES. 127 Spring St. PO Box 607. Pleasanton, CA 94566. (415) 462-4160. Freelance submissions: sometimes. Submissions Editors: Marian Green (general); Anne Shalsant (book review and travel). Circulation: 30,000.

POINT REYES LIGHT, THE. PO Box 210. Point Reyes Station, CA 94956. (415) 663-8404. Freelance submissions: sometimes. Submissions Editor: David V. Mitchell (general, book review, and travel). Circulation: 3,800.

PORTERVILLE RECORDER. 115 E. Oak. PO Box 151. Porterville, CA 93258. (209) 784-5000. Freelance submissions: seldom. Submissions Editor: Rick Elkins (general, book review, and travel). Circulation: 14,000.

REDDING RECORD-SEARCHLIGHT. PO Box 492397. Redding, CA 96049-2397. (916) 243-2424. Freelance submissions: seldom. Submissions Editors: Kip Cady (general); Laura Christman (book review and travel). Circulation: 41,000.

REDWOOD CITY TRIBUNE. 2317 Broadway, Ste. 100. Redwood City, CA 94063. (415) 365-3111. Freelance Submissions: yes. Submissions Editor: Kevin Doyle (general, book review, and travel). Circulation: 17,000.

RIVERSIDE PRESS-ENTERPRISE. PO Box 792. Riverside, CA 92502. (714) 684-1200. Freelance submissions: seldom. Submissions Editors: Michael Jordan (general); Joel Blain (book review); Bob Hirt (travel). Circulation: 159,000.

(ROSEVILLE) PRESS TRIBUNE, THE. 188 Cirby Way. Roseville, CA 95678. (916) 786-6500. Freelance submissions: seldom. Submissions Editor: Dennis Wyatt (general, book review, and travel). Circulation: 15,000.

RUSSIAN RIVER NEWS. PO Box 19. Guerneville, CA 95446. (707) 869-3520. Freelance submissions: yes. Submissions Editor: John De Salvio (general, book review, and travel). Circulation: 3,500.

SACRAMENTO BEE. PO Box 15779. Sacramento, CA 95852. (916) 321-1000. Freelance submissions: yes. Submissions Editors: Gregory Favre (general); Paul Craig (book review); Janet Fullwood (travel). Circulation: 280,000.

SACRAMENTO UNION. 301 Capitol Mall. Sacramento, CA 95812. (916) 442-7811. Freelance submissions: yes. Submissions Editors: Jerry Eagan (general); Sue Gilmore (book review); Jackie Peterson (travel). Circulation: 75,000.

SALINAS CALIFORNIAN. PO Box 81091. Salinas, CA 93912. (408) 424-2221. Freelance submissions: yes. Submissions Editors: Dave Doucette (general); Tom Leyde (book review and travel). Circulation: 23,500.

SAN BERNARDINO COUNTY SUN. 399 N. "D" Street. San Bernardino, CA 92401. (714) 889-9666. Freelance submissions: yes. Submissions Editors: Arnold Garson (general and book review); Angela Cruz (travel). Circulation: 100,000.

(SAN CARLOS) INQUIRER/BULLETIN. 1321 Laurel St., Ste. D. San Carlos, CA 94070. (415) 593-1997. Freelance submissions: yes. Submissions Editor: Grant Dubois (general, book review, and travel). Circulation: 31,000.

SAN DIEGO BUSINESS JOURNAL. 4909 Murphy Canyon Rd., Ste. 200. San Diego, CA 92123. (619) 277-6359. Freelance submissions: sometimes. Submissions Editors: Christi Phelps (general); Libby Brydolf (book review); Sue Schena (travel). Circulation: 20,000.

(SAN DIEGO COUNTY) TIMES-ADVOCATE. 207 E. Pennsylvania Ave. Escondido, CA 92025. (619) 745-6611. Freelance submissions: no. Submissions Editors: Richard K. Petersen (general); Susan Miller (travel). Circulation: 44,000.

SAN DIEGO UNION TRIBUNE. PO Box 191. San Diego, CA 92112-4106. (619) 299-3131. Freelance submissions: yes. Submissions Editors: Ray Kipp (general); Mary Hellman (book review); Phil Sousa (travel). Circulation: 270,000 daily, 440,000 Sunday.

SAN FRANCISCO CHRONICLE. 901 Mission St. San Francisco, CA 94103. (415) 777-1111. Freelance submissions: yes. Submissions Editors: Rosalie Wright (general); Patricia Holt (book review); Marjorie Rice (travel). Circulation: 700,000 (combined with the *San Francisco Examiner*).

SAN FRANCISCO EXAMINER. 110 5th St. San Francisco, CA 94103. (415) 777-2424. Freelance submissions: yes. Submissions Editors: Paul Wilner (special sections); Tom Dowling (book review); Don George (travel). Circulation: 700,000 (combined with the *San Francisco Chronicle*).

SAN FRANCISCO SUN REPORTER. 1366 Turk St. San Francisco, CA 94115. (415) 931-5778. Freelance submissions: yes. Submissions Editors: Amelia Ward (general and book review); Charles Belle (travel). Circulation: 11,000.

SAN JOSE MERCURY NEWS. 750 Ridder Park Drive. San Jose, CA 95190. (408) 920-5000. Freelance submissions: rarely. Submissions Editors: Jerome Ceppos (general); Carol Muller (book review); Zeke Wigglesworth (travel). Circulation: 250,000.

(SAN LUIS OBISPO) COUNTY TELEGRAM-TRIBUNE. 1321 Johnson Ave. PO Box 112. San Luis Obispo, CA 93406. (805) 595-1111. Freelance submissions: yes. Submissions Editors: Mike Stover (general); Bruce Miller (book review); John Frees (travel). Circulation: 38,000.

SAN MATEO TIMES. 1080 S. Amphlett Blvd. San Mateo, CA 94402. (415) 348-4321. Freelance submissions: yes. Submissions Editors: John Hubbard (general and travel); Jack Russell (book review). Circulation: 45,000.

SAN MATEO WEEKLY. 723 So. B St. San Mateo, CA 94401. (415) 373-0701. Freelance Submissions: yes. Submissions Editor: Kirk O'Neil (general, book review, and travel). Circulation: 33,000.

(SANTA ANA) ORANGE COUNTY REPORTER. 1212 N. Broadway, Ste. 250. PO Box 1846. Santa Ana, CA 92702-1846. (714) 543-2027. Freelance submissions: no. Submissions Editor: Lavonne Mason. Circulation: 1,000.

SANTA BARBARA NEWS PRESS. PO Box 1359. Santa Barbara, CA 93102. (805) 564-5200. Freelance submissions: yes. Submissions Editors: John Lankford (general); Joan Crowder (book review); Linda Bowen (travel). Circulation: 52,000 daily.

SANTA CRUZ SENTINEL. PO Box 638. Santa Cruz, CA 95061.
(408) 423-4242. Freelance submissions: sometimes. Submissions Editors: Peggy Townsend (general); Chris Watson (book review); Mel Bowen (travel). Circulation: 30,000.

SANTA MARIA TIMES. PO Box 400. Santa Maria, CA 93456.
(805) 925-2691. Freelance submissions: rarely. Submissions Editors: Don Brown (general); Wayne Agner (book review and travel). Circulation: 22,000.

(SANTA MONICA) GOOD LIFE INDEPENDENT JOURNAL.
1032 Broadway. Santa Monica, CA 90401. (213) 393-0601. Freelance submissions: sometimes. Submissions Editor: Herb Chase (general, book review, and travel). Circulation: 47,000.

SANTA ROSA PRESS DEMOCRAT. 427 Mendocino Ave. Santa Rosa, CA 95402. (707) 546-2020. Freelance submissions: sometimes. Submissions Editors: Bruce Kyse (general); Jim Fremgen (book review); Dan Taylor (travel). Circulation: 90,000 daily, 95,000 Sunday.

SANTA YNEZ VALLEY NEWS. 423 Second St. PO Box 647. Solvang, CA 93463. (805) 688-5522. Freelance submissions: sometimes. Submissions Editors: Paul Wahl (general); Pam Mowry (book review and travel). Circulation: 7,500.

SARATOGA NEWS. 12378 Saratoga-Sunnyvale Road. Saratoga, CA 95070. Freelance submissions: yes. Submissions Editor: Kim Malanczuk (general, book review, and travel). Circulation: 10,000.

(SEASIDE) SENTINEL, THE. PO Box 1309. Seaside, CA 93955.
(408) 899-2305. Freelance submissions: yes. Submissions Editor: David Bennett (general, book review, and travel). Circulation: 20,000 weekly.

SIMI VALLEY ENTERPRISE. 888 Easy St. Simi Valley, CA 93065.
(805) 526-6211. Freelance submissions: yes. Submissions Editor: Jacque Kampschroer (general, book review, and travel). Circulation: 16,800 daily, 17,400 Sunday.

SISKIYOU DAILY NEWS. PO Box 129. Yreka, CA 96097. (916) 842-5777.
Freelance submissions: yes. Submissions Editor: Sean McMahon (general, book review, and travel). Circulation: 22,000.

(SONORA) UNION DEMOCRAT. 84 S. Washington St. Sonora, CA 95370.
(209) 532-7151. Freelance submissions: sometimes. Submissions Editors: Buzz Eggleston (general and travel); Kathe Waterbury (book review). Circulation: 20,000.

SOUTHERN CALIFORNIA COMMUNITY NEWSPAPER.
8800 National Ave. South Gate, CA 90280. (213) 927-8681. Freelance submissions: sometimes. Submissions Editors: Phil Villa (general and travel); Art Aguilar (book review). Circulation: 540,000.

STOCKTON RECORD. PO Box 900. Stockton, CA 95201. (209) 943-6397. Freelance submissions: yes. Submissions Editors: Richard Hanner (general); Janet Krietemeyer (book review); Deborah Willoughby (travel). Circulation: 59,000.

SUNNYVALE VALLEY JOURNAL. 355 W. Olive. Sunnyvale, CA 94086. (408) 739-3093. Freelance Submissions: yes. Submissions Editor: Laura Wood (general, book review, and travel). Circulation: 19,000.

THOUSAND OAKS NEWS CHRONICLE. 2595 Thousand Oaks Blvd. Thousand Oaks, CA 91362. (805) 496-3211. Freelance submissions: sometimes. Submissions Editors: Marvin Sosna (general); Shirley Appleman (book review); Deann Wahl (travel). Circulation: 23,500.

TURLOCK JOURNAL. PO Box 800. Turlock, CA 95381. (209) 634-9141. Freelance submissions: sometimes. Submissions Editor: Don Hansen (general, book review, and travel). Circulation: 10,300.

UKIAH DAILY JOURNAL. 590 S. School St. Ukiah, CA 95482. (707) 468-0123. Freelance submissions: seldom. Submissions Editors: Jim Smith (general); Sae Woodward (book review and travel). Circulation: 10,000.

VALLEJO TIMES HERALD. PO Box 3188. Vallejo, CA 94590. (707) 644-1141. Freelance submissions: sometimes. Submissions Editors: Colleen Truelsen (general); Dan Judge (book review and travel). Circulation: 28,000.

(Ventura County, Inland) *Daily News see* **(LOS ANGELES COUNTY, NORTH) DAILY NEWS.**

VENTURA COUNTY STAR-FREE PRESS. PO Box 6711. Ventura, CA 93003. (805) 656-4111. Freelance submissions: very rarely. Submissions Editors: John Bowman (general); Rita Moran (book review and travel). Circulation: 56,000.

(VICTORVILLE) DAILY PRESS. PO Box 1389. Victorville, CA 92393-0964. (619) 241-7744. Freelance submissions: sometimes. Submissions Editors: John Iddings (general); Rae Dawn Olbert (book review); Larry Croom (travel). Circulation: 25,000.

VISALIA TIMES DELTA. 330 N. West St. Visalia, CA 93291. (209) 734-5821. Janet C. Sanford, Publisher. Freelance submissions: sometimes. Submissions Editors: Barry Kawa (general); Camille Nichols (book review and travel). Circulation: 23,000.

WATSONVILLE REGISTER PAJARONIAN. PO Box 780. Watsonville, CA 95077. (408) 724-0611. Freelance submissions: yes. Submissions Editors: Mike Wallace (general); Stacey Vreeken (book review and travel). Circulation: 13,500.

WHITTIER DAILY NEWS. PO Box 581. Whittier, CA 90608. (213) 698-0955. Freelance submissions: yes. Submissions Editors: Bill Bell (general); Glen Whipp (book review and travel). Circulation: 19,000.

Hawaii

HAWAII TRIBUNE HERALD. PO Box 767. Hilo, HI 96721. (808) 935-6621. Freelance submissions: no. Submissions Editor: Gene Tao. Circulation 25,000.

HONOLULU ADVERTISER. 605 Kapiolani Blvd. Honolulu, HI 96813. (808) 525-8000. Freelance submissions: yes. Submissions Editors: Susan Yim (general); Wanda Adams (book review); Ed Kennedy (travel). Circulation: 100,000.

HONOLULU STAR BULLETIN. PO Box 3080. Honolulu, HI 96802. (808) 244 3981. Freelance submissions: yes. Submissions Editors: Dave Shapiro (general); Burl Burlingame (book review). Circulation: 90,000.

MAUI NEWS. PO Box 550. Wailuku, HI 96793. (808) 244-3981. Freelance submissions: yes. Submissions Editors: Dave Hoff (general); Harry Eager (book review and travel). Circulation: 16,000 daily, 22,000 Sunday.

Literary Agents

There is no law which says that a writer must have an agent. However, for some writers the benefits of having an agent are well worth the 10-15 percent commission charged. For example, some publishers simply refuse to consider unagented manuscripts. The specific services and charges vary from agent to agent, but they usually include the following:

Before sale—Evaluates your manuscript, advises on the preparation of your proposal, talks to editors, sends out your submissions, and informs you of results.

During sale—Negotiates contract with publisher and reviews the terms with you, after which you must decide to sign or not sign.

After sale—Receives and examines your royalty statements and payments, deducts the appropriate commission, and sends you the remainder. Pursues the sale of subsidiary rights retained by you in your contract.

Merely writing to one agent does not guarantee that you will be accepted as a client, so expect the search to involve several contacts. The following information has been gathered and organized to help you in the process of finding the right agency for your work.

How to Use the Information In This Section

The first paragraph of each entry gives the basic contact information and identifies the agent to whom you should address your query.

Subjects of Interest

We've included information on the type of material the agent prefers to handle. Your chances of a positive response to your initial inquiry are maximized when you approach an agent who is already interested in your subject matter. Books that the agent has previously sold indicate the contacts and success the agent has had. However, some agents prefer to keep this type of information confidential.

Agency Policies

Many agents will handle new writers only if they have been referred by clients, editors, or other professional colleagues. Other agents will gladly encourage new writers and are eager to represent well-written manuscripts. Reading fees are charged by some agencies and do not guarantee that the agent will accept the work. Some only charge a first-time writer, and some will refund the fee if the manuscript sells. Agents may charge an additional fee to cover "out-of-pocket" expenses, such as long-distance phone calls, photocopying, express mail, etc.

Agents who do not handle all forms of subsidiary rights often will work in conjunction with other agents to get you the best deal possible. Agents will also work closely with their counterparts in Europe for sales of foreign rights, or in Hollywood for sales of dramatization, motion picture, and broadcast (performance) rights.

Agents try to respond to your submissions or queries in a reasonable length of time; make it easier for them by including a SASE.

Commission: This information represents the percentage of income from your writing that the agent takes as a fee for representing you. Most agents charge between 10 and 15 percent. You alone must decide if it is worth it to you to market your book yourself or pay an agent to do it.

Initial Contact

Never send a complete manuscript unless requested by the agent. An initial query letter may include no more than an outline or brief summary of your story and idea. For nonfiction, include your qualifications. Always include a SASE.

Additional Information

This section lists any other information the agent expects you to know, or wants you to know, about the agency.

Abbreviations

n/i means no information was given to us by the agency.

n/a means that this particular question did not apply to the agency.

LINDA ALLEN AGENCY. 1949 Green St., #5. San Francisco, CA 94123. (415) 921-6437. Agent: Linda Allen.

Subjects of Interest. Books—Fiction: juvenile; young adult. Nonfiction: juvenile; young adult. Representative titles: *Suffer the Child* (Pocket Books); *dBase 4 Made Easy* (McGraw Hill); *Visiting Miss Pierce* (Farrar, Straus and Giroux). **Scripts**—not at present. Do not want: category fiction; Westerns; science fiction.

Agency Policies. Previously unpublished authors: yes. Reading fee: no. Other fees: photocopying. Subsidiary rights: all, when appropriate; differs from contract to contract. Response time to initial inquiry: 6 weeks. **Commission:** 15%.

Initial Contact. Query letter; sample chapters. Include SASE.

BOOKSTOP LITERARY AGENCY. 67 Meadow View Road. Orinda, CA 94563. (415) 254-2664. Agent: Kendra Marcus.

Subjects of Interest. Books—Fiction: children's; young adult. Nonfiction: children's. Other—illustrated children's. Representative titles: *Letter to Letter* (Dutton); *Stable in*

Bethlehem (Golden); *Jenny* (Macmillan). **Scripts**—handled by sub agent. Do not want: adult material.

Agency Policies. Previously unpublished authors: yes. Reading fee: no. Other fees: postage; photocopying; phone. Subsidiary rights: all. Designated agents: yes. Response time to initial inquiry: 4-8 weeks. **Commission:** 15%.

Initial Contact. Fiction, entire manuscript. Nonfiction, outline, 2 sample chapters.

Additional Information. BookStop Literary Agency sells quality fiction, nonfiction, illustration and manuscripts for books for children from six months to sixteen years old.

MARTHA CASSELMAN. PO Box 342. Calistoga, CA 94515-0342. (707) 942-4341. Agent: Martha Casselman.

Subjects of Interest. Books—Fiction: mainstream; literary; will consider "women's books." Nonfiction: looking for books dealing with contemporary concerns, including politics, biography; children's and YA (limited number); cookbooks and food-related works. Recent publications: confidential, but publishers include Simon & Schuster, Harper and Row, Knopf, Holt, *Focus Magazine.* Do not want: genre fiction; computer; technical.

Agency Policies. Previously unpublished authors: yes, including short story writers. Reading fee: no. Other fees: copying; overnight mail; Fax; charge back. Subsidiary rights: all, depending on contract between author and publisher; agency controls all rights not contractually assigned to or held by publisher. Designated agents: chosen for specific projects. Response time to initial inquiry: 1-6 months. **Commission:** 15%.

Initial Contact. Phone; query letter; query with synopsis or proposal. Include brief biographical material; for nonfiction also include analysis of market for book and the competition.

Additional Information. We cannot return long-distance query calls. Therefore, it is preferable to query by mail and include a SASE. If calling locally, office hours are Monday through Friday, 9:30-4; please do not expect us to return calls in the evening. I absolutely do not want material mailed by way of a computer-generated program that is sent to every agent in the country; do not send unsolicited full-length manuscripts, fiction or nonfiction.

CHAOS LITERARY AGENCY. 6200 Wilshire Blvd., Ste. 903. Los Angeles, CA 90048. (213) 278-2002. Agent: David Reyes.

Subjects of Interest. Books—Fiction: commercial and literary, all genres; children's and young adult. Nonfiction: all areas. Do not want: poetry.

Agency Policies. Previously unpublished authors: yes. Reading fee: no. Other fees: no. Subsidiary rights: all. Designated agents (foreign or film rights): Tuttle-Mori (Japan); Agenzia Letteraria Internazionale (Italy). Response time to initial inquiry: 4-6 weeks. **Commission:** 15% domestic; 20% British and translation.

Initial Contact. Query letter; query with synopsis or proposal.

CINEMA TALENT INTERNATIONAL. 8033 Sunset Blvd., Ste. 808. Los Angeles, CA 90046. (213) 656-1937. Agents: George Kriton; Maxine Arnald; Lawrence Athan.

Subjects of Interest. Books—Fiction: yes. Nonfiction: yes. **Scripts**—episodic TV; miniseries; motion picture. Do not want: anything that deals with drugs.

Agency Policies. Previously unpublished authors: yes. Reading fee: no. Other fees: no. Subsidiary rights: all. Response time to initial inquiry: n/i. **Commission:** 10%.

Initial Contact. Query letter; query with synopsis or proposal.

RUTH COHEN, INC. Box 7626. Menlo Park, CA 94025. (415) 854-2054.
Agents: Ruth Cohen and Associates.

Subjects of Interest. Books—Fiction: quality adult and juvenile; mainstream novels; genre: mysteries, romances, historicals. Nonfiction: quality writing and well-researched manuscripts. Representative titles: *Boomerang Kids* (Little Brown); *Killshot* (Bantam); *No Way Out* (Harper & Row). Do not want: poetry; film scripts.

Agency Policies. Previously unpublished authors: yes. Reading fee: no. Other fees: photocopying; foreign cables and shipment. Subsidiary rights: first serialization; reprint; dramatization, motion picture, and broadcast; translation and foreign; English language publication outside the United States and Canada. Designated agents (foreign or film rights): Joel Gotler of LA Literary Associates. Response time to initial inquiry: 3-4 weeks. **Commission:** 15%.

Initial Contact. Query with synopsis or proposal plus 15 pages of opening of manuscript. Include SASE.

Additional Information. Actively seeking good writers of juvenile YA fiction and adult mysteries.

SANDRA DIJKSTRA LITERARY AGENCY. 1155 Camino del Mar, Ste. 515. Del Mar, CA 92104. (619) 755-3115. Agents: Sandra Dijkstra, President; Katherine Goodwin, Associate Agent.

Subjects of Interest. Books—Fiction: quality contemporary and literary fiction; mainstream; mystery-suspense; horror; science fiction; historical fiction or romance. Nonfiction: biography/memoir; psychology; health and medicine; parenting; business; art and artists; self-help; finance; travel; essays; women's studies; politics and social issues; nature. Representative titles: *The Joy Luck Club* (Putnam); *Leadership Is an Art* (Doubleday/Dell); *The Horse Latitudes* (William Morrow/Avon). Do not want: textbooks; children's; dissertations; computer books; vanity press; Westerns; poetry. No scripts, screenplays, or plays.

Agency Policies. Previously unpublished authors: occasionally. Reading fee: no. Other fees: in-depth evaluation of manuscript or proposal; fee depends on length. Subsidiary rights: all. Designated agents (foreign or film rights): La Nouvelle (France); Agence Hoffman (Germany); Rogan Pikarski (Israel); Luigi Bernabo (Italy); The English Agency (Japan); Kooy & van Gelderen (Netherlands); Monica Heyum (Scandinavia); Mercedes Casanovas (Spain, South America). Response time to initial inquiry: 3-4 weeks. **Commission:** 15%.

Initial Contact. Query letter; query with synopsis or proposal.

FELICIA ETH LITERARY REPRESENTATIVE. 140 University Ave., Ste. 62. Palo Alto, CA 94301. (415) 375-1276. Agent: Felicia Eth.

Subjects of Interest. Books—Fiction: high quality (no glitz). Nonfiction: health; psychology; history; popular science; women's issues; investigative journalism; contemporary issues. Representative titles: confidential. Do not want: juvenile; young adult; poetry; romance series; science fiction series; Westerns.

Agency Policies. Previously unpublished authors: yes. Reading fee: no. Other fees: photocopying; telexes, Fax, and Fed Ex; any extraordinary expenses. Subsidiary rights: first serialization; newspaper syndication; reprint; video distribution; sound reproduction and recording; translation and foreign; commercial; English language publication outside the United States and Canada. Designated Agents: independent agents. Response time to initial inquiry: 3-6 weeks. **Commission:** 15%.

Initial Contact. Fiction, query letter with first 30 pages. Nonfiction, query with synopsis or proposal. Include credentials and SASE.

FLORENCE FEILER LITERARY AGENCY. 1524 Sunset Plaza Dr.
Los Angeles, CA 90069. (213) 652-6920, 659-0945. Agent: Florence Feiler.

Subjects of Interest. Books—Fiction: very little. Nonfiction: how-to. Representative titles: work sold to Putnam, St. Martins, Fawcett, Harlequin, Zebra, Penguin. Do not want: n/i.

Agency Policies. Previously unpublished authors: no. Reading fee: no. Other fees: no. Subsidiary rights: all. Response time to initial inquiry: 2 months. **Commission:** 10%

Initial Contact. Query letter.

Additional Information. Films: *Out of Africa, Babette's Feast.* More films are in production.

CANDICE FUHRMAN LITERARY AGENCY. 30 Ramona Rd. PO Box F.
Forest Knolls, CA 94933. Agent: Candice Fuhrman.

Subjects of Interest. Books—Fiction: adult; commercial. Nonfiction: self-help; how-to. Representative titles: *A Kiss is Just a Kiss* (Crown); *The Recovery Resource Book* (Simon & Schuster); *Reclaiming Yourself* (Dell). Do not want: genre; children's.

Agency Policies. Previously unpublished authors: yes. Reading fee: no. Other fees: copying; postage. Subsidiary rights: all. Response time to initial inquiry: 2 weeks for queries; 4 weeks for manuscripts. **Commission:** 15%.

Initial Contact. Query with synopsis or proposal.

Additional Information. I'm especially interested in nonfiction self-help or how-to and am happy to work with new authors. Please include SASE with submissions if you want your materials returned.

MITCHELL J. HAMILBURG AGENCY. 292 S. La Cienega Blvd., Ste. 312.
Beverly Hills, CA 90211. (213) 657-1501. Agent: Michael Hamilburg.

Subjects of Interest. Books—Fiction: general. Nonfiction: general. Representative titles: *Helter Skelter; Von Ryan's Express; Logan's Run; Taxi Driver; Time after Time.*

Agency Policies. Previously unpublished authors: yes. Reading fee: no. Other fees: no. Subsidiary rights: first serialization; dramatization, motion picture, and broadcast; video distribution; commercial. Response time to initial inquiry: 3-4 weeks. **Commission:** 10-15%.

Initial Contact. Query letter first.

FREDRICK HILL ASSOCIATES. 1842 Union St. San Francisco, CA 94123.
(415) 921-2910. Agents: Fredrick Hill; Bonnie Nadell.

Subjects of Interest. Books—Fiction: literary. Nonfiction: investigative journalism; biography. Do not want: no genre fiction (science fiction, romance, etc.).

Agency Policies. Previously unpublished authors: yes. Reading fee: no. Other fees: galleys sent overseas. Subsidiary rights: first serialization; newspaper syndication; dramatization, motion picture, and broadcast; video; English language publication outside the United States and Canada. Designated agents: agents in every major country and Hollywood. Response time to initial inquiry: 4-8 weeks. **Commission:** 15%, domestic; 20%, foreign.

Initial Contact. Query with synopsis or proposal.

ALICE HILTON LITERARY AGENCY. 13131 Welby Way.
North Hollywood, CA 91606. (818) 982-2546. Agents: Alice Hilton.

Subjects of Interest. Books—Fiction and Nonfiction: sophisticated, civilized, quality material. Representative titles: *Tax-Free America* (Witlauer). **Scripts**—episodic TV; specials; miniseries; motion picture; cartoons. Do not want: children's books; violence.

Agency Policies. Previously unpublished authors: yes. Reading fee: on book-length material, $2 per 1000 words (pica) for previously unpublished authors. Other fees: no. Subsidiary rights: all, as the need arises. Response time to initial inquiry: 4-6 weeks. **Commission:** 10%.

Initial Contact. Query letter.

JLM LITERARY AGENTS. 17221 E. 17th St. Santa Ana, CA 92701. (714) 547-4870. Agent: Judy Semler.

Subjects of Interest. Books—Fiction: general, literary, mysteries, contemporary romances. Nonfiction: general, especially women's issues. Representative titles: *Ghost of a Chance, Flying Wing, Light Her Fire, The Secret Rules of Romantic Love.*

Agency Policies. Previously unpublished authors: yes. Reading fee: no. Other fees: yes, $100 fee on signing for unpublished authors only. Subsidiary rights: first serialization; second serialization; reprint rights; dramatization, motion picture, and broadcast; direct mail or sound reproduction and recording rights; direct sales rights; book club rights; English language publication outside the United States and Canada. Response time to initial inquiry: varies; include SASE. **Commission:** 15%.

Initial Contact. Query letter; query with synopsis. Include 2 chapters for fiction and a full proposal for nonfiction.

WILLIAM KERWIN AGENCY. 1605 N. Cahuenga Blvd., #202. Hollywood, CA 90028. (213) 469-5155. Agent: William Kerwin.

Subjects of Interest. Scripts—movie of the week; pilots; feature films. Do not want: episodic. Material must be original only.

Agency Policies. Previously unpublished authors: yes. Reading fee: no. Other fees: no. Subsidiary rights: first serialization; second serialization; dramatization, motion picture, and broadcast; video distribution; commercial; English language publication outside the United States and Canada. Response time to initial inquiry: 7 days, with SASE. **Commission:** 10%.

Initial Contact. Query letter; query with synopsis.

LAKE AND DOUROUX, INC. 445 South Beverly Dr., Ste. 310. Beverly Hills, CA 90212. (213) 557-0700. Agents: Candace Lake; Michael Douroux.

Subjects of Interest. Scripts—main concentration: screenwriters, directors, cinematographers in areas of episodic TV; specials; miniseries; motion picture; cartoons.

Agency Policies. Previously unpublished authors: no. Reading fee: no. Other fees: no. Subsidiary rights: first serialization; reprint; dramatization, motion picture, and broadcast; book club. Response time to initial inquiry: n/a. **Commission:** 10%.

Initial Contact. Does not accept unsolicited material.

LARSEN/POMADA LITERARY AGENTS. 1029 Jones St. San Francisco, CA 94109. (415) 673-0939. Agents: Michael Larsen; Elizabeth Pomada.

Subjects of Interest. Books—Fiction: literary; commercial; historical romance; "new voices." Nonfiction: pop psychology; business; popular science; biography; cultural affairs. Do not want: scripts; poetry; children's and YA.

Agency Policies. Previously unpublished authors: yes. Reading fee: no. Other fees: no. Subsidiary rights: all. Designated agents (foreign or film rights): yes. Response time to initial inquiry: 6-8 weeks. **Commission:** 15%.

Initial Contact. Phone; query letter; query with synopsis or proposal. Synopsis and 30 pages, fiction; proper proposal, nonfiction. Include SASE with all proposals.

Additional Information. We are looking for good new ideas and new voices. We are charter members of ILAA.

MAUREEN LASHER AGENCY, THE. PO Box 888. Pacific Palisades, CA 90272. (213) 459-8415. Agents: specialities decided in-house.

Subjects of Interest. Books—fiction and nonfiction. **Scripts**—motion pictures; TV. Do not want: stage plays; radio.

Agency Policies. Previously unpublished authors: rarely. Reading fee: no. Other fees: no. Subsidiary rights: all. Response time to initial inquiry: 1 month. **Commission:** 15%.

Initial Contact. Nonfiction, query letter and proposal. Fiction, manuscript.

IRVING PAUL LAZAR AGENCY. 120 El Camino, Ste. 108. Beverly Hills, CA 90212. (213) 275-6153. Agents: Irving Paul Lazar; Alan Nevins, associate. Not accepting any new material.

LITERARY/BUSINESS ASSOCIATES. PO Box 2415. Hollywood, CA 90078. (213) 465-2630. Agent: Shelley Gross.

Subjects of Interest. Books—Fiction: contemporary, mystery, thrillers, occult, comedy, romance, political thrillers. Nonfiction: how-to, self-help, psychology, healing, new age, pets, feminism, mysticism/spirituality, contemporary trends, celebrity autobiography, popular business, humor.

Agency Policies. Previously unpublished authors: yes. Reading fee: yes, an evaluation and critiquing fee for new authors, part of which is refundable on sale of manuscript. Other fees: marketing fee; long-distance calls; postage. Subsidiary rights: yes. Response time to initial inquiry: 4-6 weeks. **Commission:** unpublished authors 15% domestic, 20% foreign; published authors 12% domestic, 20% foreign.

Initial Contact. Query letter or complete manuscript. Include SASE.

Additional Information. We also offer a professional editing service.

LITERARY MARKETING CONSULTANTS. One Hallidie Plaza, Ste. 701. San Francisco, CA 94102. Agents: K. Allman (general nonfiction); Barbara Hargrave (religious material and fiction).

Subjects of Interest. Books—Fiction: science fiction; mystery; religious fiction of all types; some young adult; some romance. Nonfiction: religious and scholarly works; trade books with a specific, identifiable target audience. Regional Bay Area material welcome. (We look for well-defined topic and competent execution.) Representative titles: confidential. Do not want: poetry; short fiction by unpublished authors.

Agency Policies. Previously unpublished authors: yes. Reading fee: no. Other fees: handling fee after acceptance as client (sometimes waived with track record). Subsidiary rights: first serialization; reprint rights; English language publication outside the United States and Canada. Response time to initial inquiry: 1-3 months. **Commission:** 15%.

Initial Contact. Query letter.

Additional Information. Established in 1984, we are a small agency with highly specific needs. We expect accuracy in language skills (grammar) and creativity in style.

LONDON STAR PROMOTIONS. 21704 Devonshire St., #200. Chatsworth, CA 91311-2903. Agent: Lore London.

Subjects of Interest. Books—Fiction: all subjects. Nonfiction: all subjects. **Scripts**—any. Do not want: theater plays.

Agency Policies. Previously unpublished authors: yes. Reading fee: no. Other fees: no. Subsidiary rights: English language publication outside the United States and Canada. Response time to initial inquiry: 30 days. **Commission:** varies.

Initial Contact. Query letter with synopsis or proposal.

Additional Information. Include SASE.

LOS ANGELES LITERARY ASSOCIATES. 8955 Norma Place. Los Angeles, CA 90069. (213) 275-6330. Agents: Joel Gotler; Howard Sanders.

Subjects of Interest. Books—Fiction: yes. Nonfiction: yes. Other: unpublished material which we sell to film/TV companies prior to sale to publishing companies. Representative titles: *Purpose of Evasion* (St. Martin's Press); *Depraved Indifference* (NAL). *The Plumber* (Knightsbridge). Do not want: screenplays.

Agency Policies. Previously unpublished authors: yes. Reading fee: no. Other fees: extensive photocopying. Subsidiary rights: first serialization; dramatization, motion picture, and broadcast; book club; translation and foreign; commercial. Designated agents (foreign or film rights): many agents (New York, London) as well as the publishers handle my foreign rights. Response time to initial inquiry: promptly. **Commission:** 10%.

Initial Contact. Query letter; recommendation.

Additional Information. We see much of the material bought in Hollywood.

MARGRET MCBRIDE LITERARY AGENCY. PO Box 8730. La Jolla, CA 92038. (619) 459-0559. Fax 619-459-0132. Agent: Margaret McBride.

Subjects of Interest. Books—Fiction: commercial/mainstream; mass market; literary. Nonfiction: commercial/mainstream business; self-help; how-to; relationships; women. Representative titles: *One Minute Manager* (series) (Morrow); *What Men Won't Tell You (But Women Need to Know)* (Morrow); *Why Men Don't Get Enough Sex and Women Don't Get Enough Love* (Pocket Books). Do not want: children's; poetry; screenplays.

Agency Policies. Previously unpublished authors: yes. Reading fee: no. Other fees: no. Subsidiary rights: translation and foreign; English language publication outside the United States and Canada; audio rights. Designated agents (foreign or film rights): Eliane Benisti (France); Asano Agency (Japan); Raquel de la Concha (Portugal, Spain); Licht and Licht (Scandinavia); Michael Meller (Germany, Italy, United Kingdom). Response time to initial inquiry: 2-8 weeks. **Commission:** 15% domestic; 25% foreign.

Initial Contact. Query with synopsis or proposal.

HELEN MCGRATH, WRITERS' REPRESENTATIVE. 1406 Idaho Ct. Concord, CA 94521. (415) 672-6211. Agent: Helen McGrath.

Subjects of Interest. Books—Fiction: all types. Nonfiction: new-age; self-help; biography; how-to. Representative titles: *Love Me True* (Harlequin); *Mass Dreams of the Future* (McGraw Hill); *Point Blank* (St. Martins). Do not want: scripts; cookbooks; poetry; religious; textbooks.

Agency Policies. Previously unpublished authors: yes. Reading fee: no. Other fees: photocopying. Subsidiary rights: all. Designated agents (foreign or film rights): A.S. Bookman (Denmark, Sweden, Norway and Finland); Jane Conway-Gordon (Britain); Agence Hoffman (Germany and France); Michael Meller (Holland); Lorna Soifer (Israel); Erich Linder (Italy);

Ursula Barnett (South Africa); Julio Yanez (Spain and Portugal). Response time to initial inquiry: 3 weeks to 3 months. **Commission:** 15%.

Initial Contact. Phone; query with synopsis and proposal. Include SASE.

MITNICK AGENCY, THE. 91 Henry St. San Francisco, CA 94114. (415) 864-2234. Agent: Samuel A. Mitnick.

Subjects of Interest. Books—Fiction: mainstream; literary; "new" voices. Nonfiction: health; self-help; biography; science; business; cookbooks; humor; current affairs; history; Judaica; reference; history; anthropology; investigative journalism; sports. Do not want: science fiction; paperback category fiction; new age; computers; juvenile. No original screenplays.

Agency Policies. Previously unpublished authors: prefer published, but will consider only after query. Reading fee: yes, for first novels. Other fees: photocopying. Subsidiary rights: all. Designated agents (foreign or film rights): Carol Smith (Britain); Michael Meller (Germany and Italy); Lora Fountain (France). Work with several agents in Hollywood for film and television production. Response time to initial inquiry: 2-6 weeks depending on length. **Commission:** 15%.

Initial Contact. Query letter; query with proposal, synopsis, and two sample chapters. No response or materials returned without SASE. Include background experience, especially as it relates to publishing or proposal.

Additional Information. I am a former publisher (HP Books, GP Putnam's) and editor in chief (HBJ, Dell, Da Capo Press). Occasionally work as packager, for which commission fees rise accordingly.

NEW AGE WORLD SERVICES AND BOOKS. 62091 Valley View Circle. Joshua Tree, CA 92252. (619) 366-2833. Agents: Rev. Victoria E. Vandertuin.

Subjects of Interest. Books—Fiction: new age. Nonfiction: metaphysical; parapsychology; occult; lost continents; yoga; mystical; UFO; alchemy; astrology; reincarnation; biblical prophecy; crystals; channelling; health and beauty. Other: poetry; short stories; articles. Do not want: humor; cookbooks; conservative and fundamental material. Representative titles: confidential.

Agency Policies. Previously unpublished authors: yes. Reading fee: yes, depending on length. Other fees: manuscript typing service; critiquing service. Subsidiary rights: first serialization; second serialization; direct mail or direct sales; book club; commercial. Response time to initial inquiry: 4-6 weeks. **Commission:** standard.

Initial Contact. Phone; query letter and synopsis.

Additional Information. All submissions must be completed, typed manuscripts in the new-age fields, either fiction or nonfiction. We also have a beautiful writer's retreat available in the high desert on a year-round basis. Write or phone for information.

REED LITERARY AGENCY. 12089 Lopez Canyon Rd., #201. Lakeview Terrace, CA 91342. (818) 896-1769. Agent: Ellen Reed.

Subjects of Interest. Books—Fiction: science fiction; fantasy; mysteries. Nonfiction: serious and intelligent metaphysical/occult/new age; pagan. Representative titles: *The Living Myth; Ta Mera.* Do not want: anti-occult material; screenplays.

Agency Policies. Previously unpublished authors: yes. Reading fee: no, but do offer critiquing and editing services if desired. Other fees: photocopying charges. Subsidiary rights: all. Response time to initial inquiry: 1 week queries, 2 months, manuscripts. **Commission:** 10%.

Initial Contact. Query letter or query letter with synopsis.

Additional Information. This is a small, new agency with four clients. Owner is a published author. Wants a few good clients.

SHERRY ROBB LITERARY PROPERTIES. 7250 Beverly Blvd., Ste. 102. Los Angeles, CA 90036. (213) 965-8780. Agents: Sherry Robb; Sasha Goodman (fiction); Jim Pinkston (nonfiction); Vick Mato (film).

Subjects of Interest. Books—Fiction: literary, off-beat novels; serious literary novels; big commercial women's novels; mysteries and thrillers. Nonfiction: commercial nonfiction, especially in the areas of self-help. Known for celebrities: *Dreamgirls* by Mary Wilson (St. Martin's); Jacqueline Stallone's *Starpower* (NAL); also books by Betty White (Doubleday) and Smokey Robinson (McGraw Hill); *No Easy Place to Be* (Simon & Schuster); mysteries, *The Daphne Decisions* (Bantam), *Finders Keepers* (McGraw Hill); mainstream, *My Enemy, My Love* (Dell), *Mistresses* (Pinnacle). Nonfiction: *The Agony of It All* (Tarcher).

Scripts—episodic TV; specials; miniseries; motion picture; romantic comedy, both TV and features. Do not want: most poetry unless also a performer.

Agency Policies. Previously unpublished authors: yes; we've sold 60 first-time authors in five years. Reading fee: no. Other fees: Sometimes we recommend more intense editorial work and suggest a freelance editor to work with. Subsidiary rights: all (except for those handled by a publisher). Designated agents (foreign or film rights): We have 10 foreign agents around the world. Response time to initial inquiry: 2-4 weeks. **Commission:** 15% books, video, audio; 10% film.

Initial Contact. Fiction, query letter plus manuscript; except for romance, query letter plus 3 chapters. Nonfiction, query letter plus proposal. Include author biography. All queries or submissions must include SASE.

Additional Information. We edit and guide writers of fiction; help shape proposals for nonfiction writers.

JACK SCAGNETTI TALENT AND LITERARY AGENCY. 5330 Lankershim Blvd., #210. North Hollywood, CA 91601. (818) 762-3871. Agent: Jack Scagnetti (nonfiction; novel-length fiction; screenplays; television plays).

Subjects of Interest. Books—Fiction: stories must be high quality that lend themselves to screenplay adaptability. Nonfiction: how-to; sports; films; biographies. **Scripts**—screenplays; TV. Representative titles: *Highway to Heaven* (TV episodic script); *Family Ties* (TV episodic script). Do not want: poetry; magazine fiction.

Agency Policies. Previously unpublished authors: yes. Reading fee: yes. Other fees: one-way postage on multiple submissions. Subsidiary rights: all. Response time to initial inquiry: 4-6 weeks. **Commission:** 10%.

Initial Contact. Query letter; query with synopsis or proposal.

Additional Information. More emphasis on screenplays than books; more interested in nonfiction books than fiction. Signatory of Writers Guild of America—West.

SEBASTIAN AGENCY. PO Box 1369. San Carlos, CA 94070. (415) 598-0310. Agents: Laurie Harper.

Subjects of Interest. Books—Fiction: commercial mainstream woman's novel; historical (not historical romance); suspense/thriller; man's adventure; Western; literary fiction. Nonfiction: adult (except cookbooks or poetry). Representative titles: *God Was an Atheist Sailor* (W. W. Norton); *The Monogamy Myth* (Newmarket Press); *A Sheaf of Wheat* (Ballantine); *Women Who Shop Too Much* (St. Martins). Do not want: original screenplay material; romance; science fiction; fantasy; horror/occult.

Agency Policies. Previously unpublished authors: yes. Reading fee: no. Other fees: $100 one-time, nonrefundable fee for previously unpublished author signing on with agency. Subsidiary rights: first serialization; second serialization; reprint; dramatization, motion picture; book club; translation and foreign; commercial; English language publication outside the United States and Canada. Designated agents (foreign): Michael Meller (Germany, England, Italy, Scandinavia); A.C.E.R. (Spain, Brazil, Portugal); Tuttle-Mori (Japan). Response time to initial inquiry: 4 weeks. **Commission:** 15% domestic; 20% foreign.

Initial Contact. Query letter; query with synopsis or proposal. No submissions in February or September.

Additional Information. We are seeking multiple-book authors more than single-book; interested in helping to guide the writing career of an author.

SHUMAKER ARTISTS TALENT AGENCY. 6533 Hollywood Blvd., #301. Hollywood, CA 90028. (213) 464-0745. Agent: Timothy Shumaker.

Subjects of Interest. Books—Fiction: action; adventure; comedy (urban). Nonfiction: autobiography; subjects of esoteric nature; historic (you were there); WWII oral histories; sports; music and arts; archaeology; mysticism, metaphysics. Representative titles: confidential. **Scripts**—episodic TV; specials; miniseries; motion picture. Do not want: pornography; occult; propaganda of all types.

Agency Policies. Previously unpublished authors: yes. Reading fee: yes ($50 screenplays; $135 novels). Other fees: marketing expenses. Subsidiary rights: all. Designated agents (foreign or film rights): Sarah Baldwin-Benish. Response time to initial inquiry: 6 weeks. **Commission:** 10%.

Initial Contact. Query with synopsis or proposal.

Additional Information. We are deliberately a small agency whose main concern is meaningful human relations and a desire for excellence in our clients.

SINGER MEDIA CORPORATION. 3164 Tyler Ave. Anaheim, CA 92801. (714) 527-5650. Agents: John J. Kearns (special project manager); Kurt D. Singer (everything).

Subjects of Interest. Books—Fiction: romances, Westerns, horror. Nonfiction: business; computers; psychological self-help; ethnic cookbooks; how-to. Other: juvenile activities. **Scripts**—specials; miniseries; motion picture; cartoons; in the areas of international celebrities, health, and travel material for worldwide syndication only. Do not want: local histories; war; science fiction; children's stories.

Agency Policies. Previously unpublished authors: yes. Reading fee: $250 for new book manuscript. Other fees: not for published authors. Subsidiary rights: first serialization; second serialization; newspaper syndication; reprint; book club; foreign; computer and other magnetic and electronic; English language publication outside the United States and Canada. Designated agents (foreign or film rights): several New York agents. Response time to initial inquiry: 2 weeks. **Commission:** 15% domestic; 20% foreign; 50% syndication.

Initial Contact. Query with synopsis or proposal.

Additional Information. We have contracts with German and Italian publishers for romances and business titles.

GLORIA STERN AGENCY. 12535 Chandler Blvd., #3. North Hollywood, CA 91607. (818) 508-6296. Agent: Gloria Stern.

Subjects of Interest. Books—Fiction: contemporary life. Representative titles: *On the Rocks.* **Scripts**—motion picture; movie-of-the-week. Do not want: gratuitous violence.

Agency Policies. Previously unpublished authors: yes. Reading fee: new clients, $35 hourly. Subsidiary rights: dramatization, motion picture, and broadcast; video distribution; book club; translation and foreign; English language publication outside the United States and Canada. Response time to initial inquiry: 1 month. **Commission:** 10-12%; foreign sales, 15%.

Initial Contact. Query letter.

Additional Information. We also provide complete editing, consultation, and ghostwriting services.

H. N. SWANSON, INC. 8523 Sunset Blvd. Los Angeles, CA 90069.
(213) 652-5385. Agents: H. N. Swanson; Michael Siegel; Sanford Weinberg.

Subjects of Interest. Books—Fiction: yes; first novels. Nonfiction: yes. Representative titles: *Freaky Deaky* (Morrow/Arbor House); *Killshot* (Morrow/Arbor House); *Dirty Money* (St. Martin's Press); Arthur Hailey's *Strong Medicine*. **Scripts**—episodic TV; specials; miniseries; motion picture (emphasis). Do not want: individual short stories; unfinished manuscripts.

Agency Policies. Previously unpublished authors: yes. Reading fee: no. Other fees: no. Subsidiary rights: all; foreign rights. Response time to initial inquiry: variable. **Commission:** 10%.

Initial Contact. Query letter with synopsis or proposal; with referral.

Additional Information. H. N. Swanson, Inc., is the oldest literary agency in Los Angeles. Past clients include Raymond Chandler, James M. Cain, John O'Hara, Pearl Buck. We are very selective but remain committed to new and exciting talent.

PATRICIA TEAL LITERARY AGENCY. 2036 Vista del Rosa. Fullerton, CA
92631. (714) 738-8333. Agent: Patricia Teal.

Subjects of Interest. Books—Fiction: category and mainstream (the latter usually from authors with publishing credits); specialize in romance literature, both contemporary and historical. Nonfiction: how-to; self-help. Representative titles: *Bound by Blood* (NAL); *Wildflower* (Berkley); *The Enchanter* (M. Evans). Do not want: articles; puzzles; children's; YA; poetry; short stories.

Agency Policies. Previously unpublished authors: yes. Reading fee: no. Other fees: $35 marketing fee to cover postage and telephone. Subsidiary rights: first serialization; reprint rights; dramatization, motion picture, and broadcast; book club; translation and foreign; English language publication outside the United States and Canada. Designated agents (foreign or film rights): Sandra Watt and Associates for film rights. Response time to initial inquiry: 2 weeks; 4 weeks, synopsis and chapters. **Commission:** 15%; 20% mainstream.

Initial Contact. Query letter.

Additional Information. With all correspondence, a SASE must be included for a response. Include a SASE postcard for confirmation of material arrival.

SANDRA WATT AND ASSOCIATES. 8033 Sunset Blvd., Ste. 4053.
Los Angeles, CA 90046. (213) 653-2339. Agents: Sandra Watt (books, books-to-film); Robert Drake (books).

Subjects of Interest. Books—Fiction: category fiction; literary; women's fiction. Nonfiction: new age; humor; nature crime; psychology; diet; sex; general interest. Representative titles: *Lemons . . . & Lemonade* (NAL); *Sex and the Single Parent* (Henry Holt); *Hungry Women* (Warner).

Agency Policies. Previously unpublished authors: yes. Reading fee: no. Other fees: On signing, first-time authors pay a marketing fee used solely for the promotion and marketing of their work. The fee is nominal. Subsidiary rights: all. Designated agents (foreign or film rights): We are a full-service agency with foreign reps in over seven countries. Response time to initial inquiry: 6-8 weeks. **Commission:** 10% (film); 15% (books); 20% (foreign).

Initial Contact. Query letter.

Additional Information. Liberal bent; possesses integrity and is willing to work with new and, as yet, unproven talent.

WRITERS' ASSOCIATES LITERARY AGENCY.
3960 Laurel Canyon Blvd., Penthouse Ste. 219. Studio City, CA 91604. (213) 851-2488. Agents: Barbara Dempsey (screenplays); Barbara B. Stratton, (novels, print media).

Subjects of Interest. Books—Fiction: main line contemporary fiction; historical novels; short stories. Nonfiction: varied. Other: plays. Representative titles: *See the Woman* (Worldwide); *Tawny* (Marquis); *The Chateau* (C. Gunn, London). **Scripts**—episodic TV; motion pictures; cartoons; TV movies. Do not want: children's fare.

Agency Policies. Previously unpublished authors: yes. Reading fee: minimal and refunded upon sale. Only unpublished writers are so charged. Other fees: no. Subsidiary rights: first serialization; second serialization; newspaper syndication; dramatization, motion picture, and broadcast; video distribution; book club; translation and foreign; commercial; English language publication outside the United States and Canada. Response time to initial inquiry: 6 weeks. **Commission:** 10%.

Initial Contact. Query with synopsis or proposal.

Additional Information. We are especially receptive to new writers and their development.

WRITER'S CONSULTING GROUP. PO Box 492. Burbank, CA 91503.
(818) 841-9294. Director: Jim Barmeier.

Subjects of Interest. Books—Fiction: we will look at all manuscripts. Nonfiction: all. Representative titles: Craig Smith espionage story; Smurfs (Hanna-Barbera). **Scripts**—we will look at all scripts.

Agency Policies. Previously unpublished authors: yes. Reading fee: no. Other fees: no. Subsidiary rights: dramatization, motion picture, and broadcast; video distribution. Response time to initial inquiry: 1-3 months. **Commission:** 10%.

Initial Contact. Phone; query letter.

Additional Information. Mr. Barmeier is a graduate of Stanford University's Master's Degree Program in Creative Writing and provides ghostwriting, editing, and book publicity services for interested writers.

Professional Organizations

Membership in one or more professional organizations can enhance your resumé, expand your network of professional contacts, and be a source of industry information and news. No two organizations are exactly alike, as you'll see from reading this section. Membership criteria, dues, and activities vary as does the contact information.

Some organizations maintain an office where you can request information; others use branch members' homes or work addresses and phone numbers. A few organizations prefer that queries be directed to their national headquarters. In any case, with dozens to choose from, you are sure to find one that's right for your writing field and geographic area.

How to Use the Information in This Section

The first paragraph of each entry identifies the name of the organization, address and phone number of its national headquarters, and name and professional title of a contact person. We've listed the date when the organization was founded, number of members nationally, and annual dues (at the national level).

Information that applies to both the national and branch (or chapter) levels, such as membership criteria, activities, and benefits, is listed under the national entry. If the information applies only at the chapter level, it is found there.

Local Chapters

To help you find a chapter or branch in your area, we've listed the name and address and/or phone number of a local contact person. Some organizations prefer all inquiries to be directed to their national headquarters since annual elections render the current information inaccurate. Some organizations were very generous in supplying information about their activities, and thus their entries are comprehensive; others are quite concise.

Members: This figure represents the number of members of the organization and/or chapter at the time it was surveyed.

Purpose: Most of the organizations we surveyed listed a statement of purpose, which often emphasized the organization's role in the pursuit of excellence in writing, advancement of members' career goals and communication skills, and dissemination of information.

Membership criteria: Some organizations list only an interest in writing and payment of dues as their criteria for membership; others offer several types of membership and require different levels of professional achievement as criteria.

Dues: When appropriate, we listed national dues and branch dues. While some organizations require only branch dues, others require dues to be paid at both the branch and national levels. Still others require a one-time processing fee in addition to the dues.

Benefits: Some chapters offer many benefits including local programs, monthly newsletters, medical insurance, legal representation, a lending library of books or tapes, and more.

Meetings and Activities: Most organizations sponsor monthly meetings, often with guest speakers. Seminars, critique group sessions, and annual conferences are also common. If an organization lists conferences as one of its activities, there may be additional information in the Conferences section. Some organizations sponsor conferences in a different state each year. We've limited our listings to those conferences that regularly though not exclusively use California sites.

Newsletters: In addition to providing information to its members, some organizations' newsletters accept freelance material (though usually not for pay) and publish book reviews and/or press releases of events or news.

Editor: This entry specifies the name of the newsletter editor.

Frequency: The newsletter publication schedule is indicated here.

Submissions: This section lists the types of written material the publication accepts.

Additional publications: Some organizations produce a variety of publications or resources. Those publications other than newsletters are listed here.

Abbreviations

n/i means no information was given to us by the organization.

AMERICAN MEDICAL WRITERS ASSOCIATION. 9650 Rockville Pike. Bethesda, MD 20814. (301) 493-0003. Executive Director, Lillian Sablack. Founded: 1940. Members: 3100 (national); 375 (California); 190 (NCA chapter). Dues: $65.

Purpose: To promote clarity in medical communications. Membership criteria: interest in medical communications. Benefits: curriculum of workshops leading to a certificate in their specialty area of medical communications; networking; annual conference (location varies); medical and life insurance. Meetings: eight to ten times annually (chapter); annually (national). Activities: meetings, chapter events, workshops/seminars, conferences.

Newsletter: *The Pacemaker*. Editor: Judith Windt. Frequency: eight times yearly. Submissions: articles for quarterly journal only. Additional publications: freelance directory, quarterly journal.

Northern California Chapter. Contact person: President, Daniel Liberthson, Ph.D., c/o Syntex Laboratories, 3401 Hillview Ave., MSL 1410, Palo Alto, CA 94304. (415) 759-7617.

Pacific Southwest Chapter (Southern California, Arizona, Nevada, Hawaii). Contact person: President, Beverly Sloane, 1301 North Santa Anita Ave., Arcadia, CA 91006. (818) 355-8915. Members: 250. Activities: bimonthly meetings with prominent speakers, annual one-day conference co-sponsored with Independent Writers of Southern California.

AMERICAN SOCIETY FOR TRAINING AND DEVELOPMENT.
National office: (703) 683-8100. Founded: 1946. Members: 23,000 (national). National dues: $120.

Purpose: To provide leadership, service, and education for the training and development of individuals, organizations, and the community. Membership criteria: Any person who is interested in the training and development of individuals is eligible for membership. Benefits: directory.

El Camino Chapter. Contact person: Executive Director, Linda Patten, 3545 Perada Dr., Walnut Creek, CA 94598. (415) 322-ASTD. Members: 600. Dues: $50 (plus one-time $10 processing fee). Benefits: discounts on all functions/events, free directory, monthly newsletter (job referral), networking opportunities, a chance to gain insight to the active training field. Meetings: second Tuesday of each month. Activities: meetings, workshops/seminars, conferences, contests. Newsletter: *The Update*. Editor: Sandy Pokras. Frequency: monthly. Submissions: press releases and articles upon editor's approval.

Golden Gate Chapter. Contact person: Executive Director, Linda Patten, 3545 Perada Dr., Walnut Creek, CA 94598. (415) 937-5640. Members: 975. Dues: $50 (plus one-time $20 processing fee). Benefits: discount on monthly meeting fees and workshops, monthly newsletter, directory, position referral service, special interest groups, networking opportunities. Meetings: dinner meeting on second Wednesday of the month. Activities: meetings, workshops/seminars, conferences, trade shows. Newsletter: *The ASTD Reporter*. Frequency: monthly. Submissions: press releases regarding members.

Inland Empire Chapter. Contact person: Deborah Loury, c/o Riverside National Bank, PO Box 1279, Riverside CA 92502. (714) 276-8823.

Los Angeles Chapter. Contact person: President, Linda Stipancic, 10820 Beverly Blvd., Ste. A-5-101, Whittier, CA 90601. (213) 908-3020.

Los Padres Chapter. Contact person: Pam Hawes. (805) 963-5871.

Mt. Diablo Chapter. Contact person: Membership Chairperson, Kathy Block, PO Box 1646, Danville, CA 94526. (415) 932-2374. Members: 100. Dues: $30. Meetings: Third Tuesday of every month.

Orange County Chapter. Contact person: President, Lynn McCann, 195 South "C" St., Ste. 250, Tustin, CA 92680. (714) 770-8268.

Pacific Delta Chapter. Contact person: Lou Surles, PO Box 30115, Stockton, CA 95213. (209) 983-6430. Members: 102. Dues: $20. Newsletter: *The Dateline*. Editor: Gail Wax. Frequency: monthly. Activities: monthly meetings (except July), two workshops annually.

Sacramento Chapter. Contact person: President, B. B. Hill, PO Box 89010, Sacramento, CA 95818. (916) 443-4305. Members: 400. Dues: $55 (for new members). Meetings: third Tuesday of the month. Newsletter: yes. Frequency: monthly. Submissions: press releases, articles.

San Diego Chapter. Contact person: Marcie Jordan, 1360 Rosecrans, Ste. I, San Diego, CA 92106. (619) 224-2783. Members: 583. Dues: $55. Activities: monthly lunch meeting, last Wednesday of month.

AMERICAN SOCIETY OF INDEXERS. 1700 18th St., N.W. Washington, D.C. 20009. (202) 328-7110 (phone and leave message). Founded: 1968. Members: 700 (national); 110 (California). Dues: $40.

Purpose: To improve the quality of indexes and increase awareness of indexing among publishers and public. Membership criteria: interest in indexing. Benefits: informative newsletter, publications, and conferences; medical, life, and disability insurance. Meetings: bimonthly. Activities: meetings, workshops/seminars, conferences, trade shows, potluck informal gatherings.

Newsletter: *ASI Newsletter*. Frequency: quarterly. Submissions: letters to the editor, articles, press releases. Additional publications: membership directory, register of freelance indexers, many aids to indexers (national level).

Golden Gate Chapter. Contact person: President, Trisha Feuerstein, PO Box 1030, Lower Lake, CA 95457. (707) 928-5751.

Southern California. Contact person: Irv Hershman. (213) 397-9453.

AMERICAN SOCIETY OF JOURNALISTS & AUTHORS, INC. 1501 Broadway, Ste. 1907. New York, NY 10036. (212) 977-0947. Executive Director, Alexandra Cantor; President, David W. Kennedy. Founded: 1948. National dues: $120.

Purpose: to establish high ethical standards and further pursuit of excellence in writing nonfiction. Membership criteria: professional published nonfiction writers. Benefits: medical benefits package, dial-a-writer referral service, membership directory. Branch-level activities: meetings, workshops, seminars, annual conference, discussion groups, networking with professionals. Refer all requests for information to national office.

Newsletter: *ASJA Newsletter*. Frequency: monthly. Additional publications: *The Complete Guide to Writing Nonfiction, A Treasury of Tips for Writers; The ASJA Handbook*.

Los Angeles Chapter. Contact person: Isobel Silden, PO Box 35282, Los Angeles, CA 90035.

San Francisco Chapter. Contact person: Chairperson, Iris Lorenz-Fife, Star Route Box 172-A, Woodside, CA 94062.

ASIAN AMERICAN JOURNALISTS ASSOCIATION. 1765 Sutter St., Room 1000. San Francisco, CA 94115. (415) 346-2051. Executive Director, Diane Yen-Mei Wong. Founded: 1981. Members: 900 (national); 400 (California). Dues: $36 (paid at branch level).

Purpose: to increase employment of Asian/American (A/A) journalists; to assist A/A students pursuing journalism careers; to encourage fair and accurate news coverage of A/A issues; to provide support for A/A journalists. Membership criteria: includes categories for professional members; full members (journalists); associate members (non-journalists, retired, or part-time); student members. Benefits: reduced rates for organization conventions, directory, job bank. Activities: workshops, seminars, conferences. Meetings: two times annually; chapters meet monthly.

Newsletter: *Asian/American Journalists Association*. Frequency: quarterly. Submissions: press releases, articles. Additional publications: periodic studies and handbook.

Hawaii Chapter. Contact person: Nestor Garcia, 1170 Auahi St., Honolulu, CA 96814.

Los Angeles Chapter. Contact person: President, Joanne Ishimine. (213) 668-2800. Members: 150. Meetings: monthly.

Sacramento Chapter. Contact person: President, Mr. Lonnie Wong, 2705 23rd St., Sacramento, CA 95818. (916) 454-4548. Members: 30. Meetings: monthly. Activities: workshops, community service projects. Newsletter: *AAJA Sacramento Chapter*.

San Diego Chapter. Contact person: President, Milrose Basco, PO Box 882076, San Diego, CA 92108. (619) 293-3131. Members: 50. Meetings: monthly.

San Francisco Chapter. Contact person: President, David Louie. (415) 984-7227. Members: 150. Meetings: monthly. Activities: quarterly events. Newsletter: *SF Chapter AAJA Newsletter*.

Association of Business Writers of America *see* **NATIONAL WRITERS CLUB.**

BAY AREA BOOK REVIEWERS ASSOCIATION. 50 The Uplands. Berkeley, CA 94705. Contact, Henry Mayer. Founded: 1981. Members: 24. Dues: none.

Purpose: to provide a forum for book reviewers and to make the annual awards honoring excellence in books by Northern California writers. Membership criteria: freelance and staff book reviewers. Meetings: monthly.

BOOKBUILDERS WEST. PO Box 883666. San Francisco, CA 94188-3666. President, Casmira Kostecki, (415) 594-4429; Membership Chair, Bernie Scheier, (415) 477-4400. Founded: 1969. Members: 325. Dues: $75, for companies with four or more employees; $40, for companies with three or fewer employees.

Purpose: educational and social resource for book publishers and their suppliers (freelance designers and production services, typesetters, color separators, printers, etc.) in 13 Western states. Membership criteria: publishers, suppliers, or individuals engaged in book publishing or offering services to book publishers; must be located or do business within the 13 Western states; publishers must publish books with Western states imprint or register copyright in one of the states. Benefits: monthly dinner meetings, seminars, access to job bank, bimonthly newsletter, biannual trade show/conference. Meetings: monthly (except July and August). Activities: meetings, workshops/seminars, conferences, annual Bookbuilders West book show.

Newsletter: *Bookbuilders West*. Editor: Pat Brewer, Wadsworth Publishing Company. Frequency: bimonthly. Submissions: press releases rewritten for Calendar or Industry News; articles are solicited, but appropriate submissions are considered. Additional publications: *The New Directory* (includes membership and other book-production resources), book show catalog (annual).

CALIFORNIA PRESS PHOTOGRAPHERS ASSOCIATION, INC. c/o Moonlight Press. PO Box 994. Westminster CA 92684. (714) 894-8976. President, Norbert van der Groeben; Managing Director, Gene Booth. Dues: $30 professional; $15 student; $15 past presidents; $12.50 retired; $35 associate; $50 sustaining.

Purpose: A professional and educational organization for working news photographers employed by large and small newspapers and television stations in California. Activities: chapter meetings, annual meeting.

Newsletter: *The California Press Photographer*. Frequency: bimonthly.

CALIFORNIA PRESS WOMEN. 114 21st Ave. San Francisco, CA 94121. (415) 584-1455. President, Myra Bailey. Membership Chairperson, Mary Woolcott. Members: 75. Dues: $41.

Meetings: monthly board meeting. Activities: workshops, seminars, student scholarships, essay contest.

Newsletter: *Proof Sheet*. Frequency: quarterly. Submissions: press releases and articles.

CALIFORNIA WRITERS' CLUB. 2214 Derby St. Berkeley, CA 94705. (415) 841-1217. Secretary, Dorothy Benson. Founded: 1909. Members: 800. Dues: $25 annually, the same for all chapters. $20 to join.

Purpose: nonprofit professional organization open to writers to provide writing and market information and to promote fellowship among writers. Membership criteria: publication for active membership; expected publication in five years for associate membership. Benefits: workshop opportunities, monthly newsletter, discounted conference fee, contests. Meetings: monthly. Activities: meetings, workshops/seminars, conferences, contests. An all-branch meeting is held once a year.

Berkeley Branch. Contact person: Dorothy Benson, 2214 Derby, Berkeley, CA 94705. (415) 841-1217. Members: 118. Meetings: monthly. Newsletter: *California Writers' Club Bulletin*. Editor: Dorothy V. Benson. Frequency: monthly. Submissions: press releases, article submissions. Additional publications: *West Winds* (anthology).

Los Angeles Branch. Contact person: President, R. Daniel Foster, 1647 N. Coronado St., Los Angeles, CA 90026. Members: 42.

Mt. Diablo Branch (Danville area). Contact person: President, Ted Fuller, 241 Greenwich Dr., Pleasant Hill, CA 94523. Members: 73.

Peninsula Branch. Contact person: President, Barbara Foley, 2220 Avy Ave., Menlo Park, CA 94025. Members: 97.

Redwood Branch (North Bay area). Contact person: President, Mary Varley, 2305 Jose Ave., Santa Rosa, CA 95401. Members: 93.

Sacramento Branch. Contact person: William Holden, 8115 Sacramento St., Fair Oaks, CA 95628. (916) 967-7950. Members: 175.

San Fernando Valley Branch. Contact person: President, Anna Faber, 14054 Badger Ave., Sylmar, CA 91342. (818) 362-2530. Members: 150. Activities: monthly meetings, critique groups. Newsletter: *Changes*.

South Bay Branch (San Jose area). Contact person: President, Bonnie Vaughan, 411 Chestnut Park Court, San Jose, CA 95369. Founded: 1987. Members: 73. Activities: monthly meetings, conferences, contests. Newsletter: *CA Writers' Club, South Bay Branch*. Frequency: monthly.

COMEDY/HUMOR WRITERS ASSOCIATION. PO Box 211. San Francisco, CA 94101. (415) 541-5608, 751-6725. President, Karen Warner; Membership Chairperson, John Cantu. Founded: 1986. Members: 250. Dues: free.

Purpose: to provide friendship, contacts, and educational activities for comedy/humor writers. Membership criteria: actual or aspiring comedy/humor writer. Activities: dinners with guest speakers, classes, workshops.

Newsletter: part of *Cantu's Comedy Newsletter*. Editor: John Cantu. Frequency: quarterly. Submissions: press releases relating to all aspects of comedy/humor.

COSMEP, THE INTERNATIONAL ASSOCIATION OF INDEPENDENT PUBLISHERS. PO Box 703. San Francisco, CA 94101. (415) 922-9490. Executive Director, Richard Morris. Founded: 1968. Members: 1400. Dues: $50.

Purpose: trade association of small publishers. Membership criteria: must be publishers of books or periodicals; self-publishers are eligible to join. Benefits: information available on request; medical and life insurance offered. Meetings: annually. Activities: conferences.

Newsletter: *COSMEP Newsletter*. Editor: Richard Morris. Frequency: monthly. Submissions: press releases.

CUPERTINO WRITERS CLUB. 180 West Rincon Ave. Campbell, CA 95008. (408) 370-2205. Coordinating Chairperson, Barbara Johnson. Founded: 1973. Members: 60. Dues: $3 annually.

Purpose: To meet regularly to share information and to critique members' work. Selections of 10 pages or less are read aloud; critiques are written following each reading. Occasional speakers. Membership criteria: be actively writing, attend three meetings, and read at least once prior to joining. Benefits: first-book signings for members to honor a first published book; directory. Meetings: twice monthly.

EDITCETERA. 2490 Channing Way, #507. Berkeley, CA 94704. (415) 849-1110. Coordinator, Hazel White. Founded: 1971. Members: 70. Dues: $20.

Purpose: a nonprofit mutual benefit corporation designed to help freelancers improve their skills, share resources, and find work. Membership criteria: strong background in book publishing or technical documentation, freelance status, successful completion of editcetera tests and work reviews. Activities: workshops/seminars.

INDEPENDENT WRITERS OF SOUTHERN CALIFORNIA. PO Box 19745. Los Angeles, CA 90019. (213) 969-1663. President, Cheryl Crooks. Members: 400. Dues: $55 plus $55 one-time initiation fee.

Purpose: a professional service and support organization for self-employed writers, focusing on the business of writing. Membership criteria: principle occupation must be writing (professional); producers of services for writers (associates); students. Benefits: medical and dental insurance, networking, directory, job referral service. Meetings: monthly. Activities: workshops, conferences, specialty groups within the organization, including health writers' caucus and script writers' caucus.

Newsletter: *The IWOSC Independent*. Editor: Ellen Alperstein. Frequency: monthly. Submissions: press releases, articles.

INTERNATIONAL ASSOCIATION OF BUSINESS COMMUNICATORS. One Hallidie Plaza, Ste. 600. San Francisco, CA 94102. (415) 433-3400. Fax (415) 362-8762. President, Norm Leaper; Membership, Ann Fraley. Founded: 1970. Members: 11,500. International dues: $150 plus $30 applicant fee.

Purpose: to further excellence in the area of business communication. Membership criteria: qualification and payment of fees. Benefits: directory; applicants are sent a packet outlining services. Activities: chapter meetings, workshops, international conferences. Magazine: *Communication World*.

Hawaii Chapter. Contact person: Jan M. Kagehior, VP, Corp. Comm., AMFAC/JMB Hawaii, 700 Bishop St., Ste. 2100, Honolulu, HI 96813. (808) 945-8295. Members: 55. Dues: $50.

Long Beach-South Bay Chapter. Contact person: Debora M. Callaghan Spano, Northrop University, 5800 W. Arbor Vitae St., Los Angeles, CA 90045-4770. (213) 337-4455. Members: 55. Dues: $40.

Los Angeles Chapter. Contact person: Sara J. Swee, Wm. M. Mercer-Meidinger-Hansen, Inc., 3303 Wilshire Blvd., 6th Fl., Los Angeles, CA 90010. (213) 480-6423. Members: 275. Dues: $55.

Orange County Chapter. Contact person: Lisa Parks, Society of Critical Care Medicine, 251 Imperial Hwy., Ste. 480, Fullerton, CA 92635. Members: 150. Dues: $45.

Peninsula Chapter. Contact person: Kevin A. O'Connor, Comm. Rel. Mgr., Hewlett-Packard Co., 3000 Hanover St., 20BR, Palo Alto, CA 94304. (415) 857-6906. Members: 175. Dues: $35.

Sacramento Chapter. Contact person: Rick Cabral, Pacific Public Relations, 1771 Stockton Blvd., Ste. 208, Sacramento CA 95816. (916) 454-9923. Members: 31. Dues: $65.

San Diego Chapter. Contact person: Julie C. Andrews, General Dynamics, PO Box 85357, MZ C-5-1049, San Diego, CA 92138. (619) 547-9004. Members: 83. Dues: $39.

San Francisco Chapter. Contact person: President, Lin A. Lacombe, PO Box 117513, Burlingame, CA 94010. (415) 375-0275. Members: 320. Dues: $35.

INTERNATIONAL FOOD, WINE, AND TRAVEL WRITERS ASSOCIATION. PO Box 1532. Palm Springs, CA 92263. (619) 322-4717. President, Don Jackson; Executive Director and Membership Chairperson, Ray Kabaker. Founded: 1956. Members: 350 (international); 250 (California). Dues: $60.

Purpose: to provide a gathering point and resource base for professionals engaged in the food, wine, travel, and hospitality industries. Membership criteria: open to individuals, companies, and organizations maintaining professional interests in the above industries; must be nominated by a member or an officer. Benefits: access to current information on press trips and other professional travel benefits, official IFW&TWA working press card, confidential membership directory; special discounts on rental cars, travel, hotel accommodations; writer participation in *Annual Guide Book*; networking relationship with members worldwide and associate member organizations. Activities: local and regional meetings; annual conclave; awards based on nominations by regular members, including the *Golden Fork Award*.

Newsletter: *Hospitality World*. Editor: Ray Kabaker. Frequency: monthly. Submissions: press releases, articles from members. Additional publications: *Window to the World* (guidebook).

MARIN SMALL PUBLISHERS ASSOCIATION. Box 1346. Ross, CA 94957. President, David Waldman. Founded: 1979. Members: 200. Dues: $25.

Purpose: to help members publish their written, spoken, or visual materials. Membership criteria: actively pursuing business of self-publishing. Benefits: market and production information. Meetings: bimonthly. Activities: meetings, workshops/seminars, conferences, trade shows.

Newsletter: *SPEX*. Editor: Karen Misuraca. Frequency: six times a year. Submissions: press releases, article submissions. Additional publications: membership directory.

MEDIA ALLIANCE. Fort Mason, Bldg. D. San Francisco, CA 94123. (415) 441-2557. Executive Director, Micha Peled. Founded: 1976. Members: 2500. Dues: $50 first year; $40 renewal.

Purpose: to provide resources to writers, journalists, and media people. Membership criteria: none. Benefits: health plan; access to credit union; subscription to newsletter; discounts on training, computers, and events; job listings for writers. Activities: meetings, workshops, seminars, conferences.

Newsletter: *Mediafile*. Frequency: bimonthly. Submissions: press releases and articles. Additional publications: three books.

MYSTERY WRITERS OF AMERICA. 236 West 27th St., Room 600. New York, NY 10001. (212) 255-7005. President, Mary Shura Craig; Membership Chairperson, Priscilla Ridgeway. Founded: 1945. Members: 2200 (international). Dues: $65, $25 for correspondent members.

Purpose: to promote interests of mystery writers; to maintain recognition of mystery writing in publishing industry and reading public; to disseminate information and share benefits of associating with others interested in mystery writing. Membership criteria: includes categories for people actively writing mysteries, those published in other fields, those published outside the United States, and those who are unpublished or fans.

Newsletter: *The Third Degree*. Frequency: nine issues yearly. Activities: conferences, Edgar Allen Poe annual awards dinner usually held in New York City in May.

Northern California Chapter. Contact person: Karen Kijewski, 7472 Leonard Ave., Citrus Heights, CA 95610. (916) 722-1556. Members: 250. Membership criteria: unpublished writers of mystery (affiliate); professionals in allied fields—editors, agents, libraries, etc. (associate); and published writers of fiction or nonfiction in the crime/mystery/suspense field (active). Benefits: association with writers sharing common interests; access to national organization's publicity, pamphlets, marketing information; participation in local meetings, seminars; publicity efforts. Meetings: nine times a year. Activities: meetings, workshops/seminars, trade shows, manuscript critiquing service. Newsletter: *Lineup*. Editor: Meg O'Brien. Frequency: 10 issues yearly. Submissions: press releases. Additional publications: membership directory.

Southern California Chapter. Contact person: Regional Vice President, Elizabeth James, 1162 Angelo Dr., Beverly Hills, CA 90210. (213) 278-9500. Membership criteria: published writers of fiction or nonfiction in the crime/mystery/suspense field (active); unpublished writers of mystery (affiliate); professionals in allied fields—editors, agents, libraries, etc. (associate). Benefits: association with writers sharing common interests; access to national organization's publicity, pamphlets, marketing information; participation in local meetings, seminars; publicity efforts. Meetings: nine times a year. Activities: meetings, workshops/seminars, trade shows. Annual Edgar Awards Appreciation Banquet (black-tie) in spring/summer. Newsletter: *March of Crime*. Additional publications: membership directory.

NATIONAL LEAGUE OF AMERICAN PEN WOMEN. Pen Arts Building. 1300 17th Street, NW. Washington, D.C. 20036-1973. (202) 785-1997. President, Frances H. Mulliken. Founded: 1897. Members: 6000 (national); 1300 (California). Dues: $35, paid at branch level (200 U.S. branches).

Purpose: to further professional contacts and excellence in the arts. Membership criteria: rigorous qualification process. Activities: national meeting in spring (biennial).

Newsletter: *PenWoman* (magazine). Editor: Grace T. Rowe. Frequency: nine times annually, includes book reviews and professional/skill criteria updates, standards. Additional publications: national membership directory.

State President (Northern California): Vicki Lavorini, 2730 39th Ave., San Francisco, CA 94116.

State President (Southern California): Linda Aleahmad, 733 Bristol Ave., Simi Valley, CA 93065.

Berkeley Branch. Contact person: President, Opal Lafferty, 669 Dowling Blvd., San Leandro, CA 94577. Members: 18. Activities: monthly meetings (except summers), workshops, seminars, contests. Newsletter: *Berkeley Branch Newsletter*. Editor: Rosemary Wilkinson. Submissions: articles. Additional publications: membership directory.

Butte County Branch. Contact person: President, Lois H. McDonald, 14609 Skyway, Magalia, CA 95954. (916) 873-0769. Members: 20. Dues: $30. Meetings: monthly.

Diablo Alameda Branch. Contact person: President, Lucile Bogue, 2611 Brooks, El Cerrito, CA 93420.

El Camino Real Branch. Contact person: President, Madge Saksena, 3757 Macbeth Dr., San Jose, CA 95127. (408) 258-7125. Members: 27. Dues: $30. Activities: monthly meetings, workshops, seminars, conferences, contests.

Publications: membership directory.

Hollywood-Los Angeles Branch. Contact person: President, Frances Wolf, 1918 N. Whitney, Hollywood, CA 90068.

La Jolla Branch. Contact person: President, Helen Elizabeth Silvani, 5388 Chelsea St., La Jolla, CA 92037.

Laguna Beach Branch. Contact person: President, Mary Decker, 24772P Hidden Hills Rd., Laguna Niguel, CA 92677.

Las Artes Branch: Contact person: President, Trudy Duisenberg, 1010 Emerson St., Palo Alto, CA 94301.

Modesto Branch: Contact person: President, Margaret Bell, 2520 River Rd., Modesto, CA 95351.

Napa Valley Branch. Contact person: President, Toni Tacona Brent, 3051 Foothill Blvd., Calistoga, CA 94515.

Nob Hill Branch. Contact person: President, Ann Basuino, 2627 14th Ave., San Francisco, CA 94127.

Palomar Branch. Contact person: President, Helen Sherry, 11929 Caminito Corriente, San Diego, CA 92128.

Redwood Branch. Contact person: President, Cathy Ray Pierson, 132 Azalea Way, Eureka, CA 95501. Founded: 1969. Members: 12. Meetings: nine times annually. Newsletter: *Writing Behind the Redwood Curtain*. Editor: Carolyn Moore, PO Box 111, Arcata, CA 95521. Frequency: six times annually. Submissions: press releases, articles. Additional publications: membership directory.

Sacramento Branch. Contact person: President, Mary Lucille Johnson, 5346 Kenneth Ave., Carmichael, CA 95608.

San Bernadino Branch. Contact person: President, Barbara Shipman, 27075 E. Highland Ave., Highland, CA 92346.

Santa Clara Branch. Contact person: President, Thyra Tegner-Rogers, 226 Via La Posada, Los Gatos, CA 95030.

Santa Cruz Branch. Contact person: Esther Schulz, 100-63 N. Rodeo Gulch Rd., Soquel, CA 95073. (408) 475-5514. Members: 32. Dues: $30. Newsletter: yes. Editor: Beverly Levine. Frequency: monthly, except summer. Activities: monthly meetings except summers, workshops, conferences, occasional art shows. Additional publications: membership directory.

Santa Monica Branch. Contact person: President, Knarig Boyadjian, 2924 St. George St., Los Angeles, CA 90027.

Simi Valley Branch. Contact person: President, Leonore C. Schuetz, 1360 Venice St., Simi Valley, CA 93065.

Sonoma County Branch. Contact person: President, Constance Miller, 2099 Redwood Dr., Healdsburg, CA 95448-4531. Members: 35. Dues: $40. Meetings: monthly. Newsletter: monthly bulletin for members. Additional publications: membership directory.

Stockton Branch. Contact person: President, Mabel Ellen Myers, 1215 West Park St., Stockton, CA 95203.

Victor Valley Branch. Contact person: Treasurer, Wilma Vielda Terrill, 1231 N. Laurel Ave., Upland, CA 91786.

NATIONAL WRITERS CLUB, THE. 1450 S. Havana, Ste. 620. Aurora, CO 80012. (303) 751-7844. Contact person: Executive Director, James L. Young. Founded: 1937. Members: 4000. Dues: Membership, $50, plus $15 one-time setup fee. Professional Membership (credits covering sales to at least three national or regional magazines, a book sold to a royalty publisher, a play produced, or employment as writer, journalist, or editor) $60, plus $15 one-time setup fee.

Purpose: to meet the needs of freelance writers for honest, sympathetic, and authoritative help. Membership criteria: person must be serious about writing. Benefits: savings plan, group insurance, discounts on books and supplies, agent referral, acts as literary agent to small presses, manuscript criticism, correspondence courses in fiction and nonfiction.

Newsletter: *Authorship*. Frequency: six times per year. Additional publications: *NWC Newsletter, Flash Market News*. Additional publications: *Professional Writers Directory* (national; inclusion is by choice).

Note: for those interested, NWC now operates the Associated Business Writers of America. If your writing expertise lies in this area, you may become a dual member at no extra charge.

Hawaii Chapter. Contact person Robert T. Tanouye, 2419-A Pauoa Rd., Honolulu, HI 96813.

Los Angeles Chapter. Contact person: President, LaVonne Taylor-Pickell, PO Box 7155, Mission Hills, CA 91346-7155. (818) 367-8085.

Siskiyou Chapter. Contact person: Shari Fiock, 406 Walter's Lane, Yreka, CA 96097. (916) 842-5788.

Southern California Chapter. Contact person: Donna Harper, 9379 Tanager Ave., Fountain Valley, CA 92708. (714) 968-5726. President, Donna Harper (714) 636-9959; Membership, James Bardin (714) 892-9045. Members: 95. Dues: $10 plus national dues. Membership criteria: professional or aspiring writers. Benefits: to encourage writers and provide critiquing; chance to meet other writers and hear speakers related to writing; medical insurance. Meetings: monthly. Activities: meetings, workshops/seminars, conferences, contests. Newsletter: *Write News*. Editor: John Rennebu. Frequency: monthly. Additional publications: we plan to publish our first quarterly journal in the fall.

NATIONAL WRITERS UNION. 13 Astor Pl., Seventh Floor. New York, NY 10003. (212) 254-0279. Executive Director, Kim Fellner. Founded: 1983. Members: 3000 (national); 700 (California). Dues: $55-$135 (sliding scale).

Purpose: trade union for freelance writers; to gain equity, fair standards, and payment for freelance writers through collective action. Membership criteria: publish a book or play, three articles, five poems, one short story, or an equivalent amount of newsletter, publicity, technical, commercial, governmental, or institutional copy; or have similar portfolio of unpublished work, actively seeking publication. Benefits: medical insurance, collective bargaining, individual contract advice, press credentials, grievance handling. Activities: delegates' assembly annually in June, chapter meetings, workshops, conferences.

Newsletter: *The American Writer*. Editor: Ed Hedemann. Frequency: quarterly. Additional publications: Boston chapter has published *An Insider's Guide to Freelance Writing in New England*.

Los Angeles Local. Contact person: Chairperson, Sarah Arsone, PO Box 480349, Los Angeles, CA 90048. (213) 459-4373. Members: 180. Meetings: monthly. Activities:

conferences, workshops. Newsletter: *LA Writer*. Frequency: monthly. Submissions: press releases.

San Francisco Bay Area Local #3. Contact person: President, Bruce Hartford, 236 West Portal Ave., #232, San Francisco, CA 94127. (415) 654-6369. Members: 400. Membership criteria: all qualified writers, and no one shall be barred or in any manner prejudiced within the union on account of age, disability, ideology, national origin, race, religion, sex, or sexual preference. Benefits: medical insurance, negotiates union contracts with national and local publications; establishes grievance committees; job hot line for technical writers; contract advisory committee to assist authors; trade group meetings. Meetings: monthly. Activities: workshops/seminars, conferences, contests. Newsletter: *Bay Area Writer*. Editor: Kathleen White (415) 285-6946. Frequency: quarterly. Submissions: press releases, articles (from members only). Additional publications: *The American Writer* (national).

Santa Cruz/Monterey Local #7. PO Box 2409. Aptos, CA 95001-2409. (408) 427-2950. Contact person: President, Ray March; Outreach, Steve Turner; Grievance Chair, Steve Turner. Founded: 1982. Members: 75. Dues: $60 minimum (national); $12 (local). Benefits: grievance protection in or outside contracts, databases evaluating agents and publications, networking, job hot lines. Activities: monthly steering committee meetings, workshops, seminars, conferences, contests, sponsors annual nationwide poetry competition. Newsletter: *Cows Bigger Than Barns*. Editor: Cecile Mills. Frequency: quarterly. Submissions: press releases. Additional publications: *Frequent Flyer*, calendar published between newsletters.

NORTHERN CALIFORNIA BOOK PUBLICISTS ASSOCIATION.
c/o Butterfield Associates, 1339 61st St., Emeryville, CA 94608. (415) 428-1991. President, Carol Butterfield; Membership, Leigh Davidson. Founded: 1975. Members: 120. Dues: $35 (associate); $50 (full).

Purpose: forum for the communication of ideas concerning the publicizing, promoting, and marketing of books. Membership criteria: not limited to publishing industry; membership includes authors, literary agents, retailers, investment bankers. Benefits: discount on all functions, voting privileges. Meetings: 11 times annually. Activities: monthly meetings, luncheons with guest speakers, half-day spring and fall breakfast workshop, workshops, seminars, conferences, book fair (1989).

Newsletter: *News from the Northern California Book Publicists Association*. Editor: Pat Anderson. Frequency: bimonthly. Submissions: articles.

NORTHERN CALIFORNIA WOMEN IN FILM AND TELEVISION.
PO Box 89. San Francisco, CA 94101. (415) 431-3886. President, Judy Pruzinsky. Founded: 1982. Members: 2500 (national); 180 (chapter). Dues: $50 plus one-time initiation fee of $10.

Purpose: to increase equal opportunity of employment of women in film and television. Membership criteria: minimum two years' experience in film or related industries. Benefits: directory, support network. Meetings: monthly. Activities: workshops, seminars, weekly breakfasts.

Newsletter: *On Screen*. Editor: Jennifer Heuff/Kate Mayer. Frequency: bimonthly. Submissions: press releases, articles.

PENINSULA PRESS CLUB. PO Box 18596. San Jose, CA 95158.
(408) 266-1256. President, Bill Workman; Executive Director, Myrta Schuller. Founded: 1974. Members: 160. Dues: $30.

Purpose: to provide a forum for the interchange of ideas and opinions between professionals in the various news and public relations media. Membership criteria: must earn a major source of one's income or spend a major portion of one's working time as a paid employee in the one of the journalistic professions. Benefits: directory, use of a hotel pool/health facilities. Activities: conferences, contests, workshops, social networking events, annual picnic, professional awards banquet.

Newsletter: *The Peninsula Press Club News*. Editor: Jane Offers. Frequency: monthly. Submissions: press releases, articles.

PEN INTERNATIONAL. 38 King St. London, WC2E 8JT. England. Executive Director, PEN USA Center West: Richard Bray. Founded: 1921 (London, England). Members: 2000 (USA). Dues: $45 (USA Center West).

Purpose: international, nonprofit organization to promote free expression in the arts and "to protect the principles of unhampered transmission of thought and to preserve the concept of a free press within each nation and among all nations." Activities: international congresses, programs, advocacy, contests, and awards.

PEN American Center. 568 Broadway, New York, NY 10012. (212) 334-1660. Publications: *Guide to Grants and Awards*.

PEN USA Center West. 1100 Glendon Ave., Ste. PH, Los Angeles, CA 90024. (213) 824-2041. Fax (213) 824-1679. Membership criteria: open to all qualified writers and members of the literary community who subscribe to PEN's ideals and aims. Activities: international congresses, programs, workshops/seminars (co-sponsored with other organizations), and contests . Benefits: newsletter, announcements, events, awards, committee work, publicity kits for new authors, imprisoned writers' advocacy.

Newsletter: *PEN Center USA West* newsletter. Editor: Victoria Branch. Frequency: quarterly. Submissions: press releases, articles related to PEN's interests. Additional publications: membership directory.

POETS & WRITERS, INC. 72 Spring St. New York, NY 10012. (212) 226-3586. Executive Director, Elliott Figman. Founded: 1973. Members: 9500 (national), 900 (California) listed writers. Dues: none; ($5 listing fee).

Purpose: nonprofit corporation organized for literary and educational purposes. Membership criteria: publication requirements in order to be listed. Activities: Writers Exchange Program, competitions, Readings/Workshops Grants Program which offers matching grants to writers in New York and California; National Literary Information Center (NLIC).

Newsletter: *Poets & Writers Magazine*. Editor: Darylyn Brewer. Frequency: bimonthly. Submissions: articles. Additional publications: references, source books, how-to guides, several newsletters.

Poets & Writers West (West Coast Office): 1862 Euclid Ave., Box 292. Berkeley, CA 94709. (415) 548-6618. West Coast Coordinator, Stuart Robbins. Activities: readings/workshops programs.

PRESS CLUB OF SAN FRANCISCO. 555 Post St. San Francisco, CA 94102. (415) 775-7800. Founded: 1888. President, Leo Lee; Membership Chairperson, Harre Demoro; General Manager, Joyce Cirimelli. Members: 2000. Dues: varies.

Purpose: private social club to promote better understanding between cultures. Membership criteria: application reviewed by category (students, professional journalists). Benefits: privileges of club and reciprocal clubs, parties, conferences, athletic facilities. Meetings: annual and designated; no set number. Activities: junior scholarship program, meetings, press conferences.

Newsletter: *The Scoop*. Editor: Teresa Barnett. Frequency: bimonthly. Submissions: articles.

PUBLISHERS MARKETING ASSOCIATION. 2401 Pacific Coast Highway, Ste. 102. Hermosa Beach, CA 90254. (213) 372-2732. Fax (213) 374-3342. Executive Director, Jan Nathan. Founded: 1983. Members: 1200. Dues: vary; start at $75 for companies having up to nine employees.

Purpose: to cooperatively market titles and to educate the independent publisher. Membership criteria: must be a publisher or about to become a publisher. Benefits: cooperative marketing programs to libraries, bookstores, schools, and speciality markets. Meetings: monthly. Activities: workshops, seminars, conferences, trade shows, contests.

Newsletter: *PMA Newsletter*. Editor: Jan Nathan. Frequency: monthly. Submissions: press releases, articles. Additional publications: membership directory.

ROMANCE WRITERS OF AMERICA, INC. 13700 Veterans Memorial Dr., Ste. 315. Houston, TX 77014-1023. (713) 440-6885. Members: 4000 (national); 820 (California). Dues: $45 plus $10 one-time processing fee.

Purpose: support and education for romance writers. Membership criteria: must join national organization before joining local. Activities: annual national conference (1000+ attendees).

Newsletter: *Romance Writer Report*. Frequency: bimonthly.

Aloha Chapter. Contact person: Jacquiline R. Wolski, 1951 C Dicson Circle, Honolulu, HI 96818. (808) 422-0119.

Central Coast Chapter. Contact person: Sue Hogan, 585 Hacienda, Cayucos, CA 93430. (805) 995-1163. Members: 15. Dues: $12 plus per meeting charge. Meetings: monthly.

Gold Coast Chapter. Contact person: President, Bobbie Grabendike, 1215 Anchors Way, #47, Ventura, CA 93001. (805) 642-7195. Members: 30. Dues: $12. Benefits: audio tape library of conference workshop presentations, synopses packet (collection of synopses of published books). Meetings: monthly.

Inland Valley Chapter (Riverside County). Contact person: Pam Scheibe, 7556 Jayhawk Dr., Riverside, CA 92509. (714) 681-6365. Members: 7. Dues: $18. Meetings: monthly. Benefits: lending library, personal relationship, and critique at monthly meetings.

Los Angeles Chapter. Contact person: Genny Dazzo, 9027 Larke Eleen Circle, Los Angeles, CA 90035. (213) 837-4708. Meetings: monthly.

Monterey Bay Chapter. Contact person: Laura Lindsey, 1765 Sommerfeld Ave., Santa Cruz, CA 95062. (408) 462-9222. Founded: 1988. Members: 35. Dues: $20. Membership criteria: actively engaged in writing romance. Benefits: support, friendship, helpful hints. Meetings: second Saturday of the month. Activities: meetings, workshops. Newsletter: *MBC*. Frequency: monthly. Submissions: press releases, articles.

Orange County Chapter. PO Box 395, Yorba Linda, CA 92686-0395. Contact person: Sharon Brevik, (213) 377-6753; Maryann O'Brien, (818) 795-6597. Members: 244. Dues: $21 first year, $18 for renewal. Benefits: lending library of audio tapes. Meetings: monthly. Activities: annual contest for unpublished romance writers, mentor program, editors, and celebrity romance writers host special meetings.

Sacramento Chapter. Contact person: Carol H. Titus, 6368 Misty Wood Way, Citrus Heights, CA 95621. (916) 722-2507. Members: 72. Dues: $20. Meetings: monthly.

San Diego Chapter. Contact person: Chapter Advisor, Betty Duran, 585 El Miraso, Vista, CA 92083. (619) 724-5146. Members: 70. Dues: $18. Meetings: second Saturday monthly. Benefits: lending library. Activities: mentor program matching unpublished writers with published mentor, "Write for the Money" program, roses for book sales. Newsletter: *Romantically Speaking*.

San Francisco Chapter. Contact person: Olivia Hall, 43501 Ocaso Corte, Fremont, CA 94539. (415) 657-8831. Members: 100. Dues: $20. Benefits: critique groups; lending library of books, tapes, and transcripts of national conferences, seminars, panels. Meetings: monthly, first Saturday of month. Activities: hosts several romance editors yearly, conferences, workshops, seminars, contests. Newsletter: *San Francisco Area Chapter Newsletter*. Editor: Barbara Turner. Frequency: monthly. Submissions: press releases with romance writing tie-in, articles. Additional publications: membership directory.

SAN DIEGO WRITERS/EDITORS GUILD. 3235 Homer St. San Diego, CA 92106. (619) 223-3634. President, Lynn Ford; Treasurer, Betty Smith. Founded: 1979. Members: 120 (California). Dues: $25; $40 (writer plus spouse); $12.50 (student).

Purpose: to help writers and to form a professional network. Membership criteria: for professional membership, three published works for pay or one play produced or one published book (not vanity press); for associate membership, serious interest in writing. Activities: monthly meetings, annual conference.

Newsletter: *San Diego Writers/Editors News*. Frequency: monthly. Additional publications: membership directory.

SCIENCE FICTION WRITERS OF AMERICA. Contact person: President, Greg Bear. 506 Lakeview Rd. Alderwood Manor, WA 98036. West Coast Regional Director, Stephen Goldin. 6251 Havenside #4. Sacramento, CA 95831. Founded: 1965. Members: 1000 (national); 100 (California). Dues: $75.

Purpose: to inform science-fiction writers of professional matters; to promote professional welfare; to help in dealing with publishers, agents, editors, and anthologists. Membership criteria: sale to professional publishers (reduced subscription rate available to unpublished writers). Benefits: medical insurance, model contracts, legal advice and representation under certain circumstances, meeting room at conventions, bookstore discounts, free review copies of books and magazines, numerous quarterly publications. Activities: conferences, weekly meetings, small meetings at many science fiction conventions, annual awards banquet. (The annual Nebula Trophy awarded by SFWA is the most important award in the science fiction genre.)

Newsletter: *Bulletin of the Science Fiction Writers of America*. Editor: Pamela Sargent, Box 486, Johnson City, NY 13790. Frequency: quarterly. Submissions: press releases, articles. Additional publications: membership directory, *Science Fiction Forum* (letters), *Awards Report* (Nebula Trophy).

SOCIETY FOR TECHNICAL COMMUNICATION. 901 N. Stuart St. Arlington, VA 22203. (703) 522-4114. Founded: 1953. Members: 13,000 (national); 2000 (California). Dues. $75, $10 one-time initiation fee; $25 student rate, payable at national level.

Purpose: the advancement of the theory and practice of technical communication in all media. Membership criteria: be engaged or have an interest in any phase of technical communication. Meetings: open to the public in all chapters. Activities: annual arts and publication contest; annual international conference in April, held in continental United States (New York/1991).

Newsletter: *Technical Communication* (quarterly journal), *Intercom* (monthly newsletter).

Berkeley Chapter. Contact person: Ray Bruman, 2929 Lorina St., Berkeley, CA 94705. (415) 549-1509. Dues: $75. Activities: monthly meetings including speakers, field trips, demonstrations. Newsletter: *Ragged Left*. Frequency: monthly. Submissions: press releases, article.

East Bay Chapter. Contact person: Corrine Stefanick, 1833 Ninth St., Alameda, CA 94501. (415) 676-2737. Additional contact: Vince Swanson, (415) 595-1414. Meetings: first

Thursday of every month. Activities: speakers, job listings, field trips. Additional publications: membership directory, publications competition.

Los Angeles Chapter. Contact person: President, Mary Chaitt, 8655 Belford Ave., #64, Los Angeles, CA 90045. (213) 568-9116.

Monterey Bay Chapter. Contact person: Susan Dumonde, 711 Archer St., Monterey, CA 93940. (408) 372-4690.

Orange Coast College, Student Chapter. Contact person: Don Pierstorff, Orange Coast College, English Dept., 2701 Fairview Rd., Costa Mesa, CA 92626. (714) 432-5716.

Orange County Chapter. Contact person: Dorothy Duplissey, 21471 Pine Tree Lane, Huntington Beach, CA 92646. (714) 968-8663. Members: 230. Meetings: monthly (September through June). Newsletter: *Techniscribe*. Frequency: ten issues annually. Submissions: articles, press releases.

Sacramento Chapter. Contact person: President, Lance Gelein, 10304 Georgetown Dr., Rancho Cordova, CA 95670. (916) 386-1900 (work). Membership criteria: must be actively engaged in the field or interested in the field. Benefits: quarterly journal, monthly newsletters, national conferences, local programs, conferences and workshops, employment referral service. Meetings: monthly. Activities: workshops/seminars, conferences, contests. Newsletter: *Capitol Letter*. Editor: Walt Brennan and Barbara Kubichka. Frequency: monthly. Submissions: press releases, articles. Additional publications: employment referral brochure, membership directory.

San Diego Chapter. Contact person: President, Linda Oestreich, 2938 30th St., #A., San Diego, CA 92104. (619) 553-4791. Members: 200. Dues $75 (includes local and international). Meetings: monthly, September through June. Activities: participates in annual national arts and publication contest. Newsletter: *Signature*. Frequency: monthly. Submissions: press releases, articles from members.

San Diego State Student Chapter. Contact person: President, Dr. Sherry Little, English Dept., San Diego State University, San Diego, CA 92182. (619) 594-5238.

San Francisco Chapter. Contact person: President, Kathy Tobin, PO Box 2706, San Francisco, CA 94126. (415) 985-7121. Members: 250. Dues: $75. Meetings: third Wednesday of the month. Activities: participation in arts and publication contest. Newsletter: *The Active Voice*. Editor: Janna Custer. Frequency: monthly. Submissions: press releases, articles.

Santa Barbara Chapter. Contact person: President, Yvonne G. DeGraw, c/o Signal Technology, 5951 Encina Rd., Goleta, CA 93117. (805) 683-3771. Members: 38. Meetings: fourth Thursday of the month. Newsletter: *The Dispatch*. Submissions: articles.

Sierra-Panamint Chapter. Contact person: John Dunker, Code 3411, Naval Weapons Ctr., China Lake, CA 93555. (619) 939-3027 (work). Members: 30. Meetings: monthly. Newsletter: *The Petroglyph*.

Silicon Valley Chapter. Contact person: Tim Carl, 1198 S. Stelling, Cupertino, CA 95014.

SOCIETY OF AMERICAN TRAVEL WRITERS. 1155 Connecticut Ave., Ste. 500. Washington, D.C. 20036. (202) 429-6639.

SOCIETY OF CHILDREN'S BOOK WRITERS. PO Box 296. Mar Vista Station. Los Angeles, CA 90066. (818) 347-2849. Executive Director, Stephen Mooser; Chairperson of Board of Directors, Sue Alexander. Founded: 1968. Members: 5000 (national). Dues: $35.

Purpose: to serve as a network of information and support for professional writers and illustrators of children's literature. Membership criteria: full members (published writers of children's literature) and anyone interested in children's literature. Benefits: manuscript exchange, writing grants, medical insurance. Activities: meetings, workshops, seminars, conferences (national conference every August), annual awards.

Newsletter: *The Bulletin*. Editor: Stephen Mooser. Frequency: bimonthly. Submissions: from members only.

Northern California Chapter: Contact person: Bobbie Martin, 536 Thomas Circle, Suisun, CA 94585. (707) 426-6776. Members: 400. Dues: $15. Meetings: last Saturday of the month. Newsletter: *Galleys*. Editor: Alice Salerno. Frequency: bimonthly. Submissions: press releases, articles.

Orange County Chapter. Contact person: Regional Advisor, Dianne MacMillan, 7530 East Vista del Sol, Anaheim, CA 92808. (714) 637-6586. Members: 200.

Santa Barbara/Ventura/Oxnard/Camarillo Chapter: Contact person: Regional Advisor, Jean Stangl, 1658 Calle La Cumbre, Camarillo, CA 93010. (805) 482-1075. Members: 96. Activities: two conferences annually.

Southern California Chapter. Contact person: Co-Regional Advisor, Judith Ross Enderle, 29636 Cuthbert Rd., Malibu, CA 90265. (213) 820-5601, (213) 457-3501. Members: 1000. Dues: none (payable at national level). Meetings: none. Activities: conferences including Writer's Day in March, critique in July, National Conference in August, Illustrators' Day in November.

VALLEY WRITERS NETWORK. 5212 N. Valentine, Apt. #10. Fresno, CA 93711. (209) 275-5267. Contact person: Debra Lynn Chance.

WESTERN WRITERS OF AMERICA. PO Box 823. Sheridan, WY 82801. (307) 672-2079. Membership Chairperson, Barbara Ketcham. Founded: 1950. Members: 500 (international). Dues: $60.

Purpose: to advertise professional writers and help promote their books. Membership criteria: associate member must have published one book or five articles; full member must have published 3 books or 30 articles. Benefits: promotion and publicity. Meetings: none. Activities: annual conference, fourth week in June, location varies. Newsletter: *WWA Newsletter* (bimonthly) and *The Roundup* (quarterly magazine). Additional publications: membership directory.

WOMEN IN COMMUNICATION, INC. 2101 Wilson Blvd., Ste. 417. Arlington, VA 22201. (703) 528-4200. Executive Vice President, Susan Lowell Butler; Membership Director, Michele Grassley Franklin. (415) 397-5525. Founded: 1909. Members: 11,500+ (national), 600 (California). National dues: $85 plus $25 one-time processing fee.

Purpose: a national organization of women and men who work to unite all communications professionals, support First Amendment rights, recognize outstanding communication achievements, and promote the advancement and equitable treatment of women communicators. Membership criteria: must have worked at least two years as a professional in creative communications (professional status) or work 20 hours weekly in a professional capacity (associate status); student memberships also available. Benefits: networking, professional development, governmental representation, professional publications, life, medical and disability insurance. Activities: annual national convention, workshops, seminars, advancement fund for scholarship and awards programs.

Magazine: *The Professional Communicator*. Editor: Linda Russman. Frequency: 5 times per year. Submissions: press releases, articles. Additional publication: *Washington Memo* (legislative newsletter), membership directory.

Honolulu Chapter. Contact person: Didi M. L. Chang, 818 Keeaumoku St., #533, Honolulu, HI 96814. (808) 521-6135.

Los Angeles Chapter. Contact person: Bonnie Gutman, 13952 Bora Bora Way, 212F, Marina del Rey, CA 90292. (213) 305-1565. Members: 300. Dues: $50 (plus national dues). Meetings: monthly. Activities: program meetings, focus seminars, conferences, awards, scholarships. Newsletter: *The Signal*. Frequency: monthly. Submissions: press releases. Additional publications: membership directory.

North Bay Area Chapter. Contact person: Jill Feldon. (415) 898-3708.

Orange County Chapter. Contact person: Joy Mieko White, Communicator's Connection, 21651 Vintage Way, El Toro, CA 92630. (714) 770-8339.

San Francisco Chapter. Contact person: Tammy Jo Williams. (415) 578-1545. Members: 250. Dues: $25. Activities: monthly meetings, networking evenings, job bank. Newsletter.

Santa Barbara Chapter. Contact person: Louise Polis. (805) 683-2060.

WOMEN IN FILM. 6464 Sunset Blvd., Ste. 900. Los Angeles, CA 90028. (213) 463-6040. President, Marcy Kelly. Founded: 1973. Members: 1500. Dues: $100.

Purpose: to increase equal opportunity of employment of women in film and television and create greater visibility of work by women. Membership criteria: three years' professional experience in film and television. Benefits: medical insurance, contacts with professionals, other benefits outlined in membership information. Meetings: bimonthly. Activities: workshops, seminars, conferences, 10+ meetings annually. International organization with branches in United States.

Newsletter: *W/F Newsmagazine*. Editor: Melissa Miller. Frequency: bimonthly.

WOMEN'S NATIONAL BOOK ASSOCIATION, INC. 160 5th Ave. New York, NY 10010. (212) 675-7805. President, Cathy Rentschler. Founded: 1917.

Purpose: a nonprofit, tax-exempt corporation providing educational and literary programs to those interested in the publishing industry; also serves as a channel of communication for topics of interest in the book world. Membership criteria: open to women and men in all occupations associated with the publishing industry.

Newsletter: *The Bookwoman*. Additional publications: membership directory.

Bay Area Chapter. Contact person: President and Membership Chairperson, Linda Mead, 379 Burning Tree Ct., Half Moon Bay, CA 94019. (415) 726-3969. Members: 150. Dues: $15. Meetings: monthly, September through May. Activities: contests, scholarships. Newsletter: yes. Frequency: bimonthly. Submissions: press releases, articles.

Los Angeles Chapter. Contact person: Sue MacLaurin, 3554 Crownridge Dr., Sherman Oaks, CA 91403. (818) 501-3925. Members: 160. Dues: $20. Meetings: monthly (September through June), third Tuesday. Activities: annual writers conference, workshops, monthly program with speakers, annual writing contest (poetry, essay, short story). Judy Lopez Awards Dinner.

Newsletter: *WNBA/LA Newsletter*. Frequency: monthly. Submissions: press release; very short articles by members.

WORLD ACADEMY OF ARTS AND CULTURE. Contact person: Secretary General, Rosemary Wilkinson. 3146 Buckeye Court. Placerville, CA 95667. (916) 626-4166. Dues: $30 first year, $10 annual renewal.

Purpose: international organization which gathers world poets in biannual conference to promote world brotherhood and peace through poetry. Activities: liaison for information for poets, international conferences.

Newsletter: *The Voice of Poets*. Frequency: biannually (before and after international conference).

WRITERS CONNECTION. 1601 Saratoga-Sunnyvale Rd., Ste. 180. Cupertino, CA 95014. (408) 973-0227. Community Relations Director, Mardeene Mitchell. Founded: 1983. Members: 2000. Dues: $40 a year (individual); $180 a year (corporate membership for six named individuals, $30 each additional person).

Purpose: to provide a wide range of services to writers and other publishing professionals and to act as a facilitator for connections between writers and members of the publishing and film industries. Membership criteria: an interest in writing and writing/publishing related topics. Benefits: substantial discount on seminars and services, conferences, and special events. Members may also purchase books and tapes at a discount from our bookstore. Meetings: ongoing seminars and events. Activities: meetings, workshops, seminars, conferences.

Newsletter: *Writers Connection*. Editor: Jan Stiles. Frequency: monthly. Submissions: press releases, articles. Additional publications: *California Publishing Marketplace* and *Southwest Publishing Marketplace* directories; *Writing for Hollywood* and *Selling to Hollywood* documentary videotapes.

WRITERS GUILD OF AMERICA, WEST. 8955 Beverly Blvd. West Hollywood, CA 90048. (213) 550-1000. Public Relations Director, Cheryl Rhoden. Founded: 1933. Members: 9000 (Western United States). Dues: $1500 initiation; then 1.5 percent of annual income plus $25 per quarter.

Purpose: collective bargaining agency representing writers in the film and broadcasting industries. Membership criteria: rigorous qualification process. Benefits: pension plan, medical and dental insurance. Activities: annual meeting of membership, conferences.

Newsletter: *The Journal*. Editor: Bill Meis. Frequency: monthly. Additional publications: membership directory.

Conferences

Conferences are a great place to make professional contacts, discover new information, and get motivated. In this section we've listed 34 conferences covering a diverse range of writing and publishing topics.

How to Use the Information in This Section

We've listed conferences by their official names and included other pertinent information such as sponsors' names, addresses, and telephone numbers. We've also included founding dates and a contact person (often the conference director).

Place: This information pinpoints the location of the conference; location often varies from year to year.

Date: We have listed specific dates for 1990 or 1991 wherever possible. If the information was not available, we listed the time of the year the conference is usually held.

Frequency: Most conferences are held annually. However, some are offered every two years.

Length: This indicates the length of the conference, from one day to twelve weeks.

Fee: Conference fees are often two-tiered to offer discounts to the sponsoring organizations' members.

Included: The conference fee may cover tuition, accommodations, meals, and special activities, or it may cover only tuition.

Attendees: This indicates the number of people expected to attend the conference.

Theme: If a conference lists a theme, its workshops and seminars will often tie in to that theme.

Subjects: The subjects a particular conference covers may be broad, with many offerings in all categories, or the conference may be narrowly focused.

Format: This information indicates the method of presentation for a subject and how much time is allotted to its presentation. Formats vary from hourly workshops, formal and informal panel discussions, and guest speaker presentations to intensive daylong sessions. Request the conference brochure and check to see if the subject areas and format appeal to you.

Special events: In addition to educational activities, conferences sometimes include activities such as sunset cruises, banquets, wine tastings, receptions, job fairs, silent auctions, book signings, awards presentations, and informal night-owl sessions.

Faculty: The total number of guest speakers, teachers, workshop facilitators, and the like is given here.

Additional information: Any other information that the conference director wants you, the prospective attendee, to know is included in this section.

Abbreviations

n/i means no information was given to us by the conference sponsor.

AMERICAN SOCIETY OF INDEXERS ANNUAL MEETING. 1700 18th
St., NW. Washington, DC 20009. Founded: 1968. Contact Person: David Billick. (202) 328-7110.

Place: varies; Minneapolis/1991; San Antonio/1992; Washington D.C./1993. Date: June. Frequency: annually. Length: one to two days. Fee: call for information. Attendees: 100+/-.

Theme: Indexing in the '90s. Subjects: on indexing. Format: individual speakers, panel discussions. Special events: presentation of the Wilson Awards, exhibition with indexing software publishers.

ASIAN AMERICAN JOURNALISTS ASSOCIATION NATIONAL
CONVENTION. Sponsored by Asian American Journalists Association. 1765 Sutter St., Room 1000. San Francisco, CA 94115. (415) 346-2051. Founded: 1987. Contact Person: Diane Yen-Mei Wong.

Place: varies; New York/1990; Seattle/1991. Date: August. Frequency: annually. Length: four days. Fee: $150/members. Included: meals. Attendees: 600.

Theme: Challenges of the '90s. Subjects: newspaper, magazine. Format: speakers, workshops, panels. Special events: banquet, job fair, receptions, silent auction.

ASILOMAR ADVENTURE. Sponsored by National League of American Pen
Women, Northern California. 2730 39th Ave. San Francisco, CA 94116. (415) 564-9453. Contact Person: Vicki Lavorini.

Place: Asilomar Conference Center, Pacific Grove. Date: February. Frequency: biennial. Length: four nights. Fee: varies according to accommodations. Included: room and board. Attendees: n/i.

Theme: varies. Subjects: poetry, art of seeing, music, sculpture, women, image, and creativity. Special events: art show.

Additional information: individual sessions or days available at reduced rate.

BAY AREA WRITERS' WORKSHOPS. Sponsored by Co-directors Elizabeth Sprague and Laura Jason. PO Box 620327. Woodside, CA 94062. (415) 430-3127. Founded: 1988. Contact person: Laura Jason.

Place: Mills College, Oakland. Date: four workshops in the summer, June-August. Length: Friday-Sunday. Fee: $200. Included: workshops and sessions only; room and board available separately. Attendees: 15 per workshop session.

Subjects: fiction, poetry, agents/editors, translation, small press as related to larger publishing houses, writers and taxes, surviving as a writer. Format: evening readings by participants, panel discussions. Special events: welcoming reception for faculty and attendees, semiformal dinner on Saturday.

Additional information: scholarships based on quality of manuscript.

BAYCON '91. Sponsored by Artistic Solutions. PO Box 70393. Sunnyvale, CA 94086. (408) 629-4729. Contact Person: Craig Nicolai.

Place: San Jose. Date: Memorial Day weekend. Frequency: annually. Length: 4 days, 3 nights. Fee: $45. Special member's fee. Special day rate. Attendees: 2500 members/fans.

Theme: humor or comic related in the areas of science fiction, fantasy, science, comics. Subjects: for professional and amateur writers/artists (many of whom do cover artwork) spanning the above listed areas. Format: informal seminar style with fan participation encouraged. Special events: costume contest (for both professional and amateur entries), gaming, dance, and additional activities to be announced. Faculty: 175.

BIOLA UNIVERSITY WRITERS INSTITUTE. Sponsored by Biola University. 13800 Biola Ave. La Mirada, CA 90639. 1-800-75-WORDS. Founded: 1984. Contact Person: Susan Titus.

Place: Biola University. Date: July 28-31, 1991 (always in late July). Frequency: annually. Length: 4 days. Fee: $180; $160, early registration. Special members fee. Extra fees: $275 room and meals; $70/3 nights' accommodations. Attendees: 400.

Theme: Words Paint a Thousand Pictures. Subjects: beginning writing, fiction, nonfiction book writing for children, advanced writing. Format: seven major morning classes, 52 afternoon classes held concurrently, seven at a time. Special events: morning plenary sessions, professional music, evening plenary speakers and panel discussions, banquet and awards, author's autograph session, and barbecue. Faculty: 35-40.

CALIFORNIA PRESS PHOTOGRAPHERS ASSOCIATION. c/o Moonlight Press. PO Box 994. Westminster, CA 92648. (714) 894-8976. Contact Person: Gene Booth. Call for information on annual meeting.

CALIFORNIA WRITERS' CLUB ASILOMAR CONFERENCE. Sponsored by California Writers' Club. 2214 Derby St. Berkeley, CA 94705. Founded: 1909. Contact Person: Dorothy V. Benson. (415) 841-1217.

Place: Asilomar Conference Center, Pacific Grove, California. Date: July 12-14, 1991. Frequency: biannually. Length: Friday noon to Sunday lunch. Fee: $219/CWC members (approximate); $250/nonmembers; $150/commuter rate. Included: accommodations, meals, wine tasting, parking. Attendees: 400.

Theme: To be announced. Subjects: agents; mainstream, historical, romance, mystery, horror, humor, science fantasy, travel, young adult, middle-grade and children's books; nonfiction; short fiction; scriptwriting; newspaper syndication; research; revision; book proposals; synopsis; interviewing techniques; photography, and contracts. Format: panels of magazine editors, book editors, and agents; appointments with agents; one-hour seminars on the above genres. Special events: keynote speaker, wine tasting, night-owl sessions on various disciplines; bookstore where members may bring their own books to sell. Faculty: 60. Additional information: manuscript critique service available. Details to be announced.

COMEDY/HUMOR WRITERS ASSOCIATION ANNUAL CONFERENCE. Sponsored by Comedy/Humor Writers Association. Box 211. San Francisco, CA 94101. (415) 541-5608, 751-6725. Founded: 1987. Contact Person: John Cantu.

Place: local hotel in San Francisco. Date: Saturday in September or October. Frequency: annually. Length: one day. Fee: $70. Reduced rate for members. Attendees: 50+.

Theme: comedy/humor writing. Subjects: comedy/humor. Format: six speakers giving 30-minute lectures with 15 minutes for questions and answers. Special events: after hours "schmooze" session.

COSMEP PUBLISHERS CONFERENCE. Sponsored by COSMEP, The International Association of Independent Publishers. PO Box 703. San Francisco, CA 94101. (415) 922-9490. Founded: 1968. Contact Person: Richard Morris.

Place: Boston/1991; Chicago, San Francisco, and Los Angeles in alternate years. Date: October 2-4, 1991. Frequency: annually. Length: three days. Fee: $145, member rate. Attendees: 125-200.

Theme: book marketing. Subjects: book promotion, distribution, and marketing. Format: three one-day seminars. Faculty: number varies.

FIESTA/SIESTA. Sponsored by San Diego Writers/Editors Guild. 3235 Homer St. San Diego, CA 92106. (619) 223-5235, 223-3634. Founded: 1982. Contact Person: Peggy Lipscomb.

Place: Murietta Hot Springs and Spa, Murietta, CA. Date: April 19-21, 1991. Frequency: annually. Length: Friday evening through Sunday afternoon. Fee: conference fee only: $130; $210/double occupancy; $285/single occupancy. Reduced rates for members. Included: some meals, accommodations, and special events. Day rate: Saturday $60, includes luncheon; Sunday $50, includes brunch; Saturday evening $20. Attendees: 75 maximum.

Theme: Fiesta/Siesta. Subjects: fiction (various genres), screen and TV, nonfiction, computer law for writers, children's plays, photography, self-publishing, agents, publishers. Format: 1 1/2 hour workshops—approximately 14. Special events: Friday evening buffet supper, Saturday night program, plays, etc. Faculty: 8-10.

Additional Information: We vary our program year to year. We don't repeat the same speakers two years in a row, and we keep our attendance small so we can become acquainted with each other. Our speakers are there the entire conference.

FOOTHILL WRITERS' CONFERENCE. Sponsored by Foothill College. Los Altos Hills, CA 94022. (415) 949-7431. Contact Person: Richard Maxwell.

Place: Foothill College. Date: end of June. Frequency: annually. Length: six days. Fee: $25.50. Attendees: 200.

Subjects: Poetry, fiction, freelance writing, drama, film, autobiography. Format: workshops, critique sessions, lectures, panels, reading. Special events: dance/movement; performance poetry; agents and selling.

IDYLLWILD CREATIVE WRITING WORKSHOPS. Sponsored by Idyllwild School of Music and the Arts. PO Box 38. Idyllwild, CA 92349. (714) 659-2171; winter, (213) 622-0355. Contact Person: Steven Fraider, Director of Summer Programs.

Place: Idyllwild campus. Date: summer. Frequency: annually. Length: 12-week summer program, one-week classes. Fee: $300 per week. Included: tuition only. Housing $40 (camping) to $325 (private room with meals) per week. Attendees: 500 per week.

Subjects: creative writing, science fiction/fantasy, marketing and publishing, poetry, scriptwriting classes. Special events: art shows, concerts, special events related to the arts.

Additional information: beautiful 205-acre campus.

INTERNATIONAL WOMEN'S WRITING GUILD CONFERENCE, THE. Sponsor: The International Women's Writing Guild. PO Box 810. Gracie Station. New York, NY 10028. (212) 737-7536. Founded: 1976. Contact Person: Hannelore Hahn, Executive Director and Founder.

Place: Sonoma/1991. Date: March. Frequency: annually. Length: weekend. Fee: $215, $50/commuter registration. Included: room and board. Attendees: under 100.

Subjects: poetry, fiction, nonfiction, artwork, meditation, yoga. Format: workshops, presentations, networking, critiques, evening readings. Special events: appointments with agents (occasionally). Faculty: 7.

Additional information: individual days available at reduced rate.

INTERNATIONAL WOMEN'S WRITING GUILD CONFERENCE—SAN DIEGO CONFERENCE, THE. Sponsor: The International Women's Writing Guild. PO Box 810. Gracie Station. New York, NY 10028. (212) 737-7536. Founded: 1976. Contact Person: Hannelore Hahn, Executive Director and Founder.

Place: YWCA, San Diego, California. Date: January 26, 1991. Frequency: annually. Length: one day. Fee: $70/members, $75/nonmembers, $45 half day/commuter registration. Included: lunch. Attendees: 75.

Subjects: Autobiographical writing, mythology and storytelling, marketing, nonfiction, freelancing. Faculty: 6.

MOUNT HERMON CHRISTIAN WRITERS CONFERENCE. Sponsored by Mount Hermon Christian Conference Center. PO Box 413. Mount Hermon, CA 95041. (408) 335-4466. Founded: 1969. Contact Person: David R. Talbott.

Place: Mount Hermon Christian Conference Center. Date: Palm Sunday weekend—Friday noon through Tuesday noon. Frequency: annually. Length: five days, four nights. Fee: $225 tuition, plus room and board available in three levels—deluxe, moderate, economy. Commuter registration: tuition plus a registration fee and meals. Housing not required with the conference. Included: meals must be taken with the conference. Attendees: 250-300.

Theme: writing for the religious market. Subjects: fiction, nonfiction, short story, children's literature, curriculum, poetry, inspirational, major books, articles, journals, computer aids, research methods, etc. Format: daily workshops and general sessions; all meals taken together, family style; daily group critique sessions; individual appointments with faculty. Special events: author's autograph party, writer-of-the-year awards. Faculty: 35-40.

Additional information: Advance manuscript critique service included.

NAPA VALLEY WRITERS' CONFERENCE. Sponsored by Napa Valley College. Community Education Office. Napa, CA 94558. (707) 253-3070. Founded: 1980. Contact Person: Sherri Hallgren.

Place: Napa Valley College. Date: last week of July, first week of August. Frequency: annually. Length: one week. Fee: $350 per session; $50 nonrefundable deposit. Included: light breakfast and some evening parties. Some community housing available for $20 for the week. Attendees: 80-90.

Subjects: We have programs in poetry and fiction writing. The New Poetry Workshop is a working conference; participants work with each of our staff poets in workshops devoted to generating new work. They also go over a finished manuscript in a private tutorial with the poet of their choice. In the Craft of Fiction Workshop, participants work with each of the staff writers in workshops designed to develop and improve the elements of craft: point of view, characterization, plot. A 25-page manuscript is discussed in a workshop with the writer of their choice. Special events: evening readings at Napa Valley wineries, panels with editors and agents, and craft lectures by the staff poets and writers. Faculty: 3-4 poets, 3-4 fiction writers, usually a guest or two.

NATIONAL WRITERS UNION ANNUAL CONFERENCE. Sponsored by the National Writers Union. Local #3. 236 West Portal Ave., #232. San Francisco, CA 94127. (415) 654-6369. Founded: 1986. Contact Person: Bruce Hartford.

Place: San Francisco or Berkeley. Date: spring. Frequency: annually. Length: one day. Fee: $55-$75. Attendees: 130-150.

Theme: writing. Subjects: technical writing, travel writing, freelance contracting, agent/author relationship, third world authors, contracts, environmental writing, rights of writers, and others. Format: panels and workshops. Special events: keynote speaker, party.

PMA'S PUBLISHING UNIVERSITY. Sponsored by Publishers Marketing Association. 2401 Pacific Coast Hwy., Ste. 206. Hermosa Beach, CA 90254. (213) 372-2732. Founded: 1985. Executive Director, Jan Nathan.

Place: various locations. Date: prior to ABA convention. Frequency: annually. Length: two days. Fee: varies. Members receive reduced rate. Included: meals. Attendees: 300+.

Theme: A Book Publishing Course. Subjects: marketing, design, production. Format: two- and three-hour seminars, multiple tracks. Faculty: 20+.

PROFESSIONAL WRITERS LEAGUE OF LONG BEACH WRITERS CONFERENCE. PO Box 20409. Long Beach, CA 90801. (213) 423-1527. Founded: 1972. Contact Person: Mrs. Dorothea Wolford.

Place: Elks Lodge, Long Beach. Date: mid-October. Frequency: annually. Length: one day. Fee: $25. Included: meals. Attendees: 100.

Subjects: various fields of fiction, poetry, specific tips on marketing, writing the romance novel, writing for children, how to sell what you write, research. Topics vary each year. Format: three morning lectures with question and answer periods, luncheon speaker, four afternoon workshops of two sessions each. Exchange of information with faculty and other participants very popular and helpful.

PUBLISHING WEEKEND. Sponsored by Para Publishing. PO Box 4232-853. Santa Barbara, CA 93140-4232. (805) 968-7277. Fax (805) 968-1379. Founded: 1984. Contact Person: Monique Tihanyi.

Place: Santa Barbara. Date: 1990—August 25-26, November 10-11. 1991—February 9-10, May 4-5, August 31-September 1, November 9-10. Frequency: four times each year. Length: two days. Fee: $395. Included: all meals. Attendees: limited to 16.

Theme: nonfiction book promotion and marketing. Format: lecture, discussion, exercises, and tours of publishing facility. Many resources and handouts. Special events: networking with typesetters, artists, and other resource people. Faculty: 2.

ROMANCE WRITERS OF AMERICA ANNUAL CONFERENCE. Sponsored by Romance Writers of America. 13700 Veteran's Memorial Dr., Ste. 315. Houston, TX 77014. (713) 440-6885. Founded: 1980. Contact Person: Bobbi Stinson.

Place: varies; San Francisco/1990. Date: July. Length: four days. Fee: $275. Included: workshops, agent/editor appointments, meals. Reduced rates available for members. Attendees: 1200.

Subjects: romance and mainstream women's fiction. Format: keynote address, 62 workshops, writing award for contest that precedes the conference, agent/editor appointments (10 minutes each). Special events: cocktail party, banquet, Sunday brunch. Faculty: 100.

SAN DIEGO SCHOOL OF CHRISTIAN WRITING. Sponsored by San Diego County Christian Writers' Guild (cosponsored by Point Loma Nazarene College). Box 1171. El Cajon, CA 92022. (619) 748-0565. Founded: 1989. Contact Person: Candace Walters.

Place: Point Loma Nazarene College, San Diego. Date: June. Frequency: annually. Length: Thursday through Sunday. Fee: $250; rates for individual sessions. Commuter registration: $100 per day. Included: meals, accommodations. Attendees: 200 or more.

Theme: training writers to get published. Subjects: all kinds of writing by Christians. Format: plenary lectures, specialized workshops, continuing classes. Special events: closing banquet with speaker Marabel Morgan; special awards. Faculty: 24.

SANTA BARBARA WRITERS' CONFERENCE. Sponsored by Barnaby Conrad. PO Box 304. Carpinteria, CA 93014. (805) 684-2250. Founded: 1972. Contact Person: Mary Conrad.

Place: Miramar Hotel, Santa Barbara. Date: June. Frequency: annually. Length: one week. Fee: $775/single, $570/double occupancy, $300/day students. Included: room (no board), all workshops and lectures, first and final nights' al fresco dinners. Attendees: 300+.

Theme: all aspects of writing specialities. Subjects: fiction, nonfiction, scriptwriting, travel writing, poetry, juvenile. Format: afternoon and evening panels and lectures by best-selling authors; all-night panels. Faculty: 50+.

SANTA CLARA VALLEY CHRISTIAN WRITERS' SEMINAR.
Sponsored by Santa Clara Valley Christian Writers. 71 Park Village Pl. San Jose, CA 95136. (408) 281-8926. Founded: 1975. Contact Person: Pamela Erickson.

Place: First Covenant Church, 790 Coe Ave., San Jose. Date: third Saturday in October. Frequency: annually. Length: one day. Fee: $25. Attendees: 100.

Theme: inspirational writing. Subjects: basic and advanced workshops in fiction and nonfiction writing; marketing. Format: two major sessions with guest speakers (often editors) and multiple workshops. Special events: faculty book table, free sample magazines and guidelines. Faculty: 8-12.

SELLING TO HOLLYWOOD. Sponsored by Writers Connection. 1601 Saratoga-Sunnyvale Rd., Ste. 180. Cupertino, CA 95014. (408) 973-0227. Founded: 1987. Contact Person: Meera Lester.

Place: Sunnyvale Hilton, Sunnyvale. Date: second week in August. Frequency: annually. Length: weekend. Fee: $240-$360 (may increase slightly). Reduced rate for members. Commuter rate: usually $70 less than full registration. Included: full conference registration includes consultation with faculty member. Attendees: 200-300.

Theme: Selling to Hollywood. Subjects: All workshops and panel discussions provide specific information for writers interested in selling literary properties to the film industry. Format: panels of producers, story editors, and literary agents; individual presentations and workshops; one-on-one consultations. Special events: bookstore, autograph session (if appropriate) with guest speakers, individual consultations with film industry professionals. Faculty: 12-20.

SOCIETY FOR TECHNICAL COMMUNICATION'S INTERNATIONAL CONFERENCE. Sponsored by Society for Technical Communication (STC). 701 N. Stuart St, Ste 304. Arlington, VA 22203. (703) 522-4114. Founded: 1953.

Place: New York. Date: April 14-17, 1991. Frequency: annually (location varies). Length: four days. Fee: approximately $200/members; $285/nonmembers. Included: n/i.

Subjects: the changing role of the technical communication specialist with consideration for factors such as technology, literacy levels, corporate and national cultures, and international business.

Additional information: Submissions of papers, workshops, panels, and discussion topics for the conference are invited.

SOCIETY OF CHILDREN'S BOOK WRITERS CONFERENCE.
Sponsored by the Society of Children's Book Writers, Northern California Chapter. 536 Thomas Circle. Suisun City, CA 94585. (707) 426-6776. Founded: 1985. Contact Person: Bobi Martin.

Place: Asilomar Conference Center, Pacific Grove. Date: February. Frequency: annually. Length: two days. Fee: $150. Included: accommodations. Attendees: 60.

Theme: writing and illustrating for children's books and articles. Format: lectures, small workshops, critique sessions. Faculty: 3.

SQUAW VALLEY COMMUNITY OF WRITERS ANNUAL
WORKSHOP. Sponsored by Squaw Valley Creative Arts Society. PO Box 2352. Olympic Valley, CA 95730. (916) 583-5200. Founded: 1969. Contact Person: Carolyn Doty, fiction; Gil Dennis, scriptwriting.

Place: Squaw Valley. Date: second week in July (poetry); second week in August (fiction, screenwriting). Frequency: annually. Length: one week. Fee: $450 per program. Included: one dinner meal. Attendees: prose/screenwriting, limit 125; poetry, limit 56.

Theme: to help the writer attain his or her potential by providing the concentrated attention of established writers, editors, agents, and fellow participants to the writer's work. Subjects: prose, poetry, screenwriting. Format: small, intensive workshops. Special events: movies, poetry readings, fiction readings. Faculty: 25.

Additional information: separate one-week, concurrent programs for prose/screenwriting and poetry workshops. Afternoon meetings open to the public.

STANFORD PUBLISHING COURSE. Sponsored by Stanford University.
Stanford Alumni Association. Bowman House. Stanford, CA 94305-4005. (415) 725-1083. Fax (415) 723-8597. Founded: 1977. Contact Person: Della Van Heyst, Director of Publications, Stanford Alumni Association. (415) 497-2021.

Place: Stanford University. Date: July. Frequency: annually in July. Length: 12 days. Fee: $2200; $2150/Stanford Alumni Association members. Included: books, working materials, receptions, small breakfast, all luncheons, opening banquet, closing barbecue. Attendees: less than 100.

Subjects: new publishing technologies, editing, design, production, finance and marketing, functions of publishing. Format: lectures, hands-on workshops. Faculty: 65.

Additional information: application deadline beginning of May; preview videotape available for loan. Admissions standards are a minimum of three years' experience in professional publishing or a waiver granted at the discretion of the Course Director.

WESTERN REGIONAL CONFERENCE OF THE AMERICAN
MEDICAL WRITERS ASSOCIATION. Sponsored by the American Medical Writers Association. Contact Person: Michele Vivirito. c/o Herbert Laboratories. 2525 Dupont Dr. Irvine, CA 92715. (714) 752-4500.

Place: Asilomar Conference Center, Pacific Grove. Date: spring. Frequency: annually. Length: five days. Fee: $300/AMWA members; $325/nonmembers. Included: accommodations (double occupancy), meals. Attendees: limited to 50.

Theme: medical writing. Subjects: evolution of medical journals, writing in the pharmaceutical industry, on-line medical databases, what editors and writers should know about publishing, business aspects of a freelance writing career. Faculty: 20+.

WOMEN IN COMMUNICATION. Sponsored by Women in Communications, Inc. 2101 Wilson Blvd., Ste. 417. Arlington, VA 22201. (703) 528-4200.

Place: varies; Las Vegas/1990. Date: October 11-14, 1990. Frequency: annually. Length: 4 days. Fee: fees vary based on type of membership. Higher fees for nonmembers. Individual seminar tickets are available. Group discounts available. Included: some meals. Attendees: 500.

Theme: Capture the Opportunity. Subjects: advanced track for senior communicators; cutting-edge developments in broadcasting, satellite services, and telephony; TV and film; graphics and design; ethics in journalism; entrepreneur's track for those operating and planning their own business. Format: featured speakers, seminars. Special events: night out.

WORLD CONGRESS OF POETS. Sponsored by the World Academy of Arts and Culture. 3146 Buckeye Court. Placerville, CA 95667. (916) 626-4166. Founded: 1969. Contact Person: Rosemary C. Wilkinson. For conference in Turkey contact: Dr. Osman Turkay. 22, Avenue Mansions. Finchley Rd. London NW3 7AX, England.

Place: varies; Istanbul, Turkey. Date: 1991. Frequency: biannually, by invitation of Cultural Minister/Minister of Education of host nation. Length: five-day symposium. Fee: not yet set. Reduced rates available for organization members. Attendees: 300-500.

Theme: World Brotherhood and Peace through Poetry. Subjects: poetry, literature, culture, education, art, music. Format: plenary sessions with afternoon workshops and evening cultural events. Special events: side trips to museums, ancient sites, libraries, etc. Faculty: 10+.

WRITER IN THE WORKPLACE. Sponsored by Society for Technical Communication and American River College. PO Box 1292. Roseville, CA 95661. (916) 484-8425. Founded: 1988. Contact Person: Connie Warloe.

Place: American River College, Sacramento. Date: February. Frequency: annually. Length: one day. Fee: $65. Included: meals. Attendees: 200.

Theme: changes every year. Subjects: technical, business writing, and communications. Format: keynote address and workshops. Special events: reception at end of day. Faculty: 30.

Books for Writers

The following writing- and publishing-related books are available from the Writers Connection bookstore. Writers Connection members are entitled to a 15% discount off the retail prices listed. To order books, use the order form on page 281.

Fiction

WRITING THE NOVEL FROM PLOT TO PRINT
Lawrence Block
Every step is fully described. F30—$10.95

HOW TO WRITE A DAMN GOOD NOVEL
James N. Frey
A step-by-step no-nonsense guide to dramatic storytelling. F32—$13.95

HOW TO WRITE ROMANCES
Phyllis Taylor Pianka
Everything you need to know about writing and selling the romance novel, including a sample query and synopsis. F33—$13.95

THE FICTION WRITER'S RESEARCH HANDBOOK
Mona McCormick
How to locate historical data using various sources. F44—$8.95

MYSTERY WRITER'S HANDBOOK
The Mystery Writers of America; revised edition
Top mystery writers share tricks of the trade. F17—$11.95

WRITING THE MODERN MYSTERY
Barbara Norville
How to research, plot, write, and sell a modern mystery. F29—$15.95

GUIDE TO FICTION WRITING
Phyllis Whitney
Various approaches to writing and selling fiction. F9—$12.95

HOW TO WRITE TALES OF HORROR, FANTASY & SCIENCE FICTION
J. N. Williamson
How-to essays from 26 top speculative fiction writers. F16—$15.95

PLOTTING THE NOVEL (booklet)
Phyllis Taylor Pianka
Plot patterns; the seven elements of plot and how to use them. F20—$2.35

HOW TO WRITE DYNAMIC DIALOGUE (booklet)
Phyllis Taylor Pianka
Ways to use believable dialogue to improve your writing. F15—$2.35

HOW TO CREATE LIVING CHARACTERS (booklet)
Phyllis Taylor Pianka
A handbook of methods for drawing believable characters. F31—$2.35

HOW TO WRITE A SYNOPSIS (booklet)
Phyllis Taylor Pianka
A guide to writing the all-important novel synopsis. F11—$2.35

Nonfiction

HOW TO WRITE AND SELL A COLUMN
Julie Raskin
Writing and selling columns to a variety of periodicals, choosing a subject and format, establishing your credentials. NF13—$10.95

HOW TO SELL AND RE-SELL YOUR WRITING
Duane Newcomb
Manage your writing time and market your nonfiction to maximize your income; top return on your research time investment. NF8—$11.95

HOW TO WRITE AND SELL YOUR PERSONAL EXPERIENCES
Lois Duncan
Turn everything that happens to you into writing that sells. NF44—$10.95

THE TRAVEL WRITER'S HANDBOOK
Louise P. Zobel
How to travel more and make more money writing about it. NF26—$11.95

TRAVEL WRITER'S MARKETS
Elaine O'Gara
Details on over 400 markets. NF27—$8.95

TRAVEL WRITING FOR FUN AND PROFIT
Ruth Wucherer
A veteran travel writer shares her trade secrets. NF28—$9.95

QUERY LETTERS/COVER LETTERS
Gordon Burgett
How to write the most compelling queries, cover letters. NF24—$9.95

FREELANCE INTERVIEW TIPS AND TRICKS (booklet)
Pat Kite
Techniques for landing the interview and methods for putting the interviewee at ease for best results. NF6—$3.25

WRITING FAST, FUN MONEY FILLERS (booklet)
Pat Kite
How to make money on short paragraphs. NF30—$3.25

SYNDICATING YOUR COLUMN (booklet)
Pat Kite
Tips and directions for getting columns syndicated into weekly or daily newspapers. NF33—$5.00

HOW TO WRITE A QUERY (booklet)
Phyllis Taylor Pianka
A guide to writing queries and proposals for articles and books. NF12—$2.35

Desktop/Publishing

LITERARY AGENTS
Debby Mayer
A writer's guide; includes interviews with well-known agents. DP9—$6.95

LITERARY AGENTS, HOW TO GET AND WORK WITH THE RIGHT ONE FOR YOU
Michael Larsen
A guide to selecting and working with an agent. DP8—$9.95

HOW TO GET AN AGENT (booklet)
Phyllis Taylor Pianka
How to select and work with an agent. DP11—$2.35

THE DESKTOP PUBLISHER'S LEGAL HANDBOOK
Daniel Sitarz
How to make best use of your rights as a publisher and avoid infringing rights of others.
DP15—$19.95

PUBLISHER'S LUNCH
Ernest Callenbach
A dialogue revealing the secrets of how publishers think and what authors can do about it.
DP5—$7.95

THE SELF-PUBLISHING MANUAL
Dan Poynter
New, revised edition of a complete guide to the self-publishing process. DP13—$19.95

SELLING BOOKS IN THE BAY AREA
Karen Misuraca
A directory of over 2,000 listings and resources for producers, sellers, and promoters of books in the Bay Area. DP10—$17.95

HOW TO SELF-PROMOTE YOUR BOOK (booklet)
Kite/Nelson
Tips on self-publicizing for new authors. DP7—$3.25

Specialized Markets

HOW TO WRITE AND ILLUSTRATE CHILDREN'S BOOKS
Bicknell/Trotman
Covers constructing a story, illustrating, and getting published. SM10—$22.50

THE CHILDREN'S PICTURE BOOK
Ellen Roberts
How to write it; how to sell it. SM12—$18.95

NON-FICTION FOR CHILDREN
Ellen Roberts
How to create and sell "real-world" subjects to children from preschoolers to teenagers.
SM13—$16.95

AN INTRODUCTION TO CHRISTIAN WRITING
Ethyl Herr
Effective techniques and marketing strategies for Christian writers. SM6—$8.95

1991 CHILDREN'S WRITER'S & ILLUSTRATOR'S MARKET
(Available February 1991)
Connie Wright Eidenier
Constructing a story, handling illustration, and getting published. SM9—$16.95

1991 HUMOR AND CARTOON MARKETS
(Available February 1991)
Edited by Bob Staake
Over 500 listings of magazines, newsletters, greeting card companies, comic book publishers, advertising agencies, and syndicates for humor writers and illustrators. SM1—$16.95

THE CRAFT OF COMEDY WRITING
Sol Saks
Write effective comedy material for TV and more. SM2—$14.95

WRITING FOR THE EDUCATIONAL MARKET
Barbara Gregorich
A complete resource manual for writing/publishing in the various educational applications. SM18—$13.95

Scriptwriting

HOW TO WRITE FOR TELEVISION
Madeline DiMaggio
Tips and techniques from a successful screenwriter. SC23—$10.95

HOW TO SELL YOUR SCREENPLAY
Carl Sautter
Comprehensive explanation from a seasoned professional of how to sell your screenplay. SC18—$22.95

WRITING SCREENPLAYS THAT SELL
Michael Hauge
A comprehensive manual for the total screenwriting process, from story concept to marketing SC22—$9.95

THE ELEMENTS OF SCREENWRITING
Irwin R. Blacker
A no-nonsense guide for film and television writing including plot, character, conflict, crisis, climax, exposition, and dialogue. SC7—$4.95

PRACTICAL SCREENWRITING HANDBOOK
Michael McCarthy
Light but thorough "how-to" guide for motion pictures and feature films, from title page to "the end." SC2—$12.95

MAKING A GOOD SCRIPT GREAT
Linda Seger
How to get the script back on track and preserve the original creativity; a guide for writing and rewriting. SC8—$10.95

SUCCESSFUL SITCOM WRITING
Jurgen Wolff
A round-up of the best writing tips, instruction, and inspiration. SC17—$16.95

SCREENPLAY
Syd Field
The foundations of screenwriting; a step-by-step guide from concept to finished script.
SC9—$8.95

THE SCREENWRITER'S WORKBOOK
Syd Field
Exercises and step-by-step instruction for creating a successful screenplay; a workshop approach. SC10—$8.95

Resource/Reference

1991 WRITER'S MARKET
Writer's Digest
Where and how to sell what you write; thousands of markets for fiction and nonfiction articles, books, plays, scripts, short stories, and more. RR25—$24.95

CALIFORNIA & HAWAII PUBLISHING MARKETPLACE
Writers Connection
Comprehensive directory of publishers, magazines, agents, newspapers, organizations, and more. RR48—$16.95

SOUTHWEST PUBLISHING MARKETPLACE
Writers Connection
Comprehensive directory of writers' markets and more for Arizona, Colorado, Nevada, New Mexico, Texas, and Utah. RR49—$14.95

THE WRITER'S DIGEST GUIDE TO MANUSCRIPT FORMATS
Writer's Digest
Illustrated, easy-to-follow guide to all types of manuscript formats, including books, articles, poems, and plays. RR44—$17.95

FINDING FACTS FAST
Alden Todd
Comprehensive research techniques to save you hours; a gold mine of information sources and research techniques. RR40—$3.95

ASSOCIATED PRESS STYLEBOOK AND LIBEL MANUAL
Addison-Wesley
Authoritative word on rules of grammar, punctuation, and the general meaning and usage of over 3,000 terms; insight into journalistic techniques. RR1—$10.95

CHICAGO MANUAL OF STYLE
University of Chicago Press
A comprehensive, authoritative guide to journalistic and reference techniques. RR41—$37.50

A WRITER'S GUIDE TO COPYRIGHT
Poets & Writers
A summary of the current copyright law for writers, editors, and teachers. RR29—$6.95

THE WRITER'S LEGAL COMPANION
Brad Bunnin
How to deal successfully with copyrights, contracts, libel, taxes, agents, publishers, legal relationships, and marketing strategies. RR8—$14.95

EDITING YOUR NEWSLETTER
Mark Beach
A complete guide to writing and producing a successful newsletter—on schedule and within budget. RR2—$18.50

COPYEDITING, A PRACTICAL GUIDE
Karen Judd
A comprehensive field guide to copyediting, publishing. RR23—$17.95

HOW TO WRITE A BOOK PROPOSAL
Michael Larsen
A step-by-step guide from a leading literary agent. RR11—$10.95

THE ELEMENTS OF STYLE
Strunk/White
Classic guide to correct writing. RR10—$4.95

THE MENTOR GUIDE TO PUNCTUATION
William C. Paxson
Quick and easy answers to punctuation problems organized for easy access. RR9—$4.95

REWRITE RIGHT!
Jan Venolia
Most writing can be improved by the simple process of review and rewriting. RR5—$6.95

WRITE RIGHT!
Jan Venolia
The best summary of grammar available for writers. RR32—$5.95

THE WRITING BUSINESS
Coda editors: Poets and Writers Newsletter
Practical advice on the business side of being a writer. RR36—$11.95

WRITING AFTER FIFTY
Leonard L. Knott
How to start a writing career after you retire. RR37—$12.95

WRITING DOWN THE BONES
Natalie Goldberg
Guidelines for freeing the writer within. RR38—$9.95

GET IT ALL DONE AND STILL BE HUMAN
Tony and Robbie Fanning
New revised edition of time management strategies for writers and others. RR24—$9.95

THE PROFESSIONAL WRITERS GUIDE
National Writers Club
An indispensable, comprehensive guide on all aspects of the writing business. RR47—$16.95

Discover for yourself...

The hundreds of freelance writing opportunities in the Southwest

The *Southwest Publishing Marketplace* provides a comprehensive listing of resources, opportunities, and markets, some relatively new and untapped, in Arizona, Colorado, Nevada, New Mexico, Texas, and Utah.

Discover up-to-date listings:

Books—Select from small, mid-size, and large presses

Magazines—Locate new markets

Newspapers—Find submission and book review editors

Literary Agents—Choose the right agent for your book or script

Writers Conferences—Gain insights, information, and contacts

Professional Organizations—Maximize your contacts

Reference Books—Expand your sources of information

"With its comprehensive listings and cross-references, the *Southwest Publishing Marketplace* fills a gap as big as the Grand Canyon! Finally writers will be able to zero in on the right markets right away with this easy-to-use directory."

> Mary Westheimer, writer, editor, and founding member of the Arizona Authors' Association Advisory Board

"Whether your written work has a regional slant or you would just like to connect with authors and publishers in your area, this book should prove a helpful resource."

> Steve Davis, author and publisher of *The Writer's Yellow Pages*

Be among the first to increase your sales to markets in this rapidly growing writing/publishing region. $14.95, Writers Connection members price is $12.71. To order your copy, use the form on page 281 or call (408) 973-0227.

Book Subject Index

This index is alphabetized using the letter-by-letter system and is divided into three sections: fiction, nonfiction, and subsidy presses.

Nonfiction

Subsidy Presses

Magazine Subject Index

This index is alphabetized using the letter-by-letter system and is divided into two sections: fiction and nonfiction.

Comprehensive Index

This index is alphabetized using the letter-by-letter system. Magazine and newspaper listings are in italic.

How does a writer break into Hollywood?
Find an agent? Write the stories Hollywood wants?

Nineteen top Hollywood pros answer these questions and more in the hottest new resource for scriptwriters—the *Writing for Hollywood* and *Selling to Hollywood* videotapes. In the broadcast quality style of network television, these tapes provide an insiders' look at the complex and intriguing process of writing and selling screenplays for motion pictures and television.

Selling to Hollywood

86 minutes

Writing for Hollywood

83 minutes

- **Breaking In**
  written and unwritten rules of the game
  using the "spec" script to open doors
- **Protecting Your Material**
  registering scripts with WGA
  sending follow-up letters to pitches
- **Agents**
  selling without an agent
  how to find and work with an agent
- **Selling to the Studios and Independents**
  rejection/acceptance factors
  the development process
- **"Hot" Scripts**
  elements of the equation
  writing with original voice & style
- **Pitching**
  elements of a good pitch
  log lines, set pieces, plot points
- **Opportunities and Alternatives**
  production deals with studios
  getting character-driven pieces to the stars

- **The Prewriting Process**
  stepping out the scenes
  determining the major turning points
- **Structure**
  the three-act structure
  the character's journey from A to Z
- **Dialog & Characterization**
  creating interesting characters
  advancing the story
- **Rewriting**
  time sequence in scriptwriting
  questions to ask during the rewrite
- **Story Analysis and Script Evaluation**
  how professional analysts evaluate scripts
  researching for accurate period pieces
- **Collaboration**
  how to become your own worst enemy
  collaborators as allies
- **TV Sitcoms**
  the sitcom structure
  creating cliffhangers

You don't have to live in Hollywood to be a successful screenwriter. Learn how to write the stories Hollywood wants and discover how to sell them to an increasingly competitive industry where million-dollar deals are made over lunch.

Produced by Paul Edwards Production Group and Writers Connection. Individual VHS tapes are priced at $79.95 each; the set is $129.95. Writers Connection member price is $71.95 per tape; $116.95 for the set. To order, use the order form on page 281 or call (408) 973-0227.

Order Form

Information/Membership/Subscription

☐ Send me a Writers Connection newsletter/seminar catalog

☐ Enroll me as a Writers Connection member
includes subscription—$40 per year $_____

☐ Send me 12 issues of the *Writers Connection* newsletter
without membership—$12 $_____

Books/Tapes

Check the books and tapes you wish to order below. Price code:
member/nonmember price.

☐ Send me _____ copies of the **Southwest Publishing
Marketplace—$12.71**/$14.95 each $_____

☐ Send me _____ copies of the **California and Hawaii
Publishing Marketplace—$14.41**/$16.95 each $_____

☐ Send me _____ copies of the **Writing for Hollywood** VHS
videotape—**$71.95**/$79.95 each $_____

☐ Send me _____ copies of the **Selling to Hollywood** VHS
videotape—**$71.95**/$79.95 each $_____

☐ Send me _____ sets of both videotapes at the special
package price—**$116.95**/$129.95 each $_____

☐ Send me the following titles from the books for writers
listing. Writers Connection members can deduct 15 percent.
Please enter code, title, and price for each book below.

_____ $_____

_____ $_____

Book/tape subtotal $_____

Calif. residents add 7.25% sales tax $_____

Add $2.50 per book/tape ($10 max.), $.65 per newsletter for shipping $_____

Add $5.00 additional for book/tape orders to Hawaii $_____

Total $_____

Name_____

Address_____

City_____ State_____ Zip_____

Daytime phone _____ Membership number_____

☐ Check or money order enclosed

Please charge my: ☐ Visa ☐ MasterCard   Account #_____

Expiration date _____ Signature_____

Please return to:
Writers Connection
1601 Saratoga-Sunnyvale Rd., Suite 180, Cupertino, CA 95014
Phone orders using a Visa or MasterCard are accepted: **(408) 973-0227**